LIVING *In The* INFINITE

LIVING *In The* INFINITE

And Still Getting to Work on Time

A GUIDE FOR THE PERPLEXED

by Stan Smith

Lucia Press, 77 Spruce Way, Carmel, CA 93923-9609
First published in 2007 by Lucia Press

Printed in the United States of America

16 15 14 13 12 11 10 09 08 07   1 3 5 7 9 10 8 6 4 2

Library of Congress Control Number: 2006907993

ISBN-10: 0-9788124-1-7
ISBN-13: 978-0-9788124-1-6

Designed by Kara Adanalian | www.acmegfx.com
Set in New Baskerville
Cover illustration by Dynamic Graphics | © 2006 JupiterImages Corp.
This book is printed on acid-free paper

To contact the author, visit www.LivingintheInfinite.com

For my students, who are my ongoing teachers. Their commitment and perseverance amaze and inspire me.

For Russell Paul Schofield, teacher of teachers and a true center of light. He created a path of exploration; his vision of human potential has encouraged many to embrace their spiritual promise and achieve their highest purpose.

For my parents, Billie Smith and C. Chandler Smith, who placed a high value on loving to learn and the freedom to explore.

There is a light that casts no shadow because it permeates all things and surrounds them. We create illusions, however, that cast illusions of shadows, and then we believe and act as if these illusions and shadows were real. We will live these illusions until we reclaim the truths we hid in their shadows and clear our eyes to again revel in the beauty of the light within all creation and within ourselves. Only then will we know ourselves as we actually are and cast no shadows.

Contents

Preface

There's nothing entirely new under the sun: so Pythagoras taught at the dawn of philosophical inquiry. There are no truly novel ideas regarding the fundamental questions of who and why we are and where we're going. Still, ideas need expression in new ways to help us expand our perspectives. From time to time, even the highest and most enduring truths need fresh articulation, in ways as varied as the great diversity of seekers of truth. How humanity sees itself and the cosmos changes as consciousness evolves; therefore, we react to the ageless underpinnings of existence in distinct patterns in each historical period. These patterns differ in ways that make a difference, as I hope this book may make a difference despite confirming Pythagoras.

What follows has been said before in other ways. I have nothing fundamentally new to say, only my particular way of saying it based on my own experiences. I hope that this can help a few people remember something important that they've forgotten they already know. I would be delighted if this helps some seekers in the same way that those who took the trouble to speak their truths in ways I could hear have helped me.

I conceived this book in 1991; it originated in observations made during the prior eighteen years with my students in a training in spiritual transformation and integration called Actualism. This teaches each student to experience and relate to her or his own individual infinite self, also known as the higher self, divine self, or immortal being of light. In working with these remarkably dedicated and insightful individuals as they sorted through the ramifications of being both a finite person and an infinite self, I found that they were confused by this inner polarity of existence and perplexed by the paradoxes it produces, especially the human paradox. I also realized that this confusion is pervasive in our culture, which rarely entertains the notion that human beings are spiritually infinite and isn't comfortable with paradox. I felt it would be useful to write a book outlining why we are perplexed and how this affects us and presenting perspectives to help sort through this. Material for this book comes from my interactions with students and others as they grappled with the polarity and paradox of their spiritual nature.

I found I needed to draw on disciplines in which I have no expertise. I took heart reading the foreword to Johan Huizinga's *Homo Ludens*: "In treating of the general problems of culture one is constantly obliged to undertake predatory incursions into provinces not sufficiently explored by the raider himself. To fill in all the gaps in my knowledge beforehand was out of the question for me. I had to write now, or not at all. And I wanted to write."[1]

In my case, it felt more like this book wanted me to write it, and write it now. This experience relates to the subject of the book. The motivation for writing didn't come from my conscious self; rather, I felt an inner demand and sense of necessity. The process of creating the book brought forth ideas not previously in my awareness, an experience common in the writing process. These felt like they came from a deeper or higher place within me. What may be "original" (bearing in mind Pythagoras's statement) has this origin; it feels to me like a gift from my higher or infinite self. My job was to express and context that material. This, I believe, is the process of all creativity.

Researching the history of how people have conceived of themselves spiritually, I grew increasingly aware that the idea of the individual infinite self or spirit is not just an arcane matter of metaphysics and metapsychology. It's a crucially important issue related to individual freedom and responsibility and thus to solving the most essential issues of our time. It is more important than ever for each individual to take responsibility for the consequences of her or his actions. This is particularly true in the West, especially in America. We have great power, individually and nationally, to accomplish extraordinary good, but we also have the power to consume scarce resources, pollute, dominate, and destroy to a degree beyond anything previously imaginable. For instance, everyday it requires great vigilance to avoid causing environmental harm that may last for generations or prove irreversible.

Life is hard; how can one possibly take on more responsibility? The only way to take up this challenge is to know oneself. We need to know where our responsibility actually lies and where it doesn't; we need to know all the resources at our disposal for handling our true responsibilities and how to access these resources in our world and in ourselves.

Because of the media, the decline of education and the family, the frantic pace of modern life, and our culture's materialism, learning these things is extremely difficult. At the same time, more resources for knowing oneself are available than ever before. They are hidden in plain sight, a mystery until we find them, and then they present a greater mystery: why didn't we notice them all along?

If we take up this challenge, we will have the satisfaction of successfully meeting a crisis as great as any in history. In doing so, we will learn how to make our lives more meaningful and easier. It will not be easy, but if, as I believe, this is what the divine asks of us and this is what we will gain, it's a pretty good deal.

I employ both intuition and analysis in exploring the infinite self. Those who are partial to one of these may not resonate to the inclusion of the other in this book; however, the juxtaposition of the two is relevant to the subject and demonstrates some of the book's premises. I hope to engage the reader in integrating the two, because the subject calls for examination from more than one direction and its full understanding requires such a synthesis. Analysis provides a conceptual framework with which to make sense of our intuitive experiences of the infinite within us.

Chapter 1 describes the infinite self; the remainder of part 1 discusses the many practical effects of the infinite and finite intersecting in a person, why infinite and finite must be distinguished, the damage that can occur if they aren't, and the benefits of making this distinction. It also explores the modalities of our consciousness and how their interaction reflects principles that underlie cosmic existence as described by both science and religion. Part 2 goes into further ramifications of our being both finite and infinite for living a successful and fulfilling life; it concludes by examining some larger implications. Part 3 presents a series of exercises, ranging from brief and quite simple to a more intensive practice, for experiencing infinite self and for beginning a lifelong process of integrating body, mind, and infinite spirit.

It is the paradox of a book that's much about paradox that the timeless subject of the infinite and eternal needs to be placed in historical context. While this perspective interweaves throughout the text, the appendices give it full airing. They begin with a brief overview of ways human beings conceive of the divine, its relationship to the cosmos and to us, and the attributes of soul and spirit. Appendix 2 reviews how a selection of religions throughout history have described the spiritual makeup, origin, and destiny of human beings; it identifies those that have included, at least to some degree, a conception of human spiritual nature similar to that of this book. It concludes with a discussion of a crucial historical watershed in our psychospiritual development, the effects of which are still playing out.

I have placed this more academic material in appendices to avoid burdening the rest of the text, which focuses more on experience and practicality. Nonetheless, I believe that the appendices are of more than academic interest, helping readers understand where we are and how we got here. They also provide a matrix in which the idea of the infinite self can take a more definite form.

For simplicity's sake, I use the word "God" to refer to divinity. This isn't meant to attribute gender. It refers to a conception of divinity as unitary and beyond all differentiation. Divinity articulates into masculine and feminine polarities, which are often referred to as "God" and "Goddess." The word "God" has multiple meanings: historically, it meant first *a* masculine divinity and then *the*, still masculine, divinity; this evolved into a modern usage by which many people designate a genderless divinity. The word "Goddess," however, is never used except in reference to a female divinity and therefore can't replace or alternate with "God." The words "divinity" and "the divine" don't have the same immediacy of relationship as "God" or "Goddess," so they can't be used exclusively. By using "God," I hope I offend no sensibilities.

I use the word "infinity" in its most inclusive sense of unbounded space, unlimited time (eternity), the division of space and time into endlessly smaller intervals, and the Absolute Infinite. Philosopher Plotinus, mathematician Rudy Rucker, and physicist David Bohm give these descriptions of the infinite: "Absolutely One, it has never known measure and stands outside of number, and so is under no limit either in regard to any extern[al] or within itself. . . . And having no constituent parts it accepts no pattern, forms no shape."[2] "An Absolute exists by itself, and in the highest possible degree of completeness."[3] It is "the unbroken wholeness of the totality of existence as an undivided flowing movement without borders."[4]

The terms "infinite self," "higher self," "divine self," "immortal self," "being of light," and "immortal one within" are interchangeable as used here.

Other than "God," conventionally capitalized to refer to the deity of the three major monotheistic religions, I've chosen not to capitalize spiritual names and concepts such as "divinity," "divine mind," and particularly "infinite self," though in some cases this differs from common practice. Capitalization of such spiritual terms implies a separation between the spiritual entities so described and the material person and world. I believe it's important at this time to accentuate the continuity and relationship between the spiritual and the material. Conventional exceptions are proper names and specific terms customarily capitalized in a particular tradition or when, discussing a particular author, I follow his or her usage.

All Bible quotations are from the New Revised Standard Version (NRSV) unless otherwise noted. When attributing quotations from the *Encyclopædia Britannica* (*Britannica CD 97*), I use the abbreviation *EB*. Italics within quotations occur in the original unless indicated otherwise in an endnote.

To assist readers to see relationships, influences, and patterns in the development of the aspect of human consciousness this book concerns itself with, I've included the dates of most of the figures and primary sources mentioned who are no longer living, as well as other information that might seem tangential.

Acknowledgements

I am profoundly grateful to those who have taught me how to discover my own truth and who trained me to teach. They've made my life far richer than I could ever have expected.

I wish to express appreciation to Jaclyn Kanner for helping me to see myself as a writer, initiating me into the process of crafting a book, finding sources, and offering ideas, and for giving inspiration, encouragement, and critique—each in proper measure and at the right time. I want to thank Hank Berrings for long and helpful discussions regarding polarities. I am indebted to Leonard Shlain, Lynn Stewart, Alice Stearns, Steve Bankes, and Bill Twitty for time generously given reading the manuscript in whole or part and offering honest and insightful feedback; Lynn also gently and patiently helped me to refine the text. I would like to acknowledge Susan Pierce, who took the project to heart and gave hours and effort above and beyond in the later editing process, providing insights and sources, trying to make me a better writer, and preventing comma abuse. Hilary Morgan was the alpha and omega of the rewriting process, generously enduring both the raw early manuscript and many hours of final, difficult fine-tuning.

My thanks to Judy Schriebman, Bonney Grey, and Susie Vanderlip for leading me to good institutions and great people, to Joe Shaw for editing, to Kara Adanalian for her skill and creative vision in Web design, cover art, and layout, to Deborah Medvick for her keen eyes and expertise in galley proofreading, and to Maimonides for subtitle guidance.

PART ONE

A Case of Mistaken Identity

The decisive question for man is: Is he related to something infinite or not? That is the telling question of his life. Only if we know that the thing that truly matters is the infinite can we avoid fixing our interest upon futilities. . . . If we understand and feel that here in this life we already have a link with the infinite, desires and attitudes change. . . . In our relationships to other men, too, the crucial question is whether an element of boundlessness is expressed in the relationship.

The feeling for the infinite, however, can be attained only if we are bounded to the utmost. . . . Only consciousness of our narrow confinement in the self forms the link to the limitlessness of the unconscious. In such awareness we experience ourselves concurrently as limited and eternal, as both the one and the other. In knowing ourselves to be unique in our personal combination—that is, ultimately limited—we possess also the capacity for becoming conscious of the infinite. But only then!

—C. G. Jung, *Memories, Dreams, Reflections*

1

The Human Paradox

> He felt happy and at the same time sad. He had absolutely nothing to weep about yet he was ready to weep. . . . The chief thing that made him feel like weeping was the sudden, acute sense of the terrible contrast between something infinitely great and indefinable existing within, and that narrow, corporeal something that he . . . was. The contrast wrung his heart and rejoiced him.
>
> —Leo Tolstoy, *War and Peace*

Solving mysteries can be fun, enlightening, or a matter of survival. The best are all three. We're going to explore one of the ultimate mysteries. Its solution is readily accessible, yet it continues to bewilder many people, causing endless confusion and suffering. Although some of the earliest spiritual texts illuminate this mystery, and although more good and insightful people have devoted themselves to unraveling its enigma than perhaps to anything else in history, even the awareness of this paradox has often become lost through misunderstanding or forgetfulness. It has also suffered intentional suppression.

Our mystery is the paradoxical nature of human beings, the contradictory qualities that so often cause people to wonder, Who are we? Why are our lives so difficult to understand?

The usual way of stating the paradox is that we are both physical and spiritual; we live finite lives, yet we believe in and sometimes experience continuing beyond our mortality. An ancient and recurrent yet uncommon and unorthodox view, however, holds that we are infinite as well as finite beings.

Only by comprehending that we are both infinite and finite and by living accordingly can we resolve the quandaries of our paradoxical existence.

Being infinite, in the sense that I suggest, means more than having an immortal soul or being one with the cosmos. It also signifies something other than experiencing God within oneself. It means having, or more accurately, *being an infinite and eternal individual spirit* created by God. This infinite self expresses aspects of God and is itself capable of creating and sustaining an individual human being that is its own finite self-expression (a microcosm), in the same way that the universe is God's creation and self-expression (the macrocosm).

Half of this description of human beings as paradoxically both limited and infinite is self-evident: we are clearly finite creatures—we are born, and we die. We confront our physical and mental limits at every moment. These limits can be hard to accept; while finite life can be joyous and rewarding, it often seems difficult to navigate and impossible to understand.

The other half of the description is less obvious: are we infinite, eternal, and divinely creative beings? Aspects of this notion find expression in poetry and in religious doctrines pertaining, for instance, to the soul; still, most people wouldn't say that they regularly have experiences of being infinite and eternal. These, however, are surprisingly common among adults (though few are recognized as such, being projected onto external divinity or simply ignored). During infancy and early childhood, each of us experienced the infinity of our being, feeling an oceanic oneness with all and a limitless sense of self. William Wordsworth (1770-1850) described his impression of this:

There was a time when . . .
The earth, and every common sight,
To me did seem
Apparelled in celestial light. . . .
. . . .
The things which I have seen I now can see no more.
. . . .
Our birth is but a sleep and a forgetting . . .
. . . .
Not in entire forgetfulness . . .
But tailing clouds of glory do we come
From God, who is our home:
Heaven lies about us in our infancy!
Shades of the prison-house begin to close
Upon the growing boy.[1]

Most of us remember little from that time because those experiences don't fit into our adult mentality and beliefs. We didn't experience the world then as we later learned to and don't now have the words to express what we felt then. As we matured, the infinite remained with us, fully present and as available for experience as when we were infants. We became skilled, however, at suppressing or explaining away most of these experiences; we redefined them so that they made sense within the agreed-upon ordering of the finite world we had to adapt to. Still, we continue to catch glimpses of our infinite potential when we sense we're much more than the limited self we normally imagine, have greater purpose and potential, and have settled for less than we could be. Most commonly, we feel the infinite in moments of quiet reverence in nature or in responding with wonder to the boundless beauty and possibilities of the universe. When these experiences occur, we don't understand them for what they are; both our upbringing and our religious and secular education actively prohibit recognition and provide no cognitive framework or language that includes them. Not many people enthusiastically immerse themselves in wonder or lose themselves in reverence, even for a while; fewer still allow deeper, spiritually illuminating experiences of their infinite self to emerge.

Instead, *we have unconsciously learned to try to make experiences of our infinite nature fit into the limits and rationales of our finite self.* Unfortunately—and this is the core of the human mystery and the crux of many of life's dilemmas—*we can never make these fit* into the finite. The finite self and world cannot contain the infinite self; experiences of it are not of the same order as finite experiences. However, because we don't even know we're trying to make them fit, we become confused, think something is wrong with us, consider ourselves failures, become compulsive, or decide the world is perverse and incomprehensible. It's impossible to make sense of our existence until we realize that we're dealing with two orders of experience and two aspects of self, not one.

The Continuity of Finite and Infinite

Crucial to understanding the relationship between these two aspects of self is that there is no discontinuity between finite and infinite selves or between the spiritual and physical worlds; finite self only experiences an illusion of separation. This illusion can be most convincing, given that the infinite self, if it's allowed into awareness, is so intangible to the physical senses that it seems it must be separate and distant. Millennia of belief in a deity in heaven above reinforce this illusion. Nonetheless, the infinite self is within and throughout its finite creation at all times and under all circumstances, immanent and interpenetrating; it is continually creating and maintaining the existence of the finite self, which thus is never independent of it but instead interdependent with it. The finite self partakes, albeit finitely, of the full nature of the infinite self, which is unified fully and eternally with God.

We are strongly predisposed toward the illusion of separation. Western religion and science provide the framework for how the majority of people in the West think of and perceive the world, an approach that values making distinctions among discrete entities. The most advanced Western scientific thought, however, as well as Buddhist, Hindu, and Taoist religious traditions and some Christian mysticism, affirm the continuity between infinite and finite, divine and earthly, ultimate and mundane. Though most people also view physics and metaphysics as discrete endeavors, they are sounding ever more alike. Modern physics increasingly extends into the paradoxical and mystical in its pursuit of a unified theory of the fundamental forces of the universe.

The continuity between the infinite and finite aspects of self and the absence of duality or division between spirit and matter requires a profound revaluing of matter. Unfortunately, many beautiful spiritual descriptions of our higher nature involve an inherent devaluation of material existence, as if the relationship of spirit and physical existence were a zero-sum affair, such that when the one is exalted, the other requires degrading. Recognizing the continuity of our infinite spirit with our earthly form requires matter to be viewed, as in some religions, as being spiritual itself (see the first section of appendix 1).

The greatest significance of this relationship of spirit and matter is that the finite aspect of self can learn to experience and express the infinite self in bodily existence, manifesting as individuated spirituality. It can evolve to be a partner with it in fulfilling the purpose for which infinite self created the mental, emotional, and physical aspects of finite self.

Theologians often have taken the continuity of God, or infinite self, and finite self to mean oneness without essential distinction. Many mystical and metaphysical voices throughout the ages have spoken of submersion in the divine and thus of an end to individual identity (seen as finite) through union with All. The Sufi mystic Mahmud Shabistari (d. c. 1320) describes this: "There is no being save only One. . . . In his divine majesty the *me*, the *we*, the *thou*, are not found, for in the One there can be no distinction."[3] The burden of individual identity can seem heavy, and losing it in God may feel like a great relief.

Being an infinite, divine self involves more than being one with God. We don't merely partake of the energy of God or enter into the consciousness of divinity. Rather, our infinite aspect is an individual eternal identity, a *unique* creation of God expressing qualities of God in a singular pattern as an infinite self. I use the term "identity" here in its most fundamental sense: for the "I am" which we always are, which preexists all particular finite identities such as gender, nationality, profession, and family connections, and which we cannot cease to be, no matter what we do. It gives finite self a profound sense of purpose and of being worthy of that purpose.

The continuity of infinite self and finite self does not negate or lessen individual finite identity, just as our knowledge that everything in the universe is part of an unbroken space-time fabric of energy fields doesn't dissuade us from our everyday experience that distinct people and things exist in our world. Exploring our infinite identity, in fact, enhances our personal identity and reveals it to be a divine gift and blessing.

The Tripart Self

The infinite self has often been confused with the soul. It differs profoundly from this in a number of ways, however.

The infinite self is eternally existent. Having an infinite and eternal nature is not the same as having an immortal soul. A common belief is that God creates soul and body at the same time; if so, or if the soul is created any time after the beginning of the cosmos, the soul is immortal only after that, not eternal in the sense of existing through all time, before and after time, or completely outside it.

The infinite self is the creator of the mind and body and is omnipotent and omniscient within them. In contrast, the soul, while often viewed as capable of thought, feeling, will, desire, and ethical choice, is not seen in any religious system as creator of body or mind.

The infinite self is never separate from God. Many beliefs, such as Christian doctrine regarding damnation, hold the soul to be at risk of separation from God.

Having an infinite self means that the individual is, at minimum, tripartite. The three aspects of self are: personality (mind, perspectives, and emotions) and body taken together; soul (as well as, in some views, other spiritual attributes created by infinite self); and spirit (infinite self). (For a fuller discussion, see appendix 1, s.v. "Soul, Spirit, and Nature.") Other terms for the infinite self or spirit are: higher or actual self, being of light, divine self, God child, or the immortal one within.

In its union with the divine, the infinite self partakes of all the attributes of God. The individual infinite self creates the body, personality, and soul and is all-pervasive within them in the same way that God is omnipresent throughout the cosmos. Every person is the creation of an infinite self. Each infinite self relates with infinite and unconditional love to its creation, and its light pervades body and soul; this is the heritage of each finite self. Drawing on that heritage, the finite self evolves spiritually, growing in ability to discover the truths of its unique identity and spiritual purpose and to creatively embody and express its divine nature. Its destiny is partnership with its infinite self.

At this stage of human spiritual development, our most important work is not just earning a blissful afterlife apart from the body (or in a resurrected body at the end of time) or achieving the Buddhist no-self. Rather, it is to interrelate and integrate finite self (body, personality, and soul) with the individual infinite self *in this life* in a synthesis termed wholeness. Wholeness involves finite and infinite fully unified and interacting interdependently, so that finite self can learn to access and express the wisdom, love, and creativity of the higher self. The capacity for wholeness grows with heightened self-awareness.

This is not a deification of human beings, who, while being infinite selves, are clearly "all too human" as finite selves. It's also not polytheism, because while God children are infinite and eternal, they are the higher aspects of human beings (or, more accurately, human beings are the finite aspects of God children), and are omnipotent, omniscient, and omnipresent *only* within their respective creations. They are eternally unified with God and act in the name of and in alignment with the will of the divine. They partake of divine qualities, each being distinct in the particular qualities of the divine that it manifests, and each expresses these according to its own singular God-given creative purpose. They are creations of God and completely consistent with God's nature.

An Invitation to Explore

While the concept of the individual infinite spirit—the divine self—might be viewed as a religious belief, its better use is to lead an inquisitive mind to confirming experiences. It has practical value in helping to make better sense of one's life. It addresses questions that are ancient yet most contemporary: Who are we? What is our purpose and destiny?

The infinite self is not something to believe in. The idea that each of us is an immortal individual spirit, a being of light endowed by God with the ability to generate and sustain an individual human being who is that spirit's own finite self-expression, is emphatically a working hypothesis, an invitation for you to explore, experiment, and learn by means of your own experience. Hypotheses are valuable in terms of their ability to fruitfully focus attention, explain consequences, and predict consistency of outcomes. The test of this one lies in how well it enables you to sort out different kinds of experience, make better sense of your life, act more wisely and effectively, and feel more alive and joyous.

Discussing the infinite self involves all the limitations inherent in employing language to describe the ineffable. Words and the concepts they form are at best metaphors or symbols, not the real thing. Humankind, as it increases in self-awareness and knowledge of the cosmos, has continuously evolved the metaphors it uses to speak about the ultimate and its own nature. In our time, increased knowledge of the world's spiritual traditions has fostered greater open-mindedness in spiritual inquiry; together with the modern acceptance by science and mathematics of the concept of the infinite, this expands our framework of consciousness so that we can create new metaphors for who we are.

To speak and think of the spiritual part of us as an infinite and eternal self is an idea that is only now beginning to be available in its fullest sense. "Infinity," having meaning in both the spiritual and scientific realms, serves well to facilitate the rejoining of these long-separated arenas of the search for ultimate truth. Its use supports a spiritual seeker in employing all the tools and tough-mindedness of the scientific investigator, while it reminds the scientist that all truth is open-ended and in the end spiritual. It fittingly symbolizes our highest sense of self for the era we're entering. In the future, better descriptions will inevitably evolve.

As to whether the notion of the infinite self is more than metaphor, each of us must form our own conclusions based on personal experience. My own experience satisfies me that it's a valid and useful description, as much as one can say that about any representation of the unknowable.

What Is Your Experience?

It can be tempting to explain away any sense of being infinite by reducing it to a carryover of infantile feelings of having no boundaries; likewise, one may legitimately argue that whatever is said about experiences of the divine self could easily and more acceptably be interpreted simply as the presence of God. This isn't provable one way or the other. We can only rely on whether we have an inner resonance to the idea and, if so, we can experiment and pay close attention to the experiences this produces.

A brief exercise will help you explore this (exercises 3 and 4 in chapter 20 expand on this):

> Close your eyes, relax, and clear your mind. Think of your (putative) infinite self, within and all around you. For a minute or two, let yourself observe whatever qualities of this aspect of you that may enter your awareness. Then think of the infinite self of a person you know. (Your infinite self will immediately connect with whomever you think of.) Notice the distinct qual-

> ities of this person's higher self, differing from those of your own. Then do this with another person, and again note the differences. Do it with someone you dislike; you may be surprised by unexpected qualities of that person's higher self that differ from the personality you know. Try this with someone from history (immortality is obviously of help here), and compare your experience with your expectation. Now let yourself open to an experience of God. Note what is different.

Your results are likely to be subtle. Simply file them away with an open mind and without drawing any conclusions. Repeat this at other times, and base your opinion on the cumulative results of several trials. Is what you feel your imagination? With practice, you can distinguish what your mind creates (imagination certainly may enter the process, especially at the beginning) from what originates outside your mind. These have different qualities, and you'll learn to tell them apart as you repeat the exercise.

Here's an example from my own experience. I don't wish to give the impression that one should feel anything in particular; no one's encounter with the infinite will be just like mine or anyone else's. My ongoing relationship with my infinite self is very understated. It's the most important thing in my life but also unobtrusive and easy to miss. I often register my infinite self's presence only by inference from seemingly coincidental occurrences that in timely and intelligent ways illuminate my inner growth processes or questions I'm grappling with. I have a highly skeptical mind and, I'm sure like many people, tend to write off these occurrences as pure chance picked out by the selective focus of my mind. My higher self, however, can be blatant in these communications, clustering them past the point of it being reasonable to dismiss them. It will even "sign" them with a pun implicit in the structure of these events. (I'm fond of puns.)

A more direct and abiding experience is of a larger part of myself in and around me at all times. This is full and vibrant, completely respectful of the lesser me and not demanding attention, but if I focus on it (especially when I'm feeling compressed or weighed down), it's expansive and lifting both physically and in spirit. While there's no apparent boundary to this aspect of me, the expansion is usually just enough to get me beyond false limits imposed by circumstance or my internal state.

Another ongoing feeling is a sense of self—individuality and personhood in their largest meaning—that pervades me. I can't define it; it is simply "I," but it's more than the "I" that I usually identify as myself. I experience each part of me having its own unique sense of identity; however, that which I'm referring to is deeper than and common to all aspects of me. It is what's left when I factor out all particular self-definitions. Any other sense of individuality, such as arises from vocation, accomplishments, or relationships, is open to change or suspicion of being circumstantial; this one (so far in my experience, at least, and according to my intuition) is clearly not changeable. It provides a subtle and simple sense of there being a point to my life and of my having inherent value.

A fourth feeling is of being specially, forgivingly, and playfully loved. I perceive that anyone I meet is similarly loved but not from the same source. This isn't sentimental love; many of life's difficulties seem to be there to provide me a caring and cautioning reminder to be more aware and a challenge to act with deeper integrity.

There's nothing dramatic, revelatory, or extra-sensory in these experiences, but they fill my life. I feel partnered, yet interaction depends significantly on my choice and openness. If I sit quietly and go within in meditation or contemplation to focus on my infinite self, I always get a lift, an insight, or some other welcome but often unexpected change in my interior state or approach to the world. Focusing on God provides similar experiences, but these are not as personal, direct, intimate, and empowering. God provides the overall context; in contrast, these feelings and perceptions are integral to the fabric and processes of my life.

I think of this as mundane mysticism. I don't think I have a special gift; if I can experience relating with infinite self, anyone can; it just requires a little effort and attention. Each of us perceives uniquely; we each can discover how best to experience and relate to the infinite being of light we are.

A Turning Point in Spiritual Evolution

As you discover the ways that you experience your own infinite self, you'll explore personally and in your own way the mystery of your paradoxical nature. You'll also encounter the challenge of a spiritual frontier, the cutting edge of our inner growth as we enter a new era of self-knowledge and responsibility. You are called to a quest that will put to trial everything you think you know about yourself spiritually. Deeper experience and understanding of the unique infinite nature of each of us will mark a turning point in the evolution of our spiritual consciousness, one which will profoundly effect our lives and abilities to contribute to society. It will mark the beginning of a maturing process in our sense of who we are and how we can best relate to each other and to our world. It will move us toward the development of a cosmic perspective that is spiritual as well as scientific, toward recognition of emerging potentials, and toward a higher valuing of all of humanity and nature. At the same time, the accountability implicit in this recognition of our true stature will motivate us to come to terms with our recently acquired capacity to inflict catastrophic damage on ourselves and on our planet's ability to sustain life.

This quest is ancient and ongoing. The paradox that we as finite human beings have existence and purpose on an infinite scale as an individual divine self is an idea that has been recognized and explored in differing forms for more than three thousand years, primarily in Western religions and mysticism. Ancient Egyptian belief, Zoroastrianism, Platonism and Neoplatonism, early Christianity, Gnosticism, medieval Christian mystics, Catharism, and Kabbalah have all entertained to some degree the notion of a divine individual infinite and/or immortal self. (These are explored in appendix 2, parts 1-3.) Yet, we can now understand, engage, and embody our infinite nature as never before.

We have much work to do: to sort and synthesize experiences and ideas and to create a new psychological and spiritual balance for the current configuration of the human psyche. This work requires discipline and inspiration, intuition and analysis, insight and dedication, and a clear mind. It requires courage to face the experience of the full living reality of the infinite and to overcome both the fear of discovering who one actually is and the ego's terror of losing control. (While fear occurs for some people, intense joy is just as likely.) We need steadfastness to encounter our resistances and illusions. If we do this work, we can explore the human infinite self in ways never before possible. This will enable us to achieve an inner marriage of our seemingly opposite and contradictory qualities that is wholeness— the integration of finite and infinite selves. In so doing, we can profoundly alter our civilization to assure our survival, improve our quality of life, and produce unparalleled accomplishments in art and science. Otherwise, after our current flowering of relative enlightenment, we may enter another dark age of forgetfulness and mystification. What we do right now will be immensely influential in determining which path humanity follows.

The discipline and analysis of science must be part of how we approach this subject. Yet, science is as much about mystery, including the human mystery, as spirituality is. Mystery has two meanings. One suggests the obscure, bizarre, dark, scary, and impenetrable. Many people see human nature this way, particularly its unconscious and mystical aspects. Mystery, however, can also be magical and miraculous, exciting curiosity and offering a puzzle to solve, which is what motivates many scientists. The scientific process is open-ended and without final answers; similarly, our mystery as infinite and paradoxical beings will never be fully unraveled (after all, we do like to think of ourselves as endlessly fascinating.) Although in spiritual as in scientific exploration the search for answers to mysteries is endless, each discovery along the way offers great rewards. We have a clear choice. Which kind of mystery, sinister or wondrous, will we be to ourselves?

Exploring our mystery leads to self-knowledge, the ultimate foundation of peace and joy. Joy is most profound when we experience our infinite dimension, our divine self. It is this joy, and the accompanying energy and sense of purpose, which lightens the burden of responsibility in our historical moment. To deeply enjoy life is part of our spiritual purpose; to experience and express joy is to complete the world. In joy, we bring the infinite, the divine, to earth; through it, we facilitate our sacred inner marriage. By it, I mean passionate surrender to the beauty and awesome splendor of creation. Less than that doesn't serve the purpose. Surrender must involve the exercise of free-will moral choice, that is, choice that recognizes costs and consequences and therefore affects the evolution of consciousness. Only we as human beings can do this in its full spiritual dimension. Too often, we choose the inverse of joy as a spiritual path. That we are willing to suffer so much indicates both that we recognize the importance of our purpose and that, paradoxically, we will learn to choose joy of our own free will, because transcendent joy is requisite to the accomplishment of our spiritual purpose. We are sufficiently dedicated that in the end we will embrace joy, if necessary. We needn't wait, however, for completion of our purpose to enjoy ourselves. We don't have to keep looking for the light at the end of our spiritual tunnel. We can see light and feel joy wherever in the tunnel we happen to be and embrace our mystery in this spirit.

2

The Infinite Self and Its Creation

> You strike a light. . . . And you hold the light before you and say: It is I; don't be afraid. And you put it down, slowly, and there is no doubt: it is you; you are the light around these familiar intimate things.
>
> —Rainer Maria Rilke, *The Notebooks of Malte Laurids Brigge*

As infinite and eternal spiritual beings—God children—we chose to become finite. Perhaps we, as infinite beings, did this because it provided the one thing we lacked: limit. Also, perhaps we wanted to see how we and other God children would look if we had what limits would give us: faces. We would have form and substance and therefore the ability to express ourselves in the finite world. Spiritual teacher Russell Paul Schofield (c. 1910–1984) called life in the finite universe, which God engendered and in which we as infinite selves create finite self-extensions, "the cosmic learning game," to signify a playful and profound exploration on the part of infinite and finite selves together.

As finite beings, we can never fully grasp this; we can only tell stories about it based on our limited comprehension and with the constant risk of unwarranted anthropomorphizing. We call these stories myths when they are the creations of a whole culture. Stories about the cosmic learning game can get quite confusing in the use of pronouns: we are both infinite self and finite self, and "we" can mean either or both. We, as finite selves, need to learn to think in ways that include these possibilities, despite this being awkward at first. It has always been simpler to externalize and separate the infinite self as an "it," "he," or "she," but abjuring this is essential: we can only have a sense and a sensing of the truth of the nature and purposes of infinite beings because we, as finite beings, are also those infinite beings. The experience lives within us and has always driven us to create narratives to express it.

As an example, my attempt at such a story is this: The cosmic learning game in which we, as infinite beings, could create finite self-expressions seemed to us the most fun possible, a stupendous creative act to which we would add an unexpected twist: we would give our creations free will! We would always be present within them, supporting and giving them love, and we would be ready to respond if they were open to our help, but we would never contravene their free will. They would be free even to try to break the laws of the cosmos, to forget us and to deny their heritage—more accurately, to deny who they are, for they are and always would be aspects of us and therefore would always partake of divinity even if they tried not to.

And how they—we, as finite selves—would try! As finite beings, many of us chose with zest and great abandon, and still choose, to try to break the laws of the universe and to forget who we are. Thus, as finite beings, we chose to take the prodigal journey: we ate, and eat, the unnourishing husks of illusion until we, being sufficiently fed up, choose at some point to begin to remember who we are. We never forgot completely; as infinite beings, we assure that there will always be enough memory to stir finite self out of whatever kind of sleep it seeks oblivion in. Awakening and remembering, we as finite selves reclaim our heritage and enjoy the feast of reunion set by infinite self to celebrate the return of the prodigal daughter or son.

As infinite beings, we know all along that the final outcome will be this joyous feast, followed by joyfully co-creating, together with finite self, all that is good, true, and beautiful with which to bejewel God's cosmos. We know this because our finite creations have a virtual eternity (over uncountable lifetimes, if one accepts reincarnation) in which to explore to their (our) hearts' content the effects of forgetting who they are and of breaking the laws of the universe and finally to understand what is real. We know they (we) are going to get thoroughly tired of forgetting and breaking cosmic laws at last and will have learned a treasure trove of wisdom and compassion in the process; therefore, nothing will have been wasted or pointless. Moreover, we won't really have lost any time at all, because not only is there a virtual eternity in which to return to union, there's timeless union with infinite self after that.

The most important part of the story is the joy with which we as infinite selves enter into the cosmic learning game and the unfathomable love that we always have for our creations. This is a game we choose, not a fall from grace we take.

This story is only words that, given their limitations, must fail to convey the reality of higher self. They have validity only for me. Your story will arise from your own inner sensing and knowing.

The Relationship of Infinite Self and Finite Self

The interaction between the infinite and finite selves that one is constitutes the most important in our lives. It is the most fascinating, compelling, profound, mysterious, empowering (but not overpowering), and sometimes awe-inspiring relationship possible. It is intensely personal because the creation is the dearly beloved of the creator (and vice versa when we get to know our infinite self).

An ancient symbol that Judaism calls the Star of David expresses the nature of the interaction: two interpenetrating triangles that form a six-pointed star. In one interpretation of this symbol, the triangle pointing upward represents the finite self, whose spiritual impetus is to know God, to return to union with the divine, to rise and expand in awareness, and to remember its nature and purpose. The triangle pointing downward represents the divine self entering into earthly form. Together they form a balanced, stable, creative configuration.

To infinite self, its living creation is the crossroads of the cosmos: only there does infinite self fully express itself in the finite cosmos, and there it is infinitely present, in and throughout at all times. While it supports and offers guidance, it respects its creation's free-will choices as to how the latter grows and learns its lessons. Their actual design is to be co-creative partners, each bringing something essential to the relationship. Finite self creates in form, which is surface; infinite self fills these creations with profound meaning and with life-energy. Genesis portrays this creative partnership when Adam receives the task of naming (distinguishing, identifying, and thereby giving form to) the teeming and inchoate life God has created. We, as finite selves, continue to differentiate and name; the work extends to deciding what is true and important among the vast amount of sense data we experience. To fulfill its role in the partnership, finite self puts emphasis on specifics and particular occurrences; it discriminates the essential from the superfluous and has the ability to focus in one place because that's the only place it is at that moment. Therefore, it can effectively concentrate and ground energy from the infinite.

The Gift of Creative Freedom

The most essential fact for the finite self and the crux of its meaning and purpose—of our lives—is that infinite self gives it creative power, along with free will in expressing that power. In their creative partnership, they have differences in their natures and qualities but not in their relative importance. Until now, however, only infinite self has known this.

Finite self provides the ability to identify with and thereby personalize experience. This power certainly has its down side, such as when finite self forgets that it transcends its current condition or circumstance or that it can experience more. When it forgets, its very ability to focus can magnify any pain it feels. It knows the aloneness of having limits. However, the integration of the experience of infinite self mitigates this down side, expanding us beyond the moment and the specific. The pain and loneliness of the moment dissolves in the infinite sea of the energy and love of higher self.

Paradoxically, as finite self takes on greater responsibility in its cocreator role, this opens the door to greater support from infinite self, resulting in less effort, discomfort, and stress. Finite self becomes more at peace with itself as it recognizes that whatever it is doing now is the most important thing in the cosmos—to its own infinite self, albeit, in all likelihood, to no one else—so it can feel fully centered in it. Moreover, finite self realizes that it cannot accomplish its responsibilities and creative purpose alone. Fulfilling its purpose requires the participation of infinite self, which waits to be invited but provides all when asked. The person's awareness of higher self allows it to experience the cosmic context of what it is doing and to envision the larger purpose served. This purpose, while usually quite different from what finite self thinks is most important, gives meaning to the most mundane tasks and prevents feelings of isolation or irrelevance.

Without finite self, infinite self lacks grounded focus, because it is not anywhere in particular, but that very expansiveness balances the limitation of finite self. A person can have the sense that her infinite self is present anywhere—or everywhere—as well as being centered exactly where she is. When the capabilities of these two selves are integrated, a person can be fully and effectively present and centered in his particular location yet his awareness, as well as the light of the being of light within him, can expand to include anywhere else that needs his attention without pulling him off center or limiting his effective focus.

The finite mind seeks the proportionality necessary in fair and harmonious human relations, in the creation of beauty, and in leading a balanced and satisfying life. Proportion involves a ratio, a relationship of the parts of a limited entity to one another. The finite mind has developed the ability to reason (*ratio*nality) in order to achieve proportionality. Infinite mind has no limited parts to be concerned with; therefore, ratio is meaningless in an infinite context. Thus, experience of the infinite or divine often seems mystical and *ir*rational.

The divine self provides a sense of the perfection of everything. From the standpoint of cosmic totality, this is accurate, but from the perspective of finite self and in its terms, the idea that everything is ideal is obviously irrational and wishful thinking. This apparent contradiction arises because the finite mind cannot perceive things in their entirety, particularly their full development over time, unless they are of a small enough scale; except in mystical states, it also can't be aware of their full context including how their influence ripples out to engender unexpected effects. The function of the finite mind is to discriminate and to make decisions that will ideally, if not usually, lead to manifest perfection (in finite self's terms) in the life of finite self. The finite mind must distinguish and make comparisons. Infinite mind functions differently; it doesn't discriminate or make superior/inferior evaluations. The finite mind's job is to see the smaller picture, to feel exactly how specific things interact, and to take creative actions that promote perfection as best it, as a finite entity, can conceive of this. Thereby, it grows in its capacity as a creator. Infinite mind, on the other hand, does not separate: everything is contained in everything, is both void and fullness. All pairs of opposites come together and are the same, are one, in infinite mind. The infinite cosmos is complete and flawless (infinite self's sense), yet each of the component sets can be in the process of perfecting itself (finite self's experience).

Infinite self, interacting with finite self, focuses in the world by way of our experience as body, mind, and emotions; the effect of this increases if finite self is aware of infinite self. As finite personalities and biological beings, our interaction with higher self opens us out into the infinite, transmuting our personal nature and species heritage, lifting them up and expanding them to their full potential. Interacting, the two marry infinite self's context and serenity with finite self's motivation and movement and its action in service of perfecting. With their union and integration, infinite self takes joy not only in the cosmic perfection of the divine order but in the process of perfecting (a process that is itself part of cosmic perfection). Finite self takes joy in what, to it, is the progressive achievement of the goal of perfection at each step, as well as in the knowledge that cosmic perfection is assured—knowledge that is gained intuitively or through mystical experience. Finite self can obtain comfort from this assurance, yet can't rest assured—it has work to do within its life's particular circumstances and limits. The eternal perfection of the cosmos depends, paradoxically, on the finite individual's perfecting actions. Perfecting is a process in time, temporality being finite self's modality of experience; perfection, on the other hand, is the experience of higher self because it exists in eternity, encompassing the process of perfection as well as the perfect origin and ultimate result of the process. Psychologist C. G. Jung (1875-1961) states that man "in an invisible act of creation put the stamp of perfection on the world by giving it objective existence." While perfection is commonly thought to be the work solely of the divine, such attribution produces a "view [of] life as a machine calculated down to the last detail, which, along with the human psyche, runs on senselessly, obeying foreknown and predetermined rules. . . . Man is indispensable for the completion of creation . . . [and] is the second creator of the world."[1]

The individual has essential choices to make as a perfecting being, and then must leave the rest to the divine. The coexistence of finite and infinite selves provides a person with a constant creative tension. The finite aspect needs sleep and comfort and relies on habit to efficiently handle routine tasks and needs. It conserves and protects its energy, its sense of identity and self-esteem, and its emotional resources. Although we can find infinite peace and harmony in our infinite self, we may also experience our infinite nature as wild, wide open, constantly changing, perpetually prodding us, profligate with energy, forever challenging our settled ideas, and powerfully desirous. This challenging is especially unsettling when finite self labors to discover "eternal verities" only to endure infinite self shredding those hard-won truths. This serves to remind finite self that not only can it never grasp the infinite and eternal, it must always be letting go of what it has only recently learned lest this turn into doctrine and obstruct learning more.

The presence of infinite self in our finite lives keeps presenting us with paradoxes and contradictory paradigms: are we to exercise our free will, be enterprising, and make things happen, or surrender to God's will and go with the flow, resisting not evil? Are we to focus on being one with the whole of life, or are self-determination and the development of our individuality more important? Infinite self's presence is a never-ending pain in the finite anatomy, a matter that is hard to reconcile with the fact that this presence is also unfathomable bliss!

3

The Light in the Middle of the Tunnel

... Your heart complains of being thirsty
When ages ago
Every cell of your soul
Capsized forever
Into this infinite golden sea.

—Hafiz, "So Many Gifts"

Gautama Buddha (b. sixth or fifth century B.C.E.) avowed that any sentient being could potentially achieve Buddhahood, or enlightenment, instantly. This achievement does not currently appear to be occurring on any large scale. Most of us don't feel that enlightenment or even a revelation or prophetic experience is apt to happen to us or to someone we know anytime soon. Still, we can speculate on what the Buddha might have meant.

Rather than expecting instant attainment, the Western paradigm of progress through effort over time predisposes us to assume the necessity of a linear sequence of events leading, in due course, in the general direction of enlightenment. In Gautama Buddha's case, this involved first being a prince, then becoming disillusioned with his sheltered, privileged life in the midst of a suffering world, renouncing his heritage to become a wandering seeker, meditating for years, and finally achieving his great realization about the causes of suffering and how to overcome it. Those of us who aren't princes probably don't feel we are even at step one of this linear progression toward enlightenment. Joining a monastery or wandering off into the woods might be impractical. We feel quite removed from what he experienced.

Were we to decide to try to achieve enlightenment, we'd probably seek out a teaching or discipline that would provide a framework of study designed to lead to this goal and, with our best work ethic, plunge into the effort. While practicing a discipline is fruitful and often necessary in order to achieve enlightenment, moral perfection, peace, or freedom, this process can contain its own trap. By making an effort and working toward a goal, we may unconsciously be postponing achieving it until we've accomplished the things we believe we must complete in order to earn the goal. The very structure of our work ethic ultimately stands in the way of enlightenment (though it can help initially) for there is no end to effort and busyness, which of themselves don't lead to anything except more of the same. Throughout the ages, those who have achieved a degree of enlightenment or have perceived cosmic truth have recognized it as a gift, not as something they can earn. The experience has occurred for some who have sought after and prepared for it, yet it didn't happen to many others who also diligently prepared themselves, and it did come to pass for some who neither sought nor wanted it but were simply plodding along on the way to their Damascus. In this field of endeavor, there is clearly not a linear progression leading to a predictable result, and instant, unprepared enlightenment is uncommon. Sometimes, there is a mystifying succession of peak experiences followed by deep valleys of despair, with no predictable pattern or timing.

The achievement of some degree of enlightenment is not merely a random event, however; those who study and do inner work are, anecdotal evidence suggests, more likely to have illuminating or transformational experiences. (If we factor in the possibility of study and initiation in previous lives, then the insightful or revelatory experiences of those untrained in this lifetime have a possible, if highly speculative, explanation.) Neither predictable nor random, enlightenment is paradoxical; in fact, it is the highest manifestation of humanity's paradoxical nature. It involves an interaction between finite and infinite selves where neither controls the events of the relationship but where both can affect them and contribute to them.

The Buddha's astonished and astonishing utterance upon achieving enlightenment, "O wonder of wonders, all beings are Buddhas!" goes against all common observation. The following figure illustrates what he may have been getting at. Its horizontal line is our time tunnel, the progression of linear time. Along this continuum, we place the time when we expect certain things to happen and plan accordingly. Some events, such as when we might achieve enlightenment—the light at the end of our tunnel of struggle and suffering—we position at an indeterminate distance to the right. The vertical line intersects the line of linear time in the present, the middle of the tunnel. It represents the presence of our individual infinite self and of the divine. This line extends to infinite distances above and below. It indicates the potential experience within each moment that, based on the testimony of mystics and others in altered states, is enormous in both height and depth.

The vertical line diagrams the proposition that we are not trapped in a linear time sequence governed by cause and effect; rather, we have access to the divine light of the infinite at all times. It points toward the possibility of living the infinite *now* in this moment. Life takes time, but divinity is immediate.

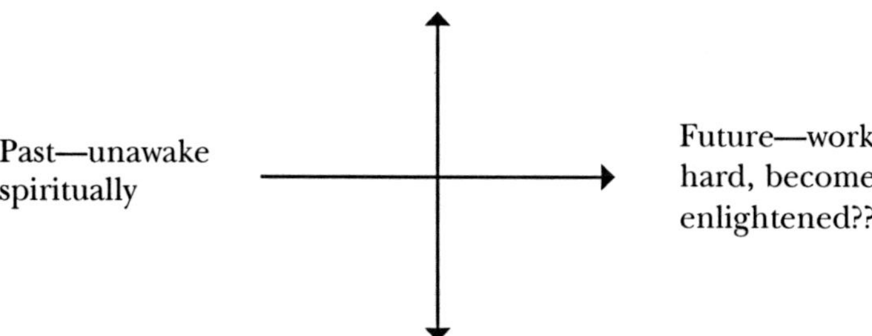

The Light in the Middle of the Tunnel Intersects Linear Time

We don't need to wait for the light at the end of the tunnel; it's available wherever we are. Thus, Gautama Buddha could assert that any sentient being could potentially achieve Buddhahood at any given instant.

Causality in linear time has been challenged by relativity and quantum physics. Quantum theory posits, and experiments with subatomic particles demonstrate, noncausal interactions of entities separate from one another in time or space; it suggests these entities are projections of a higher dimension of existence. When we engage with the higher dimension of the divine self, different parameters apply to outcomes than when we lock ourselves into cause and effect expectations. Steps we're sure are required of us may not be necessary if we've learned how to relate to infinite self, opening the door to the seemingly miraculous—a miracle being something we don't know the cause of.

Physicist David Bohm (1917-1992), a close collaborator of Albert Einstein (1879-1955), suggests a new understanding of fundamental order, based on the nature of the hologram. Each part of a hologram, and, by extension, each part of existence, records "information" regarding the total item photographed, the full "form and structure" of which is "*enfolded*" in every part of a hologram. If a part is illuminated, form and structure are "*unfolded,*" producing a likeness of the complete article.[1] "A *total order* is contained, in some *implicit* sense, in each region of space and time."[2] In the same way that illumination of any part of the hologram reveals the whole, the presence of infinite self allows for complete enlightenment in any moment. Physicist Louis De Broglie (1892-1987) states, regarding the fundamental order, "In space-time, everything which for each of us constitutes the past, the present and the future is given en bloc. . . . Each observer, as his time passes, discovers . . . new slices of space-time which appear to him as successive aspects of the material world, though in reality the ensemble of events constituting space-time exist prior to his knowledge of them."[3] Bohm describes the diagram's vertical line, De Broglie the horizontal. The Eastern spiritual approach to the same idea is given by Sri Aurobindo (1872-1950): "Nothing to the supramental sense is really finite; it is founded on a feeling of all in each and of each in all."[4]

Entering the Potential of Each Moment

How do we have access to the tremendous potential experience within each moment? We achieve it through focused awareness. This provides illumination that potentially unfolds the holographic experience of the infinite order in an instant of enlightenment. Many people have had moments that seemed to last for an eternity: of love, rapture, fascination with something, pain, or sorrow. In these, we seem to move outside of time; we become highly focused because we encounter some striking event, emotion, or sensation. At times of high creativity or even in a dream, we can instantaneously receive an inspiration that may take years to fully unfold, explore, and express, though we experienced its completeness in the instant of first apprehension. We can initiate this kind of focus ourselves. A mundane example is that when we're tired we can lie down, relax profoundly, let go of thoughts of the day, and be fully present within ourselves for barely a few minutes, arising feeling as if we've had a long nap and finding fresh perspectives on problems we've been wrestling with (see chapter 20).

Buddhism holds that our task is simply to remember that each of us is already a Buddha in nature. Zen uses koans and other means to enable the student to instantly (at some point) break through the conceptual conditioning of the mind to be aware of his "original face," while Chinese Taoism encourages trusting intuitive intelligence in order to act spontaneously, allowing one's actual nature to emerge unmediated by the mind. The key premise of Eastern disciplines is that what we need is already within us; we have only to remove or get around whatever obscures who we are. Similarly, anyone may have moments of spontaneous insight ranging from simply remembering a past event in a new light or seeing a coherent pattern in a confusing situation to experiencing sudden creative inspiration; with a little attention and practice, this and more can occur increasingly often in daily living.

Practices such as meditation, life-energy work, and other inner disciplines involving focused awareness serve to shift a person's experience from one modality of mind to another. Western minds are educated to function mostly by discursive reasoning, a logical movement from one thing to another that occurs step by step in time (or actually produces time[5]) and certainly takes time and effort. Another modality, however, grasps its subject as a whole and with immediacy. In this mode, mind does not separate itself from its subject; rather, it employs its most natural and effortless function, that of direct apprehension of something. The mind senses its subject in a most subtle way, rather than thinking about it external to itself. Words or preconceptions don't mediate this kind of knowing, which tends to be more accurate than analysis in getting at the subject's essential nature.

If, instead of setting our sights on a full-blown mystical experience (whatever we think such a thing is), we aim for the kind of accessible feeling or intuitive knowledge that actually occurs fairly frequently in normal life, we will develop a most useful and deeply rewarding relationship with the infinite right now and without further preparation. To do this, we need to pay attention to and value the occasions where we are outside the flow of time, even partially. We can give ourselves up to an experience of natural or artistic beauty. We can stare at a fire or a candle while letting the mind go blank. We can jog or walk with no goal or effort. Or, we can notice moments of reverie as they occur and let ourselves go more deeply into them. Each of us will find our own particular way; it is already happening in our day-to-day life. We can then choose to enter it more fully and consciously.

This practice involves an act of volition (paying attention, focusing awareness), followed by the action of releasing, relaxing, letting go, opening, and therefore being receptive to experience and to the response and support of infinite self. These two steps bring the two aspects of self, the finite and infinite, into effective interaction. We choose as finite beings. We then let go of the effort of choice and open to allow the infinite to respond. It will respond in a way we don't govern and usually don't expect, at a time we can't predict, but it *will* respond because we've entered into the paradoxical structure that is the nature of our relationship with the infinite.

You can practice this in the more systematic ways presented in exercises 1-4 in chapter 20.

Consistency in practice on the part of finite self opens the door to having experiences of the infinite, although, like infinite self's responses, they occur unpredictably. The injunction in Matthew 25:1-13 to the virgins, to keep their lamps filled with oil because they could not know the hour of the coming of the bridegroom, speaks to the nature of the relationship between finite and infinite within each person.

Properly understood, we don't practice a spiritual discipline in order to get somewhere, because the light we seek is neither at the end of the tunnel of effort and struggle nor at the end of the time that these take. The linear does not become the vertical by our plodding along it; the vertical intersects it. The spiritual light of higher self and its infinite understanding are available here in the middle where we are, where we can go deeply into the moment. When we do so, events and outcomes seem less in our control. Our horizons extend: not linearly but spherically around that point in time. We don't know when experience of the divine self will arrive; we can't control its coming by our efforts. We can only savor it. We can be ready, however, and we can be open to the fact that it may come at any moment, no matter how unprepared or undeserving we may feel. The moment it does, we are in some degree both in time and in eternity, but eternity is the context and is the more real and compelling.

The goal is not to achieve something. We do not permanently return to or attain union with the divine, allowing us to abandon this world and its tribulations. There is no goal, if goal implies finality. There is, rather, intersection or interpenetration. We should not try to hold on to union because it's there when we need it if we're open to it and because, when we open, it is always enough. The act of holding on closes us off.

We simply need to quit squinting and straining for the distant glimmer of a light at the end of the tunnel (which may be the proverbial oncoming train, anyway), and remember that we can flip on the light switch of focused awareness for a wonderfully bright and wholly present illumination from within, anytime.

Eastern spirituality famously enjoins us to "Be here now." Physicists have determined there is *only* here and now; in this discovery, they join mystics and meditators, the poets and lovers of life of all ages. Erwin Schrödinger (1887-1961), a founder of quantum mechanics, said, "The present is the only thing that has no end." The light always was, and only can be, in the middle of the tunnel.

4

Distinguishing the Experiences of Finite Self and Infinite Self

> We attempt, with our finite minds, to discuss the infinite, assigning to it those properties which we give to the finite and limited; but this [assigning] I think is wrong.
>
> —Galileo Galilei, *Dialogues Concerning Two New Sciences*

The infinite self is always present within its finite creation as a necessary part of the creation's life, always giving it support. Often—indeed continually—the finite self has experiences of the higher self, but because we don't have a conceptual framework that allows us to distinguish our experiences of our infinite selves from those we have of ourselves as finite selves, we become confused. The experiences of infinite self make sense only as such; they are misleading or make no sense at all if mistaken for experiences of the finite world. Bewildered, we try to squeeze what is natural for the infinite into the conditions of the finite; this can never contain the infinite, so we inevitably fail. Finally, in frustration and often in guilt over our inability as finite selves to measure up to the experiences we're having of the potentials of the infinite realm, we decide there's something wrong with us, or everyone else, or the whole world! People have often told me that they feel they don't belong on this planet and that the reality they live in doesn't match their inner sense of the way things are meant to be, a discrepancy that produces lifelong distress.

The problem begins with compelling experiences that occur at the end of infancy, before a person can speak and form the kind of memories that later can be easily accessed as adults; these are experiences that a person has when forming her fundamental sense of self. At this time, when she is still living in the feeling of being infinite, she collides with the fact that others see and treat her as an entirely finite being and expect her to behave as such. Given that these adults and older siblings are larger and thus able to enforce their views upon her, she has to abandon the charms of her interior infinite existence. A person moves relatively rapidly from a subjective, infantile, infinite sense of self to a growing objective awareness of herself as exclusively finite. As an older child or adult, the sense a person in infancy had of herself as infinite, the way that she was taught to react to these experiences at that time, and the choices she made as to how to handle the situation are mostly buried beneath her normal waking awareness. Thereafter, a person usually can't make sense of the aspects of experience that arise from her infinite nature. She tries to understand them in terms of the finite, producing no end of confusion and poor judgment.

In this chapter, we will look at some kinds of situations where this crossing of wires commonly occurs. We'll examine the consequences of this for our lives and see how these experiences appear different when we can distinguish the types of sensibilities natural to each of these two aspects of self. Once we make the distinction, we'll find that we can achieve a mutually supportive relationship between the two, one that can make living more effortless, reduce stress, and explain much about life that otherwise seems perplexing or even perverse.

The experiences we have as infinite selves are by their nature of uncommon interest, in the same sense that mystical experiences are inherently of exceptional interest, and yet they don't commonly interest many people, who automatically view the mystical as impractical and suspect. Focusing, however, on the everyday registry of the experience of the individual infinite self tends to demystify mystical experience and produce a practical mysticism that is no mystery at all, yet is endlessly engaging. The more we pay attention, the easier it is to recognize.

The Importance of Being Infinite

Recognizing and experiencing the infinite self has profound moral, spiritual, and practical implications. It is daunting to try to relate meaningfully to the God of all creation, especially if we believe that we are mere finite, flawed mortals. This belief exists because of the melding of a person's innate sensing of his own individual divine self with his experience or conception of God, attributing both experiences to a God separate from himself. Such a belief leads to the feeling of being virtually nothing; one prays to God for one's needs that seem, nevertheless, to be insignificant. It gives the sense of such a differential of power and scale as to make one feel utterly helpless except to beg God for relief from one's sinful nature or the burdens of life. So, people pray to God for all manner of dispensations. Prayer can attune a person to the divine and help him enter into a dialogue with divinity as well as help him to be open to receive its gifts; however, the sense of being puny and fallen can lead to spiritual passivity, a feeling of only being able to plead one's miserable case. All power to act and achieve results lies with God, but blame for failure resides with oneself. When the latter begins to feel too onerous, one may quit trying. Doubt even as to the goodness of the divine order can begin to creep in, resulting in loss of faith.

Awareness of being both a finite self and an infinite self leads to an entirely different sense of empowerment and responsibility. One goes beyond feeling merely limited and fallible and believing that one barely has the ability to make the moral decisions that save one's own soul (and even salvation is often seen as only by God's grace). One sees oneself not merely as finite and prone to error but also as a creative divine being, endowed with the resources to respond to the finite self's needs. The relationship that finite self has with infinite self is not one of supplication but is a working partnership. The finite self has responsibility for helping to develop the partnership, learning how to work with and embody the higher self, and bringing forth the kind of potentials that few people acknowledge or express, lacking awareness of their infinite nature.

While the individual, as finite self, must be able to recognize his limitations and foibles if he is to build this relationship to its full potency, he also needs to be aware that he exists not only as a limited and imperfect creation but, equally, as a divine and flawless infinite being. This simultaneous awareness helps keep the person from falling into despair over his obvious lacks and prevents hubris over the qualities and powers of his higher nature. It produces a balance between the sense of a need to learn and grow and the awareness of the capacity to thereby refine and perfect the partnership, which leads to a manifestation of one's divine nature in the finite world. It enables one to take seriously Jesus' (c. 6-4 B.C.E.-c. 30 C.E.) astounding words, "the one who believes in me will also do the works that I do and, in fact, will do greater works than these."[1] To see oneself in this light leads to a profound sense of worthiness and capability, and with this comes an equal sense of responsibility and enthusiasm to act in a way that expresses the fullness of self. To see one's fellow human beings this way makes it harder to devalue, control, damage, or destroy them. There is no need to do so, for one feels unquestionably that one has the ability and means within oneself to meet one's own needs. There is no compulsion to prove oneself superior to another because one already knows oneself to be infinitely worthy while being neither superior nor inferior to anyone.

Whose Experience Is This?

Even though we are infinite selves and have experience as such, when speaking of the experiences of our infinite selves, I am necessarily referring to those impressions of infinite self that finite self can register. Finite self, of course, is our reference point, the part of us we've learned to call ourselves and through which we view all things. It's the part of you engaged in reading this. In a true mystical state or in deep meditation we can, to a degree, leave the finite or expand from it and enter into the infinite; as many mystics report, however, they can bring back to finite awareness only a minute portion of what they encountered in that state. (We have a similar, related feeling when we wake up from an intense dream and feel it slipping away as we return to our normal consciousness.) Our means for forming finite descriptions of the nature and experience of the infinite are limited and produce distorted results. There is a great need for Western civilization to develop language more fluent in expressing the transcendent. Societies that from a Western viewpoint seem primitive have long understood the importance of this and have been much better at it, which is why we have misunderstood them and dismissed their "beliefs" as superstition. Eastern religions developed a lexicon for distinguishing concepts and experiences of the infinite that is as exacting as the terminology of Western science. Richness of vocabulary regarding particular subjects indicates what is important to a culture and gives its members the means to distinguish and evaluate phenomena. Religious and poetic symbolism currently provides us our primary means for describing experiences of the infinite.

The fact that we in some way continually register, as finite selves, the imprint of the experiences we have *as* infinite selves is in addition to finite self's sense of the presence and effect *of* this higher self, however limited and inaccurate the experiences and expression of them may be. Ultimately, it's how the experiences that we have as infinite selves impinge on us as finite selves that matters to us (as finite selves), regardless of their true nature and magnitude. How the infinite impacts us can vary greatly. To experience as infinite self is to experience on a vast and encompassing scale of perception and meaning. If finite self registers this, it may be felt as what is called ego death, or else as an inflated sense of self, awe that leads to a profound sense of motivation and encouragement, despair (if the person does not have a strong, healthy sense of self), peace, or exquisite beauty that leaves a profound reverence for all life. The meaning of the impact can differ from person to person. If the source, the infinite, is held to be exclusively external (for instance, if it is believed to be God, Allah, or else an impersonal infinity as in Buddhism or *Brahman* in Hinduism) the import will be vastly different and more limited and limiting than if it's understood to arise from the individual divine self. Therefore, what we will examine emphasizes, necessarily, how the experiences that we have as infinite selves occur to us and affect us as finite selves. Rather than the experience we have as infinite selves, we are concerned with the intersection and the interaction of that experience—registered in a necessarily finite and limited translation—with our finite selves. Most important is how we can integrate the imprint of this interaction meaningfully into finite life.

Much of the experience of the infinite is lost and distorted in translation to finite comprehension, but while it's hard to accurately bring back experiences that transcend our finite nature, the process of making them a part of everyday living is even harder. This is partly because integrating them can upset the finite self's status quo, force it to face painful challenges to its beliefs, make it revise its priorities and manner of living, and even change its sense of identity. Although truly dramatic change happens rather infrequently, the habit patterns of finite self resist even the possibility of this and try to sabotage the effective integration even of much less powerfully transforming experiences. The fear of change causes some people to abandon the attempt to integrate the experiences of the infinite; many more suppress these experiences before they reach awareness so as to altogether avoid feeling this fear.

On some occasions it's appropriate and useful to approach and relate to something more from the "perspective" of one's infinite self, as much as one is able. (The word "perspective" is obviously inaccurate: an infinite being does not have a viewpoint; that's what finite selves are for. Nonetheless, for the sake of discussion that's not too tortured by compensating for our lack of the means to talk easily about what is infinite, I must use such misleading terms. Likewise, talking about differences between finite and infinite self can create the mental picture of them as separate entities. The finite self is, of course, an aspect of the wholeness that includes infinite self; as a part, however, it is distinct from that wholeness.) Other circumstances require an approach more from the finite perspective. Knowing the difference and how to tell which approach is suitable has been a key aspect of esoteric training throughout the centuries. Those who've failed to distinguish the correct approach have been prone to act in ways such as grandiosity, obscurantism, otherworldliness, and lack of grounding in practical reality that at times have given esoteric study a bad name.

Uncrossing the Wires: Mortality and Immortality

A common example that illustrates the importance of the distinction is that many people, especially the young, have an irrational feeling that they are immortal and act accordingly. This is enormously helpful for military recruiters in times of war; its effect is also apparent in the way many adolescents drive, in their choosing to smoke, and in many other risk-taking behaviors. It's not that they are unaware that they're mortal; neither do they lack fear of death. Knowledge of the dangers they court can be reinforced, yet often to little effect. Because of adolescents' incomplete development of the prefrontal lobes of the brain, which foresee the consequences of actions, they are more likely to respond to another kind of knowledge that is intuitive, largely unconscious, and completely valid: they are indeed immortal beings. Unfortunately, the truth of this feeling does not apply to their bodies. This intuition is both a vestige of the engulfing experience of the infinite which occupied them as infants and the continuing inchoate sensing of the presence of infinite self, yet it's powerful enough to be lethally misleading if its origin isn't understood.

Another example is that well into adulthood, many people act as if they had all the time in the world to achieve their goals. They feel as if to get down to business would confirm their mortality; it would seem, unconsciously, to deny their equally real, though differently located, immortality. Midlife crises arise when the changes the years enforce on us make our mortality less avoidable and time more obviously limited. Benjamin Franklin (1706-1790) poked fun at himself about how his sense of his real eternal nature could undermine his good judgment as a finite self, even as an old man. When thinking he was perhaps too idle and playing at cards overmuch, he found that "another reflection comes to relieve me, whispering: 'You know that the soul is immortal; why then should you be such a niggard of a little time, when you have a whole eternity before you?' So, being easily convinced, and, like other reasonable creatures, satisfied with a small reason when it is in favour of doing what I have a mind to, I shuffle the cards again, and begin another game."[2]

Entitlement, Endowment

Children are entitled to nurture from their parents. Teenagers have to negotiate the difficult transition from this entitlement to taking more responsibility for themselves, while at the same time learning what talents and abilities they are endowed with to handle their responsibilities. This change would be difficult enough without confusing external finite parents with the internal infinite self. We have a lifelong entitlement to access the resources of infinite self, including the wisdom to guide us, the life-energy that supports our health and vitality, and the security and self-assurance that come from an awareness of being valued and having purpose and spiritual identity. The only limitation to this claim is our ability to access these resources. The age-old beliefs of aristocrats and kings that their positions were God-given arose somewhat from the felt truth of this inward prerogative. Likewise, in our time a misapprehension of our rights as the creations of infinite selves feeds the growing sense of entitlement adults feel. It occurs even in the consciousness of sincere seekers, who feel entitled to the benefits of their spiritual practices and come to doubt God or their practice when the benefits don't come through, forgetting that they must learn how to open to these, removing obstacles created by belief and habit.

A child is entitled to receive unconditional positive regard and the necessities of life and growth from her parents. Receiving more (assuming she's fortunate enough to be given these essentials) will depend on her ability to form interdependent relationships with her parents, friends, teachers, and others. This matches how the higher self structures and prods the child's progress as a finite self: she is given a basic support system of life-energy, inner guidance, and sense of purpose, although even this must be utilized. Beyond this, children vary in their endowment with the ability to learn to establish healthy relationships, although, regardless of differences, all except those with maladies such as severe autism can learn this. Endowment is not inalienable; it is more like a loan or a time-sensitive opportunity, as taught in the New Testament parable of the talents: use it to grow or lose it. The endowment increases if used and may atrophy if neglected or abused. Each child receives those gifts that will assist her in her unique life tasks and lessons, but these may seem to her of little value if they vary from the norm. Many people intuitively recognize the need to exercise their talents but may not be aware of their actual entitlement to inner resources and therefore see life as a struggle against an ungiving cosmos. Those more attuned to their actual entitlement but misled as to its source may feel disappointed at the world's failure to deliver what they feel entitled to receive. They may develop dependence on those around them or become manipulative to get what they feel is their due. The numinosity (the charge of psychic or spiritual energy that when strong can obsess or compel) of the source of their entitlement causes some people to feel specially, even divinely, singled out and expect others to treat them accordingly. Most people manage to achieve a mature recognition of the need to balance the realities of actual entitlement and endowment without any thought of having an infinite self; however, such awareness can help one to find a way through the pitfalls of overemphasizing one or the other so as to fully utilize both.

Actual Pride, Actual Humility

The importance of distinguishing the experiences we have as infinite selves from those we have as finite selves can be seen in the difference between actual pride and actual humility on the one hand, and ego-based pride and humility on the other. This distinction is essential for anyone wishing to enter seriously into spiritual training. Actual pride stems from the recognition that one is an infinite being, created by God and partaking of divine nature, as well as the beloved finite creation of that divine self. This is as grand a self-definition as one might want, but actual pride involves the further awareness that if one is infinite and eternal, one can't compare oneself in any way to any other infinite and eternal being or to the finite creation of one. Each, being infinite, is totally, incomparably unique, so one can have pride in being oneself without feeling superior to anyone else. The nature of infinity does not allow for that.

Actual humility arises from the recognition that one is also finite, limited, fallible, and involved in a learning game in which periodically falling on one's face is a given. As with actual pride, actual humility involves remembering that one is unique and has a learning curve and a style that are entirely one's own and that therefore one is not only no better than anyone else, one is no worse. Each person is a creator, is in a unique league of one's own, and is utterly beloved of one's divine self and God. Actual humility is a great comfort, relieving one of the burden of living up to an external standard and of the fear of falling short, freeing one to get on with one's own purpose and growth.

Actual pride and actual humility contrast instructively with the egotism of spiritual pride and abject humility, which arise from the confusion of the finite and infinite aspects of self. Spiritual pride, similar to what Jung called inflation and described as the personal psyche being engorged by the overwhelming energy of an archetype of the collective unconscious, involves finite self identifying with infinite self and trying to encompass it and be it, which is a lot to digest: one becomes full of oneself and puffs up. Finite self can never live up to what it's trying to be because that involves trying to be the aspect of self that it is not and cannot be. Actual pride on the part of finite self, on the other hand, could be depicted as the finite self pointing to the higher self as its heritage and goal; finite self's sense of value arises from its right relationship with infinite self.

Abject humility occurs when finite self becomes aware of infinite self but thinks it is *supposed to be that* and is dreadfully aware that it can never live up to such a standard, so it feels condemned to a life of failure. One's intuitive sense of the nature of the higher self becomes an ongoing rebuke and a reflection of one's shortcomings. There are endless accounts of sincere religious devotees who have mortified their flesh and lived in great deprivation, even reveling in martyrdom, as compensation for their sense of infinite, irremediable inadequacy. (Inflation can appear in abject humility as well; it can lead to a grandiosity of unworthiness and to feeling that one is so bad that no one could match one's extremity of worthlessness and depravity.) Actual humility involves the understanding that one is created to be finite and limited and that as such it's perfectly okay to be imperfect and fallible; however, it also includes the awareness that one is more than that—that one is not limited to finite experience but can transcend it and encompass both finite and infinite.

Many seekers, aware of their potentials and abilities, know that they're not fulfilling them. As infinite beings, we offer more than finite self could ever express. This awareness can lead to self-judgment, but it is actually the promise of things to come after we complete our current tasks. Either the negative or positive view of this fact can provide a rationale for one not to try to live up to finite self's capabilities: either one is not up to the task, or there is no need to try because it will inevitably happen sometime. Those who desire to know and develop themselves more commonly fall into the trap of self-negation than of not trying.

Actual humility and pride arise from the awareness that one is more than ego, body, personality, or what society says one is; this awareness sets one on the quest for self-knowledge and the fulfillment of higher purpose. Conversely, abject humility and spiritual pride—a deflated or inflated ego—send one on a search for self-justification as compensation for feeling like a worm, for validation as being good or legitimate because anyone cut off from his source in the infinite will always doubt himself, or for ego gratification because the needs of egotistical pride can never be satisfied. Bereft of the meaning and purpose of infinite self, one overreaches and tries to infinitely fulfill what are finite needs, doing more than is appropriate for finite self yet never being able to feel complete or do enough to justify to oneself the sense of being infinite.

Form: Limitation or Expression?

It is vital to distinguish between infinite self and finite self regarding their approaches toward the world of finite form and structure. Having the accurate intuition that self is in some way unlimited, finite self can find form, especially life in a bodily form, frustrating and limiting. A surprising number of people feel that being born into their body and circumstances was a mistake or that cruel fate has trapped them. Some people treat form and structure, such as a relationship, job situation, commitment, social structure, belief system, or any arrangement or organizing principle at all, as limiting their freedom and therefore as something to avoid, escape, or demolish. (This does have the valuable effect of driving some who feel this way to achieve greater freedom, to become more aware, and to seek higher truths.) The higher self, on the other hand, finds form to be a joyous expression of itself, an endlessly creative opportunity, a field of infinite potential. As infinite self is always more than—and more lasting than—any material form, it has nothing to fear about entering into form, much as a child may create a number of different games in the course of a day, any of which she can enthusiastically change or abandon at any time. Thus, finite self and infinite self have exceedingly different experiences of form. Each offers the other what it seeks: finite self provides the higher self with the opportunity for experience and expression within limit so as to produce shape and form, and the infinite offers finite self a sense of endless opportunity and a here-now feeling of limitless freedom, as well as the awareness that one is here by choice.

The fairly common view of form as confining has led to major religions establishing doctrines with highly negative attitudes toward earthly form and its pleasures and possibilities. Many faiths project this view onto the higher self or God, convincing people that God is the originator of attitudes that denigrate the flesh. This in turn has led to feeling justified in treating the physical world or aspects of it with contempt and violence, mortifying or martyring one's own body, subjugating women (seen as closely associated with the physical world), or disregarding the environment. It is harder to sustain these behaviors when we experience the "attitude" of infinite self, which cherishes and enjoys finite form.

Conversely, when infinite self's attitude toward form fills finite self's experience but the attitude's origin is unrecognized, the result can be hedonism, seeking unlimited pleasure in the physical world.

Lacking an understanding of the infinite aspect of self, American culture has approached the issue of form and its limitations with the emphatic declaration: "Size matters!" As a young nation, we felt impelled to become larger, expanding across the continent and into the Pacific and Caribbean. Then we touted having the most and the biggest of various natural and man-made wonders. More recently, form has been a personal matter of the size of various body parts: becoming ever bigger or more extreme (including thinness) assuages our innate sense of limitation in size, precisely as multitasking and going ever faster does for our limitation in time. It leaves us in perpetual doubt, however, as to whether we measure up. Men are especially concerned about this in relationship to women; given that the feminine aspect of our nature feels closer to the infinite, this points to the real issue: how do we measure up to the unlimited potential we intuit to be within ourselves? While for women large is good in those select aspects of the anatomy men have special interest in, for the most part the issue is measuring down, with concerns about weight and slenderness assuming pathological proportions in diseases such as anorexia nervosa. We can't be comfortable with the form we have until we take the full measure of ourselves as finite and infinite; when we experience this totality of self, we will feel no need to live up to anything but will be able to enjoy bodily existence, care for, cultivate, respect, even hold it sacred, yet not take the form we're in too seriously. Until then, we will continue to compensate, which currently means to "super size it," causing us to become the most obese population in history.

No Pain, No Gain; All Gain, No Pain

The individual whose frame of reference is entirely the finite, but who has some concept or intuition of his or her infinite existence as something to strive toward, may believe that the suffering associated with finite existence is the mark of spiritual progress. He is sure he must go through the pain to get to the joy, and he plunges into the accumulated garbage of his life with great relish. This is not without profit; he accomplishes spiritual work and clears enough of life's painful litter that he may attain illuminations and idyllic experiences. Where identification with finite self is strong, however, this reward reinforces the conviction that growth must involve suffering; the seeker dives yet deeper into the debris of his unresolved conflicts and wounds. Many a saint has inflicted harm on his flesh because of this stimulus-response bondage. Belief in the value of suffering can also motivate a person to enter unnecessarily into the pain of another person, thinking this is part of a complete relationship or essential to compassion. We do totally enter into one another as infinite selves, but good boundaries are essential to finite selves, protecting us without limiting empathetic and loving interaction.

The opposite belief holds that spiritual pursuits can quickly produce a pain-free and blissful existence. A person thus inclined identifies, as a finite self, with her infinite self or the higher aspects of her finite nature, usually having had some direct perception or indirect experience of these. The person may seek to live exclusively on this level and view disease or misfortune as an indication of spiritual failure. She may shun people who suffer and struggle in order to avoid contamination by their condition.

Our actual psychospiritual nature involves the truths at the heart of both of these experiences, relating in a dynamic interaction. Part of our purpose as finite selves is indeed to plow through the dregs of life and transmute what we encounter into finer stuff; life's difficulties become kindness, insights, and lessons learned, such as we can glean from all experience; we can then help others do it themselves. We must stay connected with the earth of our nature and its difficulties in order to grow. We don't have to suffer in doing so, however. With identity experienced in both finite and infinite aspects of self, we can ground ourselves in joy and light while engaging in the world of finite evolution. We can live in the light in the middle of the tunnel while traversing the tunnel. This is seldom pain-free; still, pain is not the point or the badge of progress, and the interaction of infinite self with finite self can minimize it. Awareness mediates this interaction; free-will choice catalyzes it.

Product and Process, Purpose and Purposefulness

People who are open to an abiding experience of the individual higher self are inclined to relate to life in a more relaxed way. This experience can provide an intuitive understanding of living as the playing out of infinite potentials over unlimited time. These individuals tend to be more pacific and have less of an urge to dominate the earth or to force things to happen. Unfortunately, historic figures who have the need to rule others or have an all-or-nothing approach to things have been liable to marginalize or destroy people who are less driven as well as the cultures that foster them. Ironically, the urge to dominate may also have at its foundation an experience of the "all" that the person is and has as an infinite self; in these cases, however, this experience of unlimited expansiveness and power gets confused with the proper goals of the finite self, objectives that aren't properly infinite and do not necessitate control or domination.

A defining characteristic of living cells is the membranes that enclose them, the integrity of which is necessary for life. It is part of our cellular foundation, therefore, for us to want to achieve closure, to wrap things up. We also have a life span within which we instinctively want to complete certain things. We want to know how things will come out; we feel a need for definite answers to life's questions. As finite beings, we are naturally outcome or product oriented.

Infinite beings are process oriented. Over infinite time, we can accomplish, by way of our finite self-extensions, every desirable outcome; for any given one, there's no hurry. What's important is *how* we do something, not the result. It's more important that the process be an expression of the qualities of consciousness and energy that are the essence of our nature. For this to occur, the methods and means of action of the finite self need to be open to the participation of the infinite self. This has remarkably practical consequences in the finite world, for whatever we do with joy or with love (qualities of every infinite self) tends to have a superior outcome in worldly as well as spiritual effects, at least in the long run.

For the higher self, there is greater emphasis on quality than on quantity; success rests more on living life in a particular manner than on accomplishment in the world's terms. In the famous Zen example, what turns out to matter to the seeker after she has achieved spiritual realization is how she chops the wood and carries the water, which were her mundane and seemingly unspiritual tasks before she set off to seek enlightenment. To these the seeker must ultimately return but with a completely new sense of what she's doing when performing them.

The ancient spiritual injunction to know oneself means to engage in a process, not to create a product called self-knowledge. It is to live fully and in full awareness the life of finite self in union with, and thereby with experience and knowledge of, infinite self. Self-knowledge is a way of life, not a goal. A time-honored esoteric dictum runs, "The life lived is the truth received."

Another way of stating this difference between the attitudes inherent in finite and infinite selves is to distinguish purpose from purposefulness. Many people feel they are on earth for a higher purpose. This sense of purpose is a deeply meaningful and motivating experience, informing their whole lives. Yet, many are painfully unable to discern their what their purpose is. They urgently feel the need to be doing something, yet are unclear as to what. Their feeling is often attributable to their awareness of the profound sense of purpose of the divine self in creating its finite self-extension. This purpose can be stated in terms of aiming for certain qualities of life-experience, becoming more aware, and learning through making choices. Despite the tendency of finite selves to concretize this and look for particular things to achieve and good deeds to do, higher purpose doesn't necessarily translate well into a specific action (although it may in some cases). For most people most of the time, actual fulfillment of the sense of purpose largely occurs by expressing certain aspects of consciousness or character, such as good will, integrity, or love, in whatever they do. Finite self imagines that purpose requires a specific set of actions and accomplishments. One can release a heavy load of false responsibility by realizing that purpose is usually more a matter of means than outcome. Instead of feeling that his current commitments are barriers or distractions keeping him from getting to his higher purpose, this recognition allows a person to see that he can accomplish his divine business while pursuing whatever his life circumstances have led him to do.

The finite self's goals acquire an undue sense of absolute necessity if the numinosity and spiritual authority of the infinite, which infuse the process orientation of the infinite, become displaced onto them. This can lead to terrible urgency, compulsion, or even the fanaticism and lack of humanity seen, for example, in terrorists. This compulsion replaces any sense of personal freedom or choice. If, however, the demands of the finite self's product orientation suffuse that self's approach to the spiritual, religious pursuits take on the qualities of mundane living and become another thing to do, a duty to perform, a commodity to have in one's life. Spirituality's ability to transform and provide transcendent experience is lost, as occurs for many members of mainstream religions.

Part of the sense of spiritual purpose many people have at this time is due, of course, to their awareness of the urgent need for changes in consciousness and behavior if we are not to compromise our environment and endanger the survival of civilization and perhaps even our species. There is a deeply felt need for a new spiritual awakening in order to avert any of a number of potential crises. While laudable, this is the perspective of finite self; it arises from the same goal orientation that got us into our current predicaments and that by itself won't get us out. We need to take action on many fronts including overpopulation, environmental degradation, nuclear waste, education, disease, scarcity of resources such as water, and the inequitable distribution of the means to live. Part of the solution, however, involves people experiencing that infinite self created finite self for a majestic purpose that has nothing to do with what they achieve or acquire. This awakening will give us a sense of meaning and value that will obviate our need for many the self-validating and self-aggrandizing actions that cause many of the problems we face. Fulfilling higher purpose has little to do with fulfilling the ego's need to feel purposeful; it requires changing the structure of consciousness that overvalues achieving goals or producing a product. The greatest part of the solution to our problems will arise from people learning to treasure and embody the attributes of the higher self that they were created to express in daily living, such as empathy and forgiveness. Gandhi had great political impact in part because he maintained a sense of purposefulness and didn't let what others did to him prevent him from living according to his principles. The time he spent at his spinning wheel was as purposeful as his political activism.

Circumstances certainly require vigorous, committed actions now, but these will address the real issues, be effective, and entail a minimum of negative unforeseen consequences only if they arise from and are grounded in consistent practice of those qualities that our higher selves created us to embody. In sum, the discipline followed is the goal achieved.

People driven to succeed and those who like to go with the flow tend to view each other with skepticism, if not distaste. Both have needed qualities, and both behave in ways that can be problematic to themselves and others if they're too far out of balance. We praise, with good reason, those who address the world's troubles energetically. Hard-driving entrepreneurs point to the achievements Western civilization has made in terms of increased living standards over the past two hundred years. The gains are obvious, but there's an accounting problem. Missing from the balance sheet are the costs in human displacement, suffering, loss of life, and environmental and resource degradation that were involved in achieving these standards so quickly. In the industrializing London of Dickens's time, members of the working class had a life expectancy of twenty-one years. This was part of the price of our current well-being. The costs to the Third World are beyond calculation. A more balanced approach might have accomplished the same thing with a greater sum of human happiness and fulfillment, not just for the winners—the writers of history. China is incurring the same costs as it rapidly modernizes.

In contrast, going with the flow obviously means that the flow goes its own way. We are created with the ability to act creatively and effectively, and every religion enjoins us to use our abilities for the good of divine creation and for our own spiritual growth or reward. Doing too little is as destructive as doing too much, perhaps more so. Each person needs to find his own balance between making things happen and letting them flow. This requires rigorous attention and continual flexibility.

To achieve this balance, the most effective relationship between finite and infinite selves is for finite self to choose a goal and take action toward it. It then needs to release that energy into the matrix of divine creativity, which will mold and shape it according to the qualities of process that are the essence of infinite self's orientation. This is the meaning of casting bread upon the waters. If finite self tries to control the outcome, the effect will be limited because finite self is limited. If it releases its energy into the boundless, the effect can be unlimited. Releasing control also relieves finite self of a major source of stress.

Of course, finite self cannot simply make a choice, set things in motion, turn it over to the higher self or to God, and then relax in the belief that whatever the outcome is will be absolutely right and the will of God. Responsibility, the ability and need to respond, merely begins with that. Having fully released the energy, one then needs to observe vigilantly. From what occurs, one gets a better understanding of the divine creative purpose; one then can respond accordingly, choosing and acting again, then once more release control of the outcome, and again remain observant and responsive. This allows for an interplay of finite and infinite selves that maximizes the choosing and acting functions of the former as well as the shaping, energizing, and amplifying functions of the latter.

Equally Important, but Not to Be Confused

At this point in drawing distinctions between the outlooks and experiences we, as finite entities, have of the finite world and of infinite self and those we have as infinite selves, it must be emphasized that neither is better or more correct. They are interactive and complementary, both necessary to living in fullness. The medieval believer viewed experience of the divine as entirely superior to the finite, and he discounted the value—and validity—of sense experience, much to the detriment of scientific development and general physical well-being. This, of course, changed during the Renaissance, the Enlightenment, and the industrial revolution, so that we now live in a secular, finite-oriented culture that discounts precisely what medieval culture valued and instead prizes sensory stimulation and physical reward. Because of this and also because, in a much larger time frame, we're slowly evolving away from separated, fragmentary consciousness toward full union with our infinite selves, many people now intuitively feel that spiritual or religious experiences are the ones they must emphasize in order to achieve balance. In the Middle Ages, balance required movement in the opposite direction, toward the world. Humankind is usually in a dynamic state of imbalance and correction. As we adjust our current imbalance, we should keep in mind the equal validity of finite and infinite, worldly and spiritual; however, while stressing their equal legitimacy and the need to integrate them, the goal of this chapter is to underscore that we must not confuse the two.

Connection, Individuation

Another area where the distinction we're examining becomes blurred involves the way that infinite selves are fully aware of their utter uniqueness and from that basis prize commonality. Finite selves, in contrast, find their grounding in the similar and from that seek to individuate.

As finite selves, we strive to distinguish ourselves as individuals. The need to excel and achieve distinction has its earliest and most single-minded expression in reproductive strategies, but we feel a broader need to find or establish our own point of view and opinions and chalk up our individual accomplishments. (Emphasis on this varies from culture to culture; in some it's quite submerged, with more of a group, tribal, national, ethnic, or religious identity. The need to differentiate, in this case from other groups, nations, or religions, is usually still in play.) This individualism is, however, almost always defined in relationship to others and to group standards, and, therefore, a person feels the need to express herself within a range that does not deviate too far from the group norm, so that identity is still defined on the basis of the familiar and similar.

As infinite selves we experience our eternal cosmic distinctiveness, which cannot be lost or limited in any way. The created finite self is also entirely unique, despite outward appearances and genetic inheritance. Thus, as infinite selves in finite form, there's more emphasis on experiencing connection, on establishing things in common, and on unifying. Having created distinct bodies, we've done the separation part. Now the question is, how do we find a way to experience union (which we already achieve admirably as infinite selves) while in finite forms? This fascinating conundrum—to achieve a more perfect union—which we as infinite selves have set for ourselves in our finite incarnations, is a focus for the highest levels of human undertaking, even while individualism absorbs the attention of much of humanity.

When finite selves experience this emphasis on union, which originates in part in infinite self (as well as in the limbic system of the brain), and think that's primarily what should be happening to them (ignoring the balancing need for finite individuation), serious problems can arise. These include having weak personal boundaries, overidentification with others, co-dependency, or overemphasizing sex. Examples such as these usually arise from specific, often traumatic, events or kinds of relationships, but they derive added power within the individual from her ongoing experience that "this is the way it is and should be"; she doesn't realize that mergence with others is the way it is for infinite self, but it can't work out the same way for her as finite self. On the other hand, if the individual suppresses the experience of the infinite and overemphasizes the finite's orientation, she may become isolated and overly self-centered.

Aloneness, Not Loneliness

Without the experience of God or of infinite self, isolation breeds loneliness. A common observation is that loneliness can occur in the midst of a multitude or even with loved ones. Some essential connection feels lacking, which a person may not experience as loneliness; a lack of connection with infinite self can produce a sense of meaninglessness, so that both self and relationships lack any point or purpose. To compensate for this, people find a romantic partner, join a group or cause, or take up a hobby. This never fills the hole because this void is infinite and will take the infinite to fill it. Loneliness is a spiritual illness, and more often than is recognized, the external circumstances that seem to cause it are actually its symptoms. It arises to motivate a person to begin to search, for he has become ready to connect in a more profound way to his higher nature. The quest may lead to what seems to be an experience of an immanent, personal God; I believe that most such experiences of the divine are even more personal: they are of the person's own divine self, his direct connection with macrocosmic divinity.

This connection eliminates loneliness (as well as the very possibility of boredom). It makes possible aloneness, which is a sense of profound connectedness. One experiences the presence of one's center, spirit, and meaningfulness, whether one is apart from others or in a crowd. Aloneness gives a pristinely clear delineation of oneself and one's boundaries; it prevents enmeshment and supports real relatedness. It also involves the need of being physically alone at times, just as every great spiritual teacher and mystic has needed to go into a wilderness or other retreat in order to partake fully of the rich interaction going on inwardly. This is the purpose of focused spiritual practice and meditation. One needs to be alone to know the inward company one keeps.

The fear of loneliness keeps many people from the aloneness that cures it. We are a social species, and to be alone can feel like social failure. We need to interact, but to experience ourselves as infinite beings we need aloneness. We must keep these needs distinct; by this alone can we end loneliness.

Free Will, God's Will

As a divine, infinite self, one is eternally unified with God and created in God's image and likeness. Therefore, one's will is identical with

God's will. The same is true of the actual design of one's will as a finite self. However, as one's experience as a finite self is limited and subject to illusion and as one has free will, personal will is often not in alignment with God's will until one achieves spiritual wholeness. In frustration or in faith a person may say, "Thy will be done," without having any idea what that will is; she may even extend this to the attitude, "Let God decide." The next step may be the notion that whatever happens must be God's will. In this, we confuse our position with that of our infinite self, which is always and effortlessly expressing God's will. In this confusion we lose sight of our responsibility as finite selves to make the best decisions we can, even if they're unsound, so we can learn and spiritually grow, thereby ultimately returning to a full awareness of God's (and our own infinite self's) will. It's important for each of us as a finite self to have the chance to find out the results of our choices so that we can see where they're flawed and where they are or aren't in alignment with God's and our infinite self's will. God and our infinite selves are, in essence, saying, "Let humans decide, so that they may learn."

On the other hand, we may conflate our experiences as finite and infinite selves in such a way as to feel that we can and should, now, be able to know and express God's will and do God's work impeccably, which leads to feeling overly responsible for others and the world. This can produce deadly seriousness and eliminate any joy we might feel in learning, replacing it with unending guilt at our inevitable failures. Or a person might feel that she—or someone she believes in—does know God's will (as each of us does as an infinite self), and she therefore may develop a fanatical attachment to a person, a doctrine, or her own inner vision. We come back to the fact that even as we take action based on our best sense of God's will, we must do so in full awareness that, as finite beings, we see at best only part of the picture.

To be free to act we must overcome guilt. Many people, despite years of psychotherapy, never transcend guilt. The feeling that one is a sinner redeemable only through God's grace can be unendurable; the non-religious have even less consolation. Guilt is a major contributor to the "quiet desperation" that Henry David Thoreau (1817-1862), in his famous phrase, held to be the condition in which most people live out their lives. Even the receiving of grace can lead to a split in the self if the redeemed sinner leaves his sin behind, because the shadow, one's negative aspect, is composed of essential parts of self and without these one can never be whole. We have to face our whole self, shadow and all, without guilt but with full responsibility, in order to transform and heal the darkened parts so we can integrate them. We must accept ourselves in our entirety; acceptance of the facts that these parts exist and that we must work with them is the first step in healing and integration. As finite selves, however, we may be hard-pressed to accept the darkest parts and may only be able to do this in union with infinite self, which accepts them all. This differs from the grace of a transcendent and separate God that accepts us into heaven purged of our sins. Infinite self doesn't leave the shadow behind but enables us to endure the knowledge of it and transmute it without creating inner separation. We can engage in this process only to the degree that we open to infinite self.

Guilt is a steppingstone in our moral and psychological awakening, but in the same way that shame, which precedes guilt developmentally, matures to guilt, guilt must mature into freedom to take action, err, and learn through mistakes. Responsibility—the ability to respond based on our highest understanding of truth—is the key to guilt-free morality. Guilt takes the fun out of freedom, learning, and growth. When it's the only impetus to moral progress available, it serves a purpose, but by experiencing infinite self's joy in our growth, we can access healthier motivations.

Identity: Differentiated and Balanced

As infinite selves, we naturally experience the whole picture: microcosm and macrocosm. Our field of operation is also the whole: we affect our entire microcosm, limited only by the free will we granted it; moreover, in union with other infinite selves and with God, we affect the macrocosm to an extent. As finite selves we can only experience and act on parts of the whole—parts of our own wholeness or parts of the cosmos. Those who identify with their finite self in the face of the infinite may feel insignificant and incapable, devalue the small part that they can do as finite selves, and therefore accomplish little, rather than experiencing what they achieve in both spheres. Others who identify too much with their infinite nature can experience psychological inflation. They may believe they are here for bigger things and loathe their insignificant lot in life; more commonly, people become impatient with themselves and with others and get frustrated with their limits.

If our identity lies more with our higher self and we lean toward an inaccurately lofty view of what we should achieve, we will miss the fact that what we do as finite selves is vital to the whole and adequate to our higher purpose. In despair of living up to an unreachable goal we think we ought to achieve, we may never accomplish what we're able to, or we may muddy with resentment the good work we do accomplish. We are a part of a whole, well designed to do our finite part. As finite selves, we have the ability to focus the wholeness of infinite self into a finite arena. While our focus and experience as finite selves is limited, we can also experience the whole by way of our infinite self as it embraces and affects our microcosmic nature and participates in the unfolding of cosmic evolution. In addition, we can experience that with certainty God's design and our own purpose will achieve fulfillment—in whatever time span is needed; this knowledge allows us the peace to learn what our specific part is and to focus on accomplishing that, recognizing that it's sufficient. Without this peace and ability to focus, a person can lose her boundaries with her higher self, identifying with it and taking on responsibility for the whole that she can't possibly manage with her finite capacities. This may cost her ability to focus—the gift of being finite. A person who is overidentified with infinite self can initially feel all-powerful and invincible, then, when this proves untrue, fall into complete identification with limited self, feeling small, weak, and vulnerable, even giving up. If she feels abandoned when God doesn't step in to rescue her, a final step may be to turn toward an external authority figure for rescue, someone she can identify with who seems to see the whole picture.

The story of Judas reveals a poignant example of finite self confusing its role with that of the infinite. One interpretation of his betrayal of Jesus is that Judas decided to try to help God's plan along, forcing Jesus to reveal himself as the Messiah by putting him in a position from which he'd have to miraculously extricate himself. Jesus knew that God's design was that he would come into the power of those who would kill him and that this didn't require Judas's intervention, and so warned him: "the Son of Man is going as it has been determined, but woe to that one by whom he is betrayed!"[3] Nonetheless, Judas, based on his own mistaken view of that design (that Jesus should become a worldly king to lead the Jews to freedom from Roman domination) and on his frustration that things weren't moving along faster toward this goal, decided that it wouldn't come about if he did not intervene. To Judas's surprise and horror, Jesus did not perform a miracle to free himself. Judas was essentially trying to take responsibility for making sure that the infinite (God) did what Judas, from his finite understanding of what was occurring, thought necessary. Judas's consequent sense of guilt and separation from God led to his suicide, which cut short the exalted but less grandiose service that was within his capacity to render.

A healthy differentiation of, and balanced identification with, both aspects of self can yield the sense of reasonable assurance that protects and sustains one through to the accomplishment of the most difficult goal.

Perceptual Mind, Conceptual Mind

This kind of terrible decision, and a multitude of other less dreadful but similarly misguided examples, occurs when we confuse two functions of mind. One of these is all too human, while the other, even though a part of finite self, has much more access to the infinite or higher mind. We can describe these as the conceptual mind and the perceptual mind. Conceptual mind is that which we in the West are educated to use and rely on: the rational, analyzing mind that abstracts concepts from experience and lives in the realm of ideas. Eastern spiritual disciplines have long considered this mind to be a trap from which we must free ourselves if we are to know self and cosmos. Perceptual mind operates more simply and directly and involves our entire nerve system, including senses, communicating nerves, and brain, functioning as a whole. By way of this system, we register much of what is incorrectly labeled *extra* sensory perception. More accurately termed *extended* sensory perception, it involves ignored but common perceptual abilities that anyone can develop. Our adult perception is largely a learned skill that filters out vast amounts of sense data; this filtering becomes part of our neural functioning, considerably reducing adult experience of the sensible world.

Mathematician Rudy Rucker suggests that normally our minds oscillate between union with the world and analysis of that experience, between what I am describing as the perceptual and conceptual minds, as often as three times per second.[4] To achieve focused use of perceptual mind requires retraining our attention; meditation and other spiritual practices help accomplish this. A number of people who pursue such disciplines report experiences that are often termed ESP: clairvoyant or precognitive perceptions or other dramatic inner experiences that cause the majority of students, who don't have them, to feel inadequate. A balanced discipline doesn't aim for such experiences, and they don't indicate particular progress by themselves, however intriguing and glamorous they may be. An accurately focused regimen promotes a mind that's open to whatever enters its field of attention and strives to extend awareness throughout the full range of the finite self.

Most inner experiences of infinite self are subtle, uncomplicated, and direct and are therefore usually overlooked by those who expect divine guidance or higher wisdom to be more dramatic; plus, the cacophony of stimuli in our lives drowns them out. A walk on the beach or in the woods, a hike in the mountains, or any quiet time spent alone without thought, such as listening to music, helps us to access this inner experience of perceptual mind, and it's often at these times that creative insights or solutions come to us, unbidden and without effort. I think that most of the truly important activities of the mind occur in this manner. If we allow ourselves to know the things we need to know, we'll know them: quiet the mind and they will come. The problem is that often we don't like what we learn in this way because it doesn't match our current agenda or expectations, so we tune it out and think that we haven't received an answer to our meditation or prayer, or we engage the conceptual mind immediately to figure out how to make it different. While sometimes with hard work we can change things to be more to our liking, experience convinces me that it's far more effective to listen to higher mind, practice profound acceptance of and harmony with one's inner truth, and take action from that starting point. There'll be plenty of opportunities for creative free will choice-making along the way to completion. This is, essentially, what it is to be a Taoist, a yogi, or most any other kind of sincere seeker of divine truth.

The openness, extended attention, and awareness required to do this involve one's emotional experience, all one's senses, and one's knowing, brought together in a mutually informing synthesis sometimes termed clairsentience: a clear, open, full-spectrum awareness without bias or with as little filtering as possible. While it's a function of the finite self, it is exceptionally open to experiencing the infinite. Just as we exist in and affect a gravitational field that's coextensive with an apparently limitless or unbounded universe, an open mind is unbounded and touched by the entire cosmos. In the same way as gravity pervades the universe, this activity of mind isn't restricted to a particular direction or area. Still, perception generally diminishes with distance (like gravity), so this perceptive mind must become very subtle and requires refined technique and an experienced operator to register and recognize nonlocal data; this occurs only with considerable training or in mystical experiences or visions.

When we pay attention to perceptual mind's operation, we find that the most direct and immediate knowing doesn't occur cognitively, that is, by way of the structure of thought. We experience truth before thought kicks in, in what's commonly called the "'Aha' experience." This knowledge is unmediated by thought or any other medium we yet know of, and therefore only our preconceptions and mental conditioning distort it. While with extended sensory perception we don't usually perceive, for instance, other people's thoughts, if we pay attention we find that we often can know enough about them—their essence and characteristics—to allow us to act appropriately and effectively. We neither read their cognitive mind nor figure them out using our own—we just know. The usual name for this is intuition.

The perceptual mind is equally open to infinite self. Its operation provides immediate knowing of divine truth. The structures of thought, on the other hand, limit this kind of knowing.

Bohm stresses the need for an essentially meditative approach to all reality. "The illusion that the self and the world are broken into fragments originates in the kind of thought that goes beyond its proper measure," thought that mistakes its creations for objective existence. Rectifying this entails developing a deeper understanding of the natural order, most importantly of the mechanism of thought. Using the faculties of sense and mind, this requires "an original and creative act of perception into all aspects of life, mental and physical . . . and this is perhaps the true meaning of meditation. . . . But original and creative insight within the whole field of measure *is* the action of the immeasurable."[5] He suggests, in effect, that experience of the full perceptual mind, achieved through practices such as meditation, allows experience of higher mind, or that perceptual mind in some sense *is* higher mind. The language structure available to Westerners, which mostly expresses conceptual mind and categorizes reality dualistically (Chinese, for instance, does not), obscures the fact that there's no dividing line between finite and infinite. Thus, it's easier to experience this fact by way of the more straightforward perceptual mind.

Developing the perceptual mind takes a heavy load off of the conceptual mind, which otherwise tends to compensate for being cut off from direct knowing of infinite mind by being too rational, too controlling, and continually trying to figure things out; it feels it must prove itself but usually ends up only confusing itself. The use of perceptual mind allows for deep relaxation and mental well-being because perceptual mind brings the experience of infinite mind to conceptual mind. Too much emphasis on perceptual mind, however, produces a lack of focus, an ungrounded condition. The two minds must interact for a person to live well and be effective.

Perfectionism, Perfecting

Lack of understanding of the relationship of finite and infinite can lead to cynicism. People lose their idealism under the weight of evidence that good things don't last, good doesn't seem to win out, and good people suffer. Because we have the sense that the possibility of the good is real, a sense that comes from the fact that it's absolutely real for our infinite self, we may feel that things should be different *right now.* Part of us, the higher self, actually lives that kind of existence. Our continuous experience, as infinite self, of the pure, abiding goodness and truth of the divine, which finite self registers while simultaneously living in the impurity, imperfection, and mutability of the real world, can be a constant irritant to the latter. This may produce an unbearable sense of injustice, leading to condemnation of God, humanity, or physical existence, if we don't understand that, from the standpoint of infinite self, the finite world is *not expected or supposed* to be that way, at least not at this point in our spiritual evolution. Our experience of the infinite can be a steady guide, assurance, and haven if we recognize it for what it is, or we can feel it as a relentless reproach.

It can also produce perfectionism. Infinite self experiences the perfection of all things in a cosmic context; that is, it knows the processes occurring within finite creation are perfect when viewed in relation to their eternal unfolding. The function of finite self is to focus on the daily decisions that constitute the gritty process of perfecting. Making distinctions and choices is what finite self is about. It needs to recognize that each choice is a creative act, affecting the other parts of creation, and that the consequences of its choices may be less than perfect from the standpoint of those other parts, but the choices need to be made, nonetheless, for perfecting to occur. If finite self doesn't identify and distinguish infinite self's experience as different from its own, it can get caught in the wide-eyed idealism sometimes associated with New Age consciousness: the notion that everything that occurs is perfect *in the context of the finite world.* This can lead to ignoring finite self's job of making the difficult decisions that help mundane reality become a bit more perfect. On the other hand, finite self can become caught in perfectionism and feel that nothing measures up to the way things should be, a judgment based on comparison of the real world with the inner experience of infinite self. This in turn can lead either to compulsive striving to achieve the perfection of the infinite in the finite world, usually accompanied by dissatisfaction with self and others, or to giving up in disgust with the imperfections of human life.

The work of finite self in perfecting often is not great fun in itself, but finite self's simultaneous registry of the infinite perfection experienced by higher self, if understood as such, transmutes it. Absent the experience of infinite self, life tends toward drudgery.

Pop psychology tells us to accept self and others as they and we are. Myriad media messages, however, bombard us with the urgency of improving ourselves and advertise the means to do so. We also often desire change in our loved ones and associates. Are these directions contradictory? Not if we live as both infinite and finite self, each aspect of self attending to what comes naturally, each appreciating and benefiting from the other: profound acceptance on the part of infinite self, the urge toward and need for self-development by finite self.

Both/And, Either/Or

We live in a universe of polarities, such as matter and antimatter and the plus and minus of electromagnetic energy. We experience these on a personal scale in forms such as masculine and feminine, action and quietude, and receptivity and expression. Within itself, finite self tends to emphasize one polarity while diminishing or suppressing the other. Infinite self already (always) encompasses both. Because finite self can sense the infinite inner fullness of the polarity that's relatively lacking in its current existence, it subliminally interprets this as a void in its life, something missing without which life may feel incomplete, even if finite self has exactly what it thinks it wants. The sublime nature of the higher self, and thus, by association, of the other polarity that's part of its completeness, can make finite self's current limited life seem gray in comparison, even unjust. This often leads to the false perception that the grass is greener on the other side of the polarity. (Of course, when the other polarity manifests in finite life, it turns out to be no more sublime than the first.)

Finite life will always be conditional and partial, never the infinite completeness that finite self nonetheless intuits to be possible. This intuition may drive finite self a bit crazy until it learns to distinguish between its own and infinite self's experiences. Infinite self includes the essence of both polarities, not the form, it being the job of finite self to bring essence into form, which it can only do in stages. Finite self doesn't fully embody both. It needs to learn that it's not its nature and purpose to have it all at one time or to bring infinite potential into finite form now, even though it can sense the potential and presence of the other polarity via its infinite self. It can better celebrate and enjoy what it does have now if it understands that the rest will become possible in due course. It can even enjoy the ideal nature of the other polarity as it exists in infinite self.

This recognition is essential for those who feel the need to have it all or else feel they have nothing. "All or nothing" drives such feelings as "I'm not attractive because she/he rejected me," "I'm a complete failure because I got fired," and similar negative (or overly positive) globalizing self-judgments based on emotionally charged events. From this frame of mind, people misperceive the specific and immediate situation to be the permanent, absolute state of affairs and base a complete self-evaluation on it. The recognition that each event is one in an infinite chain of events, occurring over time but in their aggregate constituting a fullness of possible experiences, puts an end to judgmentalism based on present circumstances and eases the sense of deprivation that exists due to the current absence of the other polarity (such as approval or recognition).

In our infinite nature, we encompass all potentials. Translated into a finite perspective, we can characterize this as *both/and.* It is finite self's job to determine which of these infinite possibilities, from among those available at the time, it will express in form within the limits of finite existence. To do this it must be able to operate in *either/or* mode, developing its ability to discriminate what is actual for it at the moment and saying no to other possibilities. Yet, once it is able to make and consciously sustain the distinction between its own nature and the characteristics of the infinite, it can safely enter into the both/and experience of total self: being both finite and infinite, functioning as both discriminating and encompassing. Indeed, it needs to do so. This occurs developmentally. In the "terrible twos" of early childhood, saying no is a fascination and a delight; deciding what one likes and doesn't like and developing good boundaries are part of growing up and forming a full-fledged finite self. An adult, however, is called upon to transcend these skills so as to be able to include and harmonize with the needs and preferences of others and to find win-win (both/and) solutions or at least tactics that are subtler than simply demanding her way or giving in. This enables her to move from the limiting and oppositional kind of relationships characteristic of the solely finite awareness, in which a person does little more than discriminate self from other and tends to objectify the other, to relationships of mutual interdependence with both her higher self and others.

If the two natures are not distinguished, both/and and either/or may merge into "all or nothing." This is either/or raised to the extreme and is a recipe for failure.

The "all or nothing" quandary classically arises in selecting a mate. People agonize about making the right choice. For a man, the problem often is reluctance to forego other women. The desire to have many women is the desire to have the essence of all women, of Woman; this is as much a part of his own infinite self as it is of any woman, and he can satisfyingly experience it in the feminine polarity, the anima, in the heights and depths of his own psyche. He is most likely to connect with this, however, in a committed relationship. Similarly, for a woman this issue presents itself as fear that her current potential mate won't have all the qualities that her intuitive mind recognizes as indispensable parts of the essence of maleness. This fear is likewise founded in the fact that such essence is part of her own divine self as well as part of her animus, the male polarity of her personality; thus, she is well informed regarding this essence but misguided in feeling that it can be found in any finite male. Consequently, she may find continual fault with her partner or reject one suitor after another in her search for "Mr. Right."

To find the essence of the opposite sex, a man may cast a wide net and a woman may be over-selective, yielding the male reluctance to say no and women's hesitancy to say yes. We can know the essence of man *and* woman best by looking within ourselves and next best in the context of a relationship where we build trust and take the risks of intimacy.

The individual with whom we join in a relationship is limited; that person's infinite self is not. Thus, while we can't have it all in this life, we can experience it all by going deeply into the finite, singular relationship that we have, for however long that lasts; union with that one can have infinite depth and breadth. Anyone we might choose is equally infinite. Our destiny is to choose; if we are willing to engage deeply, we won't lose out. Meanwhile, as infinite selves, we unify easily with an infinity of beings; in our awareness of our infinite self, we can join the cosmic dance of all beings, while as finite self we enjoy what only committed finite beings can share.

In relationships as in many other arenas, we are misled by our intensely felt intuitive experience that as infinite selves we need not choose, that we can join in transcendent union with multitudes, and that we can have it all. In fact, we do have it all, all but form, definition, limit, and the profound experience of finite choice for which we created finite selves. As higher selves, we have many infinite, eternal, and perfect loves. In finite form we desire and intuitively expect to have what we have as infinite beings, and in this we are disappointed. If we, in our defined and limited relationships that must begin with either/or choices, expand our awareness to include higher self, we find that we can live the experience of actually having it all: both the limited form of finite self and the totality of infinite self.

These examples indicate that the more we as finite selves develop the ability to live in awareness of the infinite, the more essential it is to distinguish the kinds of experience that arise from each aspect of ourselves and the part each needs to play in our lives. It becomes ever more important not to confuse their roles. The more aware we become, the greater our danger of falling into this confusion because we can increasingly sense the infinite. Heightened awareness requires developing enhanced discrimination.

Many of the previous examples are understandable in terms of our relationship with infinite divinity and do not require accepting the idea of an infinite self. Their purpose is not to convince but to offer situations for further examination. What's essential for our daily living is to distinguish the infinite we experience (whether individual or cosmic) from our finite truths and needs, and to recognize how the implications of experiences from infinite source differ from those that originate in finite self. Whatever metaphysics one prefers, the important thing is to address the cause of failing to make this distinction and to deal with its perplexing effects.

Perhaps the most common example of the confusion of finite and infinite experience, and the one requiring the greatest discrimination, is romance. Another area that causes many people great perplexity is forgiveness and acceptance. Because these are particularly illustrative of our theme and occur in almost everyone's life, they deserve separate chapters.

5

ROMANCE

Come back when you can stay forever,
Love's not really love unless it lasts that long.

—Chris Waters, Bucky Jones, Tom Shapiro,
"Come Back (When You Can Stay Forever)"

Because of our ability to sense the infinite and finite at the same time, and because of our frequent failure to distinguish them, romance was born.

Love, as distinguished from romance, is decidedly less sentimental and idealized about relations between the sexes. People often use the words "romance" and "love" interchangeably, and many readers may be initially puzzled or put off by the critique of romance that follows. Its purpose is to describe the fundamental causes of painful difficulties that afflict the course of true love, which, free of these, is actualizing and healthy. My aim is to draw distinctions to help us avoid the misunderstandings and illusions that are lumped together with actual love to produce romance. Romance as I speak of it certainly contains much that is desirable and worth nurturing. While is it based on a dangerous confusion, it provides the most common context for experiences of the transcendent potentials of oneself and of relationship. Romantic love can change people for the better as it makes them aware of these potentials, but it requires more than romantic feelings for the change to stick; when the bloom of romance begins to fade, a person will likely revert to old patterns.

In romantic love we confuse finite and infinite. When we fall into romantic love, we sense the unlimited possibilities of the relationship without fully distinguishing this inner truth from the more limited reality of connection and relationship between two personalities. In a romantic relationship, we expect the other to manifest all of that infinite promise and delight right here in his or her finiteness, and we expect the same of ourselves. We feel that the presence of this person in our life will bring forth all our own unrealized personal capabilities. We take ecstatic delight in sensing the infinite wonders of this other person. We may feel that we *as personalities* have always been connected and will be in love until death do us part and beyond. We believe this romance is forever.

In a relationship that is highly romantic, we intuitively sense the actual dimensions (that is, the dimensionlessness) of the other and of ourselves as we plunge into the oceanic experience of the other's infinity merging with our own. We feel the unconditional, unbounded love of the other's higher self and of our own. Psychologist Marion Woodman speaks of how we project our wholeness, our soul, onto our partner and how lovers therefore are each "in love with . . . [his or her] own divine inner world," which charges their sexual attraction and makes it "absolutely heavenly, but it's also a bit psychotic, and it won't work in ordinary life."[1] We lose track of our boundaries, making it hard to tell whether our positive feelings are dependent on the other person or arise from within ourselves—and whether something within the other person causes problems or something within ourselves.

In a sense, romance is an example of transference, which is central to the psychotherapeutic process. Transference is the projection of a person's unresolved issues with someone, especially parents and other early influences, onto another individual. This projection keeps a person from accurately perceiving the other and greatly limits his ability to love the person as he or she is, reducing the possibility of a real relationship. A person projects not only negative qualities but also positive aspects of himself that he then can only have by way of the other, producing an unhealthy attachment.

We don't understand that we have projected not only our issues but also our infinite nature onto our beloved. We're mystified by our inevitable inability to realize that immensity in the finite. Problems arise and disappointments begin when we feel let down by our partner's failure (and our own failure, if we're honest with ourselves) to cram all that immeasurable possibility into a body and personality and into daily living. At the least, this forcibly reminds us of human limitations: our experience of and with the other falls short of the potential we sense; we're disappointed that we are not permanently lifted out of our daily drudgery into our unlimited potential and that our lover falls short of being a god or goddess.

The letdown can be much more traumatic. First, we experience being loved and accepted by a divine being, lifting us into an exalted relationship (the sense of our infinite selves joining). If the person who stimulated this sense of our own infinity then rejects us, this can throw us harshly back into feeling confined by finite existence, producing a sense of profound unworthiness. We may fall into despair or feel a betrayal that cuts deeper than frustrated hopes of love if, in this love and especially if we lack spiritual experience, we felt we enjoyed our only possible connection to the unbounded and then were cut off from it. The feeling of losing our sole opportunity to access the unlimited can lead to deep depression or to the ultimate devaluing of finite life—of one's own life in suicide, of the other's in a lover's homicide. These vast dimensions of feeling arise from the fact that the illusion of eternal romance contains so much truth: the truth of who we are and how we relate as infinite selves.

Jungian psychologist Robert Johnson proposes that romantic love, from the male perspective, is the projection of the unconscious feminine aspect of a man onto his love interest.[2] This unfair projection is often disastrous, for it involves aspects of the man that have nothing to do with her and that she can't live up to, and, if she remains authentic to herself, won't even try to accommodate. The reverse is also true: when the woman projects her unconscious masculine aspect, the animus, she mistakes parts of herself for her partner.

Anima and animus permit man and woman to encounter life and the universe in novel, limitless ways, according to Johnson. They steadfastly move us in the direction of infinity.[3] If a man could keep the histrionics of the anima world inside himself, understanding and experiencing them as not of worldly reality, then he could let his anima lead him toward the infinite while recognizing the more specific, bounded terrain of human love in his connection with his partner.[4]

Regarding the disastrous effects of confusing these, Johnson is extremely accurate. His suggestion that we treat the life of the anima (or animus) as symbol and fantasy is psychologically effective for recalling projections and reducing the negative effects of eruptions of suppressed contents of the psyche. Doing so, however, can keep us from the full spiritual potential of recognizing ourselves as infinite beings. I find that the anima is quite complex and layered; it includes aspects of the personality, spiritual dimensions of the finite self, and even infinite self, which, if treated as a symbol, is reduced to a content of the psyche. The complexity of the anima makes its unconscious projection doubly unfair because what's projected isn't entirely finite, while the unfortunate recipient of the projection is finite and can never live up to it. All this is equally true of the animus and its projection.

The Religion of Love

There is an almost religious intensity to romantic feelings. These derive from the fact that the experience of the infinite, divine self is closer to awareness in a love relationship.

In his book, *We,* Johnson explores the religious quality of romance. He makes clear how high the stakes are for us in romance, calling it the "single greatest energy system in the Western psyche." He explores the illusions involved: another person seems to unfold life's greatest mysteries for us, with the added promise of acutely heightened sensory and emotional experience. In romance rather than religion, both sexes hope to discover "transcendence, wholeness, and ecstasy."[5]

To examine the illusion of romance, Johnson uses the medieval story of Tristan and Iseult, the first literary example of the ideal of romantic love,[6] initially written about 1150. Romance is thus quite young, even though love first received written attention over four millennia ago.

The Tristan theme probably developed a century or two earlier, somewhat after a Church council declared that a person has only a single spiritual aspect, a soul, not a multifaceted spiritual nature, a decision that helped prepare the stage for romance. The Church's decree contributed to unmooring the analytic mind because it inherently has less direct experience of the infinite divine than the intuitive mind and henceforth would also lack any basis in Catholic dogma to conceive of an individual spirit. Absent this, the rational mind had to quest externally for the transcendent, symbolized by King Arthur's knights searching for the Holy Grail. This hunt led through Scholasticism in the late Middle Ages, where the rational mind developed muscle for abstraction, to the current ascendancy of science. Science now functions quite like a religion, considering the unquestioning belief many have in it as arbiter of reality. (Scientists sometimes behave in unscientific, doctrinaire ways, treating out-of-favor ideas and data with dismissiveness similar to that led which Church dignitaries to avoid Galileo's telescope). Tristan's tale emerged just as rational thought began its development toward dominance of the Western mind; romance arose to compensate for the split of rational mind from spirit and its estrangement from intuitive mind: it bridged an ever-widening divide.

In the story of Tristan and Iseult, a love potion designed to cause a person to fall blindly in love with whoever shares it induces romance when the pair mistakenly drink it. Due to this love, Tristan sees not Iseult but rather a heavenly incarnation.[7] As Johnson describes, the two are "in love with a mystical vision."[8] Tristan looks beyond Iseult to infinity. For man, woman becomes representative of "something universal . . . eternal, and transcendent."[9]

Romance involves compulsion and suffering along with complete, permanent union.[10] The legend ends with the lovers' deaths. Romance and death have been linked in the Western psyche ever since, partly because death liberates one into the "measureless universe of spirit and eternity," Johnson writes.[11] The love potion causes entrapment in illusion; this love gives a taste of the infinite that, if made into romance with its projections instead of actual love based on self-knowledge, leaves lovers feeling all the more ensnared in their limitations. Freedom comes only through death or psychospiritual disciplines leading to self-knowledge. For those not inclined toward discipline, death—whether forced or awaited through long, desolate years—assumes romance's failed attraction as the means of escape into the eternal.

Johnson reflects on Tristan's need to distinguish his desire to wed Iseult from his need for a marriage of the human and godly qualities within himself. The marriage of this pair of qualities needs to occur in each of us. Western culture's major symbol for this union is Jesus Christ. The tremendous significance of Christ's Incarnation, "taken as symbol," is that our whole existence is sacred.[12] When Johnson treats the idea of the two joined natures as merely image and symbol, he again doesn't address a larger spiritual implication. The nature of Christ as God become human can be seen not only as symbol but as a fact, one which doesn't need to be understood in a Christian sense but goes beyond particular belief and dogma, revealing that the human and divine can interpenetrate in ways that transcend our current understanding of human potential. Jesus' statement avowing we can do all he did and more points toward not simply a psychological and symbolic realization but a physical integration and manifestation of the higher self. To walk on water, raise the dead, and arise after three days from the tomb are rich and many-layered symbols that stimulate our understanding and imagination. To suggest that we grow spiritually to the point where we're actually able to do these things is a challenge of a completely different order. Whether or not we think these specifics are attainable and regardless of our particular religious or spiritual orientation, they challenge us to go beyond psychology and symbol to a lived expression of our whole self that transcends what we currently believe possible. Every great religious and spiritual tradition presents this challenge.

Yet, this degree of challenge is missing for many people in modern religion, having been transplanted into the realm of romance. A person may long for a passion that will break through the barriers of her or his mundane world. Because he's in love, a man may believe that he can accomplish great things and fulfill his dreams; a woman may feel that she would climb mountains and swim seas to reach her love. Many people look to romance to resurrect the deepest meaning of their lives. Johnson misses the level of desperation of this situation because, like most descendants of the Enlightenment, he misunderstands what the spiritual natures of human beings now call on them to achieve. We must find not only a new order of understanding but also a transcendently new kind of being that is born from the marriage of finite and infinite selves and of the masculine and feminine, linear and intuitive aspects of finite self.

As late as the seventeenth century, the rational and nonrational aspects of Western human experience and endeavor were still able to work closely together (see appendix 2, part 4). Science served the goals of religion; the founding fathers of science held the spiritual implications of their insights and experimental breakthroughs paramount. Many sixteenth- and seventeenth-century scientists, such as Isaac Newton (1642-1727), were alchemists or astrologers. Though we deride their "superstitions," such as the belief in transmuting base metal into gold, a proud achievement in twentieth-century physics proved the alchemists' intuition of the possibility of the transmutation of one element into another correct. Science and religion having been divorced from each other for over three centuries, we have great difficulty understanding the spiritual context in which the alchemists' insight could occur. Lacking this, we fail to see the transmuting of elements as part of a larger process of transmuting the person, of achieving a new condition of being, which was the primary interest of the early scientific giants. We fail to see the spiritual implication of our ability to release the tremendous power of the atom: that we must unleash a similar power from within us, one that can spiritually cope with the repercussions of our knowledge of the human genome, atomic power, and the ability to create potentially deadly microbes. Absent this, and because of the separation of the spiritual from the scientific, it was perhaps inevitable that the first use of atomic fission would be devastatingly destructive. We have become scientific giants without a similar gain in moral and spiritual stature.

To become spiritual giants, we must come to terms not only with the illusion of romance but also with the truth, hidden within this illusion, that we are infinite selves who relate to each other and can help our finite selves awaken to their enormous spiritual potential. This truth holds great promise for both spiritual evolution and the possibility of having fulfilling love relationships. It offers the prospect of a deeper union of science and spirit and of the rational and intuitive, fusions essential for the well-being of our civilization and for our ability to join in love without freighting our relationships with a load of expectation that belongs elsewhere.

Sex and Spirit, Actual and Symbolic

The rapture of union with God and the bond students develop with their teachers or gurus offer quite similar benefits to those of a love relationship: to see and be seen in fullness. (These relationships require mutuality of seeing, just as love does.) These similarities further explain why romance has become the receptacle for so much of our religious energy. Also instructive is that certain religions, especially Tantric Hinduism and Buddhism and the ancient and modern pagan religions of the West, have long recognized and used the relationship between sexual love and spirituality. The sexual union of opposites is both *symbolic* and *actual*. (I use "symbolic" in the more common but limited sense of representation or image; less commonly but more dynamically, it refers to something that serves to transform consciousness and release energy within the perceiver, which I term "actual.") It is symbolic of the union of the masculine and feminine energy and consciousness within each individual, of the polarities of manifest existence called in Taoism *yang* and *yin*, and of the union of the person with the divine. It is actual in terms of the event that occurs as passion opens each person, whether they have spiritual training or not, to the experience and effect of the interaction of finite and infinite within each partner and each with the other. This is the experience that the infinite is actually within and throughout the finite, giving it love, continually creating it, and helping the finite self's awareness to expand into the infinite self that she is and therefore into a greater capacity to love. This event can be healing, transformative, and integrating. The degree to which these occur in sacred or mundane union depends on the depth of love between the partners and on the extent of their honest openness of mind, emotion, sensation, and body to each another. The partners' training in awareness of the presence of the divine, in being in touch with all aspects of their bodies and minds interacting, and in being able to observe the movements and qualities of their life-energies, enhances this.

Sacred love can be a doorway to the godly. The thirteenth-century Persian poet Jalal al-Din Rumi (1207-1273) wrote of his master: "Shams-I Tabriz! Your face is what every religion tries to remember!"[13] It presents the danger, however, of confusing the person with the divine that one perceives as present in him or her, and of becoming ecstatically devoted or attached in ways appropriate only in relationship to the divine. This can occur between acolytes and their gurus. When romance is involved, the practice of sexual restraint or abstention sometimes develops to avoid too great a confusion between the finite person and the divine; an example is medieval courtly love among the Cathars.

While study and discipline can improve sexual experience exponentially, even without it sex preoccupies people because it offers what may be their strongest experience of the coming together of infinite and finite. At its best, it is an earth-moving, albeit mostly misunderstood, revelation of the infinite possibilities of relationship. It offers a taste of union with the divine without having to study or discipline oneself or having to become whole or holy first. It's ironic that, after centuries of deprecation by major religions as a threat to spiritual life, romantic eroticism currently provides many people with their closest approach to experiencing the divine.

Johnson suggests that the solution to the pernicious effects of the illusion of romance is to distinguish (from the standpoint of a male) the woman within him, the anima and her raptures, from the woman he's relating to and from the mundane but stable qualities of friendship and commitment a real person can offer. The same is true from a woman's standpoint. He proposes that we cease trying to work through in external interactions what we should handle within ourselves spiritually.[14]

This is essential advice, yet there is a rich potential that starts with that distinction and then, for those who can keep it clearly in view, goes beyond it.

The sacred and spiritual nature of a relationship is evinced by the degree that it brings into play previously unattained heights and depths of those involved. These unknown reaches of self, called the unconscious but more accurately termed the consciousness that is beneath and above our normal awareness, are a daunting mixture. They contain, first, what we have personally suppressed because we fear or hate it; second, accurate observations and knowledge of environment or self (including infinite self) that our upbringing and culture don't allow or give the means to register in our awareness; and third, mass consciousness (Jung's collective unconscious). Both the collective and personal suppressed contents can have dark aspects such as racism or murderous feelings toward the boss; they also have exalted aspects, potentials that are so far beyond personal or cultural comprehension as to feel alien or threatening. The latter can include strengths or interests that don't correspond to one's self-image or social position, religious or spiritual insights that don't match one's beliefs, and unusual or extended sensory perception. Therefore, when we bring part of the unconscious into awareness, it starts out as a chaotic jumble of unsavory stuff, some of which we thought we'd left behind or that we can't believe we could ever feel or think. This stew also contains gems of insight that reveal our path of growth. It takes long, hard work, in therapy or spiritual practice, to sort out the garbage from the insights, polish the gems, work through unresolved issues, realize that some things we thought were bad are actually good and true for us and vice versa, and finally integrate the valuable parts. Meanwhile, any of this can be projected onto those around us, to the detriment of all involved, at which point solitary spiritual work may look increasingly attractive. Alone, however, we would miss a great opportunity.

As we distinguish our highest potentials, including our spiritual masculine if we are female and spiritual feminine if we are male, we can bring these into our intimate relationships, not as expectations or demands as to what our partner should be but as another level of self that we're aware of and responsible for. As each lover learns to discern within her or his animus or anima its divine components and to purify them, the partners can bring together their corresponding divine aspects to achieve the spiritual equivalent of atomic fusion. This is the transformative alchemy necessary to balance our culture's scientific, rational achievements with spiritual awakening. This potential is lost if work with anima and animus is kept strictly within the individual or in a therapeutic setting, although much of it is best done there. The challenge, of course, is to discriminate clearly and continuously one's internal process from one's partner.

While an individual can accomplish this in solitary work to bring his inner masculine and feminine into the union that is the alchemists' inner or "divine" marriage, an advantage of a spiritually focused intimate relationship between partners is that it helps each one attain heightened honesty with themselves. Such truthfulness is crucial to the process of sorting through the contents of the psyche and to identifying and drawing back projections. One's partner can bring one's attention to any lack of truthfulness and integrity, which is harder to spot if the work is solitary. Candor with one another is indispensable because it helps each to be more completely receptive to his or her own infinite self and to its energy; openness also allows for this enhanced energy to flow between all aspects of the partners.

Romantic love is blind. In contrast, the love that is the real potential contained in romance requires great clarity of vision, freedom from illusion, and self-knowledge that includes both finite and infinite self in proper relationship. With this clarity, we can see both the person and the higher self of the other, keeping them distinct in our awareness and relating to each aspect according to its nature. Couples or spiritual pairs who historically have achieved this have had a profoundly transforming impact on their cultures. Examples are Pythagoras (c. 580-c. 500 B.C.E.) and Theano, Jesus and Mary Magdalene (as implied in some Nag Hammadi texts), Peter Abelard (1079-1142) and Heloise (1098-

1164), and Francis (1181/82-1226) and Claire (1194-1253). (The transformational impact of the relationship doesn't require the pair to have romantic or sexual relations; it calls for the fusion power of deep love, profound mutual acceptance and respect, and spiritual vision.) While children often don't result from such relationships, they do engender great peace, wisdom, centeredness, growth, and community.

Given that romance has subsumed much energy that was previously devoted to religion, perhaps we can use our cultural fixation with sex and romance as a portal for return to a true and grounded spirituality, with their energy enabling us to move into the next level of our evolution. Our spiritual development can't afford so much of our energy and attention to remain devoted to just one aspect of our nature, even one as vital as personal love. Fortunately, coupling and spiritual growth can enhance each other, provided we end the confusion at the heart of romance and learn the actual design of love.

Arthur's Dilemma

That confusion has produced situations where spiritual growth and responsibility have seemed at odds with love. One example is the Arthurian legend, which emerged in written romances at the time *Tristan* appeared. This contains a theme, the intractable opposition between love and duty or purpose, which has remained central to Western spiritual and moral development and personal agonizing. It finds dramatization in Arthur's conflict between his continuing love for Guinevere, despite the fact that she betrays him with Lancelot, and his duty as king to have her executed because in betraying him she has betrayed the kingdom. For millennia, in cultures as diverse as Chinese, Egyptian, and Celtic, people believed the land and the king to be intimately connected, the intimacy sometimes expressed literally in fertility ceremonies for abundant crops. These societies viewed the *person* of the king as being in complete union with his *function* for the kingdom; in modern terms, he was unified with his higher purpose. (Many cultures considered the king a divine representative or himself divine.)

The conflict between love and duty arose as the linear mind began its lengthy process of divorce from and, in recent centuries, ascendancy over the intuitive mind. This imbalance and separation produces psychological and spiritual anguish as we try to sort out the tension between individual desires, needs, and creative impulses, and societal and spiritual roles and duties. The situation could not and cannot be resolved in the conflictual terms in which it was framed; the discord will only be worked out when the two aspects of mind can achieve a new synthesis and inner marriage, and when finite and infinite relate in the new partnership that is our present potential.

This prospect is prefigured in *Parsifal*, by Wolfram von Eschenbach (c. 1170-c. 1220). Parsifal enters the grail castle, heals its wounded king and his blighted kingdom, and achieves the spiritual exaltation of the grail vision by asking the question: "*Uncle, what is it that troubles you?*"[15] This crucial but absurdly simple query—which he failed to ask years earlier, forcing him to leave in shame and failure and embark on a quest for spiritual development—isn't a detached or dutiful investigation by the linear mind. It fulfils Parsifal's purpose but arises from the kindness, compassion, and self-awareness he achieves through many trials. It portrays the deep yet simple synthesis we need and points to the possibility of transcending romance to achieve the promise of actual love.

The Many Loves of Infinite Selves

What can one say about that potential? "Eternal romance," the stuff of novels, is as real as our hopes, dreams, and passions make it out to be, but it's real in a different way than we think. It is the loving union of infinite and eternal selves. This eternal love exists in the spiritual dimension, the vertical axis of the diagram in chapter 3—the axis of spiritual presence in the here and now—and not in the horizontal axis of historical time. The infinite self of a human being always unifies, or merges, with the infinite self of another whenever he is with or even thinks of the other. This mergence of infinite selves is a total, boundless, and eternal union and sharing of essence. It occurs whether or not the finite person is aware of or intends it. Because the higher self of each is timeless, the experience is naturally that of eternal union; however, lovers can easily misconstrue this as lasting personal romance. It's at right angles to linear reality: it is an eternity in the here and now; the possibility of reincarnation aside, it doesn't imply that the two are always meant to be together as finite selves. The two are *always* together—in the moment—because they are in *all ways* together, given that the mergence of infinite selves is the most complete connection possible. While mergence occurs in all human interactions, the biological and emotional aspects of being in love cause us to be exceptionally aware of it and to think it occurs uniquely with our love interest.

The love of a finite self is by its nature limited in duration and is inevitably somewhat conditional. Its purity depends on the level of spiritual development of the person but is usually a mixture, consisting of needs and wants from early stages of development together with adult capacities for honesty, nurturing, and giving of self. The love given by the higher self is based on complete knowledge of the beloved and is pure, truly eternal, unconditional, and unbounded in its giving. We can count on it beyond question.

In our universe of polarities, love is necessarily accompanied by its opposite, which is also its complement. The polar opposite of love is destruction and separation, things that must occur in the finite world. If we love, we open ourselves to profound loss: whomever or whatever we love will at some point cease to be there for us, or else we will lose our connection by ourselves ceasing to be. Each person in a relationship needs to be separate from the other at times, so that both can renew themselves; old forms of the relationship die or must be destroyed in order that the relationship can be regenerated in the successive stages of life. Accepting this polar opposite of love, although sometimes painful, allows love to flourish. Without an intuitive awareness of the infinite and enduring aspect of a relationship, however, it's extremely difficult to accept the transitory, painful nature of love's polarity. If we don't accept this—if we reject love's polar opposite from our definition of love—we see the two as at odds, creating an unnecessary conflict. When love's polar opposite appears, we try to conform the love we feel to an idealized sense of love based on our experience of our infinite connection with the other: we try to eliminate the negative. We hold on when we should let go, at least a little; we try to keep things from changing. We attempt to eliminate unwanted feelings, but this only serves to suppress or deny them; in line with what Sigmund Freud (1856-1939) called "the return of the repressed," rejection, detachment, or hostility reappear, but having been repressed, they reappear in forms we neither own, recognize, nor understand and are projected onto the relationship or our partner. This plays out in acts of distancing, dominating, disliking, or hating. Instead of destroying our maladaptive patterns of relating, we demolish the relationship or even the beloved, by degrees at least.

Failing to consciously distinguish the ways that infinite and finite selves love, we seek infinite love within the finite world and continue to suffer the illusion of romance. Wherever there is unconsciousness in a relationship, because of projection our worst fear will come true in some form. If we don't do the work necessary to bring this negative energy into our conscious awareness, we will risk destroying our love. Oscar Wilde (1854-1900) asserted, "All men kill the thing they love."[16]

Only if we accept love and loss, what we cherish and what must change, can we achieve the full experience of mergence with the infinite self of our partner. This provides the opportunity to delve into the beauty, goodness, uniqueness, and truth both of one's own spiritual existence and of one's beloved. These explorations are mutually essential. But, to see another as he or she actually is in full grandeur and beauty can be hard on the ego if one is not well grounded in one's own spiritual truth and value; similarly, to experience the splendor of one's own spiritual actuality without recognizing the same in the other can lead to serious relationship problems. If both experiences are present and balanced, a person can benefit from the expanded sense of self that love offers and make progress toward the spiritual stature and responsibility necessitated by our global predicaments.

An Evolving Potential

At this time in history, actual love is a still-evolving potential; therefore, we cannot fully describe it yet. The breakdown of marriage and of the agreed-upon framework of relationships in many societies, with its attendant confusion, frustration, and pain, is part of the birthing of this potential, forcing us to examine who we are and what we truly want and need.

Do we want to be rapturously ablaze with perpetual desire for the one perfect person who was always meant to bring us eternal bliss? Absolutely. We may even experience this, and it might even last a little while. Then we have to get down to work and create a relationship, and keep creating it. Actual love does not come preassembled.

Romance has been such an important part of Western consciousness for so long that we cannot and should not summarily discard it. Every element in it has an essential truth. It's simply put together wrong and has some pieces that need adjustment. We have to sort out the truths about finite and infinite selves and discover how they actually work in concert. We will still want and need candlelit dinners, cozy fireside evenings, and telling our beloved that she or he is the most exquisite being in all creation, and hearing from him or her that we are, too.

To be starry-eyed indicates either a blow to the head or an illusion. Actual love requires *dis-illusionment,* the elimination of illusion. (To be *disillusioned,* on the other hand, is still to be in the thrall of an illusion: a negative one.) Dis-illusionment allows us to achieve the ideal. An ideal is something one can successfully bring into existence and live day to day; otherwise, it's an illusion. To attain any ideal, including an ideal relationship, requires a dispassionately realistic assessment of reality. The finest gift we can give our beloved is to see her or him with great clarity as well as love. This includes perceiving her as she actually is as an infinite self, as wonderful and gorgeous as can be imagined, and seeing her as she actually is as the creation of that infinite, divine self, undeniably a most exquisite being. It also involves seeing the not-yet-perfected aspects that can cause pain and behave insufferably. Above all, it entails not letting any of these cloud our perception of the other aspects but instead keeping them all in view and distinguishing them clearly.

In addition to personal affinities such as admiration and physical and emotional attraction, a love relationship between two people who are relatively individuated psychologically and spiritually involves at least an intuitive awareness of the spiritual dimension of each other and of the depth and height of the connection that provides. It mirrors the reality of each one's own transcendent nature and unbounded potentials. Actual love includes openness to the transforming possibilities of relationship. It requires awareness of and action to overcome the nearly unavoidable tendency to commit transference. It calls for each one to perceive the person that their partner is in process of becoming and to accept his incomplete perfection. In so doing, each sees in the other the adult they are, the child and youth they remain, and the older person they'll become. Our deepest need and desire in relationship is to be seen and loved for all that we are. Love of this sort requires a broad perspective and a good sense of humor. Each part of us can then relate appropriately and without confusion to each part of our beloved. There can be maximum communication and openness when each part is accepted and validated for what it is. This means there will be much less testing and proving, distancing, or conforming to expectations.

The Post-Romantic Relationship

A post-romantic relationship may appear less glorious than our romantic illusions but will actually be much more fulfilling. The fireworks of love ultimately come from spirit, and spirit can infuse the most ordinary things, so that there will be less dissatisfaction with the mundane; instead, an abiding joy will suffuse it. When two people share both their inner and outer lives, both their actual selves and their unrealized parts, there is little need for distraction, escape, or glamour.

For millennia, the game of love has been for a woman to surrender to a strong, dominant male, ideally one she admires and finds attractive. Romantic or courtly love, from the twelfth century on, espoused the idea that the male should be gentle, well mannered, and respectful of his ladylove yet still strong and dominant. Post-romantic relationships, however, will be affairs of mutuality between people understood to have different needs, perceptions, and vocabularies. Mutuality would be easy if both partners were the same. ("Why can't a woman be more like a man?" Professor Higgins plaintively wonders.) Where differences are great, as they are, and acknowledged, as they must be, respect and gentleness in both directions are requisite for mutual openness that involves neither dominance nor surrender of power. Couples must engage each other, not engage in attempts to control one another or give up their actual needs in order to play a role. The aim is not to surrender so as to be removed from one's old life or old self or to live up to an unrealizable ideal; it is to surrender to the flow of life and of infinite self, through oneself and through the relationship. Society conditions men to suppress their capacity for emotional intimacy; love serves to unlock a man and to ease his striving to control life, so that he's receptive to life's wellsprings. Love serves a woman as a completing focus for her genius for connection, engendering the trust that enables her to forthrightly express her power within a relationship, rather than to use it covertly, thinking men are intentionally withholding relating. This does not reduce a man's power; both become more empowered. It's urgent that evolved relationships awaken and free men and women to direct their power where it will meet vital needs and address issues that will impact their descendants' ability to flourish on the planet. This will be far more heroic than any Arthurian adventure.

(An example of the difference between a romantic and non-romantic approach to relationships appears in a folk tale, "The Frog King," in the Grimms's early nineteenth-century collection. Most people know the version of the story where the princess kisses the frog and it turns into a prince. The original tale puts an unusual spin on the idea that if something is truly meant to be yours, let it go and it will return to you. In the earliest version, the princess, clearly a young woman who knows how to express her power, hurls the frog at the wall so that it awakens as a prince. The astute post-romantic princess should be prepared for both tactics. Given that it takes many frogs to find a prince, however, and in light of the alarming worldwide decline of amphibians, the more romantic approach seems preferable.)

The dominance/submission paradigm of male-female interaction has long colored the relationships of men and women to divinity and to their infinite selves.[17] The same illusions and misunderstandings affect both sexual and spiritual relationships; each kind of relationship must be healthy for the other to be so. People have largely understood spirituality as requiring submission on the part of the finite self to the dominant divine; yet, this can only engender fear and mistrust. We humans, afraid that the divine will overwhelm us or that we will lose ourselves in its infinite vastness, have always tried to control the relationship through ritual, sacrifice, supplication, or adherence to codes of behavior, in order to get the divine to do what we want and not do what we fear. (Many cultures raise boys to try to dominate any situation, and throughout the ages, legends of heroes depict them as contending with gods or wrestling with angels.) To the degree that we attempt to control the interaction, we lose any authentic relationship with the divine; we act in ways that aren't true to ourselves, and we don't allow the actual divine into our lives, which exactly parallels the relationship between the sexes. Moreover, to the degree that we distance ourselves from our higher self, we lose touch with our authentic personal needs and potentials; unable, therefore, to guide our lives confidently, we fear the power of our partner and close ourselves to him or her. In the same way sexual relationships are changing, a new form of relationship with the divine is needed and possible, one that is mutual, acknowledges and engages the power of both, and involves surrender to flow, not to the control of the other. It may seem strange to think of the divine surrendering or not being dominant, but from the beginning of our existence, infinite self surrendered its power over us by giving us free will. It has long waited for us to bring our power (and responsibility) into mutual relationship and creative partnership with it.

Even though the partners in each relationship, man and woman or finite self and infinite self, bring their power into the relationship, each surrenders control radically. Hopefully, we eventually realize—although without conscious effort this comes late in life if at all—that all we can control is our own integrity and that integrity is the only thing we need. This perfect match permits us to surrender the rest, which is necessary for finite self to work creatively with higher self and for man and woman to create a satisfying and fruitful relationship.

The fireworks of the loving relationship between infinite and finite selves, like those of the post-romantic personal relationship, need grounding in the mundane. Bursts of mystical revelations or psychic experiences are rare and unsought in mature and balanced spirituality. Instead, the relationship generates peace, centeredness, energy, humor, play, joy, insight, and a fulfilling life.

Thus, relationships with our beloved and with the Beloved, the infinite self, co-evolve and mutually inform and enhance each other. The significance of this for our personal and spiritual lives couldn't be greater. Disentangling the illusion of romance and distinguishing infinite and finite aspects of relationships is slow and painstaking; patience often runs thin. Nonetheless, in relationships as in all aspects of life, we can have it all if we understand that this occurs one facet at a time. In love with a person from whom we expect and desire everything, we must remember to enjoy each aspect of the person and the relationship as it presents itself and, having enjoyed it fully, let the next emerge. The only way we can miss out is to miss what's happening in the moment. Engaging and enjoying each aspect of our beloved, we bring the divine into life's quotidian aspects as well as into the heart of our culture's crises.

We long for union. The fullness of union, of inner marriage, rests on the individuation of each partner: first, on his and her marriage of finite and infinite selves, then on the marriage of masculine and feminine within each. This allows both partners to recognize the union of their infinite selves and work consciously to connect as personalities. Inner marriage is requisite for a marriage of actual love. In the face of this daunting task, it's tempting to drink a romantic potion or elope to Las Vegas. However, we must do this work at some point in order to have union and love. Whether one is single or in a relationship, love calls us to begin, or begin anew, now.

6

FORGIVENESS

> Having come
> the bitter way to better prayer, we have
> the sweetness of ripening. . . .
>
> —Wendell Berry, "Ripening"

Although erring is human and forgiveness divine, we humans find ourselves needing to forgive all manner of trespasses. Our non-divine selves, specialists in erring, often feel hard-pressed to genuinely forgive. Instead, we suppress, ignore, or try to forget or act magnanimously (but don't really let go). This quandary pertains to not only forgiving others but the more difficult matter of forgiving ourselves.

To forgive is, in the origins of the word, to "give up" or "give away." Its usual meaning is to give up resentment (resentment meaning, literally, "to feel or sense again"—in effect, to dwell on something) and to release the desire for, or right to, vengeance or punishment.

Run-of-the-mill grievances are usually easy enough to release. In the economy of existence, to do so may cost less than holding on to the hurt or irritation; also, seeing oneself (or being seen) as forgiving makes us feel better about ourselves. Some acts, however, are so egregious that to forgive them seems a travesty of justice and to let the offender off the hook feels like a sin against the natural order. We may be reluctant to forgive if it amounts to giving up hope that the divine will balance the harm to us through just retribution: to forgive can feel like one is diminishing one's value.

A central theme in Jesus' teaching is the forgiveness of sins. "If you forgive others their trespasses, your heavenly Father will also forgive you"[1] makes it quite clear that if we wish to be reconciled with the divine, we must practice forgiveness ourselves. This theme occurs in ancient Babylonian, Taoist, and Buddhist teachings: return love or kindness for anger, hatred, or injustice. We seem to be called to an essential task that is, in its most important instances at any rate, above our station and capacities. The act of forgiving puts one center stage in the moral ordering of the cosmos. It can feel too God-like, an interference in the laws of karma or of "an eye for an eye," as if one had arrogated divine prerogatives and responsibilities for which one lacks the necessary wisdom or insight.

The dilemma arises from the fact that we're not in touch with the aspect within ourselves that's qualified to forgive: the divine infinite self. We must admit, in all honesty, that we cannot forgive some things as finite selves; their enormity surpasses our finite ability. In these cases, a play on the word "forgive" brings us closer to its essential meaning and to the solution of our dilemma. We "give" the matter to our infinite self "for" this aspect of self to resolve. Infinite self, in turn, "gives" to finite self what it needs "for" its healing and spiritual growth.

This works because the concept of forgiveness exists strictly from the finite perspective. From the "viewpoint" of the infinite, our shortcomings as finite selves are works in progress, steps in our evolution, which we as finite beings can only perceive a small part of at a time (more on this in chapter 16). The crucial matter, from the standpoint of infinite selves, is that we are learning and cleaning up our messes, not that we receive punishment. Thus, when we pray for forgiveness, there's nothing to be forgiven for, because the higher self holds nothing against us. The effect of asking for forgiveness is that we open the door so that infinite self can give us what we need for the completion of our works in progress—for growing spiritually and setting things right. Only finite self, of its free-will choice, can open the door. Infinite self is always ready to give this: "Ask, and it will be given you . . . knock, and the door will be opened."[2]

The reason that forgiveness holds such a central place in Jesus' teaching is that our very inability as finite selves to forgive the unforgivable forces us to open to the divine. To forgive another or ourselves, we must stretch not so much our capacity to forgive but our capacity to experience and embrace the infinite and engage all our God-given capacities. This is the essential element of all spiritual growth. Not to do this amounts to staying closed to the divine, which severely limits spiritual development. Forgiveness has important benefits for human society, but its crucial importance is its implication for the kind of relationship we have with our infinite self.

For members of many religions, trying to forgive can be a challenge because the actual seat of the faculty that we call forgiveness is unavailable to know and experience—unavailable if the higher self is not part of the belief system. Consequently, the very reason for the difficulty isn't apparent, causing a person to feel unforgivably unforgiving. Jesus taught the need to forgive and demonstrated how; further, he said that others could do even better. To the degree that, for Christians, Jesus came to be the exclusive carrier of the infinite aspect of self (see appendix 2, part 2, s.v. "The Christ Archetype in Late Antiquity"), the actual ability to forgive was in effect placed not only outside the finite person (accurately so) but also outside the total self, thus limiting finite self's capacity to forgive. It's true that when a person calls upon and opens to God, she can sense forgiveness and reunion with the divine, in part because she is, albeit unconsciously, opening to her own infinite self, and her infinite self responds. However, when she opens to God as an external source or even as within her but other than herself, she experiences herself merely as a sinner who either acted heinously and needs to be forgiven or who felt angry and vengeful about being the subject of a misdeed and is struggling but failing to be forgiving. Only God's grace brings the sinner back into the fold. Finite self thereby misses the actual potential of the event: to expand awareness and experience her own spiritual stature (her infinite self), and so to discover that there is a part of her that is beyond error and is the source of what we experience as forgiveness. By turning to an external source, finite self loses an opportunity for spiritual integration. To experience forgiveness of self or another via higher self is to take on much more responsibility for one's effect on the world. It opens one to receive from infinite self the wherewithal to take beneficial action, leading to greater willingness and ability to grow and act in a responsible and healing manner.

How Not to Be a Captive of Your Past

What we do not forgive stays with us, whether the offense was done to us or by us and whether it was a sin of commission or omission. We are on the hook, unhealed; we continue to carry the burden of the event and are prisoners of the past, held captive by the experience. Lack of forgiveness by either perpetrator or victim holds back both. However harmful the original act or omission may have been, to let its harm continue through lack of forgiveness is tragic. The injured part of us—hurt by our own action or that of another—can't grow and becomes hardened and closed, cut off from its spiritual source of life-energy and enlightenment. Even though only a part of us, it ultimately holds back the growth of the whole person, in the same way that an unforgiving group—for instance, terrorists, religious zealots, or groups with old injuries to avenge—can impede the development of a whole society economically, socially, and spiritually. The need for forgiveness poses us the clearest, most consequential existential decision. Based on this decision, we'll either shrivel and diminish or expand. We have the power to choose; healing requires us to act, to forgive.

The concern that if one forgives and forgets, one is letting the perpetrator (even if oneself) get off unjustly is addressed biblically: "Vengeance is mine, I will repay, says the Lord."[3] The law of karma is usually not our responsibility to enforce; the infinite self of the perpetrator insures learning and balancing the scales. We should not forget the matter—it's not as if the infraction never happened; things are different, we've changed, and forgetting would be to fail to learn. However, we should not hold it against the other—it's quite a burden to bear. Our main purpose is to become free. We're the most direct beneficiaries of our forgiving; we become wiser and therefore less vulnerable.

Finite self must initiate forgiveness. This begins by accepting that the event occurred—not easy, if one is in denial or avoidance. The next step is for finite self to ask infinite self for help with what it cannot resolve itself, surrendering the matter to infinite self—also difficult, if one feels one must struggle to accept a grievous injury or make it different. We need to surrender especially whatever seems beyond acceptance or challenges our trust in the divine order. Often, it is the pain and damage of holding on that finally provides the necessary motivation to let go, so letting oneself feel the effect of the offense (one's own or another's) deeply can be a critical step. Releasing it lets it dissolve into the infinite where it has meaning and value as part of our eons-long growth process toward wholeness.

Through forgiveness we find grace, the experience of a deep union of finite and infinite selves wherein nothing remains unresolved to separate them. This lifts us out of our finitude for a time. We must keep asking for, opening to, and receiving forgiveness, so that it becomes a way of life. This isn't self-abasing; neither does it make us morally superior. If these feelings arise, we can release them to infinite self also. Frequent forgiving helps us avoid being overly concerned with particular events; we learn to constantly let go and give over to infinite self our resentments. We can then stay in the present and receive what's given in return, enabling us to increasingly live in the infinite, which is both our primal experience and our spiritual goal.

7

We Are of Two Minds: Paradox, Polarities, and a New Synthesis

The illusion that the self and the world are broken into fragments originates in the kind of thought that goes beyond its proper measure and confuses its own product with . . . independent reality. To end this illusion requires insight, not only into the world as a whole, but also into how the instrument of thought is working. Such insight implies an original and creative act of perception into all aspects of life, mental and physical, both through the senses and through the mind, and this is perhaps the true meaning of meditation. . . . But original and creative insight within the whole field of measure *is* the action of the immeasurable.

—David Bohm, *Wholeness and the Implicate Order*

Contraries mutually Exist: But Negations Exist Not

—William Blake, *Jerusalem*

To know ourselves, we need to examine how our minds function. Our culture values scientific, rational, linear thinking—the mode of thought that discriminates opposites—and usually states its working premises in these terms. Yet, a growing number of people in our culture feel an urgent need to put greater emphasis on a more poetic and encompassing mode of awareness and living. In response there is an ongoing reframing of core cultural truths to be more inclusive and intuitive; effects of this appear in interdisciplinary scientific work, the theories of modern physics, religious ecumenicalism, holistic approaches to healthcare, and non-traditional spiritual pursuits. Values and beliefs such as materialism, progress, gender roles, human exceptionalism, the superiority of technologically advanced cultures, and even the concepts of causality and linear time have come into question in the past century. How this restating and revisioning of truths unfolds has overwhelming implications for our society and the world.

This process is sufficiently widespread and different from our accustomed approach to the world as to cause some observers to worry about an anti-intellectual backlash and a retreat from logical, analytical, "enlightened" thinking. While at times it may be reactive, its underlying impulse isn't "anti." It's a movement toward embracing, balancing, and synthesizing these two modalities—rational and intuitive—by which we experience and explain the ultimate issues of our existence and the cosmos and which have previously seemed mutually exclusive and antagonistic.

In some of the past century's most important scientific advances—especially in astrophysics and subatomic physics—intellectual investigation has led to seemingly mystical results. This suggests that we are at a point of unique opportunity to accomplish such an integration.

If we don't achieve a measure of balance between the rational and intuitive aspects of mind joined in a unified whole, momentum away from reason and in favor of the irrational will increase. This movement may be as excessive as nineteenth- and twentieth-century rationalism and its other attendant "isms" were in their imbalance in the opposite direction. If this occurs, the results might be similarly unfortunate for us, although an extreme emphasis on intuition will probably not be as destructive for humankind and the biosphere as our present excessive use of logic and analysis to understand our world and ourselves and to solve our problems.

Our overemphasis on reason doesn't mean we aren't highly irrational in our motivation and actions, only that we expect our discourse to appear reasoned and analytical, ideally with the trappings of science, even if most people don't know what the scientific method involves or what a theory is. All this serves to hide from us the uncomfortable fact of how unreasonable we really are, which seems problematic only because we think we should live exclusively in the clear, bright world of logic. Irrationality isn't inherently negative at all, but it can cause real trouble when cloaked as something else.

We need to understand the nature of the reformulation and synthesis of truths that is in progress and increasingly encompasses and utilizes both modalities of mind. This union must involve an inclusive and interdependent relationship, interacting in fusion rather than discordant fission, based on the natural ongoing dynamic interplay of these means by which we know ourselves.

The Value of Paradox

This synthesis will inevitably be paradoxical. A paradox involves recognizing that two completely valid viewpoints can provide opposite explanations of the same matter; it embraces the coexistence of two apparently contradictory states that are equally true, which seems irrational. Because the paradox isn't neat and settled, it makes us uneasy. Our minds want to tie up loose ends. A lack of orderliness and its attendant discomfort, however, can offer fertile ground for creative insights and breakthroughs. For this reason, spiritual practices have often used paradoxes, such as those expressed in Zen koans and Sufi stories, to force the mind past its limiting rational mindset. If we're to rise to the challenge of this moment in spiritual history, we need to value paradoxical thinking and become accustomed to it.

A paradox isn't some oddity to explain away or ignore. Physics reveals that the fundamental nature of reality is paradoxical. For instance, light is wave or particle, depending on how it's measured. What we experience as solid, stable matter turns out to be composed, at the subatomic level, of energy moving at exceptionally high speed. Matter is both continuous and discontinuous. Philosophy and religion always have pointed to the pervasiveness of paradox at the very foundations of existence. Further, Rucker argues that paradoxes are intrinsic to the rational mind. The irrationality of paradoxes does not imply that the logical frame of mind they assault is fictive; rather, it indicates that rationality is incomplete by itself.[1] This is not a problem but a potential.

Regardless of the insights of physics and philosophy, we're uncomfortable with the notion that things we've believed to be antithetical should be attributes of a cohesive synthesis. We may attempt to eliminate one aspect of the paradox, but this is seldom possible, so we try to force two opposites to become one or make disparity disappear in sameness. This only produces an untenable mixture, an impenetrable muddle, and a need for divorce.

This attempted oneness differs from synthesis. Rather than creating a confused jumble, synthesis allows for the coexistence of opposites, a vigorous and transformative interplay, a relationship that energizes and clarifies both without forcing one or both into a procrustean marriage bed.

A synthesis of the rational and intuitive aspects of mind puts us in an essentially scientific frame of mind, enabling us to see that everything is open to question and to multiple interpretations and that people can see an event from differing perspectives, give it various meanings, and understand it in diverse ways. They can experience God as loving or vengeful, terrifying or comforting, judge or forgiver; they can view the same aspects of life as either heroic, foolish, or evil, depending on their bias, as depicted in Akiro Kurosawa's (1902-1994) film *Rashomon,* which dramatizes an event as remembered differently by four witnesses. Buddhist and Taoist thought and subatomic physics hold that one cannot create something without creating its opposite. Thus, one can't do a completely good act, as unexpected bad consequences may result; the same is true of a bad act with its potential good effects.

Polarities and Dualities

This ambiguity is inherent in a universe of polarities, where everything has its opposite or mirror-image, feminine its masculine, plus its minus, positive electrical charge its negative, matter its antimatter. As the infinite or divine enters into existence in finite form, it manifests as mutually interdependent polarities; this seems to be essential for physical existence. Jung declares, "There can be no reality without polarity."[2] Indologist Heinrich Zimmer (1890-1943) writes, "Is not everything, in some deep way, its own opposite? Even though ... categorizing logic ... may refuse to accept the paradoxical fact, nevertheless ... every moment of life includes, somehow, qualities diametrically opposed to those apparently implied."[3] Taoism's core is an understanding of the necessary relationship of every pair of opposites and how this relationship can fruitfully evolve. Friedrich Nietzsche (1845-1900) puts it this way: "Have you ever said Yes to a single joy? O my friends, then you said Yes to *all* woe. All things are entangled, ensnared, enamored."[4] Hindu metaphysics has long held that to achieve an enlightened state it is necessary to go, as the Bhagavad Gita suggests, "beyond earthly opposites."

This essential bipolar aspect of the cosmos is not a duality, where duality means opposites that are separate, mutually exclusive, and sometimes antagonistic—as in the common understanding of the pair good and evil, for example. Rather, paradoxical polarity implies complementarity, wherein each of the pair of opposites is necessary to the other, completes it, and is essential for its existence. Our paradoxical finite-infinite nature forms a complementarity. The mutual interdependence of complementarity is the natural relationship of any pair of polarities. Niels Bohr (1885-1962) anchored this idea in physics, holding that contradictory viewpoints may not only be equally worthy, but both may be necessary to a complete understanding of an event or process. Zimmer describes the essential dynamic tension between polarities, wherein "harmony is essentially a resolution of irreducible tensions. ... The pattern of existence is woven of antagonistic co-operation, alternations of ascendancy and decline." This leads to wholeness and integration.[5]

The distinction between polarity and duality is crucial because if we misperceive a polarity to be a duality, that is, if we think a "both-and" situation is actually an "either-or" condition and then we try to eliminate one aspect of the polarity, either the labor will fail or both aspects of the polarity will be damaged or destroyed. Neither of the opposites, being part of a natural pair, can ever completely vanquish the other. If one is suppressed, it will always come back to undermine the other.

For example, much spiritual pain occurs as people try to eliminate seemingly negative or immoral aspects of their own psyches (angry feelings or sexual urges, for instance) rather than healing and integrating them, not understanding that these are the complementarities of what they deem morally superior. We suffer if we attempt to eradicate our shadow side, which includes these repressed elements of self; the more we try to eliminate unwanted parts of the psyche, the stronger they become, potentially erupting in destructive behavior or disease. The failure to understand the distinction between polarity and duality has led to dark nights of the soul for many. Jung tells of a shattering childhood dilemma: for days he resisted experiencing something he intuited to be bad, an image of God defecating on a church. He exhausted himself trying to avoid the experience, but it wouldn't go away until he allowed it into his consciousness.[6] The German mystic Jacob Boehme (1575-1624) had a profoundly disturbing vision in which he saw two aspects or centers of nature within God, one dark (the desire nature) and one light (the imaginative nature). The dark center exists as a potential within God, with the light center expressed. This revelation, that what's normally considered a duality exists within divinity and that both good and evil are aspects of God, caused Boehme great difficulty and depression.[7] We discover how attempting to get rid of one polarity can destroy both when we eliminate plants, insects, or animals believed to be harmful and expendable but which turn out to perform vital ecological functions without which "good" species can't thrive; the absence of either devastates the environment.

The composers of the Hindu Rig Veda (1200 B.C.E. or earlier in oral form) saw the dynamic balance of polarities as essential for the well-being of society, based, historian Norman Cohn explains, upon the idea of "a divinely sponsored integration, as opposed to chaotic and conflict-ridden separateness. . . . The prototype of all human contracts was . . . a great cosmic contract that reconciled all opposites: light and darkness . . . life and death."[8] Their social order integrated as polarities what otherwise might have devolved into disruptive dualities. Ancient Taoists stressed that the purpose of a sage was to return his consciousness, through disciplined awareness, to its primal, non-differentiated condition. This renewed the balance of the internal and external natural order of polarities that man's consciousness, in its creation of the "ten thousand things" (the productions of his mental activity), had thrown out of equilibrium; the sage thereby established well-being and an enlightened social order.

Just as recognition of the need to deal with opposites appears early in history, it arises at the beginning of individual development. We learn to discriminate opposites in the initial days of infancy. Here, developmental psychologist Jean Piaget (1896-1980) identifies "the first manifestation of a duality of desire and satisfaction, consequently of value and reality, of complete totality and incomplete totality, a duality which is to reappear on all planes of future activity." This "is destined to be emphasized unceasingly."[9] The context indicates that Piaget is using the word duality in the same way that I'm using the word polarity, so that Piaget is describing the infant's discrimination of polar opposites. To negotiate her material and social worlds, a child's maturing mind continuously faces the need to make distinctions of opposites, some inherent in our universe of polarities and some artificial.

A child is taught to make these opposites into dualities ("That's bad! Stay away from it!") Duality does not allow for relationship. It obscures the character and truth of each aspect of the duality; it emphasizes contradiction and conflict. The complementarity of polarities, in contrast, is the strongest possible relationship, one that illuminates—even if only through contrast—the nature and meaning of each complementary quality. A complementary relationship is healing; for instance, a man's embrace of the feminine indicates a joining of contraries such that he becomes less narrow and partial and achieves an integrated awareness that frees him from fear that he will be lost in the flux of transformation.[10] The profound nature of the connection is indicated by the tendency for a psychological or spiritual state, if pushed to its most radical position, to flip to its opposite; Jung found this to occur both in individuals and the history of consciousness.

Nothing we do as finite beings can be completely one-sided because nothing comes into existence without the creation of its attendant opposite. Nor, paradoxically, can we do anything that is complete or ultimately whole. Perfect wholeness seems not to be able to exist in the finite cosmos; for instance, when matter and antimatter meet, they annihilate each other. In the physical universe, opposites interact incompletely. Spiritual evolution moves toward wholeness, but absolute wholeness, undivided and unfettered by the limitation of form, is no thing.

Although we know that nothing is whole or absolute, we can't treat everything as simply relative. Knowing the paradoxical nature of our existence, we must still behave as if our actions could be complete and completely good; we must still act wholeheartedly. It's the human miracle that a wholehearted embrace of our total nature can transcend the limits of our finite existence and bring us into the realm of the infinite, into wholeness beyond all distinction: the realm of the divine.

The principle of polarities expresses in living form as female and male. These polarities both occur within each individual as masculine and feminine qualities: outflowing and inflowing, dynamic and magnetic, functional and structural. The masculine polarity pertains more to activity, the feminine to beingness. The masculine stresses expression, giving, and functioning, while the feminine emphasizes relationship, structure, form, and receptivity. Men have feminine energy and qualities, such as acceptance of others, openness to inspiration, the capacity to nourish, and the abilities to elicit, draw in, receive supply, and to give shape and form to expression. Women have masculine attributes, such as the capabilities to energetically express, to function skillfully with power, purpose, and meaning, and to give support and supply to others. These all exist, at least as potentials, within every person. A person achieves her or his greatest well-being and fulfillment by bringing masculine and feminine characteristics into balanced expression. Each individual has rational and intuitive polarities of mind, associated with the masculine and feminine, respectively.

Taoist philosophers held that the relationships of the polarities of gender can produce things that cloud a person's knowledge of higher self and trap him in illusion, or they can generate a unified relationship in which all creation is in dynamic harmony and expresses its actual design. Lao Tzu (sixth century B.C.E.) instructed seekers: "Know the male [yang] / But keep to the role of the female [yin]"[11] to stay in alignment with the governing principle of the cosmos. Those who follow his advice embody the desired balance between the polarities: the feminine being the ground of existence and providing access to the infinite, the sage lives in it, enters into action (i.e., moves into the masculine polarity) by arising from it, stands on the foundation it provides from which to function, and then returns to it. As the feminine ground is the gateway to the infinite, men are inherently at a disadvantage in experiencing infinite self or in feeling connected to the divine unless they have integrated their own feminine. This may explain why women typically constitute a significant majority of the members of churches or spiritual groups and why women so often prepare the dead for burial and thus for the return to the divine. There's a parallel between male anxiety about not appearing good enough in women's eyes and the human concern that we are imperfect sinners in God's eyes: in both cases the finite feels fearful of inadequacy in the face of the infinite (or those closer to it, i.e. women), the more so the more distant the person feels from the divine. Because of their disadvantage, it's still largely the norm for a man to feel he must prove his worth to both God and woman through accomplishments.[12]

Return to the Feminine

The masculine, notably but not exclusively expressed by males, has been dominant in human societies for most of recorded history, at least four thousand years. During this time, the most powerful and influential members of humanity (men and some women) have almost universally expressed masculine (functional) consciousness and have been to that degree distanced from experiences of the infinite within. We're now moving into a period where the feminine, structural energy will take the lead. The current revaluation of the rational and intuitive aspects of mind and the movement toward their synthesis are aspects of the current profound shift in the relationship of masculine and feminine polarities and of the sexes. Other signs are abundant: the women's rights movement, changes in men's consciousness and priorities, sciences studying the interconnectedness of life, and concerns with world peace, environmental well-being, and adequate nourishment. It's no coincidence this return to the feminine occurs simultaneously with the current discoveries of physics that verge on mysticism, increased acceptance of the infinite in mathematics, and an incipient awareness of the individual infinite spirit. A return to the feminine principle in both men and women brings all people closer to the infinite source of being.

The shortcomings of the long-standing masculine-dominated order have received much attention: endless wars, hierarchies empowering the few and degrading the rest, analytic systems that too often miss the forest for the trees, and now the destruction of the forest itself in addition to many other ecosystems. (Only a dualistic mindset, however, would ignore the advances this imbalance has fostered and that perhaps could only have occurred because of it: most important, the ability to distinguish and isolate phenomena that has been at the heart of scientific and technological advances.)

Whether on a personal or historical scale, the relative emphasis on the masculine and feminine polarities changes over time; this serves a necessary rebalancing function in the evolution of human consciousness.[13] We don't want too much of either side of a polarity, or for too long, so we'll periodically make at least sampling forays to the "other side." While this dynamic imbalance is probably inevitable, the amplitude of imbalance is somewhat within our control; therefore, we have responsibility for the resulting scale of disparity within ourselves and in society. During a period of rapid change such as the present, relationships between feminine and masculine are confused and difficult (especially because they're between paradoxical complementarities, and we're not accustomed to think in paradoxes or comfortable with them), but there's an increased opportunity to establish a better balance of masculine and feminine qualities and energy in society and in each person.

We now have an existential choice that will affect the quality of life and the course of events for generations to come. For men, the most constructive decision would be to explore and embrace their own feminine nature to a courageous degree, to respect and be utterly fair to women, and to change the rapacious way some relate to the material world. A paradigm for this is the spiritual warrior, developed centuries ago, for example, in Chinese monasteries, which emphasizes balance, discipline, forbearance, non-aggressiveness, love of all life, and protection of the weak. For women, the most beneficial course is to embrace the value of the masculine, rather than reject it as the cause of much destruction and misery, to explore its potentials while avoiding regressive seduction by it (such as adopting a win-at-all-costs attitude), to seek fairness and mutuality in relationships with men rather than revenge, advantage, or separation, and to express both masculine and feminine power instead of relying on familiar methods of negotiating relationships and getting needs met.

Men and women can only develop this new paradigm together, engaged in the spiritual quest for inner marriage (personal integration and balance) and working for a society that fully employs and values both masculine and feminine. Such a society would include individuality, competition, and exploration, while taking into account the predictable negative effects of these. The welfare of the whole would have priority, and all who truly need care and nourishment would receive it (but could refuse it). Individualism could not run rampant, but neither regulations nor love could unduly stifle individual expression and enterprise.

Polarities are defined by their relationship; much grief arises if they act separately. The underpinning of the society envisioned here will be the understanding of how masculine and feminine complementarities interact in biology, society, and the psyche and how to enhance each in an interdependent dance, a new synthesis. The infinite can express itself most fully through their coordinated movements and especially in the spaces between them formed by their dance.

The rational mind has developed sufficiently to completely dominate its other polarity, to the point that science rigorously excludes spirituality. While new beliefs may be formulated that, biased to the same degree but in the opposite direction, emphasize only the feminine polarity of our nature, and while such change might feel satisfyingly radical, ironically this outcome would be based on the same dualistic thinking that caused the previous extreme imbalance. Achieving a new, more balanced synthesis will require supremely aware and insightful intervention.

The Rational Offers Keys to the Irrational

The dominance of the rational has produced, paradoxically, the mathematical and intellectual tools that enable us to enter what was previously the realm only of the metaphysical or irrational, in a way that's fruitful and illuminating for both the rational and intuitive approaches. This is evident in the science of chaos and in mathematical investigations into infinity occurring in the realms of pure mathematics, astrophysics, and subatomic physics, where scientific studies yield results as mysterious and poetic as the most profound religious insights. Using these tools to investigate the infinite, we can develop the lucid self-knowledge required for conscious rebalancing and responsibly engaging the limitless resources that our infinite nature provides.

From ancient times, the sense of the infinite and boundless, whether as divinity, spirit, or cosmos, has been part of humankind's spiritual and intuitive sensibilities. Only since the late 1800s, when mathematicians established a firm foundation for studying the infinite, could those supremely rational enterprises, science and mathematics, go where previously only philosophical and spiritual intuition had dared. In doing so, purely rational investigation revealed its own limits. For instance, at the big bang, the theoretical beginning of the cosmos, both space-time's curvature and the density of matter would have been infinite; at this point, facing these infinities, all scientific theories fail.[14] Likewise, the uncertainty principle at the heart of quantum theory indicates the limits of what we can know about subatomic particles and thus the foundations of our existence. We come full circle to where the rational mind must incorporate non-rational, intuitive insight in order to proceed. Now, both modalities of experience, rational and intuitive, must contribute equally and at unprecedented levels of competence to expanding our understanding of and relationship to the infinite.

The emerging images and symbols of infinite self present challenges to this nascent self-awareness if not handled wisely. Finite mind, controlled by dualistic thinking, can manipulate the creative power of infinite mind from which these symbols ultimately come, doing this in sometimes useful but often unnatural and harmful ways. Like the sorcerer's apprentice, it may draw on this limitless creativity for interminable production of the fictive and for boundless fantasy, absorbing and overwhelming the mind and the sense of self. Likewise, the rational mind can tap this creative power to generate ceaseless analytic distinctions, which, although intended to yield a whole truth, inevitably lead to ever finer fracturing of reality. (This is depicted in Greek mythology: whoever tried to cut off the many heads of the Hydra monster found that for each one severed, two grew back.) To reduce the strain arising from infinite potential, finite mind may also translate the infinite presence of higher self into infinite series, the aspect of infinity most easily accessible to the analytic mind. Divine infinity is confused with limitless numbers of things; an effect of this frame of mind is our near-infinity of stuff, such as endlessly mass-produced goods that require continual work to produce, acquire, care for, pile in the garage, and get rid of.

If finite mind is loving rather than fearful, it can remain open, supple, and comfortable with the paradoxicality of polarities, and so refrain from making dualities of them. If it's fearful or unsure of love, it will try to create and control dualities by hardening the boundaries between them. This produces a vicious circle: hardened boundaries separate us from something, so we can't know it, and because we fear the unknown, fear increases, causing us to further harden our boundaries. Ironically, the fearful mind's attempt to maintain control leads to it being in the thrall of its dualities because it takes them too seriously. The greater the fear, the more misleading and damaging the dualities created, such as finite/infinite—this being the most damaging because the most profoundly untrue. If open, however, the mind can receive enough support from infinite self to handle even what it misbegets under dualistic illusions that tap into infinite potential. Another Greek myth dramatizes the need for this: the mortal Psyche mistrusts her divine lover, Cupid, which causes him to leave her. To win him back and appease Venus, his angry mother, Psyche must sort a huge mound of small grains into piles by nightfall. She faces a symbolically infinite task to perform in a very finite span of time. Fortunately, countless ants come to her aid. Thus, infinity is required to deal with infinity, and Psyche's test is to learn to accept the support of the infinite.

Given that everything is paradoxical, that dualistic thinking can dupe us into misusing the creative power of infinite self, and that, being finite, we can't fully understand our infinite self, what's left to guide our behavior? While it's tempting to fall back on the false clarities and easy answers of duality and doctrine, we must rely on our humanity: on the totality of what we are in our heights and depths, our light and shadow, our limits and our boundlessness. We have, therefore, a compelling need to discover who we are. We undertake a quest in which nothing is cut and dried, nothing guaranteed. This enterprise takes courage. We may not be able to sort it out rationally, but we can experience much more of ourselves than we can describe or explain, and we must act based on the truth of that experience.

Both Sides Now

The primary reason to discuss the infinite self is to give our dominant rational mind a plausible rationale for opening and widening the doors of experience. To be receptive to experiencing infinite self and to meaningfully incorporate the experience into our everyday awareness of ourselves, however, requires that we engage it with both the intuitive and rational aspects of mind. This involves engaging both sides of the brain: the spiritual, intuitive, artistic right-brain and the analytic, rational, left-brain with its methodology of science and mathematics. (This is a crude distinction: cutting-edge science and math involve much intuition and creative insight, and dreams have had a prominent role in many breakthroughs in technology and science; artistic vision requires careful analysis. Also, the difference in the functions of the brain hemispheres isn't clear-cut.). Utilizing both enhances our ability to distinguish experiences of infinite self from those of finite self and to integrate both into a sense of the whole self.

We need to learn to think in new ways that incorporate the infinite, just as humanity's whole frame of reference had to change to incorporate the theories of Nicolaus Copernicus (1473-1543) and Charles Darwin (1809-1882). Our thinking has yet to catch up with many discoveries of the twentieth century. Changing how we think entails more than having new thoughts; it requires new processes of mind, and these necessitate new relationships between the aspects of mind, a marriage of left and right brain. Though thinking about the infinite challenges our conceptual framework, this is indispensable to our mental and spiritual evolution. As each aspect of mind becomes more practiced and comfortable navigating the infinite, the two united can have increasingly illuminating experiences of infinite self. In this marriage the rational mind will increasingly recognize the usefulness and accuracy of intuition as well as its limits, while accepting it own limitations; the intuitive mind will value the clarity and discrimination of its counterpart. Their strengths are complementary; they also illuminate each other's deficits, helping curb hubris in each other. The rational mind is particularly prone to arrogance, but many intuitive people, perhaps compensating for our culture's prizing the rational, can be dismissive of the analytical mind; religious fundamentalism takes this to dangerous extremes.

To think in new ways requires new educational methods. Secular education tells us little about our paradoxical nature; likewise, traditional Western spiritual instruction about the soul doesn't delve into the complexity of our makeup and the moral questions this raises. Doing so would require a far different educational process than our technological culture deems necessary, although in many "primitive" and "less advanced" societies the nature of paradox is learned readily. It would necessitate increased attention to and sophistication about dreams, symbolic language, art, ritual, and fantasy and entail a different sense of who we are spiritually, rather than only having an intellectual understanding of what it is to be fully human, though that would be a welcome first step. (Although for hundreds of years China has mostly been in the role of recipient of influences from the West, its growing presence on the world stage makes it likely that aspects of its culture and philosophy will have increasingly global impact, including, one might hope, its comfort and facility with paradoxical polarity.) Understanding the human paradox is essential to freedom, love, personal growth, and release from suffering, but both religious and classical scientific thought have made it hard to approach the subject. Still, we can anticipate increasing numbers of people finding it easier to understand and accept the existence of infinite self and its continuity and active interrelationship with finite self because science demonstrates continuities between what were considered completely separate realms: mind and matter and even spirit and matter.[15] Awareness of these continuities is gradually suffusing our worldview. This will eventually produce a conceptual framework within which new spiritual experiences can become conscious.

The Scientific Mind and the Experience of the Infinite

Considering, however, that the very concept of infinity was long subject to scientific and religious debate and is still cause for uneasiness, the idea of relating to an infinite being that is an aspect of oneself has probably evoked profound skepticism in some readers. This reaction arises in part from the way our rational mentality operates, discriminating and separating things into categories. Descriptions based on these discriminations, as we've seen, yield classifications framed as completely opposite to each other, such as one and many, true and false, etc., which tend to become dualities. Where finite and infinite are concerned, their difference and mutual exclusivity seem so profound as to make the idea of the infinite seem incomprehensible: something to speculate about but not understand, directly experience, or relate to in any "real-world" way. The logical mind recognizes that it can't adequately conceptualize the infinite and so feels that it may as well give up. It's prone to deny the reality of what it can't grasp on its own terms.

An examination of numeration, the most precise expression of the discriminating, left-brain function of our minds, may shed light on the rational mind's discomfort with the idea of the infinite. Once we've distinguished one thing from another, we can count things, and in counting we affirm and make more concrete their differences—this is number one, that's number two, etc.—making an abstract reality of what at first may be only tentative separations. We also distinguish orders, categories, and sets. These groupings take on their own reality; the more definitely we name things, the more real the separations seem.

That which is countable seems by definition finite; it's distinguished and separated from other things, and separation delimits it. One way to view the infinite is as an unending series of finite things. Looking at it as such leads to doubts about its reality because it doesn't seem to be part of our lives, which consist of countable things. We have trouble seeing the connection between a group of limited things, however large, and infinity, which seems different. Our discriminating minds suspiciously see many apples forced together to make one (awfully big) orange. To the rational mind, an infinity of successive units may seem like a confusing fragmentation and complexity, an unending, unendurable length, or a geometric or logarithmic increase that boggles the mind. In no time, infinity gets completely out of hand.

Another way of defining the infinite, however, is *the whole*, the undivided matrix or fabric from which all creation arises. Its nature is in its wholeness, not in its vast accumulation of parts, and every part partakes of its wholeness. In this sense William Blake (1757-1827) wrote of seeing infinity in a grain of sand. Hindu and Buddhist philosophies have long held that the cosmos is oneness and that perceiving distinctions between seemingly separate things constitutes the veil of illusion; Taoism emphasizes the unity behind the multiplicity that our minds distinguish in the world.

Implicit in Isaac Newton's law of universal gravitation and Einstein's general theory of relativity are reasons to question the ultimate reality of dividing things and, in a sense, even of numeration. Newton theorized that everything in the universe exerts a reciprocal gravitational pull on everything else in an undivided web of mutual attraction. Einstein stated that the fabric of space-time *is* gravitation. Non-divisibility also appears in quantum physics, where, as Fritjof Capra says, "it is the whole that determines the behavior of the parts" and, at subatomic levels, "it becomes more and more difficult to separate any part of the universe from the whole."[16] Physicists have begun to hypothesize the interdependence even of matter and mind, seeing these as noncausally connected "projections of a higher reality which is neither matter nor consciousness."[17] The connectedness of all things in the gravitational space-time fabric raises potential questions about there being any actual dividing line between anything. Such separations would seem to be arbitrary, as would the definitions we use to categorize things. Clearly, these distinctions have reality of a certain order and great practical value, but they aren't the ultimate reality.

Given that scientific consensus holds the universe to be infinite, these theories in effect suggest that the finite self can perceive, relate to, and participate in the infinite because it is an integral part of the unbroken infinite fabric of the cosmos.

Relativity proposes that the fundamental property of existence is the *field*, not *things* as we usually think of them. Einstein doesn't treat matter apart from its gravitational field; matter and space are interdependent aspects of a whole, a totally interconnected unified entity without division. The vacuum of space itself interacts with the atoms within it and must be receptive to their radiation for them to emit it. In quantum physics, what we consider solid objects are understood to be "wave-like patterns of probabilities, and these patterns, ultimately, do not represent probabilities of things, but rather probabilities of interconnections," explains Capra.[18] Thus, the fundamental qualities of physical existence may lie more in interrelationships within a field than in particles. Rather than describing *what a thing is* and what it's composed of, perhaps we can only explain *what a field does* and its interconnections.

This puts questions about our ability to know and experience infinity in an interesting light. If reality is field-like, can we ever definitively "know" a finite thing? Apparently not, given that, as Capra explains, "everything in the universe is connected to everything else and no part of it is fundamental. The properties of any part are determined, not by some fundamental law but by the properties of all the other parts. Both physicists and mystics realize the resulting impossibility of fully explaining any phenomenon."[19] So it seems that we, who've clung to the finite and have historically resisted the concept of the infinite, can only truly know the whole, the infinite, rather than any finite entity!

In experiments involving collisions of subatomic particles at extremely high energy (high velocity), the particles break up but not necessarily into smaller pieces. When subatomic particles are "split" in particle accelerators, they transform into other particles, which may then change back to their prior form. The energy used to split the particles is absorbed (mass and energy being interchangeable) to create other heavy particles. The particles can therefore be seen as both destructible and indestructible.[20] Instead of units being either fundamental and indivisible or infinitely divisible, there seems to be endless transformation in the quantum field. In fact, energy can create particles out of "nothing"—in pairs of matter and antimatter. This occurred in prodigious numbers at the big bang. Whence came the energy? Stephen Hawking replies, "the total energy of the universe is exactly zero. The matter in the universe is made out of positive energy. . . . In a sense, the gravitational field has negative energy."[21] Matter and gravity nullify each other, so matter can be added or destroyed without violation of the law of conservation of energy. Infinite quantities of particles emerge from the vacuum and cease to exist continuously and endlessly. In the realm of the exceedingly small, there is infinite potential, a field or void that plays out a zero-sum but infinite process of creation and destruction.

Although quantum mechanics is excellent at predicting outcomes across a group of events, Bohm speaks of the "irreducible lawlessness of *individual* phenomena in the quantum domain."[23] At the subatomic interface with the void, the infinite is profusely creative. The uncertainty principle of quantum physics indicates that rather than being empty, a vacuum contains infinite energy and thus potentially infinite mass. Indeed, any number of universes may continually be in the process of creation, at any point in space, each with total energy equaling zero. Physicist Alan Guth summarized the bottom line of cosmic existence: "The universe is the ultimate free lunch."[22]

Perhaps we know and experience the infinite more directly than we think, given that everything we relate to is a field of infinite potential in flux, within which the creation and destruction of matter are continuous. The uncertainty principle and the spontaneous materialization of virtual particles locate the horizon of the infinite emerging into finite being, a horizon that exists within and all about us, always.[24]

The fact that the void has infinite energy, which isn't apparent because matter and gravity balance and cancel each other out, can by analogy help us to understand why, if we are infinite and have infinite energy, we feel so little of it. We're constantly using exactly that energy in prodigious amounts to block and nullify the experience of the infinite, which our training and conditioning cause us to deny and suppress. We're performing an isometric exercise that neutralizes energy, which, absent the blocking, we are told could move mountains.

In sum, the problem the rational mind has in seeing how it could relate to the infinite and the infinite self arises from the fact that the infinite whole and the endlessly numerous constitute a rationally unexplainable paradoxical polarity that the analytical mind tends to construe as a duality, and any dualistic construct posits separation. Whereas infinity conceived as an infinite series can seem interminable, infinity viewed as the undivided matrix of all things has immediacy that is centering and relaxing. Instead of trying to mentally grasp an enormity, we can entertain the sense of wholeness within, the energy of which flows through us and out into life. We feel our natural place in the cosmos.

We should always question our experiences but with scientific openmindedness, never dismissing any out of hand. Scientific thoroughness requires that we be honestly open to any experience, physical or spiritual, evaluate it as best we can, test our explanatory hypotheses, and move forward based on results. In the scientific paradigm, argues Rucker, "any system of knowledge about the world is, and must remain, fundamentally incomplete, eternally subject to revision."[25]

Infinity and its Discontents

Nevertheless, mathematicians have long been uncomfortable with the nature of the actually infinite, which allows, for instance, lines of vastly different lengths to have the same number of points.[26] Only with "great artificiality," in Rucker's words, could they escape having infinities in the foundations of their discipline. Infinities continue to crop up in quantum physics and relativity, and mathematicians tend to dismiss equations yielding infinite results as flawed or meaningless, even though between 1874 and 1884 Georg Cantor (1845-1918) produced a conclusive mathematical theory of the actual infinite.

Cantor's theory contains attributes of the infinite that have interesting parallels to the relationship posited here between infinite selves and God. Cantor established that there are an infinity of infinities and gradations of infinity. This differs, Rucker explains, from the common and "naïve" notion of there being a single infinity "unattainable and not quite real. Cantor keeps this naive infinity, which he calls the Absolute Infinite [which is inconceivable], but he allows for many intermediate levels between the finite and the Absolute Infinite . . . [which] correspond to his *transfinite numbers* . . . numbers that are infinite, but none the less conceivable."[27] These numbers, less than the Absolute Infinite and existing within us, sound a lot like a mathematical description of infinite selves. The transfinite numbers can occur in the physical world; they are infinities that, as Cantor wrote, "are clearly limited, subject to further increase, and thus related to the finite."[28] According to Rucker, set theory demonstrates that "once one has an infinite Absolute, one must also have many conceivable infinities as well."[29] This principle indicates that any possible attribute of Cantor's Absolute also characterizes a lesser set, which resembles the relationship of God to infinite selves possessing the attributes of God.[30]

Rucker observes that people still maintain a "primitive" notion of the infinite and approach it almost as they do religion;[31] it often induces "such feelings of helplessness, futility, and despair that the natural human impulse is to reject it out of hand."[32] Cantor addressed the psychological implications of infinity: he wrote that fearing it "is a form of myopia that destroys the possibility of seeing the actual infinite, even though *it in its highest form has created and sustains us, and in its secondary transfinite forms occurs all around us and even inhabits our minds.*"[33]

The possibility of experiencing the infinite, and the infinite self, is within reason and is approachable according to the scientific method. There's no need—it's not even helpful—to be convinced of the reality of infinite self. What is desirable is persistent receptiveness to fresh experience, made possible by unbiased rationality coupled with attentiveness to the subtleties of intuitive experience. This marriage of the two aspects of brain and mind, as with all good unions, yields more than the sum of the parts. Together they can solve our greatest mysteries, especially the human enigma: who we are.

If there are infinite universes generating more universes of infinite variety, we'll inevitably have to reassess our place in the cosmos, but we'll have difficulty coming to grips with this new cosmic reality without searching for the corresponding infinity within us. This must be sought spiritually as well as scientifically; without that deep grounding, we will have a hard time keeping our psychological and social balance.

When finite self is open to this infinite within us, our minds are best able to function in both modalities: the finite rational mind that counts finite objects or amounts, and the intuitive mind that engages the unlimited as a whole. We can analyze any movement as an infinite sequence of finite actions, or we can relate to it as one whole flowing movement. This joining of modalities lets us spend time in the comfortably finite rooms of the mind, which daily living requires, while still enabling us to go outdoors into the radiant sun of the infinite when we desire; we can keep the windows open to that sunlight all the time.

PART TWO

Living in the Infinite While Having a Life

I
Do not
Want to step so quickly
Over a beautiful line on God's palm
As I move through the earth's
Marketplace
Today.

—Hafiz, "Today"

8

Golden Rules and Evolving Ethics

May I be the friend of that which is eternal. . . . May I know good men and follow in their footsteps.

—The Prayer of Eusebius

Nothing is of more practical significance to humans than how they relate to one another. This is usually determined by their culture's ethical and moral standards, and these arise from how people see themselves psychospiritually. We can easily trace the historical development of human consciousness in the expansion of the spiritual vision embodied in each period's ethical concepts. The first for which we have a clear record is "an eye for an eye"; early expressions of this code developed in Mesopotamia roughly four thousand years ago.[1]

"An eye for an eye" is an ethical norm well suited for developing a self-aware, non-narcissistic view of the world. It fosters awakening to the fact that the ego is not omnipotent and its actions have predictable, inescapable consequences occurring in a period of time that extends beyond its span of attention. This standard describes a consistent and congruent response by the world to one's actions, regardless of one's wishes or fantasies. It facilitates a moral evolution parallel to the development of an infant from its sense of being infinite and without boundaries to becoming a child able to recognize and accept its limits.

Later, a new ethic appeared within numerous religions, supplanting "an eye for an eye." In the West this is most widely known as Jesus' "golden rule": "In everything do to others as you would have them do to you."[2] It appears much earlier in various forms. Confucius (551–479 B.C.E.) put forward the practice of *shu,* "likening to oneself," not doing to others what causes oneself anguish[3] (the so-called negative golden rule). Buddhism states this identically: "Hurt not others in ways that you yourself would find hurtful,"[4] as does the Hindu Mahabharata: "Let no man do to another that which would be repugnant to himself."[5] It was similarly articulated by Zoroaster, Herodotus, and, in Judaism, in the apocryphal book *Tobit*,[6] by Philo of Alexandria (c. 20 B.C.E.-50 C.E.), and by Rabbi Hillel (first century B.C.E.-first quarter of first century C.E.): "That which is hateful to you, do not do to your neighbor. That is the Torah, the rest is commentary."[7] Positive statements of it occur as early as Homer (ninth or eighth century B.C.E.?) and ancient Taoism.

This ethic promotes comprehending that there are not only *bodies* out there, which, if you do harmful things to them, are likely to hurt you in return, but that there are *persons* out there. It expands the ego's awareness of the fact that other egos exist that have needs similar to one's own and need to be taken into account. This is a tremendous advance in consciousness, yet it operates on a level of awareness that remains egocentric; it still measures the world in terms of oneself. Within this moral milieu, perspective (seeing the world from a single viewpoint) entered art. This ethical framework views man as the measure of all things. Only now, in the context of our increasing ecological sensibility and our growing awareness of an infinite universe and of life possibly existing elsewhere, are we beginning to challenge this view.

Whereas the ethical paradigm of the period from around 2,000 B.C.E. to the origins of the current era arose from and instructed the infancy of our egoic consciousness, the ethic of the roughly two-millennia-long era now concluding addressed our egoic childhood. The standard of the latter era is appropriate to the developmental level of a child who feels the limits imposed by her finiteness and seeks to orient herself within a larger, yet still finite, context. In this larger environment, time appears to be finite, beginning with Creation and ending with Judgment Day. Eternity exists around this, and Christian and Islamic doctrines maintain that we participate in eternity only after our measured lives, either in perdition or in bliss. We have no active, creative role in the eternal or in how it forms and affects our finite existence. The summary effect of our choices is limited to which of the eternal places we end up inhabiting.

We're at the beginning of a new stage in the growth of human awareness. As a culture we've contemplated at length and have learned to some degree to live the old paradigm of the golden rule. Having completed the ethical work of the past age (albeit imperfectly), we're ready for a yet more evolved ethic. In fact, not only are we ready, we see around us the increasingly dire effects of the limitations of the golden rule and are beginning to recognize the need for a new ethical standard. Its assumption is that what others need or want is the same as what we need or want. We've become rather good at behaving toward others in ways we want them to act toward us: we do unto others as we would have them do unto us whether or not that is what they want or need us to do to them. Unfortunately, they often do not.

While the ethic of the past age helped humanity to develop a sense of the other as *like* self, which assisted the development of empathy, in the coming age we'll be called on to see each other person as *unique*—not alien, not other, quite akin to ourselves yet also individual, different, and autonomous. We'll increasingly be able to relate to each other in the manner of adolescents in the process of becoming adults. (Adolescence seems to be a relatively modern invention, derived from the luxury to extend education and put off becoming a full member of the economic system. This has proved so necessary and enduring, if not endearing, that what used to last a few years now may take a decade or more.) As adolescents, we must learn to balance the need to develop a sense of individual identity with the need to fit into peer groups and society. We learn to distinguish how others, particularly of the opposite sex, are like us and unlike us, so that we do unto them according to who they are, not according to how we believe or would like them to be. As spiritual adolescents, we will assume the increasing responsibility appropriate to being mature enough to see ourselves as unique infinite beings in the context of other unique infinite selves. We'll recognize that we must act in ways that meet the actual needs of our own and others' finite selves. We will begin to see ourselves as potential spiritual adults, a status that requires yet greater awareness of others as both similar to and different from ourselves. In future eons we may expect to achieve full maturity, then wisdom, and then perhaps true self-realization. (I'm speaking of humanity generally; in every period, individuals have attained each of these stages.)

The limitation of the prior ethic is that it doesn't challenge us to see the other's uniqueness of feeling, perspective, cognition, and purpose. The past age is littered with holy wars, wars of conquest, and ideological wars, the intent of which was, in part, to do unto others as their initiators would have had the others do unto them. The belief is truly convoluted, allowing conquistadors of the sixteenth century to do whatever necessary to the Aztecs and Incas so that they would become as the Spanish were (as to religion, not power or wealth). In other contexts, the same rationale has motivated Muslims, communists, capitalists, and various cultures and nationalities, etc. In each case the believers felt that they should make the others exactly like themselves and that the others should want this. This rationale persists.

One expression of this ethic, favored by the Aztecs, involves sacrificing others for their own good and for the good of one's God or ideology. The converse manifestation of this is the ethic of self-sacrifice, martyring oneself for the good of others as if one didn't count for anything oneself. (Inevitably, one defines what is good for them; as one's belief still counts for everything, one is still being highly egotistical.) One suffers martyrdom or sacrifices self in smaller ways in the name of what one would want them to do or be—for the sake of God, doctrine, or even love, as in the case of many parents.

We need an ethical paradigm that reflects the fact that we've grown to be able to see ourselves in the context of relationship with other unique selves. We can begin to see ourselves living in a *field* of selves in which there is no single valid perspective but in which observers value the fact that each person has a perspective, recognizing that all perspectives have some essential validity. This ethical understanding parallels the past century's developments in physics, such as relativity theory, Einstein's insight that the key to understanding existence is not matter but field with particles being modulations of the field, and the theory that the whole of existence is enfolded into each part.[8] Likewise, twentieth-century art offers a counterpoint to Renaissance perspective, from Cubism with its fractured perspective to abstract field painting and the elimination of perspective.

Making man the measure of things and holding one's religious belief to be the one true faith is absolutism that can be seen, in the context of field theory and relativity, to be based on limited perspectives. It's another instance of confusing the experiences of the two aspects of self, finite and infinite: the absolute relates only to infinity, but we can't apply it even there; the finite is the world of the relative, and this pertains even to the expression of the divine within the finite and thus to religious beliefs. In practice this means that one is free to have absolute faith that one's own belief is true, at least for oneself, but must recognize that this is subjective; therefore in relationship to others, one can't act as if it's any more or less true than anyone else's.

We can say that man is *a* measure of all things, but we must also recognize that *so is everything else.* We discover the universe in a grain of sand and find that all things contain the divine completely.

A New Ethical Paradigm

The following is an attempt to express the new paradigm we need: *Give to others according to their actual needs, and give to yourself according to your own needs, which are equally important.*

A corollary is: *You are no more or less important than anyone else in the great scheme of things, but you have the prime responsibility for taking care of yourself so that you flourish and achieve your spiritual purpose.* (This does not imply that your prime responsibility is to take care of yourself, only that you are responsible for doing that.) *Just do this in a way that helps or at the very least doesn't hinder the flourishing of others.*

Of course, knowing the other's actual need, or even one's own, is an inexact science at best; discovering how to do this and developing awareness of egocentric blind spots will be the cutting edge of moral and ethical development for the next spiritual era. We can only do our best to achieve some insight and discernment, humbly recognizing the inevitable deficiencies of our understanding of others and not imposing ourselves on them. Despite our awareness being limited and any new ethic being imperfect, we can confidently expect to develop our abilities to see beyond ourselves.

Practicing this ethic leads to seeing the whole person. This includes the unique infinite self, the exceptional and unblemished actual person as created by infinite self, and the negative effects of the conditioning, beliefs, traumas, etc. that can produce attitudes and behavior that are dramatically different from the actual nature of the finite self. Perceiving all this at once, we neither dismiss nor idealize a person; we are able to see much more clearly what the person actually needs. Seeing ourselves in the same way, we realize more accurately what we need and how that's different from others' needs, and we understand that this difference is natural and acceptable.

Paradoxically, in valuing others as themselves, we will be able to see and value ourselves in our own incomparable individuality. We will be less likely to become psychologically enmeshed with others and can maintain better emotional boundaries. We will be better able to meet our own needs, which will give us the means to better assist others. In addition, we'll see a sharp decline in all forms of martyrdom.

9

Desire, Will, and Purpose

Birds make great sky-circles
of their freedom.
How do they learn it?
They fall, and falling,
they're given wings.
—Jalal al-Din Rumi

A discussion of the relationships between desire, will, and purpose necessarily raises the ancient, vexing question of whether we have free will. Positing the existence of an omniscient, omnipotent God has always created problems for the idea of human freedom. Ancient Stoic philosophers believed that a ubiquitous fate determines all circumstances and we must endure or enjoy it with equanimity. Plotinus (205-270) believed that we have free will but that its exercise, as expressed by translator Stephen MacKenna, "is simply an index of our ignorance and imperfection. If one knows the best . . . then one can only act in accordance with it, not out of any external compulsion, but by the operation of one's own will."[1] Augustine's (354-430) emphasis on predestination became Christian orthodoxy and received new impetus in the sixteenth century from Protestant reformers such as John Calvin (1509-1564).

Modern psychology has raised similar issues. Conditioning, i.e., learned stimulus-response pairing that has become habit, substantially governs our patterns of thought and behavior. Conditioning significantly determines what we believe are our desires, needs, and aversions. We tend to think and do things that activate the pleasure centers of the brain; we like to contemplate whatever makes us feel good about ourselves, secure, and in control, or else we worry about things we need to resolve to get control of our lives back. (Neuroses compel people to excessively dwell on fears and anxieties or to avoid success, yet such agonizing behavior helps maintain a feeling of security and control.)

At the same time, we expend time and energy on things that have little to do with achieving our dreams or meeting our basic needs. While we speculate about and question the incongruity of this, usually our attention, distracted, quickly wanders elsewhere, and we don't focus on the anomalies long or effectively enough to explore their implications, much less decide to do something about them.

The result of our conditioned thinking and behavior is the dissipation of energy and awareness. All activities of the brain, including analyzing, planning, worrying, fantasizing, or reflecting on a pleasing turn of events, expend awareness and energy. (The brain uses twenty percent of our oxygen, though it's only four percent of body weight.) Worse, conditioning produces patterns of energy and consciousness that may be adverse for health, well-being, and fulfillment. These patterns tend to structure behavior in ways that ensure the survival of the conditioning. The ill effects of these can range from imperceptible to debilitating or even lethal.

The varieties of our conditioning, and the stimuli that trigger reactions causing us to lose focus or react detrimentally, are legion and very hard to resist. Many people find it difficult enough to concentrate at length on a plan or a problem, even when the result would be rewarding. Under normal circumstances, it's nearly impossible for people who lack practice to focus awareness for any length of time, free from the pull of random thoughts and impulses. Employing processing techniques such as inner light-fire can dissolve the conditioning and beliefs that limit our freedom. (An explanation of these techniques follows in the next chapter; details are in exercise 2 in chapter 20.)

Increasing Spiritual Energy

Freedom to focus awareness is the freedom to retain and increase spiritual energy. It is the freedom to act: not to *react* in a conditioned, predetermined way but to *respond* authentically to present circumstances. It is freedom of will.

Historically, many have thought that the best way to focus awareness was to repress or eliminate desire, even treating it as sinful; some disciplines still try to accomplish this through suppressing or avoiding certain feelings, needs, or wants. However, seeking to become disciplined and even holy is still a desire, subject to the same conditioning as more mundane desires, and it can become a habitual pleasure-producing activity itself: the pleasure of feeling oneself to be a good or spiritually advanced person. This habit, like any other left unaltered long enough, can undermine a person's overall inner balance and health. The problem lies not with desire as such but with the conditioning and habitual lack of awareness that affect it. Desire, like love, is a divine force: God desired to generate the cosmos; infinite selves desire to create finite selves and to support them.

Desire is not the same as the thing desired. Equating it with the object of desire causes us to say, "My desire is that car/beautiful woman/cute guy/job/vacation." Desire is simply a force we can focus or that becomes attached to something. We observe this most easily in an infant: his desire to have something can be all-consuming, but when he gets it, he drops it and abruptly redirects his desire to another item beyond his grasp. Having the object doesn't eliminate the desire; the force of desire is still going strong and can easily shift to something else. Opposite yet equally instructive is the experience of those who have a passion to attain something but feel empty and lack a sense of fulfillment once the goal is achieved, at least until they conceive of another goal that gets the force of desire flowing again and makes them feel alive.

The observation that an awful emptiness can follow achievement or, conversely, that desire is not necessarily quenched by gaining its object has motivated many spiritual and religious seekers to learn to reside in pure spiritual desire and spurn directing desire toward any aspect of the world. They have sought to remain in infinite bliss. Many have chosen the life of a hermit, monk, or nun in which they don't have to worry about such mundane desires and needs as getting to work on time or earning a raise.

Most of us are all too familiar with the opposite extreme: squandering time and energy in the chase after worldly desire fulfillment. In America, we have a decent chance to achieve what we desire, but while we may succeed in our chosen field and reap rewards, we often still have nagging doubts as to why we do it. Our desire fulfillment isn't always deeply fulfilling.

Many people think of this situation in what amounts to dualities: acquisition versus renunciation, chasing after the good things of life versus giving them up for cloistered bliss, religious or otherwise. To live in the infinite and eternal, to enjoy infinite bliss, doesn't demand such choices, because it doesn't need an eternity or even a lot of secluded time. An alternative to avoiding or denying desire is the practice of suspending gratification and maintaining focused awareness without suppressing the experience of desire, so that one comes to reside in desire itself, sometimes experiencing it as complete fulfillment or the love of God. To momentarily touch the infinite with our full focus of attention turns on tremendous voltage that can infuse all the other moments of daily living. To do so with high focus requires this suspension of the habitual urge to satisfy desires or scratch the itches of worry, irritation, ego abrasion, etc. It entails experiencing within us the wherewithal—infinite self—to gratify these and yet just remaining in the experience of being that source, that potential, without necessarily exercising the potential. We can develop detachment from outcomes and experience unity with right process because desire is a force we can direct, not the thing desired. We needn't refrain from acting on or pursuing our important desires, because our task at this time in spiritual evolution is to marry heaven and earth; therefore, we can't just withdraw to heaven.

Over many centuries, humanity has learned fairly well how to seek inwardly and thereby find and experience the heaven within. The challenge for the coming age is to bring the heaven within into the ordinary aspects of daily life. Our spiritual work requires a back-and-forth process of building the relationship between heaven and earth. By suspending desire gratification, we build energy and focus; we increase our potential to act decisively with clarity and timeliness. Then, when we act, we're empowered by the tremendous force of the desire of the infinite divine. We have not only great power but also the ability to direct our actions precisely, because we're free from personal need or attachment to a given outcome. (A way to conceive of this is that we enter into union with infinite desire, which acts through us: we become a lens to focus the desire of God, or our infinite self, in the finite world. Our desire is for whatever outcome may arise from that focus; our fulfillment lies in the desiring.) It's our free will choice as finite beings as to what we focus our lens on, while staying unattached to the result. Following our action, we can disengage from active desiring and return to *being*; or we can decide to redirect the force of our desire to another goal.

Far from being a path of renunciation or severe discipline, this is the most desirable experience possible. It's not difficult to learn to consistently choose what to desire, rather than to be willy-nilly smitten with it so that it flows in directions not of one's selection. We've all experienced learning to like something for which we initially had no fondness; we can quickly list many acquired tastes and aversions. As Shakespeare (1564-1616) puts it:

> Things base and vile, holding no quantity,
> Love can transpose to form and dignity.
> Love looks not with the eyes, but with the mind.[2]

This applies to broccoli as well as to our love interests.

Choosing what to desire is a bit like shining a spotlight on something, then moving the spotlight to something else. We're motivated to move in the direction of the spotlighted thing as long as we spotlight, that is, desire, it. Desire causes its object to become bright and radiant. We can, however, shift the spotlight to something else so that the desired thing doesn't govern us. Thus, to shift metaphors, desire can function as a motor that empowers us to move, while we choose the destination.

Will You Choose?

Will and will power have negative connotations for many people. In interpersonal relations, the subject of will usually comes up in terms of conflicts of will or of one person exerting his or her will over another, such that the issue is power or control. In our internal experience, will, struggle, and failure are words that are often uncomfortably connected. Most people have decided at one time or another to exert their will power to change a bad habit or make themselves do something they think is proper and good but which they don't want to do or find unpleasant and difficult, such as losing weight. Many have discovered that their will power doesn't take them far. Then again, they may succeed in their goal but find their grim effort of will has taken much joy and spontaneity out of their lives. This occurs due to common misconceptions about what will is, what it can do, and what are its appropriate uses.

The proper expression of will lies in making choices, not in forcing things to happen. There's a prevalent and rather moralistic misconception that we stir ourselves to action or self-development with will power. Many who believe this are frustrated to discover how little their will power actually moves them—to exercise, stop smoking, or do anything that creates anxiety. This is because *will has very little power.* Its job is to direct the power of desire. It chooses where to focus desire's energetic spotlight. If our desires are so strong that we don't really exercise choice but simply go along, we don't experience a distinction between desire and will; they seem to be the same thing. Will comes into play when we have conflicting desires or an approach-avoidance situation (such as desire for a forbidden object and simultaneous desire to avoid potential adverse consequences), and we have to make a choice. Skillful parenting helps a child find something positive to choose when being told what she can't have or do; she learns to use will to focus desire elsewhere, where it can be fulfilled. Absent this, the child may use will power such that one part of herself blocks or forces the expression of another part, thus being false to herself by doing what is against her nature or making a choice that creates division within herself. Or, she may exercise her will contrary to the will of the parent. Both obstructing self and resisting authority can become maladaptive habits that limit actual free-will choice.

As used here, are will and choice the same? In most situations, yes. A difference between them that's sufficient to matter arises with moral, ethical, or spiritual decisions that necessitate learning to know oneself more deeply, exploring what kind of person one is, and discovering one's own truths. This leads inevitably to studying one's relationship with God and perhaps to the recognition of one's own psychospiritual makeup. If one merely chooses to do what one's philosophy or religion says a person should, the personal will, in the sense I'm outlining, isn't actually involved, although "will power" (with its considerable limitations) might be necessary to force oneself to try to conform with its doctrines.

The highest act of will is to choose to know oneself and one's own truth and to act accordingly, that is, to make up one's own mind. To question and carefully consider something requires focusing awareness, which involves the free exercise of will. To do this is to go against our conditioning and challenge what people generally accept without examination. The issue of will arises regarding such spiritually crucial choices as whether to opt for the harder path and whether to intend the best outcome for all concerned. When we exercise will in this way, we may feel a fresh, chill, and wild spiritual wind blowing through us, for we have dropped our protective conventionality and are exposed to the divine.

In the face of this icy draught, many deeply spiritual people feel impelled to surrender their will to God or to their own infinite self, based on the idea that the divine knows better, being omniscient and perfectly loving. Less idealistically, they may base their submission on the idea that God is omnipotent, omnipresent, and rumored to be vengeful, so surrender would be prudent. These purposes are achievable either through the classical mystical approach to God by means of the annihilation of the self or through releasing oneself to God—being meek before the Lord—while being strong in the world to achieve God's purpose. A more modern, abstract way of putting this is to search for one's higher purpose and then surrender one's will to that. Such methods still have one foot in the old spiritual paradigm; an additional step is required of us now, which is only possible because of the spiritual development that has preceded us and is our foundation.

We need to transcend the traditional model by developing a strong, integrated sense of self such as never has before existed except in rare individuals. A more highly integrated and self-aware identity is necessary in order to relate more responsibly to the divine. The essence of our purpose as finite beings is to make choices and thereby exercise our free will, the divine's greatest gift to us. It matters much less in the end *what* we choose than *that* we choose, if we do it sincerely and honestly. This is not to minimize the need to choose wisely and with love. If, however, we overemphasize this, feeling that we absolutely must do what's good or that there's a right choice we have to identify and make at all costs, we'll be inclined to abdicate our free will, choosing the certainty of divine dictate. The doctrinal threat of damnation has made many people risk-averse in the arena of free will and all too willing to adhere to dogma. One can avoid many difficulties and challenges by giving up free will. If, however, surrender to God's will is motivated by fear of error or failure or by self-doubt, these same resistances will contaminate and subvert the good effect of letting God's will be done or letting things flow. Surrendering for these reasons, people avoid aspects of themselves that need to heal and grow; this may be easier and appear more holy, but it doesn't create wholeness. Those who shun their difficult aspects often are unconsciously influenced by these very aspects to act in a manner that's opposite to their conscious intent.

The same combination of fear of retribution by authority and willingness to avoid the difficulties attendant on exercising free will produces problems for hierarchical groups. The health of a system requires the active, choice-making, risk-taking participation of its members. Democracies require this to survive. Its absence enables dictators to maintain the acquiescence of their subjects but drains life from the society. In the same way, lack of vibrant, risk-taking choosing drains an individual.

Our ability to learn improves if we fully embrace the choices we make (even if we're unsure whether they are the right ones) and follow up on them in good faith. Abundant alternative choices exist in our infinite potential, but as finite selves we must put these aside and focus on the choice we've made (at least until it's plain that another direction is needed). Such single-mindedness (not to be mistaken for closed-mindedness) produces clear results that can teach us who we are and what we need to learn about how we make choices.

We can see this in the search for the love of our life. We seek an ideal relationship, not knowing that the ideal we intuit is the kind of relationship we have as infinite beings. We must, however, choose a finite relationship, warts and all. Some lovers are blinded by an intuition of the divine beauty of their partner's higher self and easily fall in love. Yet, if they think the finite relationship should be like that and be that easy, they soon start projecting fault onto their beloved. At some point they have to decide to wholeheartedly choose their relationship, even though it isn't ideal and requires work. A finite relationship calls for an ongoing choice: *we must will it.* A person may fail ever to really choose, instead living in the subjective infinity of possibility; not fully engaged, she feels victimized by her circumstances. Love is a continuous act of creation.

We may feel that Love (usually meaning an experience of the relationship of the infinite selves involved) has chosen us. We must return the favor, however. (Our infinite selves relate with many infinite selves. As finite selves, I believe, it is ours to choose; whom we love is not fated, even if we're fated to encounter certain people.) In that choice, in the course of creating love, we learn about our strengths and shortcomings and about the actual hierarchy of our needs, desires, and purposes. A clear choice yields lucent feedback. If we dump the person upon finding out that he or she isn't as perfect as we thought and search for another who is and who doesn't require work, and then another, we learn only to be disillusioned, and we discover little about ourselves or about love.

The Virtue of Making a Mess

Only free will choice making serves our primary evolutionary purpose as spiritual beings. Choosing is a process that is as much creative as moral. It is the paramount way that we learn about ourselves and about divine creation. We must choose based on the interface of our ideals and potentials with our needs and desires. If we learn best by making "mistakes," an essential for any creative endeavor, then there is a case to make that we're here to fall flat on our faces. As discussed earlier, we need on occasion to make a mess of things and then pick ourselves up, repair what's damaged, and learn. The divine is utterly forgiving, asking us only to do this and to grow in forgiveness of others and ourselves for ignorant choices; this serves our higher purpose and we can move on in a state of grace. If we don't creatively choose, we thwart the purpose of infinite self in granting us free will.

Our actual purposes are to evolve and serve. We can't know the overall purpose for which our infinite selves created us, for the same reason that we can't completely know higher self: because it is infinite. Similarly, we're unlikely to discover that we're tasked with detailed purposes, for the simple reason that infinite self usually doesn't get that specific. We can learn and serve in any number of different ways and arenas. What's most important is to know that our infinite selves create us with purposefulness, that we must make choices based on our best understanding of who we are, and that we come to know more about our purpose and higher self by experiencing the results of our choices. We don't *give up* our will to the will of higher self; rather, we *engage* higher will by exercising our will. Our purposeful life is an essay, a series of trial runs, not a perfect outcome.

The idea of purpose is part of our Western paradigm of progress toward a foreordained end. For centuries believers envisioned this exclusively in religious terms, such as the Christian millennium; now it also emerges as a potential secular economic paradise, with technology leading the way toward unparalleled abundance and health. Many people feel that their primary purpose is to participate in this paradise through acquiring wealth. On the other hand, as we've noted, the object of purposefulness resides not so much in a successful conclusion and completion but in the process, in the means and not the end. This implies that the scale, local or global, of our expression and accomplishment is usually unimportant, scale being irrelevant in the context of the infinite. Rather than having to strive hard to accomplish a purpose and produce a grand result within a limited time, we're given a lifetime of opportunities to express purposeful qualities (the way we do whatever we do and the quality of the consciousness of our effort); acting in this way is sufficient purpose for each day. In fact, purposefulness involves experiencing a rich abundance of purposes that give us a sense of meaning rather than a feeling of having accomplished a particular goal. We simply need to continue expressing and perfecting those qualities that as infinite self we created finite self to embody. While the process may involve certain accomplishments that are important in the world and worth completing in a timely and occasionally urgent way, to infinite self these are usually of secondary importance to how they we go about doing them, which, moreover, often has a more lasting and important impact than the product itself.

Partnership with Infinite Self

The spiritual goal of wholeness is achieved when finite self learns that it's truly free and creative and begins to work in partnership with infinite self, with each providing what its nature must provide for the partnership to be fruitful "in earth as it is in heaven." If we're submissive to the higher, we fail in our choice-making responsibilities in this partnership; what it needs is our cooperation and self-knowledge. Moreover, in sublime irony, when finite self finally comes to fully know its actual truth and how to work with the divine, it discovers that its actual will and the divine will have been the same all along; the seeming differences and the agonizing they caused were only the effect of illusion and conditioning. It also discovers that its deepest, truest desires are exactly those that lead it, like signposts, to the divine within. Having been created by infinite self, it only makes sense that finite self's actual desire nature would be congruent with infinite self's desire nature. Desire serves as a sort of DNA in our consciousness, but unlike physical DNA, actual desire never mutates. If we purify (decondition, dis-illusion) ourselves through self-examination, meditation, or life-energy work, we find that desire's actual design is as complete and true as ever. Thus, it's essential to explore and express desire even in its distorted form, for we learn to discern what are distortions by observing the results of acting on our desires. Expressing our finite, misguided will and making fallible choices serve the same purpose. We don't achieve the freedom to be whole by abandoning will or desire in the face of divine will.

Two venerable spiritual disciplines designed to bring a seeker into accord with the divine are the practices of full surrender and total engagement. Each, through dedication to its approach, seals out random (according to some religious beliefs, evil) influences. An example of the first approach is taking vows of obedience to a religious order; an example of the other is a life dedicated completely to service or simply to doing whatever is one's calling with the greatest attention to excellence. At this point in our spiritual development, more and more people find themselves moved to bring aspects of both into their lives in simultaneous practice. This means that when we choose a course of action, we follow through with complete commitment; then (surrendering our effort, not our will), we release what we've done into the flux of the world, to the will of the divine, to shape and expand on. We wait to see what results from it—what infinite self returns to us. If we try to control the outcome, we limit its effect; the result is the infinite's way of communicating back to us, so we must be profoundly open to it. Then it's our responsibility to respond to this and let higher self respond in turn. In this back-and-forth manner, we continue playing out our purpose, choosing, willing, and creating, and releasing with total devotion to the task. This approach allows the spiritual aspirant to be fully engaged *in* the world while not becoming *of* it, fully attentive to the divine without losing self and individuality.

When one desires and chooses to relate to infinite self, one's will serves to align finite self with a power that can move mountains. While we must take full responsibility for our choices, and while these may sometimes require painful soul-searching, such choosing opens the door to the support of the infinite. It is God's desire and the desire of each person's infinite self that she be as fully abundant and fulfilled as her finite nature will allow, so alignment is all that's necessary. This is the purpose of inner work and the fundamental purposefulness of each life: that we remove all barriers and distortions to the original and still-potential natural alignment that allows for supporting force to flow from the source of power, the higher self. Thus, our actual "will power" is *willingness to be empowered.*

One of the great spiritual truths for the coming age is that we can have our cake and eat it too. This found previously expression, more elegantly but seldom understood, in the instruction that we seek the kingdom within and all else will be added. When our desire arises from our unifying spiritual center, we naturally seek the kingdom (the cake, which is union with the divine within) first; when we are centered, it's unlikely that the "all else," added so we may "eat it too," will distract us from our purpose.

Next, we'll examine a means to achieve centering and empowerment.

10

Transformation through Living in Two Modalities Simultaneously

> I am learning to see. I don't know why it is, but everything penetrates more deeply into me and does not stop at the place where until now it always used to finish. I have an inner self of which I was ignorant. Everything goes thither now.
>
> —Rilke, *The Notebooks of Malte Laurids Brigge*

Those who wish to grow spiritually or assist the evolution of human consciousness have as their task at this time to "bring Light into the marketplace." This means integrating the spiritual and the worldly in a most profound way. The "marketplace" refers not only to commercial activity or one's job environment; it means mundane life on earth in all its varieties. This project involves living in a new consciousness in the totality of one's life. We have examined elements of this consciousness: the linear, practical, discriminating, rational functions on the one hand, and the meditative, aesthetic, inclusive, and expansive functions, on the other. The challenge is to put them together, to live in a meditative awareness that includes one's whole self, the love of God, and the vast context in which one's life is occurring, while not losing one's edge of practical focus or the ability to function in business, scientific research, athletics, etc. The goal is to synthesize all aspects of oneself.

This is an end in itself, a satisfying and encompassing mode of personal living. It is also a method to achieve the goals of personal spiritual transformation and of healing the rifts that beset our culture—rifts such as those that divide us from the natural world, religion from daily living, and politics from meaningful dialogue and problem solving.

It will be helpful to explore an example of such a method of synthesis. The purpose of the following illustration is to try to describe the essential elements of the transformational process so the reader may use this description to determine the soundness of whatever system, approach, or discipline she may consider. In discussing this particular form of inner work, I'm not advocating that the reader take it up. While it's a valid and profound transformational process and the one I'm most familiar with and thus best able to use as an example, there are many others—happily so, because different personality types and orientations need different approaches.

Russell Schofield developed a form of transformational life-energy work designed for modern minds and life-styles. This teaches a person to go within to experience the life-energy (spiritual energy, also called light-fire or inner light) and enlightened awareness of his own higher self. It asks the person to pay attention to the mind's contents, the issues he faces, and every charged emotion, thought, and sensation. He works on himself by bringing all these together in a minute-to-minute interaction of the spiritual and the mundane. Spiritual awareness and energy exist within the self and are constantly available, but many people hold these separate from the routine aspects of life and the business of making a living, if these enter into awareness at all. They usually avoid or repress the more challenging manifestations of spirit.

Whenever a person brings spirit, in its functional capacities of love, life-energy, and enlightened awareness, into relationship with any aspect of her body, mind, emotions, or mundane life, transformations occur. It's difficult, however, to simultaneously hold both spiritual and mundane elements of life in mind; in fact, our rational minds are trained to avoid contamination by these non-rational, fuzzy elements, and many people feel that they shouldn't clutter their spiritual sensibilities with the chaff of daily living, much less pollute them with dark moods and thoughts.

Schofield laid out a system of inner focus that addresses this quandary by altering how the mind relates to experiences. In this method, one thinks of specific sources of spiritual energy in order to call them into play. One focuses this life-energy on a problem or a discomfort and then simply *lets go of the thought of doing that,* while staying fully present in order to observe and experience what transpires as the two elements interact. Further directive thoughts may be necessary as the stages of the work progress, in order to shift focus, redirect the energy, and release negative conditioning. It's the energy, however, not the thought or the finite mind, that does the work of clearing and transformation; thus, each time the thought has done its part (focusing), one again lets go of it and continues to stay with the experience. Focused observation grounds the power of the life-energy. One must always be ready to move from one modality (thinking or experiencing) to the other, and not go too far into either.

Spiritual energy is always within us, even though we don't experience it (sometimes even when we begin to use it). This lack of experience of it and the fact that we may have little idea of what to do with it isn't a problem. The energy derives from infinite self, which knows how to use it and what it needs to do. The energy comes into play simply by our intent to invoke the energy. Infinite self then responds, using the energy to accomplish the work needed and gradually remove what kept the experience of the energy outside of awareness. (See chapter 20 for specific exercises and experiences you can explore.)

With practice, the two modalities of awareness become simultaneous experiences, so that the inner light or life-energy operates in the "marketplace" of the active mind. Life-energy by its nature functions in accordance with what Schofield called the "actual design" of the person who's working with the energy. Actual design is the innate healthy, purposeful, fulfilling nature of the person as created by the higher self. The practitioner doesn't need to figure out what the result of the life-energy work should be; it unfolds, leaving the mind free to observe the inner changes or to deal with life. Maintaining the activity of the life-energy in the marketplaces of the mind and the daily round of business produces gradual illumination and purification, so the person's actual design and potential more fully express in every aspect of life.

As one uses inner light, there's a growing awareness that one is the source of the energy and of the wisdom regarding how to use it, as well as the recipient of it. This inner light illuminates the fact that one is an infinite being that is constantly present in the finite body, mind, and emotions. One's sense of identity begins to expand to include much more than the previous identification with the body, mind, or feelings. Familiar but false or inadequate labels and definitions of self, around which one usually orients one's life, gradually lose their influence when experienced in the context of infinite self and can be dissolved by the life-energy.

Continued use of this also dissolves the conditioned, habitual patterns of behavior, thinking, and feeling that are the residue of experiences, recent or long past, particularly those that have been traumatic. The process of growing up, being educated, and seeking to establish an identity in the world leaves one with false pictures of oneself and limiting perspectives and ideas about the world. As life-energy removes these, one may feel a refreshing sense of freedom, meaningfulness, and ability to recreate how one lives one's life. In addition, there sometimes arises an experience of inner vastness, of immeasurable potential, and of having infinite value. Still, one continues to live in and attend to the mundane world, one inhabits a limited body, and one's sense of value doesn't make one superior to anything else: everyone and everything is also of infinite value.

The experience of being both finite and infinite enables a person to feel at home in humanity's expanding awareness of the universe because it allows for a sense of a correspondingly vast microcosm within. An individual's inner world is as complex and interesting as the outer universe. Awareness of oneself as a microcosm in a macrocosm engenders an enhanced and transforming sense of the relationship that one has to one's entire environment and of how each action affects a much larger context than one's personal sphere, just as one's gravitational field literally moves all things in the cosmos, albeit minutely. The awareness that one's undertakings have surprising impact leads to heightened moral and ethical attentiveness, considerations that don't have a dogmatic basis but instead rest on an experiential foundation and are therefore more compelling.

Living in the two modalities simultaneously nurtures a persistent sense of the transcendent value and potential inherent within each act and every moment. This is a most significant and fulfilling development in a person's consciousness, yet any attempt to describe the experience inevitably creates a false picture of what takes place because it's usually not a distinct experience that begins at a particular time. Like other spiritual experiences, it may be hard to say when one first had it; the transformation often seems to have occurred outside of time. It's rarely an exalted event. It sneaks up on one, and yet one's sense of oneself has changed; one simply becomes aware that something has effortlessly and subtly occurred. There is more to one, and greater self-assurance. This addition exists at right angles to one's flow of awareness: a constant potential for unbounded amplification of meaning and experience. Daily life doesn't allow time for much musing on infinite significance; one needs to stay grounded and attend to business. Instead, the abiding experience is there beside one, within one, and backing one up, providing a sense of fullness and richness regardless of the particular circumstances of the day. It supplies a context within which to evaluate things; it helps one not to become too caught up in the frustrations of the finite. It advises that this too shall pass and points out what will persist, reminding that both the transitory and eternal are to be cherished.

Sensing One's Interface with the Infinite

The use of life-energy and the practice of focusing awareness bring finite self into closer relationship with infinite self. Finite self must experience the infinite in some kind of finite form, however rarefied, on order to register it. We may encounter this in dreams, in the form of transcendent or religious experiences, in the recognition of a profound truth, or in the envisioning of our true purpose or life path. Of course, no form can encompass the infinite or fully express it. Infinite self gives us what we need of itself at every moment. This might be a revelation of the cosmic infinite, as expressed, for example, in the Buddhist Avatamsaka Sutra. As described by Thich Nhat Hanh, in the *Avatamsaka* realm, which is the infinite, each lotus flower comprises

> more than one thousand petals, and . . . [each petal] is another lotus flower with one thousand petals. And each of those petals is also a lotus of one thousand petals, and those lotuses are not smaller than the first lotus flower. It continues on like that forever. . . . The ideas of bigger and smaller are just not present, nor are the ideas of one and many. . . . We see the many in the one and the one in the many. . . .
>
> Indra's jeweled net. . . illustrate[s] the infinite variety of interactions and intersections of all things. The net is woven of an infinite variety of brilliant gems. . . . Each gem reflects itself in every other. . . . Each gem contains all other gems. . . .[1]

Or, it may be a direct experience of our essence, as J. A. Symonds relates: "Irresistibly . . . [the mood] took possession of my mind and will, lasted what seemed an eternity. . . . It consisted in a gradual but swiftly progressive obliteration of space, time, sensation, and the multitudinous factors of experience which seem to qualify what we are pleased to call our Self. . . . At last nothing remained but a pure, absolute, abstract Self. The universe became without form and void of content. But Self persisted, formidable in its vivid keenness."[2]

This kind of experience, while not uncommon, isn't an everyday affair. Its most intense form can allow a finite self to starkly and totally feel infinite self and "download" knowledge at such a rate that a brief vision or other kind of experience informs and gives meaning, direction, and utter conviction to a person's whole life. Practiced attention, however, increases registry of more frequent, highly practical perceptions of infinite self interacting with finite self. Simply meditating on the presence of the infinite being within may yield sensations such as tingling of the skin, expansion, inner vibration, warmth, or a loving embrace. (By "meditating" on infinite self, I mean thinking of it, then releasing the thought, feeling what occurs, and accepting this without trying to imagine or create an experience.) Other experiences include lightness or being lifted, an impression or conviction of being exactly where one should be, awareness of being centered rather than imbalanced or pulled hither and thither, or a sense of repose and relaxation. Emotionally, one may feel joy, peace, unconditional love, forgiveness, or great good humor regarding the absurdity of our paradoxical existence. One may register validation of self while at the same time feeling strongly moved to reach one's potentials. Any number of other sensations, emotions, or insights can occur. Uncomfortable sensations may come up due to feelings such as fear of something so incomprehensible and vast or from a mindset that denies the possibility of an infinite self. Negative emotions or beliefs may block the experience of the higher self. These might need clearing away before experience of infinite self is accessible; meditation or other inner work can help to accomplish this.

Our interactions with infinite self also commonly take the form of symbols. These arise in dreams or in waking visions, daydreams, intuitive flashes, the process of artistic creation, etc. Symbols mediate between the inexpressible infinite and our own modalities of experience. They can be extraordinarily useful as long as they remain adaptable and transparent, that is, as long as we can reach through them, so to speak, to feel the living, indefinable infinite. Jung emphasized the importance of symbols for providing "meaningful shape to life" and dealing with moral ambiguities by marrying polar opposites.[3]

A symbol must remain alive and fluidly adaptable if it is to convey the boundless nature of the higher self. The infinite has long been seen as creative and dynamic.[4] Eastern mysticism, whether speaking of it as the "Emptiness" or "Void," whether conceived of as *Tao, Brahman,* or *Dharmakaya* (ultimate existence in Taoism, Hinduism, and Buddhism, respectively), holds it to be infinitely alive, inventive, and generative. It comes into existence in countless shapes that then dissolve. We find consistent attestation of the relationship of *Brahman* with movement despite the fact that it is beyond form. Plotinus taught that each order of the divine naturally would emanate the next order. In modern physics, the quantum field creates and reabsorbs its endless array of virtual particles.

While the infinite is dynamic in giving us the created forms we need in order to relate to it, the experience is interactive. Just as physics demonstrates that the observer always affects the observed and that our theoretical approach determines what occurs in experiments,[5] so we help shape what we experience of the infinite. We need to be deeply receptive to the dynamic, expressive nature of the infinite so that we are fertile ground for what it sows, but also we must be dynamic in response. If our response is true to what the infinite has sown in us, we'll find that the infinite is also most fertile, for what we release to it (if we do relinquish control) returns greatly increased. To maintain a relationship with the infinite requires creativity and a willingness to experience the ongoing tension of feeling, at the same time, both humble and filled with strength and authority.

Symbols in Need of Renewal

Representations of the infinite have a shelf life. Any such articulation in finite form, however true, is useful only for a generation, an era, or at best an eon. (I use eon in the Jungian sense of a period of about two thousand years; each eon has a specific psychospiritual organizing principal or archetype, experienced symbolically.) This also applies individually: we need to let go of our old ideas and experiences of the infinite or at least reexamine and deepen them periodically rather than trying to have repetitions of a previous experience, illuminating or uplifting as it may have been. In time, older symbols, individual or cultural, tend to become crystallized and opaque, no longer leading beyond themselves. They cloud the interface with the infinite, providing experiences only of themselves; we must discard or transform them. All formulations of religion and spirituality need periodic renewal. This doesn't necessarily mean abandoning the religion, only that old forms need release or development. For example, in the Middle Ages and later, profound mystical experiences, such as those of Meister Eckhart and Jacob Boehme, offered revivification for Christianity (though they were mostly ignored), as did Francis of Assisi's love for God's creation. Kabbalah provides a similar example in Judaism, as does Sufi mysticism in Islam.

As individuals, we have our own symbols of ourselves. These are mostly implicit in how we think of ourselves and are therefore unexamined. Some may be limited and limiting; based on our parents', friends', and teachers' hopes, fears, or needs, they often distort who we really are. Others may be actual expressions of our infinite self: penetrating self-perceptions that enable us to live deeply felt and richly textured lives with the flexibility that a living symbol allows. Our individual symbols and expressions of infinite truth, like those of religions, need renewal so they provide avenues for regeneration and growth. If we hold on to limiting symbols because they're familiar or safe, we will eventually feel out of sorts with ourselves, which may progress to feeling stifled or depressed or to a mid-life crisis.

Many individuals or groups, ranging from fundamentalists to New Age seekers, feel they have *the* truth in their dogma and symbols or in their rejection of doctrine in favor of open-mindedness to all spiritual expression. While most expressions do contain truths that are worthy of attention, no symbol, doctrine, or attitude can encompass the infinite or appositely formulate it for all people, and none can be an adequate window on the infinite for very long.

Our experience of these religious truths, whether sensory, emotional, or intuitive, can make it possible for us to determine their veracity and usefulness. We can similarly check out inner experiences, for instance dreams or inspirations, by which we suspect the infinite is communicating with us. Actual communications, direct or symbolic, often feel radiant and alive and continue to unfold over time. As we penetrate them, they yield deepening, unexpected experiences; we may sense expansion, opening, connectedness, and inexhaustibility. Such symbols enhance each person's sense of self as an aware and growing being with potentials to discover and explore. Symbols that are past their expiration date leave an aftertaste of staleness, limitation, repetition, dampened enthusiasm, or closing off, though they also provide the comforts of familiarity and certitude.

Useful, living symbols, being impermanent, will not cause one to come to conclusions about anything—oneself, truth, or life. A conclusion is an ending, the shutting down of a sometimes unsettling process of questioning and questing. Living experiences such as symbols always leave one with the sense that there's more and that one had best not get too settled or comfortable with oneself or one's beliefs. Living symbols and visions empower an individual or group. With empowerment comes responsibility, for both individual and group, to recognize the limits of received vision, both in time and scope. When we sense the eternal verity of the divine truths illuminated by the symbol, we must not make the error of supposing that a symbol pointing to divinity partakes of divinity or eternality itself.

The Star of David symbol is a living and expansive form that symbolizes these essential qualities of symbols. We discussed one interpretation of it previously: the lower triangle as the earthly nature rising to know the divine, the upper as the divine penetrating into the earth to uplift it. A further meaning is that the descending triangle requires interaction with the lower, earthly nature or it will remain unformed, ungrounded, and immaterial; through the lower, it achieves substance. The lower triangle, earthly matter, requires interpenetration with the upper if it's to achieve meaning and purpose; without the expansive inflow of the upper (which enters our experience as the energetic qualities and consciousness of love, good will, etc.) it would congeal and become moribund. The six-pointed star represents two continuing movements, a ceaseless mutual penetration that transforms and evolves both.

We need continually to test symbolic forms to make sure they demonstrate the qualities of living symbols. Otherwise, we may live according to a symbol that was once a portal to infinite meaning but has gradually become dull and impervious, leaving only an image of the past. Worse, the psychic energies of fear, hatred, and outrage may co-opt symbols so that they become regressive, pulling us backward to what we've outgrown spiritually, culturally, or personally, as the Nazis did with the ancient swastika sun symbol. These symbols may be attractive on the surface, evoke strong emotional responses, and often make excellent sense (from the standpoint of the old order of understanding) but also can lead to catastrophes such as the world wars of the twentieth century. They are identifiable by the way they feel: isolating, limiting of personal choice (offered in return for security and freedom from personal accountability), or excluding rather than inclusive. They are milky rather than clear, easily definable (black and white), forced, lacking deep resonance, smug and inauthentic, divisive of self or group, or energizing in a hyper sort of way rather than providing calm and lasting energy. People become numb to this sort of symbology, but as one begins to work spiritually, a vibratory difference in the energy of the symbols becomes apparent, and bodily reactions give overt clues.

Always Perceiving the Infinite

The idea that infinite self is within and throughout us raises several questions. If the divine is immanent, as theists, pantheists, and panentheists assert (see appendix 1), why do God and the infinite seem so difficult to perceive? In one sense, the answer is obvious: perception is the act of finite creatures, and the finite cannot apprehend the infinite. Why don't we experience it at least partially? We do, in all our experience; in the view of pantheists and panentheists, we perceive God whenever we experience anything at all, because all is of God. Why don't we recognize that we're experiencing the divine? We in fact can, with training or though grace, but mostly we don't because we're educated to discriminate—to distinguish this from that—rather than see the living whole. A further reason is that, trained as we are to think so analytically, worry so much, and consider the body unspiritual, we pay only perfunctory attention to our intuition and sense experience.

William Blake, in *The Marriage of Heaven and Hell*, urged consideration of the following:

> 1 Man has no Body distinct from his Soul for that calld Body is a portion of Soul discernd by the five Senses, the chief inlets of soul in this age
>
> 2 Energy is the only life and is from the Body and Reason is the bound or outward circumference of Energy.
>
> 3 Energy is Eternal Delight[6] [*sic*]

Energy comes from the body that itself is a part of the soul accessible to the senses. We must return to our senses if we wish to enjoy eternal delight as well as to perceive our soul (not to mention the divine).

My favorite answer to the question of why we can't see God comes from a biography of a child of six or seven. Learning that we perceive an object's color because it reflects that color while absorbing all others, she realized that God, loving everything, reflects (rejects) nothing, and thus is invisible.[7]

11

Sacrifice and Abundance

> "Abundance is scooped from abundance, yet abundance remains." So runs a fine old saying of the Upanishads. . . . Since the supernatural potential [of eternal being] cannot be diminished, no matter how great the donation it pours forth, abundance remains.
>
> —Heinrich Zimmer, *The King and the Corpse*

The conception and practice of sacrifice developed in tandem with the dominant moral ethic of each period of history. The word "sacrifice" comes from words meaning to make sacred. In prehistory and early history, to sacrifice usually meant to give up or kill something of value: an animal, the first of the harvest, valuable objects, or a member of the tribe or another group. It often meant a loss (still the most common meaning). Divinity was seen as separate from the one who sacrificed; the purpose of the sacrifice was to make the individual or group who offered it sacred, pure, or consecrated to the divine recipient, giving items of worth so as to stay in proper relationship to the divine order and keep things running smoothly and advantageously. The sacrifice was a gift that served to propitiate or meet the needs of the forces or deities that could assure a safe and prosperous life.

In the most recent eon, what was sacrificed was oneself or a part of oneself: one's life if a martyr or holy warrior, one's sexuality if a priest or nun, one's joy in physical life on earth if devout, or certain foods and behaviors at specific times if pious. The Crucifixion exemplifies this for Christians. The purpose of such acts was to bring about personal union with God by getting rid of one's ungodly nature or showing commitment to the divine by demonstrating lack of attachment to lesser things. (In Jesus' case, this involved facilitating others' union with God by helping to get rid of their ungodly natures, namely their sins.) Based on Jesus' example, much self-sacrifice occurred and still occurs, often in the context of service to humanity or to one's family (typified by the all-giving parent or spouse). These contexts often produce guilt-laden or anger-ridden recipients of the sacrifice. This anger arises because the sacrifice is nominally for the recipient, but the benefactor's prime if often unconscious motivation is his own spiritual or moral elevation and the alleviation of his own guilt which the recipient then takes on.

As we move into our next spiritual stage, which involves a more cosmic sense of self, we can clearly recognize that it's inappropriate to try to sacrifice oneself—after all, such a thing is hard to do in any real way if one is infinite and eternal—and it's not an expression of good will. (The idea, occurring in both East and West, that the divine sacrificed itself by entering into physical manifestation, arises from a jaundiced view of life held by people, not by the divine or by infinite selves.) In this next stage, we can understand sacrifice in the context of the cosmic learning game that we play as fully creative finite beings aware of our infinite nature. The cosmic learning game is a way of describing the fundamental nature of the cosmos wherein infinite selves create microcosmic finite selves to live within it; each has free will, gets deeply and forgetfully involved in form and matter, and then evolves back to aware union with its divine creator as a fully realized creator in its own right. The concept of sacrifice is evolving to mean freely letting go of the nonessential and the distracting. It is thus neither self-sacrifice nor a sacrifice of anything of actual value, though this kind of sacrifice is far from easy or painless. It involves surrendering what gets in the way of being one's actual self, that is, what is not oneself but what one has clung to out of fear, ignorance, or identification. This sort of sacrifice requires the discovery that what one is giving up never really was meaningful or satisfying.

Sacrifice in this sense is the release of limits. We give up something we've outgrown in order to receive something greater—a more complete awareness of self, a more generous sense of what it's okay to possess materially, a more universal truth. We give up the world we've grown comfortable with so we can live in full view of the cosmos. The purpose of this kind of sacrifice is the evolution of self-awareness; we sacrifice what pulls us away from ourselves, what keeps us off center, what causes us to forget who we are. We seek the kingdom within and discover that all else is added because, having released and sacrificed what limits and is untrue for us and having centered ourselves in our infinite nature, there's no reason not to have all that's joyful and beneficial to us. It can no longer pull us off our spiritual center because we remember who we are. Sacrifice frees our spiritual memory. The origin of the word "memory" has a connection to offering thanks, gratefully giving back to life or to the gods or spirits.[1] Thus, to offer sacrifice is to remember; what the sacrificer offers up and releases reconnects him with the source of abundance, blessing, and grace. Remembering through sacrifice is to become a member again of the blessed, abundant circle.

Sacrifice is, paradoxically, the quickest way to have it all. We lose nothing of real value to us and gain everything worth having. Ultimately, we give up our exclusive identification with our finite self and gain awareness of and identity with the fact that we're also infinite. Previously we sacrificed the finite to the infinite. Now we need to sacrifice what devalues the finite relative to the infinite and what keeps them apart.

This new meaning of sacrifice was the potential of sacrifices carried out in all previous ages; it was the essence of all sincere attempts at sacrifice. Many martyrs gave up their lives from a place of elevated consciousness, recognizing that their bodies weren't their enduring selves; many of those who sacrificed wealth, sustenance, or comfort awakened to the fact that they could do so and not give up their essential identity. These were steps toward learning who we are as human beings and what is truly necessary to sacrifice as well as what's not. We're at the point where such sacrifice for its own sake is no longer to the point and arises from perspectives that we've outgrown.

Bread on the Waters

A yet deeper meaning of sacrifice emerges in the metaphor of casting bread upon the waters. Here, sacrifice appears in its fullest, most nonlinear, non-finite context. It requires a vision of oneself as a creator in the cosmos. Its meaning is to send forth in good will something needed by others. It requires completely releasing it without expectation of its return; paradoxically, one may do this with the full knowledge that such an act has a multiplying effect so that when one is in need it will return, increased. It's not a sacrifice but an investment in the divine order, a participation in universal interconnectedness; this investment pays dividends. To cast bread on the waters is to release—to sacrifice—the limitations of the cause-and-effect relationships of the finite world and move into a higher order of relationship such as physics describes: Bohm's "'sea' of energy," an "undetermined and unknown flux, that is also the ground of all definable forms of matter" and intelligence.[2] This is not the same as sacrificing an ox to propitiate the gods; there's no anticipation of a direct causal connection to any effect. Only one who lives in awareness of the divine infinite can practice this kind of sacrifice.

In its fullest meaning, sacrifice ultimately involves giving up nothing, for as infinite beings we can't lose anything. It means that as finite selves we release control, allowing our action of casting bread, of sacrificing, to expand beyond the range we could control, anyway. The fact that we work from a centering awareness of the infinite self within amplifies our action. The deed, a seeding, expands beyond linear cause and effect to the infinite flux wherein infinite self can multiply the effect ten-fold, one hundred-fold, or any-fold. By letting go of control, we also let go the conceptual and emotional limitations that conditioning has placed on our capacity to receive, so that we're more open to what the infinite returns to us. Casting bread on the waters places us in the most open relationship we can possibly have to infinite self. This kind of sacrificing, based on knowing who we are, enables us to explore how we can act with the greatest positive effect, which is in partnership with infinite self.

As finite creatures we can only embody a limited aspect of infinity. We can long for what we lack, or we can plunge into the experience of what we currently have, knowing that in the fullness of time we'll enter into the experience we currently don't have. To sacrifice is to release trying to have that now, to accept the finite self's limits and, in letting go, to effectively allow the cosmos to ripen and bring to fullness what will also eventually come one's way. When we try to grasp what isn't timely for us, we stunt its development. If we center ourselves in our divine self, in that which is all and has all (yet, paradoxically, according to many traditions is no-thing and has nothing), we can experience that the finite aspects of self and of our lives are facets of a whole that reveal our infinite nature over time. The whole exists complete in four-dimensional space-time but unfolds sequentially in our experience of linear time. Each facet has its place in time, and all occur in good time.

Sacrificial Fires

In summary, in earlier ages when people had far less material abundance, they sacrificed the best possessions they had in order to bring about the highest level of purification or the most beneficial response. As the sense of the value of the individual increased, self-sacrifice carried the greatest weight. Now, our growing understanding of our infinite nature and creative potential means that the most efficacious sacrifice is the relinquishment of the not-self, of whatever gets in the way of full self-awareness and spiritual purpose. In previous eras, human beings sacrificed on the fires of external gods, goddesses, or forces; later, they sacrificed to God (still external to themselves). Now, we sacrifice to infinite self, which is part of oneself. Previously, people sacrificed aspects of divine creation (such as cattle or humans—even joy, which some sacrificed, is a gift of the divine); the not-self we will sacrifice in the future is what we have created as finite selves: self-images, agendas, beliefs, and so on. These current shifts both arise from and help us enter into a dawning sense that abundance is our heritage and destiny.

Disciplines from around the world use inner divine fire: agni yoga, the transmuting fires of alchemy, Taoism's Circulation of the Light, the *Dumo* or inner heat of Tibetan Buddhism, and various forms of lightwork. In these, the practitioner gives the worst of himself—the false and the negative—to the divine self to place in fires of transformation. The fires do not destroy what he gives; they purify and return it to him in a form that heals him and leads to increased self-awareness. When we cast bread on the waters, giving our goods and good deeds in service and sharing, we can also cast that which is negative and self-negating into the fires. In both cases, we receive an abundant return of what we actually need.

Sacrifice of the nonessential is increasingly necessary for modern men and women. As finite selves in relationship to the divine, what we say no to is crucial. This defines an essential purpose and imperative for our finite existence: to know our true boundaries, our form, our face, to identify what's of highest importance, to know what we are and what we are not, and to choose to express exactly that. First, by sacrificing certain possessions, we said no to having everything we could have. Then we said no to the world and or particular ways of relating to it in acts of self-sacrifice. Now we're ready to say no to what isn't our truth. The ritual purification of the ancient sacrifice has come full circle to the need to be purely one's true self.

In contrast, what defines the relationship of infinite self to its creation is its absolute "Yes!" to all that is good and beautiful for its creation. We sacrifice in order to be available to that yes.

Here, as in other areas we've discussed, it's imperative not to project our finite nature and its imperative onto infinite self and see the divine as restrictive and nay-saying. Likewise, it's essential that we not act, as finite self, as if we were infinite by saying yes to everything at once.

Abundance

An increasing openness to infinite self's yes as well as current economic trends will likely produce tremendous changes in our definitions of abundance and plenty over the next decades and centuries. Throughout history, people have struggled to overcome scarcity; most historical events involve securing limited resources, just as oil currently drives world affairs and water will imminently. A perception of actual, impending, or potential scarcity continues to be the mindset of much of the world, with abundance seen as precarious and difficult to sustain.

The relationship of a significant part of humankind to goods and services is changing both materially and spiritually. It seems probable that this will progress in a positive direction, despite temporary downturns and barring global ecological catastrophe or war. The middle classes of China and India are growing dramatically; globalization, including rich countries' outsourcing of production to cheaper labor markets that then can emerge as industrial or service economies in their own right, will cycle through much of the developing world over the next century or two. These changes are a mixed blessing, involving social disruption and human suffering and could be accomplished in far less painful ways, but the outcome will most likely be a rise in living standards for many. While the poor may always be with us, their numbers in all probability will decline. Humanity may well remember the coming age as the beginning of an extended eon in which lack will no longer be a consideration. Even if this doesn't prove true generally, it's already true for the largest number of people in history. While nothing is certain, especially economic forecasts, it's worth examining problems that are already arising from increased abundance and exploring how awareness of infinite self can shed light on them and illuminate the deeper significance of the opportunities abundance offers.

Over time, humanity's frame of reference may shift to confidence in the availability of abundance, with scarcity seen as an aberration. Along with changes in economic reality, the deep psychological basis for this fundamental change in outlook will be the emerging awareness of the infinite. As long as we see ourselves only as finite beings, we'll inevitably perceive the reality we live in as having limited resources, interpreting our finite capacity to receive as limitation of supply. As we gain conscious experience of ourselves as infinite beings acting in an infinite universe, we'll take comfort in understanding that unlimited resources are available to us.

Members of the 1960s counter-culture, having grown up in the post-war boom in which affluence in America steadily increased and looked to do so forever, rebelled against the conformist culture of the 1950s. They began to make individualistic choices regardless of economic considerations and social mores (dismaying parents who, raised in the Depression, had a deeply anxious outlook based on scarcity). These mostly young people felt they could take for granted abundance founded in parental wealth, well-paying and easily obtainable jobs, inexpensive higher education, and a social safety net. It had taken only one generation for a figure-ground reversal to occur in the perception of the relationship of scarcity to abundance. One could drop out and sample experiences of scarcity because abundance was all around. The end of fixed exchange rates, the cost of the Vietnam War, and the oil crises of the 1970s changed America's economic situation, but the previous economic environment had imprinted itself individually and culturally. The very expectation of abundance has helped to sustain a level of relative abundance, observable in the stock market surge of the 1990s and continuing consumer confidence after the 2000 stock market crash and even the 9/11 attack and Iraq war.

Thus, many Americans are already well into the shift to a new sense of abundance, which raises novel problems, some because of holdovers from the old mindset and some inherent in the new abundance paradigm itself. Looked at from a perspective of scarcity, abundance represents an opportunity, indeed a compelling need, to get while the getting is good. The fear that the chance may evaporate and not return drives people to acquire and hoard material goods or have as much of a particular experience as can be crammed into available time. An increase in abundance can actually create difficulties as great or greater than scarcity, as a finite person who's still in scarcity mentality tries to stretch his capacity to contain what he doesn't realize is flowing from a potentially infinite supply. This problem manifests in America in the epidemic of overeating, as our genetic ability to store large numbers of calories when they're available and then endure what used to be inevitable scarcity encounters a constant supply presented in gargantuan portions. Another example is the predicament encountered by people, such as lottery winners, who become suddenly rich. Many people complain of just having too much stuff.

Even with awareness of the infinite availability of goods and experiences, a person may feel limited as to the time he has to enjoy this: limited by death. It seems a cruel irony to attain in abundance all one has dreamed of but not to be able to stick around to enjoy it. Putting aside the possibility of medically achieved physical immortality in full health, an important solution to this seeming sad twist of fate is to recognize that, being eternal, we're much more than this single life experience. In fact, we have ample time to savor the pleasures of living, so we can accept life's trials without feeling that they'll reduce our full measure of enjoyment. This applies to those who posit reincarnation as well as to those who practice living moments of limitless presence as described in chapter 14. The latter are able to vastly expand their capacity to enjoy the abundance of each moment (see exercises 1, 5, and 6 in chapter 20).

If we attain both the state of mind of abundance and recognition of the illusion of death, we'll engage the primary spiritual lesson in the new eon of abundance, which is honing the ability to choose, to exercise one's will. Recognizing prosperity and the fallacy of extinction allows one to be relaxed about things—the better, paradoxically, to seize the moment with focus and effectiveness.

Too Many Choices!

Abundance means abundant choices. Despite the value we place on freedom of choice, choosing is an uncomfortable proposition for many people because it exposes them to the risk of being wrong, failing, or losing. Some people live hemmed-in lives because they're unconsciously so frightened by choice that they avoid even the awareness of alternatives and will argue vehemently against the idea that they have more latitude than they think; yet, they lament their constrained situation.

We aren't well educated about actual choosing. We learn to choose the right answer, but abundance means that some choices may not have a wrong answer. There may not be a way to lose, but only an answer that's truer to one's actual self, purpose, potential, and need. We can look ahead to a time when being wrong, failing, or losing are far lesser concerns than they are today, when, instead, we will face an increased need to identify and choose which of very good options is best. This will require a depth of self-knowledge unheard of previously, except among a few. Anyone going though a single day's mail and email realizes the wealth of opportunities not only for consumption or gaining information but also for service by giving time or money; with this comes the quandary of the time it takes just to read them. Possibilities abound for play, exploration, and knowledge, the Web is an ocean of information, and all this is creating new kinds of stresses: abundance overload, a glut of options, and the angst of freedom of choice. We have vast opportunities for self-improvement physically, emotionally, mentally, and spiritually. For a growing number of people, material possessions are the least of what constitutes their abundance issues.

In an age of affluence, abundance of choice, and the stresses these engender, we face the danger of relying increasingly on mass media, especially advertising, to make our choices for us. The media keep our attention focused on trivial choices among consumer products. We need to lessen this influence, except where the media help us distinguish what's clearly and distinctively true for us. Being utterly unique, we can't emulate choices that work well for someone else or even for most. Movements for voluntary simplicity, "slow food," "Buy Nothing Days," and preservation rather than consumption of resources are examples of attempts to reduce choice stress and focus on choice-making that's free of the fear of scarcity and honed to one's actual needs.

In this environment, the search for an identity that serves as the basis for making choices becomes an urgent quest. Because identity is no longer a given, lifelong, unchanging aspect of the social station or class one is born into, the void is filled by products of mass culture. People need a focus of identity to center themselves and process the superfluity of possibilities. Multitudes of magazines, most of which used to be informational, now are essentially about identity, about being the kind of person who has a particular interest. Groups, lifestyles, pastimes such as video games, and mass-produced and -advertised products meet this need for identity but only superficially; buying into these defines a surface persona but does not result in growth of self-awareness.

We have a compelling need for self-knowledge and a comprehensive synthesis of the totality of self to provide the core sense of identity we require to make best use of our abundance. Lacking these, individuals find themselves wrenched by competing desirable opportunities for abundance, or else they become blasé or numb, not actually making choices and not really enjoying the opportunities. As abundance becomes a given, we'll need a spiritual center that incorporates, balances, and integrates all our potentials. We'll need to balance abundance's centrifugal force with the centripetal, attractive, organizing force of the identity of our spiritual core. (Exercises 1, 5, and 6 in chapter 20 are helpful in this regard, too.)

Since our abundance of options can't fit into our time-space lives, we must expand into the eternity of our infinite selves to integrate them. These possibilities are part of us and can't be lost. Our task of exercising choice is neither to struggle to attain all possibilities (based on fear of lack) nor to try to cram them into the time we have (based on fear of death and loss) nor to deny or avoid them (based on fear of making a wrong choice or having inadequate capacity). It's to choose the mix that exactly expresses who we are and what we need *now.* When we have what we don't need, it burdens us with its storage and care. Modern business inventory practices reflect an understanding that's part of all spiritual traditions: God will provide, with just-in-time delivery.

Choosing this mix is profoundly creative—playful and without perfectionism—and must derive from understanding our spiritual purpose. Our sense of abundance will rest not on how much we have but on selecting what's precisely right for us at the moment, no less and no more—abundance will mean precision, just as a relatively few carbon atoms in the form of a diamond are worth much more than a ton in the form of coal. The value lies in the atoms' exact crystalline arrangement, and their value paradoxically increases with the removal of some to form facets that reveal the diamond's beauty. We will want each aspect of life to be like a work of art, requiring no addition and sacrificing whatever isn't necessary.

This paring away will assume ever greater significance; as we attain more material wealth, increased abundance of opportunities, and an excess of choices, it becomes increasingly difficult to focus on what has real importance. We will need to become spiritual warriors in the face of distraction, ruthlessly wielding a fine edge of awareness and willing to peel off anything that doesn't serve our spiritual purpose and actual needs with supreme accuracy. Our demons will be less what is obviously evil and destructive than what is merely passable, comfortable, satisfactory, or even quite good. Our test will be to discern and serve our greatest truth and joy. We'll need continuously to sacrifice much that is of high quality in order to make room for what's absolutely the best we can achieve and have. Evil as we currently know it may prove to be the easier challenge!

Instead of seeking enjoyment in an overabundance of stuff, a crass parody of the infinite abundance of our actual self, we can experience abundant enjoyment even of something small, taking pleasure in its myriad qualities and meanings. We do this in the contemplation of music or the intricacies of nature or savoring fine cuisine. This requires only our attentiveness, one of the goals and rewards of inner development. Meanwhile, we can also enjoy the prospect of the great multitude of other possibilities latent within our infinite selves, potentials held in readiness for us. This approach to abundance will resolve the greatest threat to continued abundance, the overcomsumption that damages the environment.

Sacrificing the unnecessary is not at odds with seeking the kingdom within so that all else will be given, or with having one's cake and eating it too. While it's a comfort and joy to know how much is available to be given, waiting in potential, it's a relief to know that, even though our centeredness enables us to handle it, we don't have to. The infinite gives all, but the finite self gets to make the aesthetic and practical choices of receiving what will produce an artful life.

12

Grieving

Thou, over whom thy Immortality
Broods like the Day ...
    A Presence which is not to be put by.

—William Wordsworth, "Ode. Intimations of Immortality from Recollections of Early Childhood"

Grieving is a unique and essential process because it is the response of the finite, in the face of its infinite aspirations, to encountering its limits. Through this process we accept our finitude and therefore our loss; through it we're reconciled the fact that we can't have all that we love, want, or need here and now, largely because our finiteness can't contain it. Grieving allows us to feel and honor the fact that we loved what we lost or what we wanted but never had. Therefore, paradoxically, it provides an opening to the experience that we are infinite and always connected to what we love, and love inevitably attracts what we love but don't have—in good time.

We naturally grieve at the loss of a loved one, a pet, a stage of our own or another's life, a treasured possession, an opportunity, a job, our innocence, etc. Yet, for many people this is one of the most unexamined and inarticulate sets of emotions, something they hope will pass quickly and then not return. It's seldom or awkwardly spoken of by others to the one who grieves (due to guilt or avoidance or being ill-at-ease with the subject), and the griever may be embarrassed by her ungovernable feelings or distressed by her vulnerability.

This emotion is unlike other unpleasant feelings, for while it's painful and wrenching, it has a necessary and unalterable purpose and truth and a distinctive progression. (Most negative feelings also have an element of truth at their core, but this is expressed in destructive or self-defeating ways; in effect, we must rescue their truth for healthier expression, unlike grief, which while unpleasant is constructive.) Suppressing grieving can have unfortunate consequences, because grief serves the processes of healing and coming to terms with the inevitable.

(See Kübler-Ross, 38-137, for one view of the stages of grieving.)

Grieving becomes a negative, unhealthy event only when it's not allowed to proceed naturally. Grieving that is accepted and even embraced (but not held onto) is healthy grieving; such grieving is neither hurried nor hindered, forced nor controlled, but simply allowed to progress in a way that's specific to the individual. When healthy grieving has run its course, a person can freely move on to the next stage of her life. She may find that grieving deepens her love of, commitment to, and reverence for life, as well as her self-knowledge. It might seem paradoxical that a loss-induced, painful process can help open the heart and expand the capacity to love, but the ability to accept loss enables a person to be open to attaining and embracing her heart's desire. When one truly grieves, one is no longer afraid of loss, change, or being mortal and finite.

For many people, however, simply letting themselves grieve is extremely difficult, due to cultural conditioning and mixed emotional messages from family and friends. These can keep a person from allowing himself to feel the grief and other emotions that are part of the process and can keep him from letting go of grief when the time is right for him. The person's own tendencies to dramatize negativity or to suppress "bad" or painful feelings can also affect the process.

Suppression or distortion of the natural grieving response first occurs early in life. The infinite aspirations of the finite self are most obvious in infancy, when each newborn claims the world, first as an undifferentiated part of herself and then, as she distinguishes herself from others, as her limitless possession. The infant may become enraged when she encounters the limits and loss that are the proof that she is, in fact, finite. Learning those limits is the most crucial transition in human development.

Moving from an original, infinite sense of self to a finite sense of self is obviously essential, but we were trained to leave the experience of infinite self behind completely and made to feel that it was infantile, selfish, silly, and bad. In effect, we were informed that it was nothing to grieve over and told, "Just grow up!" Our earliest need to grieve was disallowed; the capacity to grieve never fully recovers in many people. The experience of the infinite was largely lost to us, repressed due to the pain of being removed from complete immersion in it—perhaps the most grievous parting of our lives—and due to the often wounding, shaming nature of this aspect of our upbringing. We can't remember it because we have no language, other than poetry and art, to express the experience. Having forgotten the infinite, neither children nor adults can grieve its absence.

A more spiritual kind of childrearing would enable future generations never to have to endure abandoning the Edenic awareness of the infinite in order to grow up. This would allow children to taste the apple of finite awareness, whereby they can know good and evil, without having to hide from the divine self or having to conceal the naked fact of their finite/infinite wholeness. (For a description of the experience of a child leaving this garden, see Kyber, 2-61.)

As adults, we must recognize that we had no choice but to leave; we had to wander in an existence that for many people never feels quite like home or seems fully real. (This sense of not belonging finds reflection in the many fairy tales about children, often royal, taken from their homes as infants and raised by strangers, as well as in the aforementioned common feeling that one doesn't fit with the rest of humanity or belong on this planet.) We desperately need to grieve this loss so that our hearts can open for a return to the experience of the infinite within. In doing so, we'll find that we haven't lost anything; we weren't cast out of our inner Eden. We only forgot. We can regain the experience of wholeness, of being finite within the infinite garden.

The Daily Art of Grieving

We need to learn to grieve, to recognize it as an art, and to practice it as part of our daily lives. When we break something, miss a chance to see someone dear to us, lose an opportunity—anything that carries for us an emotional sense of loss, however small—we can and need to grieve. The process can take as little as a few moments of acknowledging the event and our feelings about it, but it requires that we recognize that it truly was a loss. To do this is to acknowledge an empty place in our life and to feel a wound. In our modern busy-ness and ethos of pain avoidance, we habitually fill such emptiness with something else, usually doing this so quickly that we miss the chance to grieve. Unfortunately, this doesn't mean that the need to grieve has passed; we merely submerged it. We urgently need to break this habit.

To practice this may seem self-indulgent, as it certainly can be. We should treat grieving as a discipline, in the sense of giving it the attention it needs but no more than that. It may take practice to find the line between avoidance and indulgence.

Loss demolishes the fiction that we can control our circumstances and somehow avoid life's hurts. This fiction encloses us and separates us from life, love, and profound joy; thus, each loss opens a door in our walled-in existence, providing access to the vastness that is beyond our control, to the freedom of not-having, and to the unimagined possibilities that lie outside our finite boundaries. Every loss can open the heart in unexpected ways. If our grieving is healthy, it exposes us to new potentials and deeper self-knowledge. It creates unexpected connections. It helps us to recognize that we're rooted in earth and in the rhythmic ebb and flow of the physical cosmos, where loss and death are inevitable. Its still greater potential is to open us to our own infinite self and to keep our boundaries open to that limitless life that we can intuit but not possess. In accepting that loss and not-having are inherent in being finite, we find the way to enter the realm of totality, where there can be no loss, and live these two experiences simultaneously.

The paradoxical nature of human existence is clearly seen in this: the pain of grieving is the discomfort of awakening to greater life and greater completeness and of stretching our capacity to embrace more of these; acceptance of loss is the gateway to the infinite love that cannot be lost. As people, we grieve for loss; as infinite selves, we rejoice in what finite selves experience and learn and in the infinite possibilities that await us. Both feelings are real; both are vitally important. When we accept both simultaneously, we experience the liberation of being whole.

13

Play: Sensing Infinite Possibilities, Desiring to Be Limitless

> We should pass our lives in the playing of games . . . with the result of ability to gain heaven's grace.
>
> —Plato, *Laws*

Are we having fun yet? The question contains an internal contradiction. It puts the questioner within a time framework (at a point in time when there is expectation or hope of having fun, whereas previously fun wasn't happening), while on the contrary, the very nature of fun and the playfulness that creates it is that they're creative, spontaneous, unreflective, and essentially outside of the flow of time. When we genuinely play and have fun, we aren't aware of the passage of time. Play is free of the expectations that cause us to predetermine the kind of experiences we'll have. As long as we wonder about having fun, we can't have much. In true play, which adults rarely engage in, we're unbounded by the limits of time, space, and identity. Thus, a child can be an astronaut, then a mom or dad, a dinosaur or firefighter, all without the hindrance of self-consciousness.

Play needn't be humorous, but real humor is always playful. Something that's funny often juxtaposes things that don't belong together, and this opens a breach in the expected order of things, vindicating our innate sense that all things are possible. We're momentarily enchanted, giddy, out of our minds—"mindless" in the sense of the Buddhist "no-mind." This juxtaposing of antithetical things makes humor quintessentially paradoxical.

Play, itself paradoxical, constitutes an essential part of human behavior because it allows us, for a while, to transgress the limits of our world that restrict us to being finite. Play offers a glimpse of exciting, uncontrolled, and endless potentials, providing a porous interface that lets in regenerative energy from our infinite self. Having finite and infinite aspects that are not fully integrated creates tension and a painful sense of absurdity. Finite human existence seems absurd if a person intuits infinite self without understanding the actual relationship of the infinite to the finite. Tension dissolves in the paradox of play and humor; laughter releases the stress of nonintegration, and absurdity shifts from painful to hilarious. Humor lets the interface breathe.

In *Homo Ludens* ("Man the Player"), Johan Huizinga (1872-1945) defines play as activity that involves freedom, creates order, and isn't a part of ordinary life but is set apart in time and space. Distinct from normal life, play has direction and meaning unto itself. "Into an imperfect world . . . it brings a temporary, a limited perfection."[1] Huizinga asserts that play is a fundamental, irreducible aspect of our nature and as such lies at the bedrock of culture, ritual (and therefore religion), and creativity—even business enterprise, scientific and philosophical investigation, and the legal system.[2] He wonders whether reasoning itself involves play and its rules and finds medieval university scholarly life and modern learned disputation to be, fundamentally but not pejoratively, game playing.[3]

Both playground and sacred ground are places to experience and try out that which flows from the deepest, highest part of self, however attenuated and unrecognizable it is when expressed. "Just as there is no formal difference between play and ritual, so the 'consecrated spot' cannot be formally distinguished from the play-ground. . . . [Both are] hallowed, within which special rules obtain." He quotes the poet Paul Valery (1871-1945): "No skepticism is possible where the rules of a game are concerned, for the principle underlying them is an unshakable truth."[4] Huizinga sees an ancient and exalted purpose in play: "In the form and function of play, itself an independent entity which is senseless and irrational, man's consciousness that he is embedded in a sacred order of things finds its first, highest, and holiest expression."[5] Thus, finite self, all too often constrained and trapped by its own beliefs and certainties, reminds itself in play that it's embedded in a larger existence and within the rules of play can safely throw off its normal constraints for a while and taste unlimited freedom. A door opens to the boundless resources of the infinite, for while the time for play or ritual is limited, its effect is not; it has changed things. Play takes us both inward to our eternal spiritual center and outward spherically from it to experience the infinite field of alternative potentials that surrounds linear time.

Naturalists report play among species as diverse as wolves and ravens. This might seem to contradict the idea that play is a means for human beings to experience acting as individual infinite selves. No teaching to my knowledge maintains that animals have individual infinite selves. However, it has been suggested that animals have species infinite selves, an idea that has parallels in Native American religions, among others; these talk about the "spirit" of buffalo, of coyote, or any species. Whether individual or group, this spiritual self is the spirit of play, so to speak, and, in fact, we speak of a spirited game or of jests or antics arising from being in high spirits. For animal or human beings, when energy and time are available beyond that necessary for survival needs, play—activity that yields no benefit as regards life's immediate mundane requirements—will occur.

The Divine at Play

The impulse to create a playful order is divine, as indicated by the idea of the cosmic learning game, and human beings have always seen divinity as creating or maintaining order in the world while remaining somewhat aloof and free to override its rules. Plato (427-347 B.C.E.) has his version of this game: "man ... has been constructed as a toy for God, and this is, in fact, the finest thing about him. All of us, then, men and women alike, must fall in with our role and spend life in making our *play* as perfect as possible. ... What, then, is our right course? We should pass our lives in the playing of games ... with the result of ability to gain heaven's grace."[6] Thus play, far from frivolous, is a sacred and momentous endeavor.

Fun is always in some measure playful, although play is not necessarily fun. (Holy ritual is a form of play.[7]) Fun of any kind involves the unexpected. We can have fun exploring, trying new things, meeting new people, or just hanging out, open to whatever. It's fun if, by our choosing (for fun and play must involve our active volition or at minimum our tacit assent), we've cracked open the shell of our accustomed experience enough that something may enter that will change our lives, at least a little. Most important, something is fun if it opens us to the untamed, free realm of infinite self, so that we feel assured we can still contact it, which amounts to contact with life itself. (This realm can also scare us half to death, which can also be fun.)

In play, a person can create completely new life scenarios (children may do this several times an hour), analogously to infinite self creating the life of finite self. As the one who plays, she experiences herself as the unchanged creator; she can then leave behind the identity she assumed and move on, knowing who she continues to be, ready to create new identities for new games. Play confirms that she engages in, but is not wholly of, the finite world or trapped by time or the law of cause and effect.

Play and art are essentially alike. Huizinga sees play as strongly connected to aesthetic activity, which he suggests might be the same as the inclination to fashion structures embodying order, an urge that gives life to play in every form.[8] Like a child at play, an actor or fiction writer can breathe life into a character, inhabit it, allow it to freely develop, and feel it spontaneously mature outside his conscious intent, so much so that it may create the artist while he creates it.[9] This is exactly what we do as infinite selves—we enter into and give freedom to characters we create (our finite selves) with which we then have reciprocally influencing relationships. Finite self is infinite self's means to be at play in the cosmos. Play is the work of the divine in finite incarnation.

Huizinga states that play exists beyond the dualities "of wisdom and folly . . . of truth and falsehood, good and evil."[10] It gives us an experience of resolving such dualities. In play we not only reconcile to some degree our finiteness with our innate if unconscious sense of infinite possibilities and desire to be limitless; playfully we also move from duality to polarity and create a richer, healthier relationship between the polarities of finite existence.

Our culture has confused play with entertainment and distraction, which by design take the consumer away from himself and his stresses and concerns. Entertainment is in many ways the opposite of play; while stimulating, it removes the consumer from his center or at least gets him no closer. It serves to numb discomforts and distract from an unfulfilling, unhealthy life that's not focused on higher-order needs such as aesthetic or spiritual pursuits. Play helps a person identify his core needs. It awakens the participant; at its best, it challenges his perspectives, beliefs, and sense of identity. It takes energy and focus but is regenerative, refreshing, and restorative. When other people are involved, play is interactive; entertainment often isn't, such as that involving a performer and a passive audience. Of course, some entertainment contains elements of play, but true play is never merely entertaining. Real playfulness in adults is often dishonored and mistrusted as childish.

Play is serious business for children; it's a primary means for self-discovery, exploring the world, and developing skills. Adults have a grave need to relearn playfulness in its unconstrained creativity and serious lightheartedness and to distinguish play from frivolity, entertainment, or being silly. (We speak of the play of light on something but not of the silliness or frivolousness of light.) Our long work hours, the complexity of modern living, and the dulling effects of most entertainment alienate us from ourselves, draining energy needed for play. To rediscover what nourishes and balances us and to divine our spiritual nature, we must recognize the inanity and fruitlessness of what we give significant amounts of time and energy to and get down to the important job of playing. A child's wonder, founded in her experience of the infinite within, finds renewal in the adult as reverence for creation, centeredness in the deep self, freedom of expression, and a sense of ever-expanding possibilities. As finite selves, our play's the thing that creates a bridge back to our infinite selves.

14

The Meeting of Two Eternities: The Spiral of Time and Moments of Limitless Presence

All that is straight lies. . . . All truth is crooked; time itself is a circle.

—Friedrich Nietzsche, *Thus Spoke Zarathustra*

There is no linear evolution; there is only a circumambulation of the self. Uniform development exists, at most, only at the beginning; later, everything points toward the center.

—Jung, *Memories, Dreams, Reflections*

We wonder why there are so few happy endings in life, why we cannot make moments of hope, transcendence, or joy last, and why they so seldom lead to greater happiness. We are baffled because our paradigm of progress specifies that, with only minor regressions, our quality of life should be constantly improving; when it doesn't, the American ethos of individualism indicates we have failed and thus must be morally or spiritually lacking.

Novels and movies present us a linear time structure for life in which issues are stated, difficulties arise, decisions are made, actions are taken, and a climax occurs, the outcome hinging on good people (or at least people we identify with) being strong or wise enough to do the right thing or having luck smile on them. All this ends with a denouement: tension is released, the protagonists achieve insight and understanding, and each collects her just rewards. We aim to live a life similarly structured, where we receive compensation for our efforts and increase our fulfillment as we go forward. We form a habit of experiencing time accordingly.

We can observe this habitual scenario playing out within any length of time: the unfolding of a lifetime, an event, or even a few minutes or seconds. It affects how we experience all time frames. If I have a task of any length, I can watch myself go through it with this dramatic structure, dealing with problems and building to the climax of accomplishment, followed by the denouement of relaxation and afterglow ("Great, it's done!"). The degree of my emotional involvement in this structure has changed over time as I've grown in self-awareness; my need for accomplishment to give me a sense of self-worth has lessened. Yet, it continues as a configuration of awareness that's part of pacing myself and keeping track of where I am in my time flow. I notice this structure as it imposes itself on minutes-long events and over years; it applies to tasks within tasks as well.

What Times We've Had

This time framework is ancient. Most civilizations before about 300 B.C.E. perceived time as cyclical and essentially unchanging, with occasional disturbances.[1] The Near Eastern, Indo-Aryan, Northwest European, and Egyptian senses of time involved an unending conflict between forces of chaos and life-sustaining order; neither side ever won, though one or the other might at times predominate.[2] In Egypt, time was, according to Cohn, "not so much endless, unchanging duration as periodic regeneration and rejuvenation, repeated endlessly."[3] Philosopher and historian Jeremy Naydler writes, "Time was less measured than *marked* by significant events that were of cosmic stature."[4] A variation on this cyclical time was the Great Year: the cosmos ends in divine fire from which a new universe arises, recurring eternally.

Probably the first divergence from cyclical time was Zoroastrianism in Persia. Zoroaster (Zarathustra, traditionally c. 628-c. 556 B.C.E., possibly as early as 1500[5]) taught that twin spirits fight for supremacy within "limited time." When this battle ends, the cosmos will completely change in "the making wonderful," when the world is purged of evil and healed to begin a blissful eternity. Zoroaster was perhaps the first to emphasize the cosmos's purpose more than its origin and nature: time moves forward toward a moral reckoning, when the cause of evil is sealed off eternally.[6]

During the Babylonian exile, Jewish thinkers abandoned the ancient idea of unchanging conflict between order and disorder. They developed a historical view with Yahweh as the "lord of history," guiding the world toward an apotheosis.[7] To assist this and be on the right side of it, prophets emphasized rigorously observing the timing of holy days.[8] The Jews saw their God as lord of space and time; given the succession of invaders who ruled the land (space) and defiled it, attending to sacred time became vital.[9] To the Essenes (an esoteric Jewish sect) especially, calendrical precision was essential to coordinate heaven and earth. Influenced by Zoroastrianism, they viewed time as a closed-end historical framework with the future already determined. Humankind makes moral choices to seal evil out of historical time. God dispenses rewards at a last judgment, when the fate of all things will be judged according to their comportment with God's timing and order;[10] even stars receive punishment if they're out of synch.[11]

Time is linear and goal-oriented for Zoroastrians and Jews. This theme is essential for the Christian vision of history as leading to a final reckoning, as in Revelation.[12] The sealing of time from evil became the work of medieval monastic orders, accomplished through highly structured daily rounds of prayer, Mass, and work. The Protestant version is the work ethic, developed as much for religious as economic purposes: shutting out evil by dedication to good work and proving, through worldly success, worthiness of heavenly reward after evil's final defeat at time's end. The closed-end time of Zoroastrian, Jewish, and Christian belief requires accomplishing spiritual work, whether to overcome evil, stay aligned with the divine calendar, or save one's soul. This sort of limited time poses, literally, one hell of a deadline. The experience of time became one of effort and struggle; modern stress over lack of time has ancient roots. Plotinus even held that time is created by the soul's striving to establish individual identity.[13]

In contrast, Chinese alchemy, as early as 500 B.C.E., entailed a profoundly different way of working with time for spiritual growth. The alchemist's goal was, according to sinologist Joseph Needham, "to telescope time by reducing the grand overriding cycles of the universe to . . . allow of their contemplation by the adept—leading . . . to perfect freedom in perfect fusion with the cosmic order."[14] Understanding divine time allowed alchemists to unify with it in order to achieve immortality within its cycles. Needham's description suggests that Chinese alchemists had a more relaxed and effortless relationship to their non-linear time than those operating in closed-end, linear time.

Einstein demolished the scientific construct of a single linear time frame, no longer differentiating past from future. Time is individual, relative to whoever experiences it.[15] Based on current theories, time's movement is a misapprehension; the entirety of time is present at once in space-time.[16] Buddhist thought agrees. Lama Govinda (1898-1985) states: "If we speak of the space-experience in meditation, we are dealing with an entirely different dimension. . . . The temporal sequence is converted into a simultaneous co-existence."[17]

We've largely forgotten the original sacred context of our Western time structure with its hoped-for rewards. We now expect compensation within the time frame of this world, not beyond time in the next.

We laud the work ethic of an athlete, whose highest expected reward is a lucrative endorsement contract; we work harder and longer with less time for family or play, hoping to retire early. Many people wish a bit of enjoyable "evil" would break through the all-too-effective seal that their work ethic places on their appointment calendars. Those for whom the afterlife reward has less reality than for previous generations wonder what other kind of compensation can justify their daily exertion to improve their lives.

Moments of Immoderate Presence

We're unlikely to return to the ancient cyclical, static sense of time, attractive as it may seem from our current state. Awareness of our infinite existence outside time leads to another alternative to linear time as a framework for meaningful life. This involves giving more value to our most consequential or moving moments, not as steps we expect will lead to increasingly magnificent experiences or a life-vindicating final chapter but as centering points which inform and color the rest of life. Realizing that linear time cannot lead us to the infinite and eternal but that an experience of the boundless and timeless can erupt into the finite in any moment, we can develop a more spherical sense of time. We move at right angles to linear time flow, along the vertical axis of the illustration in chapter 3, into any point on the time line and out around it in an unlimited spherical expansion to include all time. We can let our lives take shape around these moments of heightened awareness that produce a sense of intense presence; they serve as points at the center of the sphere of time that are loci for the entry of our pure beingness into linear time. These can be moments of epiphany, in both senses of the word—moments of profound insight regarding one's life and of heightened awareness of the presence one's infinite, divine self.

Such a moment of immoderate presence allow a person to experience something beyond the moderate and mundane, something profoundly significant that serves to reveal his spiritual nature. He can immerse himself in this as a central point of his life and inhabit it fully, giving a non-linear form to his sense of time (see exercise 5 in chapter 20). If one inhabits a point in time in this way, the essence of the moment ripples out into past and future. It transforms the meaning of previous events and lets the quality of the moment suffuse all subsequent events, regardless of the shape they take. From this moment of centering, one can expand awareness to include past and future in relation to, or as part of, the present, rather than having past or future pull awareness away from the present so that one is "not all here."

Thoreau valued this sense of time: "In any weather, at any hour . . . I have been anxious to improve the nick of time, and notch it on my stick too; to stand on the meeting of two eternities, the past and future, which is precisely the present moment."[18] John of the Cross (1542-1591), speaking of the way God penetrates the soul in "touches," writes that merely "one of these intoxicating consolations may reward it for all the labors undergone in its life—even if they were numberless."[19] Jung relates that while recovering from an illness, he experienced "the ecstasy of a non-temporal state in which present, past, and future are one. Everything that happens in time had been brought together into a concrete whole. . . . One is interwoven into an indescribable whole and yet observes it with complete objectivity."[20] In Catholic theologian Karl Rahner's view, "Eternity is not an immeasurably long-lasting mode of pure time, but a mode of the spirit and freedom which are fulfilled in time, and hence can only be comprehended in the light of a correct understanding of spirit and freedom." These allow us to live not looking forward or backward but looking toward our center.[21] One moment is a unit in an eternal series of moments. Yet, paradoxically, as mystics have always reported, we can deeply penetrate one instant to experience and embrace the whole of eternity.

Moments of epiphany do not necessarily change the course of our lives; indeed, not expecting this is exactly the point. They can, however, flavor and perfume all the rest of our time. Time ceases to make us slaves to self-justification or achieving salvation. Instead, time becomes ample in its opportunities for us to enter into joy. We no longer have unproductive, wasted moments because production is no longer our reason for existence. Any available moment is an opportunity to move to our center, to interact with the infinite and eternal.

The Center of Time

In current traditional cultures and, we may suppose, in prehistoric ones, experiences of time included and include something akin to moments of radical presence. The ancient Egyptians experienced time not as a length to be divided and quantified but as distinctive *times*, such as hours and seasons, each having its own unique qualities.[22] Their cyclical experience of time was marked not at the ends but at the center in recurrent epiphanal moments, often connected to the seasons, sealed and sanctified not by individual acts of morality and duty but by group rituals.

Cyclical time, marked with meaningful ritual, can be intensely evocative, framing and highlighting unique moments. Ritual events create space/time in which an experience of the divine can most easily and beneficially enter life; they facilitate interaction with it. Ritual opens participants to transformative experiences and insights that transcend personal limits.

For many Westerners, however, even some who still participate in religious ceremonies, "ritual" has become synonymous with" empty" or "meaningless," and the significance of cyclical time has devolved into the merely repetitive or the yearly marking of the process of getting older. We seldom experience holidays as transcendent events; rather, they're a series of tasks and encounters we'd prefer to avoid, involving little feeling or significance. Even our usual concept of eternity, time endlessly extended, removes us from encompassing time and from the moment deeply experienced.

Despite ritual's bad reputation, linear time causes us still greater problems. People frequently experience it as an interminable series of hours or days, inhabited habitually. It's rather boring, so we compensate with increasingly sensational recreation, drugs, scandals, or conspiracy theories. Its focus on future reward takes us away from ourselves and our roots in the past and thus is both alienating and seductive; cyclical, ritual time circles back on itself and returns us regularly to core aspects of ourselves and our relationships so these can be enriched and unfolded.

Because we've mostly lost the feeling for numinous ritual and are unpracticed at experiencing non-linear time and uncomfortable with it, we compensate by trying to force its infinite potential into linear time—the horizontal axis—and thus endeavor to cram more and more activities and events into our schedule. This only makes us feel we have less time. We try to solve this through ever-faster technology, some of which enables us to do several things at once, as if by operating at nanosecond speed we could create time. Time disappears again, however, as even more demands are made on it—or else our hard drive crashes. Breaking time into ever-smaller units leaves us feeling fragmented.

We also compensate for our inability to include the vertical axis of the eternal here-now in our experience of linear time by attempting to extend the timeless over time. We allow ourselves to touch into intensely numinous experiences only at a surface level, conceptualizing them as quickly as possible so that we can remember and think about them. Some spiritual energy does enter our lives this way, but this is at a low enough amplitude at any given moment that it does not force us deeper into ourselves and doesn't challenge us to transform our consciousness or our lives. In effect, we amortize the power of our brush with the infinite, thereby dissipating it, and life goes on as before. Or, we may have an experience of extreme presence, but instead of letting it affect us however it may and letting it recur when it does, we despair of its passing and of ever having such an event again. We're uncomfortable not being able to control its occurrence and try to hold onto it. For example, if our kids do something remarkable, we immediately rush for the camera and thereby take ourselves out of the experience. In so doing, we deprive the event of its living quality; we produce a stuffed specimen of an experience to post on the Web.

The same thing occurs daily at any national park. Instead of being still and attentive to awesome natural beauty, many people hurriedly photograph the scene and move on; having captured it, they don't need to participate in the moment. When I first visited the Grand Canyon, at the viewpoint where most people see the canyon itself for the first time, I noticed that there were many joking comments like "Don't fall in!" but little in the way of truly looking. It's such an overwhelming presence that people don't quite know what to do with it. I found I needed to sit at a quiet place on the rim for an hour so that my awareness could slowly expand from its more narrow, practical focus to take in the magnificence of the place. Later, I observed a small child approach the rim. She ran up to it and said simply, "Mommy, it's perfect!" One who hadn't lost the inborn capacity for moments of epiphany put tourists, both the joking and meditating kinds, to shame.

Spiral Time

We're stuck in time and need to develop a new consciousness that successfully synthesizes cyclical and linear time to address our current condition. Consciousness developed from its original group context in cyclical time into an individualistic focus in historical, linear time that emphasizes personal development over time through acts of will and conscience. Beginning with the Zoroastrians, the first to exercise free-will choice in a historical contest between good and evil, and with the Greeks, individuals became agents responsible for their own fates. The development of individual agency culminated during the last millennium with the full formation of the autonomous intellect, leading to our scientific mentality and vastly increased technological capability. We're accustomed to think of modern, rational individualistic human beings as the pinnacle of evolution, no longer changing except in our technological prowess. The development of human consciousness, however, is unlikely to end with our current condition. Discoveries such as those about the size and fate of the universe, in addition to the challenges to our survival produced by our technology, make it inevitable that consciousness, including our time sense, will continue to evolve. Each stage of consciousness creates the problems that force it to look beyond itself to find its saving complement. We are in a period of transition, and therefore what we do has particular significance for the coming age. While this may seem a decidedly historical, linear view, derived from the paradigm of human progress, that's true only on the surface.

A synthesis is more than the sum of its parts and can be startlingly different from those parts taken in isolation. The structure of language causes us to talk of parts as distinct, although by nature they're indivisible. Precisely the time it takes to speak or think of different aspects of a whole introduces the illusion of separation. What we conceptualize as separate, we will likely experience as such—we experience the ends, so to speak, but not the joining middle because we do not talk that way.

Linear time and cyclical time are complementary components of a synthesis. I've been describing them separately, but they make up a whole and are equally essential to it. (Thoreau succinctly expressed the interwoven nature of linear and cyclical time: "As if you could kill time without injuring eternity."[23]) A useful term for the synthesis is spiral time. The structure of a spiral is a movement through space with a periodic return to a position corresponding to a previous position but expanding on it. Similarly, one property of time is historic movement and the progressive development of human awareness, but another is a cycle of return to enduring themes and processes.[24]

We can observe the structure of time as a spiral not only in history but personally. Biologically, we progress through several cycles, including the ninety-minute brain wave cycle, diurnal cycle, menstrual cycle, and life cycle. Within and beyond each of these we maintain an ongoing continuity and advancement of awareness as a developing and progressing person while regularly revisiting certain kinds of experience. Even the linear dramatic framework discussed at the beginning of this chapter recurs as a cyclic event, producing a spiral: stimuli that repeat from time to time evoke the dramas, and by means of these the evolution of consciousness takes place. The natural structure of time seems inevitably to absorb and transform whatever artificial order we impose on it.

The concept of time developed by Middle Eastern cultures twenty-plus centuries ago determined the spirit and direction of much human endeavor since. We've now spiraled back to re-examine time, both scientifically and in terms of how we live our lives. Paradoxically, the directional, progressive concept of time fostered the development of the very attitudes, methods, and skills that have produced the scientific breakthroughs that have led to linear time's scientific demise. We probably will soon experience the temporal effects of relativity on space travelers, so that linear time's theoretical demolition becomes a tangible experience for us. This will change how we think about our lives and our relationships to one another and the cosmos in radical and unpredictable ways. The effects of physics' understanding of time are yet to have significant impact beyond scientific and philosophical circles; nonetheless, they are time bombs in our psyches.

We now explore infinity and eternity in physical terms, rather than, as in past eras, as attributes of divinity. Knowing that the gravitational field of one's body extends to infinity, that the universe is boundless and time extends eternally, and that there may be infinite numbers of universes created all the time, we can now recognize that we don't need to die to enter eternity and infinity: we are in it. The idea that we ourselves could be infinite and eternal will become increasingly common, opening the way for more conscious, spontaneous experiences of this "spiritual" truth.

This profoundly different picture of us will generate a more focused but less hurried sense of time, centered and mindful in moments of limitless presence. The awareness of unbounded and non-absolute time/space will destroy the paradigm of having, conquering, and knowing it all or needing to "get somewhere." We will be able to enter the moment, not to remove ourselves from the necessities of the phenomenal world or to be blissed out but to ground our infinite selves effectively in the world. We will understand that the effects of our actions extend in all directions in time and space, generating a holistic relationship with the cosmos. Rather than frenetic activity and expenditure of personal energy to get more done, a greater ability to focus in the moment will to provide us energy from infinite source within; rational mind and linear thinking will then serve their proper function, to connect this into the world. We'll be able to do less yet accomplish more that's of actual consequence; linear-time consciousness by itself leads to efficiency only as regards the inconsequential. Given that now is the only place we can ever be or take action, the more present we are, the more effective—and playful—we can be. Athletes and performers are at their best when immersed in the moment, not concerned that the current opportunity to excel may be their only one or how it might affect their career.

In *but Not* of *Time*

We no longer believe the heavens circle the earth, yet all such convictions long held by humanity contain some intuitive truth. An understanding of cyclical time will enable us to return to being the center of the cosmos in a new way. During intensely focused moments of timeless presence we are at the center of eternity, at the center of the spiral of time, experiencing how time moves around and through us but also seeing that all other beings are likewise at the center. We find ourselves in a cosmic field where we simultaneously are and are not the center, are both cause and effect, both the unmoved mover and the moved.

The belief that there will be closure and resolution to history also has intuitive truth, even if an apocalyptic end of days does not occur. History itself may end, rather than the world: an end, not of days but our way of reckoning them. We may be approaching the end of our familiar sense of history, ready to entertain a new experience of time. We will use time's cycles as recurrent markers to evaluate our development through linear time. We'll immerse ourselves in eternal moments, mark cyclical returns, and make linear progress, all in a rich interplay of time senses that integrates infinite and finite. We'll be able to maintain awareness of the infinite pattern as a whole, as *our* wholeness, as we act in time as finite beings, in but not of linear time. We'll be able to spend time in mundane reality without leaving our true home.

Nietzsche wrote: "Round every Here rolls the sphere There. The center is everywhere. Bent is the path of eternity."[25] Living in non-absolute time/space will bring magic back into our lives and a finer sense of play than we have known for some time.

15

Human Evolution

> I have learned to be afraid with real fear, fear that increases only when the force that engenders it increases. . . . [I]t is so utterly inconceivable, so totally opposed to us, that our brain disintegrates at the point where we strain ourselves to think it. And yet, for some time now I have believed that it is *our own* force, all our own force that is still too great for us. It is true we do not know it; but is it not just that which is most our own of which we know the least? Sometimes I reflect on how heaven came to be and death: through our having distanced what is most precious to us, because there was still so much else to do beforehand and because it was not secure with us busy people. Now times have elapsed over this, and we have become accustomed to lesser things. We no longer recognize that which is our own and are terrified by its extreme greatness.
>
> —Rilke, *The Notebooks of Malte Laurids Brigge*

Despite Stephen Jay Gould's (1941-2002) compelling arguments that evolution is largely due to accidents, we like to see our species standing on the pinnacle of evolution It's nonetheless quite possible that the feature that we see as most important to our status—our extremely developed brain—will prove an evolutionary dead end.

Older parts of the brain provide instinctive protections from behaviors that are problematic for evolutionary success, such as unnecessary violence against members of one's own species. Despite the fact that the neocortex, the most recently evolved part of the brain that allows for reason, planning, judgment, and self-awareness, had already grown to unprecedented size in chimpanzees and prehuman hominids millions of years ago, it still lacks full integration with the older brain and can override it, which is good for innovation but not necessarily for staying out of trouble.[1] Dudley Young suggests that the newly expanded but unintegrated, largely underemployed capacity of the brain experienced boredom with the old instinctual order (cf. Origen's views on the fall of spiritual beings in the next chapter), so, endowed with faculties for imagining new possibilities, it invented things to occupy itself. In chimpanzees, according to Jane Goodall's research, this innovation includes murder, genocide, and group hunting expeditions unnecessary for nourishment but instead offering emotional release, including frenzied killing.[2] Human beings likewise have invented aspects of culture and technology, such as the capacity to kill on an incredibly large scale, that far exceed what is necessary or desirable for survival.

Critiques of our cultural and technological inventiveness are ancient, offered by those such as Lao Tzu and the Buddha who sought to understand the sources of human foolishness and suffering. They pointed to the mental artifacts that the mind produces and clings to and that become a web of illusion entangling it. Young contends that religion developed as a means to rein in the neocortical tendency to override instinctual limits on intraspecies violence.[3] The neocortex, with its boundless ingenuity, has nevertheless subverted religion's purpose of limiting and structuring aggression and instead uses religious differences as reasons for more violence. The neocortex's cleverness in devising rationalizations for conflict is matched only by its knack for developing ever-greater means of destruction to keep it entertained; together, these may ultimately end our evolution along with that of many other species.

One of the most perplexing things about human beings is the painful discrepancy between our primal urges and spiritual inclinations. Because the neocortex and lower brain areas have an underdeveloped and not always harmonious relationship with each other, certain of our physical tendencies—sex and aggression for instance—are often in conflict with our spiritual sensibilities. The spiritual and the primal are both strong and vital aspects of our nature, and equally valid. Our higher evolutionary purpose is to live a spiritual life in a physically viable, creative, and satisfying way while integrating our instinctual heritage to support survival and the expression of spirit.

We assume at our risk that having a large brain is evolutionarily beneficial. Darwinian proof is in survival. We are an evolutionary test case, the first creature on the planet able to reflect and plan. *Homo sapiens sapiens* is a young species and largely unproven. Our neocortex may turn out to be no more desirable than the evolution of a species into a very specialized niche that's prone to elimination by environmental change. Our large brain, in search of amusement, has created quite a number of means to put its survival in jeopardy. We're the first species to have an aware choice regarding our evolutionary outcome, and we've yet to conclusively decide whether we'll do what it takes to survive.

The religious view that we have God-given dominion over the earth yields the idea that we're incapable of evolutionary termination. Religious attitudes toward our instinctual urges prevent some believers from forthrightly engaging, transforming, and integrating their urges, instead rejecting them as evil. The neocortex may ignore or belittle those needs or project their problematic aspects onto other humans or species, but they nonetheless *will* get our attention—destructively if we disregard them, preventively and instructively if we pay attention. Rejection of them for any reason, religious or otherwise, is the surest way to guarantee their expression in ways that threaten our survival. These very instincts, however, provide the fertile soil we need to work, using our intellectual and spiritual capacities, if we're to keep our species healthy.

Part of our sense of evolutionary importance may come from another quarter, one that has less to do with our braininess, dexterity, upright posture, or divine appointment than with being the incarnation of an infinite self. Some esoteric writers describe us as unique on the planet: we are individual spiritual entities, whereas all other species have a single spiritual source each. (If this is so, a guess as to when we began to have individual infinite selves would be between seventy thousand and thirty-five thousand years ago, when *Homo sapiens sapiens* greatly expanded its capacity for abstract thought, evidenced by artistic expression and consistent burial of the dead, often including grave goods, which suggests spiritual concerns.[4]

The number of neural synapses in the human brain may exceed the number of atoms in the cosmos. Our brain's capacity to generate things to occupy and distract itself is so great that the only thing available that can contain and structure it is the divine, whether conceived of as higher mind, infinite self, *Atman*, God, etc. Thus, for thousands of years spiritual teachers, seeing that a bored mind of such prodigious capacity provides the proverbial devil's playground, have urged their followers to focus their minds in prayer, yoga, meditation, or contemplation, in order to avoid sin, error, confusion, or forgetfulness of first things, or whatever the culture considered the least desirable of human capacities.

These practices have persisted for good reason. Studies (fostered by the Dalai Lama and carried out by Western neuroscientists) of the brain activity of Tibetan Buddhist monks in meditation indicate considerable ability to alter brainwave activity, increasing the kind that connects distant areas of the brain. In this research, the left prefrontal cortex, locus of positive emotions, far outstripped the activation of the right corresponding area, generator of negative feelings. The results confirm that inner cues such as focused awareness, as well as physical activity, can induce neuroplasticity, the brain's capacity to alter its form and function.[5]

The physical relationship of the older and newer parts of the brain may evolve toward greater integration. To get there, however, may require that we engage our spiritual nature to save us from the demonic potentials of a supercomputing neocortex inadequately connected to its instinctual grounding. We do not know where our Darwinian evolution may lead, but visionaries and prophets throughout the ages have indicated where our spiritual evolution is headed, and getting there requires the right use and proper structuring of our intelligence. Such right use requires, in turn, spiritual discipline by which to interact with the divine and rewire our brains for wholeness.

16

The Problem of Evil

All things are fair and good and right to God; but men think of some as wrong and others as right.

—Heraclitus

Those who are innocent always strive to exclude from themselves and to negate in the world the possibilities of evil. This is the reason for the persistence of evil.

—Zimmer, *The King and the Corpse*

At cost of lives and treasure, we wage hot and cold wars against an "evil empire," an "axis of evil," and the "evildoers" that threaten us with terrorism. We react to the idea of evil as if we knew and agreed on what it is. Yet, philosophy and metaphysics have long struggled to answer crucial questions regarding it: What is evil? Why is it there? What can we do about it? And, where was God when it happened? If we're to consider waging war on evil until we eliminate it from the world, as suggested by President George W. Bush in 2001, we'd best know what we are taking on and the likelihood we can succeed.

The most fundamental question about evil is, does it exist? The answer seems obvious; most people's lives and their reading of the news or history provide them compelling evidence that it must. The Holocaust, the Rwandan and Cambodian genocides, the September 11, 2001 and other terrorist attacks all happened. This answer raises a yet thornier problem: how could a good and omnipotent God create or allow evil to exist? The existence of evil seems inevitably to lead to one of three general conclusions. First, God is not entirely good, which is hard for most people to accept. Second, if God is not responsible for evil, there must be some kind of cosmic duality of Good and Evil, and therefore God, the Good, isn't omnipotent, a conclusion that can lead to some unease. Third, God may be entirely good and in his goodness allows evil to occur for good reasons that surpass our understanding but in which we must have faith. This issue of theodicy, of how to posit a righteous and loving God in the face of evil, is more than a philosophical question. Unresolved, it can create mistrust, fear, and separation between a person and God and by implication between the person and her infinite self. These feelings may not be fully conscious but can undermine and diminish the relationship nonetheless, causing a decrease in receptivity to the flow of support and life-energy from the higher self. This has its own painful effects that amplify the perceived reasons for mistrust, in turn leading to greater reduction of relationship.

As present as evil seems to be in the world, a comprehensive definition and understanding of it is surprisingly difficult to achieve. In the abstract the issue becomes quite elusive, leaving unanswered these vexing and agonizing questions. Without an appreciation of the paradoxical nature of human existence and the relationship between infinite and finite, these problems simply cannot be understood or satisfactorily addressed. Responses to the calls of political or religious leaders to fight against evil will tragically miss the mark absent deeper insight into the nature of this beast.

Ideas concerning the nature of evil have varied widely. Earliest on, as well as in current traditional cultures in our time, occurs the sense of contamination and impurity: things not being in their proper place and relationship. This includes "invasions of divine violence,"[1] where the divine itself, out of place, defiles and damages. "Sacred" means "set apart," based on the primordial sense that the divine is dangerous and must be sequestered. Contamination is resolved through ritual cleansing, sacrifice, and scapegoating.

Ancient stories about what we would call evil involve deities that were morally ambiguous rather than radically evil, for example the Egyptian Set, seen as destroyer of life and source of chaos but also as preserver of the world. Similarly ambiguous is the Native American trickster Coyote.

Zoroaster made a cosmic conflict of good and evil deities central to his theology, influencing Western religion to this day. For him, evil essentially meant the lie: the self-deception of creatures seeing themselves as their own creators and as the origin of the blessings that flow from the divine.[2] The notion of self-deception occurs in the Hindu Vedas in what philosopher Martin Buber (1878-1965) describes as "the uncanny game of hide-and-seek in the obscurity of the soul, in which it, the single human soul, evades itself."[3] Buddhist and later Hindu philosophies view good and evil as part of the same whole; distinguishing them from one another is illusory. The Buddha's main concern was to address the causes of suffering. He taught that everything is impermanent and suffering arises from resistance to this fact, in the form of trying to cling to things, people, or concepts. In Taoism, the consequences of what we call evil arise from the mind stopping the natural flow of life and dissipating it in the mind's myriad creations that distract, perturb, and imbalance us. Yin and yang, dark and light, are both essential; their interactions progress through natural transformations in a dynamic balance with one or the other accentuated at any given time.

In Platonic doctrine evil is the privation of goodness, caused by misuse of free will. For Judaism and Christianity, evil entered the world with the disobedience that led to the knowledge of good and evil. There is no notion in early Judaism of a cosmic power opposed to God. Even Satan, in the Book of Job, is an important angel who serves as Yahweh's advisor and representative. At times he prosecutes individuals; *satan* in Hebrew means "accuser" or "adversary."[4] Judaism and other Middle Eastern religions sometimes equated evil with chaos, especially that brought on by invading armies. In post-exilic Judaism after exposure to Zoroastrianism, evil takes on a different character. The invading armies still symbolize an evil force inherent in adjacent non-Jewish peoples, but this has become cosmic and absolute.[5] The figure Mastema in the *Book of Jubilees,* written c.175-140 B.C.E., presents the first Jewish description of a spirit embodying hostility to divinity and intentionally resisting God's will; this became the Christian Devil.[6]

The Christian theologian Origen (c. 185-254), following Philo of Alexandria, proposed that evil began when the spiritual beings first created by God, originally good and reasonable, "became 'sated' with the adoration of God" writes Henry Chadwick. Partly through pride, they fell away from God into neglect and boredom, "gradually cooling in their love."[7] For Origen, the tribulations that we deem evil are there for our spiritual growth.

Modern views regarding the nature of evil are highly diverse.[8] These include having an independent existence as Radical Evil, a dynamic power in the cosmos sometimes personified as the Devil. It is regarded as a force of evil per se within human beings, or as negativity that a person has suppressed. It may stem from the impact of sociological and cultural circumstances on the evildoer, such as abuse or lack of education. It is the absence or lack of fulfillment of good, or it is anti-life. It results from divine self-limitation for the purpose of human freedom and growth. Either the intent of the evildoer or its effect on its victim may define it. Its manifestations range from degradation, humiliation, suppression of spirit and joy, or denial of the necessities of life, to overt cruelty and destruction. Evil may be practical (a means to an end, for instance torture to get information), or perverse (having no end beyond itself: torture for sadistic pleasure).

While a common nineteenth-century hope was that science and rationalism would banish evil, the twentieth century's wars and genocides plus the psychological insights of Freud and Jung have led to the idea that evil is a fundamental part of human nature and is inevitably related to consciousness. Both religious and humanistic thinkers maintain that it's essential that people strive to bring into awareness their negative aspects, whether seen as purely evil or as the psychological shadow. Each person must face these, whether simply to contain them or to transmute them into good. Many beliefs include the idea that engaging evil with love produces greater wholeness and maturity. This may occur either by choosing not to give it energy or by transforming and integrating it.

Philosopher Hannah Arendt (1906-1975) famously wrote of "the banality of evil." If evil is banal, why is sin so attractive? Why is Satan the most engaging figure in *Paradise Lost?* In English, as noted frequently, evil is "live" reversed. Evil (understood as part of a duality with good) is devoid of life, a vacuum. Anything not nailed down tends to be sucked into this vacuum, including the aspects of ourselves that we suppress or deny and that tend to be the interesting, creative bits. Wickedness, because of its resulting mixture with these rejected parts of life and nature, can be enticing, fascinating, and exciting; however, as Arendt's remark reflects, evil in itself, without drawing to itself such parts, lacks life and creativity. Sin, reduced to its core, is anything but original.

For any discussion of good and evil, a serious and often unrecognized problem is that we mostly define these in terms of what we feel is good or evil for ourselves, our family, group, nation, or species. This definition has two shortcomings. First, what we think is good or bad for us may turn out to be the opposite. Second, this self-centered viewpoint doesn't adequately take others or our environment into account; even if we discount their importance in themselves, they're important for our enlightened self-interest.

According to one particularly relevant view, good and evil are inextricably connected because consciousness and the awareness of good and evil arose together in human evolution and likewise arise simultaneously in each individual's development. Good and evil interact in important ways: each can produce the other; evil finds definition in relationship to good (the absence or destruction of what is good), and meaningful living derives from the need to choose between good and evil. From this perspective the attempt to extirpate evil is both foredoomed and foolish. The issue is how to manage it.

With this in mind, we can reformat our subject into three tiers:

GOOD
good *and* evil (as polarities)
Good *or* Evil (as dualities)

GOOD, in this schema, is pure being: the level of the divine and the infinite self. This pure good involves no reference to evil, being undivided and undifferentiated; it is the source and resolution of polarities which emerge from it and return to it eternally. This is not "good" as people generally think of it; it does not have to do with morality or favorable outcomes. It is pure love, in no way sentimental or conditional. It does not necessarily have anything to do with our hopes, needs, and desires; therefore, the experience of it can be quite hard for us to endure, and although mystics have encountered and written about it, most people require considerable training to experience it. However, if we strive to live in accord with its nature, it increases our joy, peace, and spiritual delight.

The second tier, good *and* evil as polarities, involves the mutual interdependency characteristic of all polarities. They are necessary to each other, interact, transform into each other, and are inseparable. Buber calls them directions, not substances.[9] Boehme's vision of two aspects of God, one light and one dark, involves these polarities. Taoism's description of the interplay of yin and yang, one increasing as the other decreases in the changing flow of life, describes these polarities' relationship. In fact, the Chinese language has only the word *yinyang*, with no conjunction that would indicate separation. A modern version of Taoism's insight is Nietzsche's statement that "it is quite possible that the very value of . . . good and honored things consists, in fact, in their insidious relatedness to . . . wicked, seemingly opposite things—it could be that they are inextricably bound up, entwined, perhaps even similar in their very nature."[10] His proposition seems outrageous when it is understood to apply to Good and Evil as dualities; as regards polarities it makes perfect sense.

Self-interest (or selfishness) is a useful example, considering that it's maligned as the root of many other sins. From one perspective, it would seem self-evident that it's of the evil polarity; after all, selflessness is what makes for saintliness. From another perspective, however, it's equally self-evident that attending to one's actual needs is essential for one to function at all, much less in a saintly manner. Further, all life is divine creation and deserves love and care; the part of creation one is best qualified to care for is oneself. Absent the effects of conditioning or trauma, people who care for themselves well and thus are healthy and self-aware will naturally reach out to others to love and serve them because that is fulfilling—it's in our genes. Selflessness taken too far leads to imbalance, ill health, resentment, and inflexibility of response. Enlightened self-interest balances self and others, allowing a dynamic interaction between selfless and selfish, each ebbing and flowing so that over time neither dominates. Complete self-abnegation partakes of neither holiness nor wholeness. Even a mystic on a mountain must distinguish the barley that is moldy and has "gone bad" from the fresh, the "good to eat," but whereas person who thinks dualistically may feel revulsion and fear at the dangerous food that's "bad" for him, the sage, while recognizing the difference, will bless the mold as part of the natural cycle.

Another example is the natural world. Nature provides all our resources and the physical means of life itself, yet it resists our efforts in many ways and can be destructive. Non-dualistic cultures have tried to work and live with nature in a sustainable balance, respecting (even worshiping) its violent side, accepting losses while trying to minimize them. Our more dualistic culture tries to conquer nature and make war on its costly, annoying, or inconvenient aspects; our faith in scientific and technological successes makes us forget that we haven't subdued it and probably never can. Believing we can, we lose respect for it and expect we can always come up with a fix for the damage we do. The law of unintended consequences—such as widespread use of antibiotics producing resistant bacteria—should have disabused us of this by now.

We see these polarities through the filter of our needs, causing us to misconstrue them as dualities, ignoring the fact that different people, or one person at different times, can see the same act or quality as either good or evil. Heraclitus (c. 540-c. 480 B.C.E.) observes: "Every good and evil are the same. Thus physicians, cutting and cauterizing and torturing sick men in every way . . . complain that they do not get as much pay as they deserve from the sick men; for what they do is good for those diseases."[11] Buber argues that nothing is in its essence good or evil; instead, each thing is both in a unity. Jung emphasizes how important it is that we not "succumb" to good any more than to evil, lest it become an addiction rather than an ethical value.[12] To succumb is to identify with one aspect of a polarity and thus split it from the other aspect to create duality.

Good *or* Evil as dualities, the third tier, are a human invention, the result of separating polarities in our awareness. Most people understand the pair in this split form, with a chasm dividing them. We have great difficulty containing good and evil, as polarities, as a totality in our rational, discriminating minds; so, opposites that are only potential within something emerge through our intervention: the particular (though not necessary) way our minds operate divides the opposites. Jung is explicit: "all division and all antagonism are due to the splitting of opposites in the psyche."[13] This allows us to imagine the nonreal; feeding on that, imagination quickly gets out of control. We try to regain our footing by bonding to whatever of our illusory creations seems most desirable. These attachments trap us in a fabricated world, not the world of divine creation. Imagination creates a seeming infinity of fictions that we fear and hate for its inherent chaos. Because our imaginings are seemingly infinite, we attribute divinity to them; the traditional name for this was idol worship.[14]

Reifying and Deifying

Thoughts, such as "good" and "evil," are structures of consciousness; each thought structure has its shape and form. Because of this, we tend to treat abstract concepts or even patterns of psychic energy as separate things in their own right rather than as parts of an interacting pattern. To the degree that we treat them as such, they take on a life of their own; they seem to operate independently of us and affect us powerfully. We first *reify* abstractions and patterns, treating them as real things. Then we *deify* them (thus the capitalized Good or Evil). This used to occur literally, such that gods and goddesses ruled people's lives; now our concepts control us, enduring and sacrosanct. The polarity evil, having no existence or meaning apart from its counterpart good (and vice versa), thus appears, as a duality, to exist in itself. As such, it appears dangerous, and if we react to it and thereby give it power, it becomes so. The nature of this movement from polarity to duality reveals itself in the development of the ultimate expression of Evil, the Devil. This entity, which as Satan was once an integral part of the court of God, mutates a few centuries later into a completely different figure, separate from God and cast into another realm, no longer able to interact with the divine.

Having created dualities, we see them as implacable enemies. Most people, of course, seek to identify themselves with the side of Good and may feel called to separate themselves from Evil and eliminate all its manifestations and causes, internal and external, from themselves. They may do this for religious reasons or to have the "good" life that by dualistic definition is what fulfills their needs and wants. Because the pair is, however, simply a misinterpretation of the polarities, it's an illusion that Evil could be eliminated— the only way to do so is to get beyond the dualistic notion of Good or Evil.

In short, the creation of the duality of Good or Evil—the separation of the polarities—is the fundamental cause of much of what we think of as Evil.

Buber, Jung, Taoism, Buddhism, and Christianity's more subtle insights all point to the need to overcome dualistic ideas of Good or Evil by way of reintegrating evil. They accomplish this by embracing evil with love, compassion, or forbearance in order to reestablish wholeness: the mutually interdependent interaction of polarities. When we return dualistic Evil and Good to their actual relationship as a polarity, they transform; together they constitute a wholeness that transcends the original wholeness (before splitting) because the process involves spiritual growth; thus, the dualistic Evil we created will serve a good purpose in the end.

Jung suggests that while God has both good and evil aspects (after all, in Job, Satan is God's son and convinces him to do seemingly unjust things), God is an antinomy, "a totality of inner opposites" rather than split between good and evil.[15] These antinomial aspects become conscious only in people, not in God, because they collide when finite beings have to make moral decisions.[16] Jung asserts that it is "naive" to impute consciousness to divinity. "Divine unconsciousness and lack of reflection . . . enable us to form a conception of God which puts his actions beyond moral judgment."[17] Since "all opposites are of God," we gain in understanding of the divine through irresolvable discord and tension.[18] Job, afflicted, is able to comprehend and accept this: he asks, "Shall we receive the good at the hand of God, and not receive the bad?"[19] Like a Zen koan, this divine paradox forces one past dualistic thinking. Jung states: "Only through the most extreme and most menacing conflict . . . can . . . God become man."[20]

Jung views the development of Christianity as bringing to full consciousness the good and evil polarities but at the same time attempting to divest the divine of evil; God becomes purely good and loving,[21] so unlike the Old Testament Yahweh that some early Christians felt theirs was a different God. As part of the divestiture, Jesus sees Satan hurled from heaven.[22] Even so, Jung asserts, Christ didn't trust God to be completely free of evil impulse, praying "Lead us not into temptation."[23] Jung sees this division as needing resolution.

In contrast, Buber contends that God is aware of "the opposites of being, which stem from His own act of creation: He encompasses them, untouched by them." The knowledge of good and evil is "the primordial possession of God." Man's knowledge is different because in him good and evil can't coexist at the same time. Nothing is inherently good or evil, but something becomes one or the other by our awareness of contraries; through humankind's knowledge of good and evil, "the opposites which are always latently present in creation break out into actual reality."[24]

Buber goes on to propose that the human tendency toward rampant evil is not due to us having evil souls but to the invention of "imagery."

In gaining the knowledge of good and evil, that is, opposites, a person "is driven out into the boundless possible, which he fills with his imaging, that is evil because it is fictitious. . . . In the swirling space of images, through which he strays, each and every thing entices him to be made incarnate by him; he grasps at them . . . not with decision, but only . . . to overcome the tension of omnipossibility."[25] (We might say he is caught in the virtual infinity of duality that has no resolution in wholeness and no inherent balance, so he can only clutch at ephemera.) Reality risks being overwhelmed by the swirling images, which God deems to be evil because they divert attention from the actuality He presents.[26] God gave limit to the unbounded possibilities by instituting death, not as punishment but to prevent "full demonry"; humankind careens into the world of opposites (dualities) as a path—history—on which ultimately to return to God.[27]

Buber considers our "evil urge" to be as essential to us as the good (Buber is thinking in polarities); only because we have divided it from its counterpart, good (thereby creating dualities) has it become the evil we know. Therefore, we must not try to eliminate our evil but to bring it back to union with good. Evil and good are not opposites—our evil is to conceive them as such—but are passion and direction, respectively, which we must embrace together to create wholeness. Passion left to itself is directionless and leads to error; direction without passion lacks real-world creativity.[28] However, good and the evil that human beings make are fundamentally and structurally dissimilar in the human realm. One is a path, the only one; the other isn't a path at all but rather indecision.[29] Buber acknowledges that the good that comes from walking God's path is not that negative happenstances cease but that these are negative only if seen apart from God; the "punishment" for bad people is that they "experience their non-existence."[30] When events are "irradiated" by God's wisdom, all, even the adverse, reveal themselves as successful; the knowledge of God's way is sublime joy. The goodness that flows from God consists not of reward but the revelation of His nature.[31]

Buber's "tension of omnipossibility," the ability of our large brain to override instinctual guidance and compulsively grasp at the myriad things it can conceive of, may arise in part from the evolutionary quandary described in chapter 15 but also from the failure to differentiate the experience of the infinite within from the imaginings and ideas of the finite brain. Accordingly, these imaginary creations take on some of the numinosity of the divine, making them even more compelling. The mind can't contain or structure this confusion of energized potentials. This mistaking of the products of finite mind for the infinite, due to the lack of conscious awareness of infinite self, energizes and legitimizes the reifying and deifying of these products that lead to duality. We need to develop the ability to differentiate what's legitimately numinous from what's simply the product of the finite brain and to recognize those experiences of the infinite that can give guidance to the mind as to what's worth its attention.

Dudley Young suggests, as previously noted, that religion first developed to provide an alternate restraint system to compensate for the loosening of instinctual limitations. "The primate [instinctual] codes that forbid intraspecific violence, defusing it through rituals of dominance and submission, are destabilized in the inventive complexity of the chimpanzee neocortex (as in our own)."[32] Early religions treated the divine itself as potentially dangerous, violent, and defiling if not contained properly. Given that most modern people do not see violence and defilement as associated with the divine or with the spiritual aspect of humanity (even though God may still be spoken of as wrathful), what was different in relations with the divine early in our development?

Evolving Evil

Perhaps the newly capacious neocortex was a bit taken with itself and its growing imagination. It found the hormonal and neural communications from the older brain areas (the limbic, "mammalian" system that involves emotions, territoriality, and aggression, and the oldest, "reptilian" brain that regulates body functions and wakefulness) to be obstructive, foreign, and sometimes scary. No part of the brain being definitively in charge, sometimes the cortex would have its noninstinctual way; if a bad outcome occurred, which instinct would have helped to avoid, it may have felt like retribution. At other times, the limbic emotions would overwhelm the functioning of the cortex, as if an unknown power possessed the higher brain, a power that only ritualized behavior could calm. The emotions arising from the limbic area range from murderous to ecstatic; whichever, their awesome force, experienced as chaotic, polluting, devouring, or supernatural, could engulf the nascent reasoning capacity of the cortex. While its effect can be terrifying, the older brain is also essential to life-maintenance and reproduction. To ancient peoples its force was both threatening and necessary (like the Egyptian god Set), so protection from it and contact with it were equally essential. When ancient humans observed both violent power and fecundity in nature, these stimulated strong emotional reactions; at other times, similar emotions were self-induced by aggressive or sexual urges. Whether subjectively or objectively aroused, the experience produced by the limbic system was the same. The fact that these reactions were literally all in their heads wasn't obvious, so they attributed the unknown cause to something external, either demonic or divine.

The cortex had to strive to gain some freedom and control. This clearing of the mind and creating some mental space plays out in a multitude of myths about the primal separating of sky and earth that marked the creation of an orderly cosmos out of chaos. In this clear mind-space, the cortex did what it does best: it abstracted and imagined, producing representations of the energy of these old brain functions so as to engage and contain them: it created gods and goddesses. (What distinguishes the modern relationship to the divine is the greatly expanded development of the abstracting, rational mind in the last millennium.) It could relate to these by way of rituals to govern their comings and goings and by way of sacrifices to appease or induce them to provide divine energy. If that energy got out of hand and defiled the people, they could project it onto some thing or animal and eliminate it through scapegoating, sending it back to the divine and sealing it off with taboos. Later, projecting the defiling energy onto a person who would be banished accomplished this purpose; alternately, sacrificing a pure individual neutralized the energy.

These gods and goddesses represented human psychic energy, including internal responses to external stimuli. For most of their existence, they have been expressions of the ambiguous, paradoxical, interactive polarity of good and evil— the mixed bag nature gives us. By at least twenty-six hundred years ago, a dualistic division of divinities into Good or Evil began to appear. During that millennium, descriptions of a divine nature that surpasses all divinities also emerged: the Hindu *Brahman* (that which is within everything and more than everything, including the gods); the Buddhist *Dharma* (the Absolute, suchness); and Plato's unnamed creator god. The Hebrew divinity, at first implicitly acknowledging the existence of other gods, became the sole God, creator of a cosmos devoid of any other divinities. Humanity's spiritual awareness became capable of distinguishing what I term the GOOD. This is always present and an embedded part of our experience, but before spiritual disciplines such as yoga developed, while experiences of the GOOD must have occurred spontaneously, they most likely couldn't be understood as such or approached systematically. The earliest record of its recognition is the monotheistic Egyptian religion of Akhenaton in the fourteenth-century B.C.E.

We have two kinds of experience of the divine, mixed and confused: one from the finite instinctual brain, the other from the actual divine and the presence of infinite self. A lot has changed since that confusion first began: the sense of good and evil moved from polarity to duality while simultaneously a profound new vision of one divinity as source and sustenance of all creation emerged. Nonetheless, the confusion remains. God may mean things as diverse as a transcendent or immanent non-personal divine principle, or, as in a cartoon, a white-robed, long-bearded personage at a computer ready to press the "SMITE" button as a sinner appears onscreen. Until each of us has sorted out our experiences, our mixed feelings and beliefs will limit our relationship with the divine, and nagging questions will persist: is God vengeful and rewarding, or beyond all that? If we fear God and think it's dangerous to get too close, how can we be totally open to the divine within? Without sorting finite from infinite, good and evil will continue to be a matter of unholy confusion.

Misfortune, Immorality, Ungodliness, and Perverseness

The question of how a good divinity created evil or how evil occurs in divine creation has long perturbed the relationship of human beings with God. We have looked at the possibility that the problem with this question lies with defining good and evil from a finite perspective and expecting this to hold for an infinite God. If we experience the issue from the standpoint of infinite selves, we will see the problem in a completely different light.

Webster's defines evil as follows:

1. Morally bad; sinful; wicked; corrupt; perverse.
2. Causing pain or trouble; harmful; injurious.
3. Threatening or bringing misfortune; unlucky; disastrous; unfortunate.
4. Caused by or considered as being caused by immorality.[33]

These definitions involve two distinct themes: an undesirable outcome (matching the original meaning of the Greek term for evil, *kakía*: harm, misfortune, pain, sickness), and sin or immorality. Sin and immorality in turn are defined as transgressions of accepted codes of behavior, with the exceptions of ungodliness and perverseness (in the sense of a person deriving pleasure or satisfaction from pain or destruction, particularly if the person intentionally causes it). Much that is deemed evil, therefore, involves what we don't want to have happen to us and what we should avoid doing so as to get along with one another because these reduce our well-being and cause suffering. Suffering, then, is what usually receives the label evil, apart from ungodliness and perverseness; with those two exceptions, we can reframe the question of why God allows evil as why God allows suffering.

Buddhism explains that suffering arises from grasping, holding on, or attachment to what by nature is transitory and impermanent. We do this out of ignorance, which is the mind's propensity to categorize and separate things even though they're actually interconnected and in flux. In their attachments human beings are trying, in effect, to make eternal what is finite and temporary. An example is dying: in the United States, many elderly people endure tremendous suffering because, while we have technology to keep people alive past the natural point of death, we have difficulty deciding when to allow them to go. We try to perpetuate life as if death were unnatural and wrong and as if we should avoid it at all costs; we are reluctant to abandon the notion that we should be eternal in our finite forms. This clinging increases suffering.

Things *are* eternal in the sense that they're part of the cosmic whole, the body of God. Everything, however, including relationships, treasured possessions, and life, is in eternal flux, so the form of something or one's connection to it will inevitably change, meaning loss, decay, or death from the perspective of a finite observer, though not in an infinite context.

We increase suffering by avoiding it or resisting the natural flow of events, for example, putting off going to the dentist for a toothache, not wanting the bother of an appointment or the discomfort of a filling. Postponing the inevitable increases the sum of pain experienced: both a protracted toothache and the pain of treating a condition worsened by delay. Still, we put that out of mind as we defer action until the discomfort becomes too great to ignore.

We confuse suffering with pain. I define suffering as pain that serves no a life-sustaining purpose, is usually protracted or chronic, the experience of which lacks meaning, and which, because of our beliefs or conditioning, seemingly can't be remedied by our actions. Human beings are particularly prone to pain made chronic by failure to change behaviors or circumstances that produce the pain; the culprits are the peculiarly human maladies of addiction, anxiety, denial, belief/disbelief, and the medical means for extending life.

Pain occurs throughout nature, at least in higher forms of animals. It serves to stimulate immediate action to prevent avoidable harm or death, protecting and maintaining life. Animals are naturally motivated to cut pain short, and when they're unable to do so, some biological mechanisms do it for them to a degree. A sick or injured animal is likely soon to fall prey to predators that put it beyond suffering; also, endorphins serve to counteract pain. Among animals associated with man, suffering is widespread and largely human-induced.

Suffering, of course, can be emotional, deriving from the human abilities to remember and project into the future. Much emotional suffering derives from the feeling that something is unjust and shouldn't happen that way. Emotional suffering also stems from an affront to our sense of self-worth or to our conviction that life is predictable and we're somewhat in control. This would simply be pain if it came and went, having been dealt with, but we may hold on to judgments, anxieties, and wounds to self-esteem for a lifetime; this is suffering. Often, the memory and anticipation of pain, as well as the maladaptive behaviors, anxieties, and even neuroses that can result, produce suffering that far exceeds the real pain. Even someone's experience of protracted physical pain is greatly affected by the way the person relates to it; it can be reduced by acceptance of it and the circumstances that caused it, or increased by resenting its injustice or by resisting, hating, or fearing it. Feeling that one has some choice in how to respond is highly beneficial. Thus, a lot of suffering is a matter of attitude or perspective, which makes the difference between pain and suffering extremely significant for resolving questions about evil.

Who's Responsible Here?

While God created pain, human beings in large part create their suffering, through their choices and attitudes. But God created us. Isn't God still responsible?

We have received the gift of free will through an act of self-limitation on the part of God and our infinite selves, so that we may become aware co-creators through exercising it. We have the right to create awfulness; God may, many believe, mitigate the results if they get too bad (through grace); however, we still have responsibility for the cleanup. Yet, even though most people accept that they have free will and though they like their freedom, some are still unwilling to accept responsibility for what they do with it. Many balk at the idea of a good and merciful God creating a cosmos in which people inflict horrendous suffering upon themselves and others, even though they could choose not to.

To address this, we need to examine more deeply what suffering is. Let's return to the dentist's chair, this time as a five-year-old. The appointment seems to last forever, and the pain feels unendurable. The child's awareness at this age is still immersed in the full experience of the moment, not yet having fully developed adult defenses such as thinking about other things or remembering that this will soon be over. When the work is complete, an emotionally healthy child will largely forget the event, in which case her pain is limited to the moment and she won't suffer, at least until the next appointment is near.

As she grows older, the very nature of time changes for her. Moments become generally less fresh and engrossing as her time sense expands, so that painful times exist in a much larger context. She knows she'll get through the visit, can predict the duration of the pain, and can focus on what pleasures may come later. She isn't so completely present in the chair and therefore not so fully in the pain. Thus, the finite human mind learns how to reduce the experience of pain; it may suppress it to a degree and work it through later. For a healthy mind, the result can definitely be useful, handling it in increments over time rather than all at once. (Of course, being less in the present moment comes at the price of reducing pleasure.) Pain that's overwhelming for us as children becomes quite tolerable for us as adults. We learn that this too shall pass, and unless we've developed anxiety, post-traumatic stress, or phobic reactions, or feel that what's happening is wrong, acute pain isn't usually a big deal. In the larger context of life with its interests and pleasures, pain isn't evil or even particularly troubling. A day's gardening will have its scrapes, bruises, or cuts, any of which might cause a child to cry but which an adult hardly notices. A workout at the gym produces aching muscles, but these are welcomed as indicators of increasing fitness.

Extrapolating to an infinite context (or even a very large finite one), the negative significance of even the most horrendous pain or suffering becomes trivial, especially considering its positive utility, just as normal, daily pain is insignificant to an adult. In the same way that the terrors of childhood, such as a dental visit or getting a shot, are part of growing up, the pains of the life cycle, of natural disasters, and even the suffering humanity imposes on itself are growing pains that recede in significance as we expand into our spiritual adulthood as unified finite/infinite beings.

Our infinite selves are present within and throughout our finite selves at all times. Therefore, our infinite selves (and, on a macrocosmic scale, God) experience our pain, but because they do so in a vastly larger context, they don't suffer. (This is the true meaning of compassion: *suffering with*, which is to be present for and involved with the experience and, most important, to provide the sufferer a reminder of the larger context. It doesn't mean *suffering for* him, that is, getting pulled into the tribulation of the sufferer so much that one is immersed in it and only adds to and magnifies the sum of suffering, as with the comic/tragic situation where the comforter is so immersed in sympathy that the sufferer feels obliged to console him.) While we as finite selves do suffer at this point in our development, when we're fully evolved we may fondly chuckle at it, the same way we do at our childhood experiences, understanding how our painful times ultimately served our growth.

Right now, though, our suffering is real enough to us. Though we may acknowledge that we created it with free will and that there will effectively be an end to it when we reach our spiritual evolutionary destiny, we may not be ready to let God off the hook if we believe we haven't received the means to end it now.

People usually view the termination of suffering as the light at the end of the tunnel of spiritual development, but the light in its middle is always available. By expanding from linear time into the timeless, time-encompassing awareness of infinite self, we can live through suffering as finite beings learning our lessons and simultaneously hold it in the larger context of infinite self. Even the expanded perspective of our whole finite self helps. Either way, we can experience the purposefulness of our pain and dilute it with the cosmic laughter of infinite good humor. Yogis and those who have sacrificed themselves for conscience or religion demonstrate that humans can do this to an extraordinary degree. People who've had near-death experiences or report seeing their present suffering in the context of previous lives recount examples of how completely the experience can change.

A minute for the very young child is an *eternal moment*; it then passes without specific memory. An older child begins to remember, fear, judge, and resist, while at the same time starting to lose his innate experience of infinite self and eternity; then a whole range of suffering becomes possible. When still older, linear time sense develops based on expanding memory, allowing for the mitigation of pain but also, potentially, for more complex forms of suffering. For adults, spiritual maturation (if this happens at all) leads to *eternal awareness*, the expansion of memory and consciousness to include our total finite experience as well as remembering who we are as infinite beings. This awareness requires that we leave the innocence of the child; we must journey away from the Garden of the eternal moment and enter into suffering, that is, into a linear time frame of reference. Only when we have expanded linear time out in all directions and made it spherical and encompassing can we as adults become as little children, returning to eternity not only through total involvement in a moment but through a comprehensive awareness centered in the eternal present. Through life-energy techniques, meditation, or other means, we end suffering by being aware of both aspects of our paradoxical nature simultaneously.

One meaning of innocence is lack of experience, and thus lack of awareness. We lose our innocence to greater awareness. Our destiny is to become fully aware through manifold experiences. Primordial innocence is neither our destiny nor a desirable state.

This line of argument, about how we create suffering and have the capacity to end it, falls short in at least one area: people who are in great pain and have no ability to change their circumstances or attitude, in particular due to grave mental illness. Schizophrenia is an excruciating malady. Its onset may involve both genetic and environmental factors (such as family dynamics) and can be a life-long condition. Mental illness is hard to evaluate in terms of my criteria for suffering, as we have much to learn about what produces it and about how and to what degree volition is impaired. The same is true of disorders where extreme anguish has altered brain function. (In fact, the more we learn about brain chemistry, the more the distinction between it and free will seems due for a salutary review.) In these instances there seems to be great suffering with no apparent possibility to reduce it in the ways that I've described, absent the sufferer being able to see a purpose or meaning in it. For those observers who resonate to them, reincarnation, karma, or the soul's choice of growth experience (such as for developing empathy) give possible meaning to this; my own experience recommends these to me. For others, such possibilities will appear only to be subjects of faith and provide no satisfactory answers.

Ungodly and Perverse

We've explored how the experience of suffering is, at least to a significant degree, a temporary function of the finite, linear mind and part of our growth process, and we've examined how to overcome it. We have now to consider the journey of spiritual maturation just described as it relates to the remaining aspects of the definition of evil: ungodliness and perverseness.

First, to say that evil, as a polarity or paradox, dissolves in the infinite GOOD is not to dismiss the problem. I mean to put responsibility securely where it belongs—with us—and to show how to keep our confused ideas about evil from limiting our ability to respond to it. We must engage it fully, effectively, and constantly. The web of illusion our minds weave is the greatest source of suffering and dualistic Evil. We can extract ourselves from this web only by knowing who we are, so that we can use the power of our infinite nature to free our minds and allow us to act in accord with it in order to open to its grace. At this point in our development, we can take on greater responsibility for our actions because we can be more aware of our motivations and the effects of our actions. We must do this, given our capacities to produce evil on a grandiose scale.

What is ungodliness? Humankind is created in the "image" and "likeness" of God,[34] which as argued here means that we are each created by our individual infinite self as an embodiment of certain of the divine qualities of infinite self with the purpose of expressing those qualities. The origins of suffering and what we call sin derive from the state of consciousness that produces the illusion of separation (duality). The primary illusion is the sense of separation of finite self from God and from infinite self. This delusion is the creation of finite self and is perhaps inevitable considering the gift of free will. While illusory, this separation seems authentic to finite self, which behaves accordingly. To be ungodly is to be untrue to our actual nature, untrue to our image and likeness. It is to be fractured and not whole; it is to treat the desire, need, or choice of one part of oneself as if it were the entirety and thereby to become unbalanced, treating other desires or needs as unimportant, although they also express aspects of infinite self. It is to *separate ourselves from ourselves:* the separating of finite self from infinite self and from its support, which is our birthright. This leads inevitably to separation and division within the person and thence to painful separative attitudes, feelings, and outcomes in relationship to others.

Separativeness is an underlying theme of many, otherwise divergent, views of evil. It may take the form of a separation of self from God through disobedience, mind from heart through rationalism, person from community through overemphasis on individualism, or belief ("What I'm doing is good or obligatory") from objective reality (causing unnecessary harm to others) through excessive idealism.

The separation of finite self from infinite self and God, despite being illusion, is our primal anguish, the most painful experience possible. Whether conscious or unconscious, it denies us the feeling of self-worth and the sense of purpose and place in the universe. We're left with the agony of meaninglessness; it creates an emptiness that we're compelled to fill but can't. Separation from infinite self ramifies into all relationships. We're unable to experience life in its nature as polarities, so we fill the void with busyness, the detritus produced by duality. Lacking the genuine flow of life that occurs within polarities, we resort to the inauthentic in order to feel alive, producing what Edgar Allan Poe (1809-1849) called an "unfathomable longing of the soul to vex itself—to offer violence to its own nature—to do wrong for wrong's sake only."[35]

The pain and emptiness of separation are so traumatic that, while we long to return to union, we close off that avenue, fearing another separation like the one in infancy. The domain of ego, which we create in part to fill the vacuum, is a hard-won and proud accomplishment, and we protect it from the infinite, lest it be reabsorbed and leave us vulnerable again. Thus, we come to stand against the divine in the manner of Lucifer; yet, because we seek a way to rejoin it, we become at odds with ourselves.

The theme of separation is ancient and fundamental. It lies at the heart of tragic drama in the flaw that undermines the protagonist, dividing the person against him- or herself. Tragedy developed in Greece from religious rituals in which the god divides and in effect kills himself and is thereby born anew (as the New Year killing the Old Year; divinity, inherently timeless, has to divide into polarities to enter time) and reunited through this self-sacrifice.[36] In the ritual, the divine manifests into polarities to accomplish a purpose essential to life and its wholeness. In contrast, the dramatic protagonist achieves understanding and acceptance of his fate but does not have his life renewed. His reconciliation with the divine takes the form of enhanced wisdom but not reunion; painful separation remains, which he has learned to endure through insight. Tragedy arose in the sixth century B.C.E., contemporaneous with the origins of science and philosophy in Greece and with the formulation of wisdom traditions such as Taoism and Buddhism and within Judaism. This manifestation of new human mental capacities by which to approach both divine and earthly worlds included powerful abilities to abstract and to separate, including creating dualities from polarities. Developing from ritual, Greek tragedy both marked the arrival and dramatized the effects of this innovative mentality. Following this, Plato increased this abstracting ability by helping convert the dynamic fluidity of the older Greek language into propositions about the nature of things, relying on novel uses of the verb "to be."[37] This provided the basis of our language structure and thought: instead of describing relationships (including how good relates to its polarity evil), we speak of what a thing *is*, which allows for the reification of abstractions into codified beliefs and doctrines, such as Good deified and separate from Evil.

(An early prefiguration of this mental and spiritual division appears in *The Odyssey* of Homer. In Homer, although Pallas Athena is the goddess of wisdom, she is also famous for deception. Odysseus, her favorite and a great deceiver himself, despairs of ever recognizing her through her disguises; he mistrusts her, thinking she is mocking him. She places him under such a spell that he cannot even recognize his long-sought homeland when he returns at last.[38] Likewise, when another divinity gives him good advice to help him out of mortal peril, he agonizes: "O damned confusion! Can this be a ruse / to trick me . . . for some god's pleasure?"[39] Thus, Odysseus, whom Homer calls "canniest of men" and "the great tactician" who conquered Troy by guile, has difficulty discerning true divine guidance when he gets it. Homer is prophetic of the separative consequences of Greek philosophy and science (and our own) when he has Athena exclaim about Odysseus, "Always the same detachment!"[40])

The illusion of separation and its effects can be overcome by finite self when, after experiencing enough of the pain of spiritual isolation, it again seeks contact with and support from the divine. To separate from oneself—finite self from infinite self—is to take the prodigal journey. This is the journey of finite self in search of the meaning of the greatest gift, free will. What does it signify to be free to make all choices? Can one make a wrong choice? If one chooses a given possibility merely because one can, is this compulsion? What happens if one chooses to deny or separate oneself from the giver of free will, and has one been truly free if one does not try to do so? On the other hand, can one consider oneself free and yet always choose what is actually true for oneself: the imprint of the actual design of the divine?

On this subject it's worth stating again Plotinus's view, in MacKenna's words: "our exercise of 'free will' is simply an index of our ignorance and imperfection. If one knows the best . . . then one can only act in accordance with it . . . by . . . one's own free will."[41] Thus, freedom *of* choice in its purest manifestation crucially involves freedom *from* making choices that aren't relevant to one's higher nature and purpose, choices that arise from lack of awareness of one's nature and purpose. Actual freedom involves steadfastness in choosing to act in ways that are congruent with one's deepest truth. Any lesser expression of freedom is merely a place on the path of spiritual development, which one will surpass. Nietzsche wrote regarding artists: "only when they do nothing 'willfully' and everything 'of necessity' does their feeling of freedom, subtlety, [and] full powers . . . reach its height. In short, that necessity and 'freedom of the will' are one and the same when they create."[42]

From the standpoint of infinite self, all roads of the prodigal journey lead home to the feast of the fatted calf, which is the celebration of the awakening of finite self to infinite self. This honors not only the homecoming but also the fact that the prodigal daughter or son returns of her or his free will and brings priceless treasures of experience and self-knowledge. To infinite self, there has been no evil in the ungodliness of the journey, the separation, the behavior unworthy of one with such a heritage, or the forgetting and denial. This is the play of cosmic children who grow by means of their cosmic learning game. And whether finite self takes the spiritual high road or, as a prodigal, chooses the low road that leads to sleeping in pigsties, learning takes place, which assures the return to union with the higher self, there being no limit to the time available for this eventually to occur.

Origen allowed that, since the spiritual beings have assurance of their redemption, these in their freedom might once again become sated and neglect God, setting up a potential eternity of fall and return. (Origen didn't distinguish infinite self from soul in his spiritual beings. Neither infinite selves nor the higher aspects of finite self fall into separation. Infinite selves recreate their finite forms repeatedly; aspects of these creations do backslide as well as grow.) In saying that in the near-infinity of finite possibilities and a near-eternity of time it is inevitable that we must return to union, it's quite as logical that the opposite occurs (or both). This, however, neglects the nature of free will that Plotinus distinguished from simply having a choice, saying that it's the freedom from compulsion to choose what is not one's highest path. Why choose the highest course? We do this because that's who we are. Our nature and purpose is hard-wired in us by infinite self. We choose otherwise when we're early on our path or caught in illusion, but a vector of inner truth moves us toward self-knowledge and the freedom to be ourselves, unerringly in the end. Our cosmic existence offers us the time to do this; once free of illusion and ignorance, our free will choice is an eternity of union with infinite self, beyond time. Why would we then choose otherwise?[43]

It's easiest for us to conceive of this vector toward self-knowledge as functioning over time: to think of it as a linear progression toward a goal achieved at a point in future time. As we've seen, however, physics understands time to be non-linear; past, present, and future exist en bloc. As the linear movement of time is our illusion, we might say that we achieve our goal at any time or even at various times. While we perceive these times as constituting a progression toward the distant goal, they may in fact function within the infinite space-time continuum as a pattern of cumulative achievement of the goal that occurs at no particular time or rather outside time as we perceive it. Our linear time experience might juxtapose periods of utter entrapment in illusion with periods when we choose our highest path, leaving us with the feeling that we are not getting anywhere. However, from infinite self's standpoint, perhaps it is the accumulation of choosing the highest that counts, a tapestry of such choices, rather than a final ability to choose at some point. This addresses Origen's quandary of redemption and fall as well as the personal experiences of numerous sincere and struggling seekers who have their moments of illumination followed by times of frustrated groping in the dark. It's in alignment with the many spiritual disciplines that emphasize there is only now in which to live a spiritual life, and all choices are made in the moment. Does this contradict the idea of a vector of inner truth moving us toward freedom? I think both are true in a paradoxical relationship best described by the spiral of time. We go back and forth *and* move forward; from outside time, "when" we do something is meaningless, but from our perspective, there is a vector of time that provides a moral context to inform our choices.

The Source of All Evil

The ultimate origin of what we call evil is separativeness, awareness that's limited and compartmentalized, leading to suffering, ungodliness, and blasphemy. Thus, the author of Job puts forward as most evil not the calamity visited upon Job and his family or even the unjustness of it all but the possibility that Job, having had all this foisted on him by God, would curse God to his face. Job refuses such blasphemy, despite his anguish. "Curs[ing] you to your face"[44] is a succinct and graphic description of making God an "other," seeing God as separated from self. (Moses pointedly was not allowed to see God's face; to be face to face is to relate to an other.) To the author, this would be the epitome of evil.

The prodigal journey leads to degradation, despair, and suffering, prods that awaken finite self to the fact that it is separated, in its awareness, from infinite self. The crucial moment occurs when the prodigal finite self feels the necessity to swallow its pride and admit the humiliating fact that it's not doing so well alone and needs infinite self, though still conceiving this as external to itself. This test of pride can lead to rebellion and refusal to accept being merely part of a whole that includes both infinite and finite. In its rebellion, finite self insists it can be the whole and can deny and overthrow the order that relegates it to what it sees as lesser status; this amounts to an impossible attempt for finite self to be infinite and to claim divinity. It can see itself as able to usurp divinity because it is in fact divine in its infinite aspect, which it is in rebellion against; yet, it can only become divine in a lived, manifested way through integration. It usually projects this split and the resultant war within the self as a belief in a cosmic conflict between Good and Evil.

The war within the self also projects out, on a smaller scale, in the form of the last definition of evil, perverseness, defined earlier as a person deriving pleasure from pain or damage, especially if intentional. This form of evil is the hardest to come to terms with: the evil of a terrorist, torturer, or serial killer. How can we conceive of a human being with a divine aspect perpetrating such cruelty, and doing so within a cosmos created by a good God?

Scale is not at issue. The biblical statement that God knows when the smallest bird falls makes clear the relevant characteristic of the infinite: it is equally within the least and the greatest. It is the nature and quality of the event that matters, not the quantity; evil is evil, on whatever scale. This means that perverseness is all too available to study. The small cruelties of everyday life are the schooling for larger manifestations.

Some people have great difficulty containing their pain and may have little willingness to do so. They solve this problem in two ways.

First, they project. Unconsciously, they deny and suppress emotional pain regarding failures, shame, and guilt and start to see these in other people. Every person has an imperative need to protect at least some core positive self-image, and there's a strong drive to expand that core. This is basic, healthy narcissism, necessary and beneficial if progressively integrated into a maturing personality. If, however, it's wounded or threatened, it may defend itself by attacking the self-image of others by projecting what it has suppressed.[45] There will typically be some truth to a projection. The part that projects, itself largely unconscious, quite easily reads what's unconscious or unexpressed in others and targets somebody with a similar negative trait, even though the recipient may not be expressing it. What one suppresses functions as a sensitive antenna for this in others, and, finding it, justifies self-righteous demonization of them.

What we project onto another we temporarily avoid having to deal with in ourselves. But even if we, individually, divorce or distance ourselves our targets or, as society, suppress, jail, or kill whomever received our projection, we'll have to find another person or group on whom to pin it. Moreover, the other will probably react to our projection, projecting back in a self-perpetuating cycle that serves to avoid the real issue. What we separate ourselves from, through suppression internally or projection externally, we can't resolve. We can work on it only within ourselves, personally or societally.

The remarkable human capacity for self-delusion enhances the success of the suppression of knowledge about self and the projection of negative traits onto another. For example, research has shown how a wide range of Germans carried out the Holocaust with pride in doing a good job while in complete denial that they were perpetrating anything untoward, much less abhorrent.[46] Also relevant is the increasing awareness within the criminal justice system of the unreliability of eyewitness accounts, borne out by DNA evidence; likewise, studies of human perception demonstrate that the brain fills in gaps in our vision, so we experience seeing patterns that our eyes are not actually viewing. Human beings are well equipped to blithely sustain their suppression and projection.

The second way we solve the problem of what to do about pain that we can't contain involves transferring it to others. We discover early how to give it away. Those who've suffered abuse as children are more likely to abuse. Children learn to pick on and stigmatize certain kids on the playground. People discover how to damage almost anything in another person, from spiritual integrity to emotional well-being, from the ability to perform mentally to physical health. The payoff lies in the obvious difference between the other's experience and one's own. A self-aware friend told me how he noticed that he would involuntarily smile at seeing an animal that had been run over, because it reminded him, quite simply, "It's dead, and I'm not." Seeing distress in others relieves suppressed internal anguish, especially emotional pain, albeit temporarily; causing it feels like being in control of allotting pain. This can occur on an individual or group level. Projection and denial help here too: "They deserve it"; "It's good for them"; "They're not really human, so they don't matter." If we don't bear our own cross, the pain of living in finite form, we'll find someone or something else to crucify.

Psychological projection and the actual transfer of pain to another both necessarily involve a separation of self from other. This involves the same disconnect between subjective reality ("What I'm doing is right or mandatory, and anyway it doesn't hurt me") and objective fact (the suffering produced) that rationalization and denial facilitate. One may be aware of the pain but doesn't feel it empathetically. This can be due to brain anomalies or to separation from one's infinite self or fragmentation as finite self; a person who experiences her infinite self will have more empathy and be that much less able to project or offload pain.

To reiterate, separativeness, the self-isolation of finite from infinite self, is not evil from the standpoint of infinite self; it is growing pains. Nonetheless, within our separated and compartmentalized experiences as finite beings, we experience it as Evil through and through. It is an illusion, but it's dreadfully real to us; while it lasts, and while we act based on it, we must take it and its consequences extremely seriously. Simply to recognize that it's not evil in an infinite context doesn't let us as finite selves off the hook! We end Evil (the dualistic kind—and only we can end it) by removing the blinders placed on our awareness by separativeness. It is our choice to make: not to end pain but to experience it in a godly manner, and so to end suffering, as Buber suggests. Until we can do this thoroughly and act from transcendent awareness, we'll need to develop an ever more refined sense of morality and an acute awareness of the consequences of Evil. To see it as growing pains requires taking on much greater responsibility for our actions and being increasingly accountable for awakening from the illusion.

Does evil exist? Taking into account man's paradoxical nature, we can now answer definitively: yes and no. It does exist for us as finite selves in finite existence: necessarily as a polarity, and through our intervention as a duality; it does not exist for us as infinite selves. The dualistic, truly problematic kind is an illusion that finite selves create and then, when they're able to open to the grace and assistance of infinite self, dissolve. It is real to those who believe it and give power to it, and only we give it power. From no other standpoint does its existence make sense.

Did a divinity of good will create evil or at least allow it? From the standpoint of the wholeness of finite and divine self and taking responsibility for all aspects of self, we can say, yes, we did.

Resist Not Evil

Evil exists for us until we walk with God as whole beings. Until then, how shall we relate to it? We must not reject evil, despite its danger and the fact that to dwell in or express evil, whether as polarity or duality, is inappropriate to our nature. Evil and good as polarities are latent within God, and the negative polarity must come into existence with the positive when infinity manifests existence; evil is part of God's and the universe's wholeness. It could end only if good ended, polarities combining as pure being. The cost of trying to fashion something purely good is creating an Evil.

It's as bad to hate evil (which, if we do, we make into Evil) as to dwell in it because we become what we hate, join ourselves to it, and give it our energy. Hatred is a tie that powerfully binds, and the object of hatred will return repeatedly until we stop hating it; rejection and separation set up a fatal attraction and fascination. Neither can we afford to hate those whose behavior we deem evil, because this can help bind them to it as well as us to them; we must remember that it's not their natural path and they're simply on the prodigal journey. Love helps draw them back to their path.

Both good and evil deserve respect. The negative polarity is a teacher and worthy adversary that strengthens us, exposes our blind spots, and reveals who we are and are not; spiritual seekers often consider it a gift of the divine that spurs and guides growth. The positive polarity is our medium for manifestation. If we love evil rather than resisting it, if we accept it as part of God's wholeness, we can pass it by and not give it the power to be a force in our lives. In addition, love can produce unexpected results. The poet Novalis (1772-1801), discussing fairy tales, noted that in many examples,

> the moment one impossible thing becomes possible, simultaneously another impossible thing becomes unexpectedly possible: the hero overcoming himself simultaneously overcomes nature. A miracle occurs that grants him the contrary agreeable thing the moment the contrary disagreeable thing has become agreeable to him. For example, the conditions of the spell on a prince changed into a bear cease to exist as soon as the bear is loved for its own sake. Perhaps a like transformation would take place if a man could become fond of the evil in the world. The

> moment he could bring himself to cherish illness or suffering, he would hold in his embrace the most charming delight.[47]

Similarly, the Norse myth of the beloved god Baldur tells how Loki, a jealous trickster god, has him killed. The other gods try to arrange bringing him back to life, but this is possible only if all living beings agree. All do, except one ugly and neglected creature who refuses because until that time nobody ever visited or cared anything about her. So, the most beautiful and joy-bringing god couldn't live and bring pleasure to others because, in paying exclusive attention to him, they ignored the other polarity.

Nietzsche stated: "What is done out of love always happens beyond good and evil."[48] Love accepts and thereby heals separativeness, reunites us with the divine, and creates wholeness within us, encompassing positive and negative.

Yet, in the face of the enormities of evil in the past century alone, it seems more than a bit blithe to speak of the healing power of love, as if love allows us to turn bad into good and live happily ever after. What can love offer to deal with our astonishing capacity for evil? My answer is that because love must encompass the fact of potentially losing what we love, it gives us the power to grieve and forgive our losses. Because evil takes something valued from life and is usually seen to do so unjustly, it's desperately hard to forgive (or be forgiven for) these losses and trespasses, but grieving and forgiveness are the difficult and lengthy work required of us that we may live with evil and not dualize it. To grieve or lament carries us in an organic process from wound and sorrow through healing to greater wholeness. Young suggests that lamentation originally developed as a means to contain the ritual violence of sacrifice, keeping it from spreading; lamentation is part of the renunciation and transformation of violent energy.[49] In the terms used here, we renounce acting out one polarity but do not separate ourselves from it; by grieving its effects and not separating, we transform its energy and transmute its consciousness without dividing the polarities.

Who laments? Traditionally, women, their iconic exemplars being Mary and the Egyptian goddess Isis. As our culture moves from masculine to feminine emphasis and as women move into greater power and traditionally male roles, it's essential that they remember how to lament, that they teach men, and that men embrace this. Who forgives? Again, traditionally, women more than men. Forgiveness is likewise vital for men to learn to do more willingly and quickly than in the past, considering that they usually wield the guns. Men, especially but not exclusively, need to learn what's actually involved in receiving forgiveness. Forgiven by his woman, a man often feels he need only apologize (if that), rather than look within himself for the source of his behavior and determine if it has basis in higher truth and, if not, change it. (The change won't necessarily be what the forgiver has in mind). Women, too, have room to improve. Learning to forgive and receive forgiveness is crucial because the most evil thing about Evil is that it perpetuates itself by eliciting reactions. Love's powers of grieving and forgiveness cut this short.

Because the rituals that structure grieving are downplayed and overlooked in our culture, many people are at a loss to understand what's happening when they're in the grieving process. In some cultures, death rituals celebrate, memorialize, and express thankfulness for the person's life, helping the deceased on her way and giving expression to the feelings of the mourners. Ancient Egyptians, mesmerized by death, had a keen appreciation for the value of ritual. Their myths tell how grieving enabled Isis to transmute the effect of the god Set's murder of her brother/husband Osiris. Through grieving, she bore Osiris in mind so that he was, in Young's words, "present in his absence,"[50] and she thus sustained his being, which in turn nourished the land's fertility. To *bear in mind* is to maintain awareness. Dualistic thinking and the conflicts it engenders degrade and limit awareness. To love, which includes grieving, is to remember. Isis bore Osiris in mind gently and persistently, searching for him when he was missing and later when Set had dismembered him. Missing the missing, remembering the dismembered, she was able to piece him back together; he was changed but not lost to her or Egypt. This is not just a woman's task; it is a capability of the feminine within each of us: to lovingly, consciously bear inevitable pain willingly, rather than suppress, reject, resent, or put it onto another. It is to sorrow but also to enhance life. We love, grieve, forgive, and accept so that we may receive divine grace. No loss is inherently Evil. If we accept love's joy and grief (the latter mitigated by lamentation and forgiveness), we keep both polarities in play in our awareness. Then, the negative polarity can serve its purpose as an essential of life (the same way that Set was a preserver of the world as well as a force of chaos), rather than turning against life as it does in dualistic Evil. Set and Horus, the sun god and son of Isis and Osiris (after she reconstituted him), were always in conflict, but this conflict maintained a dynamic balance and thereby sustained the world, a very different relationship than the later one between God and the Devil.

The questions we've examined in this chapter are age-old yet fresh in their urgency as America makes war on terror. The idea that we can eliminate evil is a spiritual illness. We *can* eliminate the dualistic kind by learning to think in polarities; this would greatly benefit domestic and international affairs but would require that we abandon our great modern quest to eliminate all the negatives of life, from inconveniences up to sorrow and death. Our belief in progress and happy endings serves us poorly here. We can and should try to mitigate these negatives and transform their energy, but wisdom teachings perennially instruct that the greatest benefit comes not from making war on them but learning how to live with them. They'll always be with us, and we'll always have problems; liberation from Evil requires that we no longer make enemies of our problems.

If we want the beauty and joy of the divine in our lives, we can't deny, repress, lose, or cast out any part of self, of our experience, or of the divine. The good shepherd doesn't look for the lost sheep out of sentimentality. Whether lost sheep or ugly wretch, we'd best go find what's missing or ignored, make his or her acquaintance and make things right, or there will be Hell to pay.

17

FAITH

Faith receives, love gives. No one will be able to receive without faith. No one will be able to give without love. Because of this, in order that we may indeed receive, we believe, and in order that we may love, we give.

—*The Gospel of Philip*

Give all, for all is yours!

—Hadewijch, *The Garden of Perfect Virtues*

Eve initiated an important stage in our evolutionary journey with what has been interpreted as an intrepid and courageous act.[1] She saw, according to Genesis, "that the tree was to be desired to make one wise"[2] and took fruitful action.

Our spiritual evolutionary destiny is to return to the Garden of Eden, that is, to union with God. When we have fulfilled this, we'll still carry the imprint of our experiences in exile. We'll still have eaten the fruit that gives knowledge of the duality of Good and Evil and won't have forgotten this knowledge. Moreover, we will then eat of the other tree, of eternal and infinite life, with God's joyous blessing. This second tree started our journey; our expulsion was not due to disobedience in eating of the first tree but because we couldn't remain in Eden lest we eat of the second also—at that point in our evolution. When we were in the garden, according to Genesis, we could have eaten of the second tree as long as we refrained from the first, the only forbidden fruit.[3] Through eating it, "the man has become like one of us" in his knowledge;[4] to have both that knowledge and the eternal life of the second tree would have been detrimental to our evolution then. The second tree will mark our completion; through it we embrace eternal life, regained by reunifying with infinite self.

(To add to the debate over the plural first-person pronoun used by God in the Genesis verse just quoted, I suggest this indicates an intuitive, perhaps unconscious, recognition by the authors that the decision was taken not so much by God as by God children, the infinite selves. God children are omnipotent and omniscient within and throughout their finite self-extensions and are most directly concerned with their creations' evolution. They are the creators of those involved; earlier God says, "Let us make humankind in our image, according to our likeness."[5])

At the time of our Edenic union with our divine nature, we weren't fully formed; we lacked self-awareness. Only by eating the fruit that gives knowledge of duality did our eyes open in self-consciousness so that we knew shame for being naked, for being so innocently unaware that we were finite and had limit and form when a moment before we were in full union with the infinite. (Being naked only matters if you think it does; once you think it, everything changes irrevocably.) With this knowledge, we passed into the exclusively finite world of the dualistic mind. Only then could the choice of hiding from God, that is, of making the divine a part of a duality and then separating from it, present itself. Only then could we conceive of lying, of being false to ourselves in order to avoid awareness of the enormity of this transformation. (Adam says he lied due to fear of God because of being naked[6]— that is, because he hadn't known his limits. Remembering our recent unawareness of our limits, we suddenly felt exposed to the possibility that we'd overstep ourselves; later, guilt covers and protects us from the knowledge of our shameful exposure.) At that point we recognized that God is different from us, unlimited in power, but we didn't know what that meant and so were afraid; we won't understand until the end of our long exile's journey of separation.

Previously, not only were we oblivious to our limits as finite beings, they didn't matter. Only with the knowledge of Good and Evil as opposites could we do ungodly and perverse Evil. If, as finite selves with finite minds, we had knowledge of the possibilities of Good and Evil but no knowledge of their consequences (which we would gain following our expulsion from Eden), we couldn't eat of the tree of eternal life lest we access the unlimited resources and duration of the infinite self without the experience to use them wisely. In this condition, we would have been capable of wreaking cosmic havoc and likely would have done so. To avoid entrapment in this evil eternally by eating of the second tree, we would need to leave Eden. To avoid Buber's "full demonry," we would know death, thereby gaining the knowledge of the consequences of Good and Evil as we make our slow return to Eden. Even so, at times our technical knowledge and destructive capacity outstrip our moral maturity.

Duality offers the rational mind possibilities so seductive that we fell far into its labyrinth of concept and analysis before gaining enough experience to begin to find the link to our divine nature, the golden thread that leads us out of the labyrinth. As we came to know the nature of Good and Evil by acting them out, we gained the perspective necessary to see our greater self clearly; through our long, painful experiences outside Eden we've grown to where we can integrate finite and infinite selves in wholeness and say, as in the New Testament, "the Father and I are one." Had we stayed in Eden, we'd never have fulfilled our destiny of knowing both infinity and the finite world of limit and consequence.

When we've achieved sufficient experience, we'll at last eat of the tree of life. The two trees represent the two aspects of self. The first signifies the finite self and its purpose of learning by way of free will and the results of choices (and, perhaps inevitably, by separating for a time from infinite self). The second tree symbolizes our eternal self. Eating of it upon our return to the Garden equates with the feast of the fatted calf on the return of the prodigal, which is the celebration and reward for completion of this passage to awareness and self-knowledge. Understanding the Eden story relative to finite and infinite selves, the action of the prodigal's father seems more justified than it might otherwise. The complaint of the brother who stayed home, upset at the use of a fatted calf to celebrate his miscreant brother's sudden reappearance, betrays his own lack of understanding of the nature of the infinite. Not only has this brother partaken of the father's wealth all along, but the father as infinite self has infinite resources to bestow; the use of a calf in no way diminishes what's available to the sedentary sibling. This brother hasn't learned to relate to the infinite in a way that would enable him to receive what is his, while the prodigal progeny was able to ask for and receive his inheritance, the resources of the infinite. This request parallels the eating of the fruit of the first tree; receiving his inheritance, the prodigal goes away, like Adam and Eve, and gains the experience, often painful, of finite life of all kinds. In doing so, he fulfills his purpose, however smelly the process, and returns bringing the gift of experience to infinite self. What he has learned allows him to receive even greater good and goods, bestowed joyously by infinite self upon its creation and limited only by finite self's (that is, either son's) capacity to receive.

Faith Is a Kind of Perception

There was a period during our prodigal journey, the journey away from Eden, when we felt most separate from infinite self and when we thus especially needed to have faith because in our separation we were blind to our own truths. Those who were further ahead on the path and had clearer vision described, for the guidance of the many who had little perception, the truths that they perceived. This was necessary at the time;

most members of humanity needed to believe—to have faith— in these descriptions from teachers perceived to be good, wise, authoritative, or righteous. People often accepted them in blind faith because they were lost in the midst of their blindness; however, blind faith is never necessary because there is always in each person the guidance of inner resonance to spiritual descriptions that are at least close to the mark, even if the person can't explain the resonance. Nonetheless, at that point a large measure of belief was necessary, and those who lost this faith were truly lost because their own inner knowing was still insufficient to guide them.

As humanity has grown spiritually, inner eyes, ears, and other senses have started to open, and we begin to recognize that the foundation of mature faith is perception, that its basis is increasingly a clearer discernment of what truly is. Hebrews expresses this: "what is seen was made from things that are not visible."[7] Likewise, "faith is the assurance ["substance" in the King James Version] of things hoped for, the conviction ["evidence"] of things not seen";[8] assurance and conviction are mental conditions, while substance and evidence are perceived, albeit subtly. Abiding experience—mental, sensory, as well as emotional—of one's actual nature and infinite self is the foundation of actual faith. This kind of faith requires radical openness to one's deepest inner truth and the willingness to act on that with perseverance. Faith opens the finite heart to the "heart" of the infinite, and finite mind to infinite mind. This inner experience combines with extrapolation from what we have experienced in life to determine how much effort and resources to put into pursuing a particular course of action. To expand knowledge requires journeys into an unknown. Faith carries us though the unknown; therefore, faith precedes and leads to knowledge, which comes from well considered and closely observed experience. We must choose our journeys wisely and pay attention along the way.

As our faith becomes less blind, we develop greater confidence in ourselves and our ability to interact consistently and truthfully with our higher self. We envision our spiritual path ourselves, rather than relying on others' visions. In this vein, Lao Tzu urges,

> Exterminate the sage, discard the wise,
> And the people will benefit a hundredfold.[9]

We learn to extrapolate from our spiritual experiences to plot a course for ourselves. We realize that our sense of purposefulness, the amorphous sense that our existence has meaning, is the finite evidence that guides us toward full realization of our purpose.

Less blinded, we realize that the value of faith doesn't lie in achieving absolute truth. Rather, growing faith in ourselves and our relationship with higher self allows us to be open to the unknown and unexpected, to the process of finding ever-greater approximations of truth. It facilitates our discovering, undaunted, that we've largely been wrong in our prior assumptions and beliefs. We become more open to others' truths, not as *the* truth that we should follow but as an expression of truth that works for them and may open our eyes in new directions. Faith provides penetrating vision of self and others, not in judgment but in awe. Spiritual seekers have long recognized faith as the way to know the infinite, not comprehensively—impossible for the finite mind—but with insight into its essence.

Through faith, we become more responsible for ourselves, a major purpose of our prodigal journey. This sense of responsibility can produce uncomfortable reactions. One is uneasiness with and distrust of external authority as a person becomes aware of her own authority and wants to express it. Another is unworthiness, guilt, or despair over the added responsibility or over perceiving spiritual potentials that she's not living up to yet—those on the path of awakening experience at any given time more of their innate capabilities than they believe they can manifest, because awareness precedes full expression; without understanding this, they may feel like spiritual underachievers. The latter reaction is a hazard of the path that can motivate regression toward external sources of absolute spiritual authority.

Humanity has grown spiritually to the point that we must go beyond a faith based on resonance and on extrapolation from experience. We're capable of truly understanding. Part of our new responsibility is to examine the reasons for all commandments and ethics presented by others or tradition. We've become more conscious, and we must have conscious confirmation of what we hear and resonate to. We must ask not so much, "What is Good?" but "What is the good it produces?" This is in keeping with Matthew, "You will know them by their fruits,"[10] and with modern scientific methodology: we cannot know the thing, only its response to experimental stimuli. Faith guides us in the direction of things hoped for and things intuited but not seen; now we need to get there and examine for ourselves the evidence of the good produced.

Faith's evolution requires that intuition and science mutually inform each other, since either alone can be—and often has been—incomplete and misleading. Posited as science versus religion, there can be no real meeting ground. Science and actual faith, however, are on remarkably similar footing, both founded on experience—physical and intuitive—and on the formulation of predictive hypotheses based on that experience. We must keep faith in the value and validity of faith: not blind but eyes-wide-open, experience-affirming faith. Then we can make a good-faith effort and maintain faith in ourselves while we cross the chasm between choosing to act based on our best guess and carrying the action through to completion, by which we know the truth of the matter. Faith perseveres; it provides a bridge between beginning in the reality we know and finishing in the actuality we intuit to be possible when we can't know for sure how or whether we'll succeed in getting there. Faith that is not blind allows us to keep our senses open to experiences that differ from our initial prediction; we can thus change course as needed, without losing faith. Faith enables us to wholeheartedly participate in the cosmic learning game.

18

Why We Lost the Infinite Self, and What to Do with It Now That We've Found It

What's freedom for? To know eternity.
—Theodore Roethke, "I Knew a Woman"

Ideas and perceptions of the infinite self have been available to human beings at a minimum for two thousand five hundred years, going back at least to Zoroaster. These ideas produce freedom and an expanded sense of self. This also raise challenging questions: If they're so beneficial, why have they led such a precarious existence? Why has the infinite self been so strongly resisted by human beings?

Part of the reason may be the previously discussed theory regarding the prevention of invasions from the divine realm. Another part is that authoritarian power structures can't abide such a vision of individual human worth and dignity. Throughout the centuries, the implications of the idea that every person is creative, eternal, divine, unified with God (at least in some part of themselves), and therefore able to directly experience divine truth were recognized as threatening to the power of political and ecclesiastical hierarchies. Widespread awareness of this divine aspect of self would have imposed inconvenient limits on the justifications that theocratic, aristocratic, or totalitarian elites could use to validate concentrating power in their hands. Dictatorial force must be definite and unquestionable; therefore, authoritarian ruling groups often have kept the paradoxical nature of humanity and the cosmos unexplored or hidden. Church and state have at times worked hand and hand to destroy, conceal, or deride this knowledge or make its study dangerous. Examples are abundant, such as the war against Zoroaster, who taught a democratization of religion and a blissful immortality that included women and the underclass as much as the privileged and priestly. Others include the murder of Pythagoras by a local tyrant, the crucifixion of Jesus, the destruction of non-canonical writings in the newly-Christianized

Roman Empire, the excommunications of Origen and Meister Eckhart, and the crusade that exterminated the Cathars.

An extraordinary aspect of human nature is the willingness of people to hazard agony and death to speak their spiritual truth; in myriad instances throughout the ages, they have risked all to espouse their view of humanity's relationship to the divine. A person's spiritual truth can be so totally compelling that to deny it, even in the face of death, would feel like cutting off half of himself. In spiritual fact, it *would* mean this; when a person is aware of his spiritual totality, separating finite self from infinite self or the divine feels like a greater death than loss of the body.

Despite this remarkable readiness to sacrifice for belief, another large part of the reason why the idea of the infinite self meets such resistance is that many people don't want the responsibility that goes with self-knowledge. As amazing as the willingness to die for truth and God has been, equally notable is the compliance of multitudes in allowing the usurpation of their freedom and its attendant responsibility by those who claim to show the way or provide protection. Many people have readily, even desperately, given away their freedom and power.

What is it about freedom and responsibility that's such a hot potato? Part of the answer lies in the effects of early development on the very structure of human finite consciousness in its interface with infinite self.

Facing One's Limits: Early Development and the Loss of the Infinite

We begin life immersed in the infinite. It takes a lot to entice us out.

Newborns have no discrimination of subject and object, according to Piaget.[1] He describes the consciousness of earliest infancy as having little of our adult sense of time, space, or causality. He saw in infants the beginning of an ability to distinguish opposites; the experiences of lack, the emptiness of hunger, and being less than whole cause an infant to begin making differentiations such as those necessary for nursing.[2]

It takes time before an infant's developing ability to discriminate dominates and submerges the experience of undifferentiated oneness, but this ability is essential; each person has to learn to filter the barrage of sensory stimuli she encounters and to sort out what's significant, learning this directly through pain and pleasure or from significant others. When the discriminating mind finally achieves ascendancy, it allows only a minute fraction of available sense data into awareness; lost to maturing consciousness is the oceanic infinite and its limitless love, light, and passion for life. The ability to make distinctions is the foundation of adult awareness and its cognitive and verbal structures, and since at the time of our earliest experiences we mostly lacked this capacity, we have no access now to early memories. Great effort is required, often through spiritual discipline, to reestablish sustained and conscious contact with the childhood oceanic experience and more still to synthesize it with adult awareness.

During a child's first stage of development, she progresses from a sense of being infinite (undifferentiated from her environment), through feeling omnipotent, to experiencing her limits as her parents and others become less immediately responsive. Within this stage, psychoanalyst Erik Erikson (1902-1994) asserts, the child must develop a "basic trust" of the world. This stage "seems to introduce into psychic life (and become prototypical for) a sense of inner division and universal nostalgia for a paradise forfeited. It is against this powerful combination of a sense of having been deprived, divided, and abandoned—that basic trust must maintain itself throughout life."[3] This crisis of growth presents the need to be able to develop a realistic sense of self and one's boundaries.

Erikson sees the goal of the next stage of a child's development as autonomy, with shame and doubt the dysfunctional alternatives.[4] Shame is one of the earliest "civilizing" human emotions. It appears at the developmental horizon where an individual's self-awareness as an actor in the world begins. He says that shame results from being seen by others before one is ready; the child becomes enraged at her powerlessness to force others not to look at her. Shame is that rage turned in the only safe direction, at self.[5]

In this second developmental stage, the child still is close to the sense of being infinite and omnipotent and may fall back into it readily, but he also begins to sense being a self-governing person interacting with others. These two senses are contradictory (paradoxical): being omnipotent, yet having to deal with physical limits and with people who have their own will and thus limit one. Erikson states, "Shaming exploits an increasing sense of being small, which can develop only as the child['s] . . . awareness permits him to note the relative measures of size and power."[6] If he oversteps himself, misjudging his finite strength, influence, or competence, others may make him feel shame. If his incipient self-awareness, still somewhat unified and identified with his infinite self, drifts overmuch into a sense of boundlessness, others may give him an abrupt and rude yank back into the finite, reminding him that he's subject to its limits and that when immersed in the infinite, he risks incurring harm or the negative reactions of others. Ridicule, anger, or punishment for this may make him feel fraudulent in his sense of limitlessness, causing him to forever after associate those painful feelings with the experiences deriving from his infinite self. He can't escape the fact that his small body is not infinite and instead has a face, which blood immediately rushes to, making him red-faced with shame. The heat of the flush serves as a powerful reminder of a person's vulnerable skin—of his limits and exposure to danger.

This shaming firmly and effectively, if sometimes traumatically, shifts identity to a child's finite, humiliated self. If the shame is too intense, the child may retreat to the familiar pleasures of the previous stage. If she is found out in this regress, her shame will greatly increase and may produce timidity or anxiety due to unsureness that she will not forget herself again. If others are empathetic or shame her only mildly, she will have a chance to expand her identity to include both finite and infinite selves.

The normal response by a child to his conflicting experiences of his nature is the development of autonomy, providing a sense of "his privileges and his limitations, his obligations and his rights," in Erikson's words; this assures him that autonomy is a good and safe thing to develop in preparation for adulthood.[7] Most people get through the psychological aspects of this change in reasonably sound fashion, becoming relatively happy and productive adults, but another element of healthy growth in this phase—maintaining awareness of the infinite—lacks societal recognition and is enormously difficult to achieve in Western culture. Thus, while a person may mature psychologically and socially, creating a functioning, self-accepting finite personality, she does not fully mature spiritually.

Healthy parenting supports a child so she's not overwhelmed by the feeling of having failed, with resulting loss of face, to present the proper (finite) part of herself to those she's dependent on. This support sustains the certainty of unlimited love her family provided in her first stage of development, and that feeling will allow her to stay connected or later reunite with her internal source of unlimited love, her infinite self. She can then face the world with confidence, aware of but unfazed by her limits. She can unashamedly aim for the stars without losing her footing in the world.

A Challenge to Our Boundaries

All living form requires boundaries, such as skin and cell walls. Consciousness has the same imperative; the developing psyche must establish a sense of being an autonomous self, secure within its limits. One of our first great accomplishments in life is to establish a stable and distinct individual identity. Then it takes years to define one's own thinking and distinguish one's opinions and perspectives from those of parents, teachers, and cohort. These are exacting and painful tasks, requiring much attention and energy, and we vigorously defend what we achieve.

Our original infantile experience of oceanic infinity represents at every step a double challenge to the successful completion of these essential undertakings. Its enticing undertow threatens to draw us back into its indeterminate but still embracing and comforting limitlessness, yet we learned very early how frightening and shameful giving in to that can be and how valuable it is to strive to emerge as a distinct person among other finite selves. If we navigate these waters successfully, we develop a fluid, creative mentality that enjoys the richness and vast potential of the paradoxical nature of finite existence. Those who mistrust themselves and fear they'll be submerged are prone to substitute for paradoxical awareness the security and rigidity of dualistic and exclusively rationalistic thinking, forming the impermeable boundaries, between opposites such as self and other or limit and wide-openness, that lessen the stress of the responsibility of freedom and self-knowledge. Through the struggle for individuality, we mature spiritually, but for those in the process, infinity can feel like terrifying chaos, messy imperfection, or a gaping maw to escape or avoid—the maw of regression to the vulnerability of infant oceanic immersion.

This struggle goes far toward explaining why human beings have had limited awareness of infinite self, and why they have so often opted for authoritarian religious or political leaders to impose laws that keep boundaries safely unyielding. Now, however, we approach a new step in our spiritual maturation with greater security in our individual identity as unique finite selves. We're entering an era in which we'll recognize that while God is neither dictatorial nor personal, wholeness involves a personal relationship with the divine, experienced cognitively, emotionally, and viscerally throughout us. We'll discover a spiritual and psychological existence that in the past only a few could embrace: a highly developed and individuated finite nature that's an integrated part of a whole and doesn't have to fight to establish its egoic separateness. Ego isn't inherently separative; it can evolve to include our actual identity, it serves important spiritual functions, and it can appreciate wholeness as our highest calling, so that we can cease endlessly trying to get ahead and stop the incessant activity of finite mind churning out mental and material clutter.

Every generation seeks its own identity, character, and distinctiveness (in ways often distasteful to the previous one), as does every person; the irony is that we've been hiding—have had to hide—from our actual identity, in order to develop a strong ego and a firmly established autonomous sense of self as an individual. Now we need to find our infinite self again to know our complete identity, lest we fall prey to despair or pointlessness, individually and collectively. The separative egoic sense of identity for which we've struggled so long is now our greatest obstacle as well as an essential achievement and steppingstone.

Before taking this or any spiritual step, each person must honestly evaluate where she is in her development and exactly what she's ready for. Psychologist Abraham Maslow (1908-1970) laid out a hierarchy of needs that an individual must meet before she can fulfill those of a spiritual nature; Roberto Assagioli's (1888-1974) psychological system likewise emphasizes that personal psychosynthesis must occur before spiritual psychosynthesis. Mental, emotional, and physical preparation necessarily precedes fruitful integration of the infinite: sorting out dreams and desires, building health, creating a balanced life. More and more individuals have done enough work that, secure in their individual identity, they're ready to experience a larger identity. There's no hurry, however, and from a spiritual standpoint, there's no place a person ought to be other than where she is; no one's getting ahead of or behind anyone else. We should move at our own best pace.

Your Experience Is Paramount

I suggest the idea of the infinite self simply as an approach to common experiences to help make sense of them, give them context, and aid in making decisions based on the truth of who you are. Your own experience is what counts. If the notion of the infinite self leads to clearer perception and a better understanding of yourself, it will have served its purpose.

Its most important utility lies in giving a person a greater sense of individual significance and potential. This leads to an enhanced feeling of responsibility for our world's fate and greater confidence in having the capacity to engage it, using the tools within us provided by infinite self.

As we've seen, to posit the existence of God children, infinite selves of unique and divine identity, is to say something substantially different than that we are all one in God. How we look at these things is extraordinarily important; the evolution of these views is most consequential for the history of human consciousness. Bitter words and bloodshed have long attended such differences, yet doctrinal conflicts have their basis in false premises because all spiritual statements are only approximations. For example, to say we are one in God is in its way as true as to assert that we are unique God children, which are infinitely diverse and eternally unified with God. To emphasize the no-self of Buddhism, on the one hand, or to posit personal and divine individual identity, on the other, is only to accentuate a particular aspect of a paradoxical complementarity. We can never finitely express the entire truth of the infinite, but we must keep trying, continuously refining our conjectures while recognizing their inherent limitations.

The infinite self, or even the infinity of the divine, is a dangerous idea. Many ideas are perilously misleading if decoupled from their counterpart polarities and made literal and absolute. Currently ominous is the belief that, because God is infinite and will provide infinitely (either now or after the end of days), there's no need to conserve resources or address overpopulation. The truth that the infinite divine can provide infinitely is lacking its complement: that the finite is the expressive agent of the infinite and must find ways to make those infinite resources available and generally act in a prudent manner. (A less spiritual analog was the dot-com bubble of the late 1990's, based on the idea that information technology was so radically different that it could somehow create wealth endlessly, so economic principles and business plans no longer mattered.) Just as experiencing the infinite is dangerous to a young child if it inhibits her developing her finite autonomy and boundaries, so the solutions that enable her to do so become harmfully imbalancing later if she doesn't go beyond them to fluidly encompass her full paradoxical makeup and the polarities of her world and its crises.

No absolute statements can be made about the nature of self or cosmos because these are mysteries past words, not in the sense of being hidden or confusing but of being beyond rational comprehension, subject only to intuitive, mythic, or poetic unfolding. We can take paradoxical experiences as working truths and embrace them wholeheartedly without making them absolute. Dualistic thinking currently posits a particularly pernicious false opposition: spiritual perception or religious conviction in conflict with relativism. Dualism denies that one can have complete faith in one's own experience or belief while accepting, even supporting, the experiences and beliefs of others as valid for them. Instead of this false opposition, we need a sort of loyal opposition, which is a core principle of the democratic process enabling civil interaction between differing views to persist over time and bring forth greater truth. The responsibility of the minority party isn't to vilify and undermine the governing party but to develop and advocate new and better ideas. To demean, revile, or kill someone who disagrees with one's truth is to misunderstand the process of progressively penetrating and unfolding an ultimately unknowable truth. This process should be the new paradigm for all investigation, scientific or spiritual.

Nonetheless, what we hold to be true is crucially important. Though we may recognize that the infinite truth of cosmos and divinity contains all possible statements without bias, at particular times one or another statement can have extraordinary utility. To declare that we exist as distinct infinite identities helps to clarify our vision of ourselves. It supports the evolution of our paramount aspirations and helps us take greater responsibility for wise and loving outcomes.

19

Conclusion: Politics, Ethics, and The Infinite's Manifestation in Polarities

In the last analysis we arrive at the circle of infinity, that utmost limit to which in every sphere of thought the human intellect is brought if it is not playing with its subject.

—Tolstoy, *War and Peace*

As I began to be politically aware in my late teens, first embracing the politics of my family and then swinging 180 degrees, I experienced, each in turn, that the basic philosophies of both sides of the political divide were compelling. How could I not appreciate the virtues and values of individual responsibility, morality, opportunity, lifting oneself up through one's own efforts, and standing in defense of democracy against attack? Yet, how could I not see the darker aspects of unbridled capitalism and self-interest, the need to protect the inevitable losers in the economic free-for-all, and the obligation to address racism, sexism, and environmental degradation? Both obviously expressed truth. Each side said the other was wrong and a bad lot besides. Having stood in both camps, I felt there was more going on than one or the other's enlightened idealism or idiocy, honesty or knavery, self-interest or sincere concern.

I realized that the political left and right between them have a whole truth. Each has part, intermixed with a lot of fantasy, wish fulfillment, dogmatism, and programs for self-aggrandizement. Each projects the problematic concomitants of the truth onto the other side. Each can feel wholly virtuous and insightful based on the veracity of the half-truth that it holds to be self-evident. Each sees only what's missing in the other side's world-view.

As I studied other political and social systems and developed some historical perspective, I saw a persistent pattern. In any situation, the whole truth will be divided between competing groups or individuals, regardless of what they're competing for: scarce material resources, recognition, spiritual "election," love. It doesn't matter how similar the religion, race, ethnicity, or any other distinguishing characteristics of groups or individuals may seem to outsiders, because a dividing line can and will be found. Each lays claim to one side, and on the other each has an enemy against which to fight the good fight. Many instances of racism between members of the same racial group or sub-group are as virulent as those between races. What's on one's own side becomes one's truth to defend; most anything on the other appears false, reprehensible, and dangerous. We split hairs and from that manage to create a cosmic dualism.

For example, many observers suspect America of needing to have an antagonist, an evildoer to be its foil and a target for its fears—an enemy to receive, in psychological terms, its projected shadow. We're unsettled and anxious when we don't know whom to blame or fear. Two generations had definite and dangerous enemies, fascists and communists, who helped define our national agenda and political debate. In the nineties, after losing the second of these, we made unsatisfying attempts to fill the role with immigrants (legal and illegal), Japanese industrialists, Chinese communists, and terrorists (more remote and appearing far less lethal than now). The September 2001 attacks provided an enemy whose shadowy, amorphous nature is well suited to receive our projections.

This phenomenon of division and antagonism makes sense in light of the manifestation of the infinite in polarities and the dualities we create from those. Contrasting world-views will develop within any human grouping. The nature of polarities understood scientifically as electromagnetism, philosophically as yin and yang, and psychologically as masculine and feminine can similarly be seen in politics and other arenas of competition: the polarities of honest opinion are complementarities, and neither polarity can or should attempt to exist without the other. Their coexistence is essential for defining and articulating a range of options and solutions. Crucially, how they interact is more important than the outcome of the specific issues they contest .

A political point of contention is not a dividing line but an interface, an opportunity for mutual interpenetration and creative interaction. In politics as in any aspect of life, the complementary interaction of polarities offers a chance to move beyond the limits of finite self and transcend differences to work for the good of the whole. A specific outcome regarding a budget deficit, school prayer, or gun control is secondary to the healing of community the process can engender. When, because we have little training in paradoxical thinking, we see left and right as constituting a duality rather than polarities, it's hard to get beyond identification with particulars. Dualistic thinking leads to gridlock. We don't recognize the creative potential missed if we see politics as inherently dirty and unspiritual. It loses civility and becomes a winner-take-all fight rather than a dynamic, interactive process.

Enlightened Self Interest Is Enlightened Responsibility

The spiritual evolutionary step we're taking, moving beyond duality, requires increased recognition of our actual responsibility for nurturing all people and all life that we affect directly or indirectly. This, as we've seen, needs the counterbalance of enlightened self-interest: taking full responsibility for one's own well-being and recognizing the limits of one's responsibility toward others, thus avoiding unnecessary self-denial or self-sacrifice. These two arenas of responsibility appear to be a primary duality separating right and left, but because recognizing the infinity of self expands enlightened self-interest to include all that we affect and that affects us and leads to thinking in terms of whole systems, they constitute a polarity. Thus, it's in our greatest self-interest to find solutions that work for both self and system.

If narrow self-interest causes us to view political interaction as a combat zone in a zero-sum game necessarily producing winners and losers, the natural flow of infinite life between the polarities will decrease, escalating antagonism and scarcity. What should be an area of interpenetration becomes a sticking point producing tension, defensiveness, and hostility. If we define our side as good and the other as bad, what remains is half a truth resulting in half a loaf as the best possible outcome. Duality always diminishes us.

If the zone of interaction is seen as a nexus where the infinite interrelates with itself by way of its polarities of manifestation, those on the other side appear in a different light, and we can recognize their half of the truth as what's missing from our own. A win-lose situation transmutes into an inspired, generative, and revelatory process serving the enlightened self-interest of both parties. The point of interaction becomes an opening to the infinite and to previously inconceivable solutions for the seemingly unsolvable.

This may sound too idealistic and impractical for real-world problems, but the Constitutional Convention that created the United States provides an example of such a process and such a solution. The delegates achieved a progressive ideal, the inclusion of all the people (using the then-current definition of "people") in the political process, giving each person fundamental rights and seeking the common good, but they did this by means of a conservative recognition of human nature, that people act in what they perceive to be their own self-interest. They employed and elevated self-interest as the driving force animating the checks and balances between the branches of government. A previously unheard-of structure of government came from men with conflicting views of politics and human nature, employing the truths offered by each side in the debates. The event still amazes us because we so rarely allow polarities to actually interact.

What would make this more typical? While our system of government has held up remarkably well, it's being sorely tested by an overemphasis on self-interest expressed in lobbying, earmarks, buying influence through large political donations, etc. Politics grows increasingly "polarized," that is, dualistic. In view of the adage that people get the government they deserve, to achieve more just and beneficial outcomes we need to educate people to understand how each part of a system affects a larger context, which in turn affects the part as well. This must begin with the individual as a system: understanding our own physical, emotional, mental, and spiritual components and how the needs of each of these parts, including those we reject, affect and are affected by the totality of self. We can then recognize how our individual interests interact with our larger interests as a member of a group, taking into account the disempowered. If we learn to experience that spiritually we're infinite, we will recognize our interests are large indeed. The combination of healthy self-love and self-respect, derived from experiencing infinite self's love for its creation along with educated awareness of what creates the healthiest environment for the person, yields the enlightened self-interest necessary for the democratic process to thrive. Educated self-interest motivates a person not merely to achieve greater personal abundance and quality of life but to recognize that this can't be at the cost of others doing without. It teaches that compassion furthers self-interest and vice versa, personally and evolutionarily. Primate studies indicate that "unselfish" actions have survival and reproductive benefits for the benefactor. The reciprocal relationship between self-interest and unselfishness takes nothing away from either; rather, it both promotes virtue and grounds it in reality.

Freedom to act from enlightened self-interest is limited by the good/bad duality that produced our culture's long-running project of sealing evil out of history and reduces our ability to know where our actual interests lie. This has cost us our healthy relationship to the earth and our body; limiting the infinite's manifestation through polarities has sealed out so much energy and creativity that life is laborious and unsatisfactory. Static good/bad or right/wrong definitions can never keep up with life's dynamic nature.

Still beyond Comprehension

If, whether personally or as a culture, we think dualistically and don't include both polarities of an issue in a solution, the rejected aspect will find a way to express itself, usually undermining the solution. Those who think dualistically reject the other polarity because they believe it can only produce negative results, having projected their own shadow onto it. Because rejected, it does, not for the anticipated reason but because of its exclusion. Dualism creates the harm it expects.

Teachings about not resisting evil, loving one's enemies, and turning the other cheek, best known in the West from the New Testament but expressed two thousand years earlier in Babylonian literature[1] as well as in Homer, Taoism, and Buddhism, are sufficiently radical that our civilization has never fully digested them. They run so fundamentally counter to the "us vs. them," "good vs. bad" duality belief system as to be completely incomprehensible to anyone in that frame of reference. These precepts provide a methodology for keeping polarities relational rather than becoming dualistically oppositional. A person under attack doesn't enter the frame of reference of being assaulted and needn't become defensive or counterattack. Rather, he receives the attack without participating in the fight as such or putting energy into it; he thereby transforms the other's energy. By loving his enemy—touching into the truth of the other polarity—he forms a relationship rather than a division. The point is never to assent to a duality but to relate to the situation as a complementarity.

The transformational response to physical attack has been most highly developed in oriental martial arts. The idea is to not react but to use the energy of the attack to deflect it. If the attack is non-physical, the person can transform its energy (for instance, anger, hatred, or judgmentalism) through meditation, life-energy work, or psychological techniques. Not trying to harm in return offers one's opponent a chance to see things from a different perspective; at the least, one hasn't invested energy in the attacker's aggressive modality, while protecting oneself. Those most adept at this defense relate to the center of the opponent's being, which is by nature beyond duality. This requires that one focus and act from one's own center.

This relational, transformational response to what many would resist as Evil is the act of an enlightened warrior, not capitulation or a sign of weakness. It requires that one know the nature of one's opponent as well as one's abilities. Gandhi indicated he would not have fought back against Hitler had Germany invaded India: a sublime principle but perhaps an arguable application. If one fights back, the principles of neither hating the aggressor nor causing greater harm than necessary still apply, as they do if one is in conflict with oneself

If each side in a conflict has only a portion of the truth (not necessarily equal portions), each side will have to question the remainder of its own position. The good/bad duality is seductive because it spares us the work of transforming ourselves and of separating truth from fiction in our beliefs. It also avoids the unpleasant and sometimes humbling labor of relating to our opponents, changing our view, acknowledging their piece of the truth, and helping them to see their own fictions without judging them. The New Testament admonition, to deal with the beam in one's eye before attending to the mote in someone else's, speaks to this.

It's easy to slip into dualistic thinking and action when dealing with polarities, yet if we respect our opponent and have insight into his measure of truth, we'll perform a holy act, creating a moment of wholeness—a moment in which the momentous can occur. Such a deed is both creative and heroic; however, the embodiment of the infinite requires an ongoing process of polarities interacting. It's a practice rather than a feat. Our primary work is spiritual transformation; producing outcomes is ancillary. We live in the world of paradoxes to express our divine nature via the polarities of our finite nature and move toward wholeness. This is the most engaging and important work we can do, whether in families, communities, national politics, or international relations. Not doing this, we're merely biding our time and missing the point.

With liberal capitalism now ascendant in much of the world and communism and socialism widely discredited, it's time to take a fresh look at the Cold War dualism between capitalism and its adversaries, given that socialism's intent is to enable all members of society to have a full stake in the power and wealth of society. Capitalism's successes in creating abundance for many and its defeat of communism don't mean that it contains the whole truth; the philosophical underpinnings of communism and socialism involve a humanistic and ethical philosophy lacking in pure free-market capitalism. Considering that dualistic thinking is ultimately self-defeating, we shouldn't ignore the principles socialism and communism intend to embody, any more than we should disregard their failings. The modern European socialist/capitalist hybrid arguably has no greater flaws than American capitalism, just different ones. As the rising tide of capitalist wealth creation, instead of raising all boats, leaves many moored to the bottom and most people working increasingly long hours and short-changing their families, we can see the part of the truth that the capitalist side of the polarity lacks; socialism as its complementarity may offer solutions. Only by engaging these two as polarities can we create something greater from them, though each may not always have the same validity or relevance. Treating capitalism as a polarity to socialism, we can view it in a more balanced way and question its fundamental assumptions and practices, including governmental and corporate decisions based on narrow economic metrics that emphasize the gains of a relative few and fail to account for human, infrastructure, and environmental costs, as well as the legal underpinnings and structure of corporations that give them the rights of persons and disempower their broad base of shareholders. We should continue to be value capitalism, however, for its substantial virtues, such as flexibility, efficient markets, innovation, and individual empowerment.

This approach would open the way for an ethical and compassionate synthesis incorporating the truths of each system in an economic and social order matching the emerging vision of human spiritual nature outlined here, a synthesis offering each person a realistic opportunity for mental, emotional, physical, and spiritual realization of his or her potential. Difficult as this would be, proceeding dualistically is far less likely to succeed. At the end of 2006, the possibility of such a course finds demonstration in a lessening of the dualism between science and religion, as a growing number of Christian evangelicals find, in Biblical teachings on stewardship, a reason to address global warming. Similarly, many scientists and people of faith are speaking out about their refusal to dualize evolution and theism (or "rationalism and irrationalism" as they are dualistically characterized), recognizing there are areas of inquiry that science by its nature doesn't address and seeing no reason God couldn't have created the laws science explores.

Nothing could be more absorbing, rewarding, or revealing of the divine within each of us than to engage in such an undertaking, demonstrating how spirit and earth, rationality and intuition, principle and practicality, and infinite and finite work together and serve one another.

PART THREE

Developing Your Own Experience: Practices

The absolute tranquility is the present moment. Though it is at this moment, there is no limit to this moment, and herein is eternal delight.

—Hui-neng, *T'an-ching*

20

How to Deepen Your Awareness of Your Infinite Self

> Nor do I myself comprehend all that I am. Therefore is the mind too strait to contain itself.
>
> —Augustine, *Confessions*

Infinite self manifests in our experience in three modalities. The first is awareness. Many people have moments of exceptional clarity, understanding, or transcendent insight, intuition, or illumination. Such events can be exceedingly brief yet so dense with meaning as to be endlessly instructive, each a constantly unfolding source of creative inspiration or self-knowledge. Another kind of experience in this modality is an unfocused, expanded awareness that allows a person to feel at one and at peace with everything, light and floating. Muted versions of these and similar occurrences are common. In these, one touches into and receives the touch of infinite mind.

The second modality is energy—the energy of life itself. It goes by many names, ancient and modern: *chi*, mana, inner light, life-energy. Energy is the most basic experience we have and is not mystical or psychic. We feel more energy on good days, not enough on others; it's clear and buoyant when pure; it can be heavy or murky when polluted. It's what makes us feel alive.

Identity is the third modality. When we make a statement beginning with "I am," we're expressing a sense of identity. Seekers of enlightenment in every age have struggled to answer the question "Who am I?" One of the injunctions carved over the entry to the ancient Greek temple at Delphi was "Man, Know Thyself." People commonly consider identity in terms of nationality, family, religion, political persuasion, occupation, etc. It may center on special bodily attributes, such as beauty, strength, or sex appeal, or on mental ability. Different cultures have arrived at a variety of answers to the question of identity. For the classical Greeks, it was being a person capable of rational thought. For Jews it is being God's chosen people. Gautama Buddha's great illumination was that personal identity is an illusion. Devout Christians find their principal identity as souls saved and known by Jesus.

Many religions and spiritual disciplines hold that one's actual identity is hidden and forgotten; they teach methods that enable the seeker to penetrate to his spiritual self. The statement in the Hindu Upanishads, "That art Thou!" and the Hindu and Buddhist methodology of *neti-neti*, "not that, not that" (a way of divesting identity from all aspects of the phenomenal world and attaining the truth by negating all thoughts about it) serve to focus awareness on the identity in the center of one's being or of existence. Past all attributes that can be described, a sense of "I-ness" remains that simply is and never is not. A Zen Buddhist seeks to remember his "original face" as a means to illumination.

As proposed here, the deepest core of identity is infinite self. When one recognizes it, connects with it, and unifies with it, this identity provides a profound sense of belonging, validity, and value, regardless of deeds or position.

The following exercises lead to direct and accessible experiences of your infinite self. Each exercise achieves this by means of one or more of the modalities of infinite self's manifestation. What you observe may seem simple and familiar; you may have these experiences every day but overlook them and underestimate their value. They provide the foundation of a growing relationship with your infinite self, which you can enjoy in the middle of your busy life.

It's best to allow yourself to have whatever experience comes to you, however subtle. Try not to look for a particular experience or attempt to visualize something, even if nothing seems to be occurring (which is normal, especially at the beginning). Relax and let things happen as they come.

Exercise One. Infinite Mind Enlightens Your Finite Mind

(About five minutes.) Sit or lie in a quiet place; it's easiest (but unnecessary) to have your eyes closed. Bring your attention to a place six inches directly above your head. In this peaceful and clear part of yourself, you can access the awareness of your infinite self. Focusing here initiates a flow of this higher awareness into your personal mind, especially your brain. It gently and effortlessly gathers your knowing awareness into the here and now, focusing, refining, and enlightening it. Let this happen; experience subtle changes in the activity of your mind.

Now experience the flow of your higher awareness into your nerves, where it soothingly gathers, refines, enlightens, and then expands your sensory awareness. Let this continue for a minute or two, and notice how your sensory experience changes. You'll find that this brings you more into touch with your body and with non-physical experiences.

Next, focus your higher awareness into your heart and liver. We hold much emotional energy and awareness in these organs, and you can experience changes in your feelings here as your higher awareness lifts, refines, enlightens, and expands your emotional awareness. Let this continue for a minute or two; simply be present and aware without effort.

Finally, feel the changes in your experience as your higher awareness interacts with your knowing, sensory, and emotional awareness throughout your body and around it, focusing, enlightening, and expanding all your awareness.

To ground yourself after this experience, focus your enlightened awareness in the place six inches above your head and in your hands and feet.

Do this once or twice a day. You can repeat it briefly and informally as often as you wish, especially when your attention is scattered or you need to be alert and focused.

You're unlikely to observe any dramatic changes while doing this, other than being somewhat more aware and clear; likewise, from day to day changes will be gradual. Over time, however, its accumulated effects will help you to be noticeably more centered and discerning and to have an abiding sense of the presence of your infinite self and its awareness.

Exercise Two. Tapping into Your Infinite Life-Energy

(Ten to twenty minutes.) Do exercise 1 first.

In this exercise you work with crystal-clear inner light or life-energy from your infinite self. The purpose of this energy is to purify, cleanse, and illuminate. It reveals and clears away beliefs, attitudes, feelings, and ways of looking at things that aren't healthy for you because they're not true to who you actually are. Life-energy is able to reveal and remove these because its ultimate source is your infinite self, which is present and omniscient throughout you and actually does the work with the energy.

Have your legs and arms uncrossed. After doing exercise 1 to interact with your infinite self's awareness, bring the focus of the awareness you've enlightened to the place six inches above your head. Here you'll find the source of the crystal-clear life-energy. Observe this point of light; it naturally responds to your awareness and grows to a three-inch form that looks rather like a star should you see it with your inward vision. (It's best not to *try* to see or visualize it; instead, let the experience come to you in whatever way it does spontaneously, including visually.)

Now, think of your star releasing liquid life-energy to flow straight down, into and throughout your body and out the soles of your feet, relaxing your feet so they're open. Focus your attention in your head. (Wherever you focus your enlightened awareness, the life-energy intensifies.) You don't need to work at this or try to make something happen; the energy does the work for you. Just pay attention. (It works even if you don't pay full attention, although not quite as deeply, and you won't experience as much). It's best to *think* of focusing the life-energy in a place, then *let* the thought go, so that you can *observe* and *experience* what happens. Let your life-energy continue to purify this area for a minute or two, helping release tension from your head, clearing and illuminating your mind.

Then move down to other areas of your body in turn, such as your lungs, heart, liver, nerves, digestive system, etc., especially areas where you notice pain, tension, or other discomfort, like a sore muscle or joint. Work in each area in the manner described. Discomfort may temporarily increase as you focus there and as the cause of discomfort surfaces; let the life-energy work, dissolving what causes the discomfort. Observe feelings, sensations, memories, or concerns that may cross your mind. They're not distractions; they're part of the process of cleansing the body and its energy and of illuminating your consciousness. Just notice them without reacting or becoming involved with them.

When you reach your feet, continue to experience the flow throughout your body and out your feet for a few moments; then think of your feet closing off, so the flow of life-energy fills your body to reenergize you, overflowing to fill the space around you for protection. Soak this in for a few minutes.

You can do this exercise once or twice a day. Do it more briefly whenever you wish (with or without exercise 1 first) to cleanse, re-energize, and refresh yourself. You can maintain the flow of energy from your star continually: simply be aware of it every thirty minutes or so to keep it going. If you forget about it longer, it will become inactive; if this happens, you can turn it back on with just a thought, even when you're busy.

This exercise has many practical benefits, including stress reduction and increased energy; like any exercise, the effects build up gradually with regular practice. It will serve you in more subtle but important ways as well, such as making it possible for you to increasingly feel the presence and nature of your infinite self, freeing you from negative conditioning or the effects of past trauma, and enabling you to act in accordance with your actual purpose and character. You can use the star's energy all the time because its source is your infinite self and therefore the energy is unlimited. As you experience the energy, it will help you open to more of the boundless resources of your infinite self.

Exercise Three. Experiencing Your Infinite Self

(This requires little time, but you can also do it at a leisurely pace.) It's best to do his exercise after you do exercise 1 for at least a minute or two; you will experience it most clearly after both exercises 1 and 2.

After exercise 1, or 1 and 2, let the awareness you've enlightened attune itself to the unique identity of your infinite self. Be present and receptive without focusing on anything. Sense the presence of your higher self, which has always been in the depths of your awareness. This deeper, higher self is more essentially you than any interest, attachment, or circumstance of your life. Experience that if these attachments or conditions were different or taken away, you would still be this same you. Notice that any idea or picture of yourself can change, yet you are still this you. Be aware of your emotions as you experience this; also observe the sensations in your body, such as lightness, tingling, or expansion.

With eyes open but unfocused; be aware of your peripheral vision, your entire field of vision. Notice sounds and smells around you, without focusing on anything in particular. Observe your whole field of attention without focus, letting impressions float through without attachment to them. You, the infinite self, are everywhere within you and around you for many feet in every direction and nowhere in particular. Feel your infinite self floating freely yet deeply and completely present within and around you. Your actual finite identity partakes of this infinite identity.

You can do this exercise by itself whenever you wish, especially when you lack confidence, feel defensive, unworthy, or off center, or when others unduly sway you. The more you do this as a focused practice, the more effective it becomes when done briefly at need.

Your impressions will probably be vague and elusive. Again, as you practice this over time, you build up a definite, if hard-to-define, impression, a kind of living and abiding sense of the calm and certainty of being something that doesn't need justification or explanation. It's a sense of yourself that's steady and unassailable and which therefore allows you to have assurance and flexibility.

Exercise Four. Connecting with the Infinite Selves of Others

(You can do this briefly or at length.) This exercise works well by itself anytime during the day, but for maximum experience do at least exercise 1 first, and ideally 2 and 3 also.

Experiential evidence suggests that infinite selves readily unify, or merge, with others, in addition to having eternal union with God. Whenever we think of, or are present with, another person, our higher selves join. In this union, the uniqueness and identity of each persists. This isn't a union of personalities, so you can do it with someone you might not want to connect with as a person. There's no exchange of personal energy involved in this merging.

Choose a person; think of your infinite self unifying with his or her infinite self. Let the thought go and open yourself to whatever experience comes: bodily sensations, emotions about this connection, or vague impressions of the nature of this infinite self (which may be distinctly different from that individual's personality; you may also notice that this infinite self differs from your own).

Do this with as many individuals as you wish. Notice variations in your experience with each. Do it with the infinite self of someone you miss and haven't seen recently, to get a sense of this inner connection that transcends time and space. If your experiences are subtle, don't discount them; as you may expect by now, they will grow with practice.

Experiment with the infinite selves of coworkers; notice how things at work may change for the better if you do this regularly. It can be especially useful to do with anyone you have trouble getting along with; it can provide you a higher perspective and even lift the quality of your interactions a bit. Try this in the morning with anyone or everyone you'll be seeing that day (it can be done quickly with each or all at once), or when you're with them—it takes no more than a thought to bring into awareness the union that's already occurring as infinite selves and therefore to make this effective in you interactions. Try this when you're with those you love; it adds a higher, spiritual dimension to the relationship.

Exercise Five. Experiencing Spherical Time

(Duration depends on the activity chosen.) The purpose of this exercise is to move from a linear experience of time flow to an experience of timeless, spherical time. Do it anytime, but also try it following exercises 1 through 3.

Pick something you do that's routine or requires little thought and has a natural end-point (or else set a timer). Alternately, simply be still, doing nothing. As you engage in the activity or the stillness, enter the allotted time as you would enter a room, feeling its spaciousness. Be aware that you don't have to make any effort to get to the end of the time; you need only be there within the time. Bring as much attention as possible to observing the process of doing what you're doing. Notice your sensations as they occur; observe as thoughts and emotions come and go. If you're being still, notice the urge to be doing something productive, but don't fight the impulse. Let it pass through you.

Sink into the moment as deeply as you can, like settling into a comfortable chair in this room of time. Occupy the moment fully. Let your awareness expand throughout the room. Experience that all else that makes up your life is outside this room of time, and you can be completely inside it. Deepen into the moment whenever your mind begins to wander, relaxing body and mind in order to release any effort you make to try to move things along. Continue to observe what you're doing and all that's around you now. Observe any impatience or boredom without engaging these; let them waft through your awareness while you sink deeper and more of you becomes present. Think of your infinite self at the center of you, immovable and timeless, aware and completely present, loving what you're doing. Open to your infinite self, and let its energy fill this moment. Expand your attention ten or fifteen feet spherically around you and experience your presence throughout this space.

When the time or task is completed, notice the different experience of time flow that you've developed. Try not to jump back into your usual time modality; linger in this room.

The goal is for this to become a way of living rather than an exercise, but that requires regular practice. You can do this anytime, regardless of what you're doing: thinking of the diagram in chapter 3, notice your experience of linear time flow; then, like the vertical arrow in the diagram, plunge into the depths of this moment, into whatever you are doing, so you experience with full awareness each part of each passing moment. You'll probably notice that normally you feel squeezed by time and tense about its limits; perhaps you habitually push to speed things up. Practice releasing such effortfulness whenever you're aware of it; your sense of being in time will change.

Exercise Six. Rapid Re-Energizing

(Three to five minutes.) Start the flow of life-energy from your star. Lying or sitting, take a sort of catnap. Begin by completely releasing the world. Let go of your connection to all you've been busy with, turning it over to your infinite self, one part of your body at a time if necessary. Notice that the world continues around you without any effort on your part. Let yourself drift; let your body go. You probably won't go to sleep but may enter a kind of half-sleep. Think of your infinite self pouring its energy into you. Float in this and soak it in deeply. Feel yourself adrift in time, not engaged with it; your sense of time flow may become much slower. At the end of the time, to be grounded before getting up, focus awareness six inches above your head and in your hands and feet.

You can learn to recharge and refresh yourself in this brief time. In fact, time has nothing to do with it; a profound openness to your infinite self allows for near-instantaneous re-energizing. Some people can do this without any thought of infinite self, having the natural ability to open within, but paying attention to your infinite self increases the revitalizing effect.

Exercise Seven. Walking the Talk

(This is an alternate version of exercise 3. Do it whenever you wish, for as long as the spirit moves you.) Ideally, do this in a park or in nature, away from people. Do exercise 1 first, briefly. Early on, you may have only fleeting moments when you feel some sense of your infinite self, but these can be deeply moving and instructive.

Go for a walk. Experience moving. Notice what personal matters are on your mind interrupting this experience. Now, expand your awareness to include your actual finite self, that is, finite self as created by your infinite self, which we often intuit to be our "real" self and which is freer, creative, more generous of spirit, and has more of a sense of innate value than the burdened, anxious self we usually experience ourselves to be. Let go of your personal concerns for a few moments and, as you move in the more timeless natural world, experience this pure you that's beyond personal history.

Next, think of and then let yourself experience walking as an infinite self, present within finite self and observing the world by way of it. Don't imagine this; simply open without critique to whatever comes to you. Experience this divine aspect of yourself around as well as in you, enjoying the movement of the finite you, interested and even amused by your concerns and choices, and entirely loving.

Shift your focus back to being finite self (actual and otherwise), and open to and experience the love that flows through and fills you as you walk along. Although this is always present, you must actively partake of it or its effect will be minimal. Now shift back to your infinite self, unmoved but experiencing the movement of finite self, treasuring each step of finite life. Now, experience being both. Experience your union as infinite self with God; observe the paradox that you're infinitely unique and yet are a part of all.

The following occurred on such a walk. I include it both for its relationship to this exercise and as an example of my experience of the interplay between infinite self and finite self.

My sense was that my higher self wished to add a concluding thought for the text: "So much awaits each of you, suns and galaxies to explore, time enough for all that your heart holds in its fullness. This will come in good time; therefore live your life as it is now with zest and grace. Give your best efforts to improving your life and yourself, but in the moment of that best effort, accept whatever the outcome will be so that you do not deny yourself the delight and value of what is." (These are the best words my finite mind can find to express the experience.)

My finite mind, being less than overwhelmed by this, pointed out that my higher self hadn't said anything novel (nothing is new under the sun, after all); this had not only been said many times before but far better. My higher self allowed that this was true. It pointed out, however, that we do need reminding, and, anyway, originality and brilliance aren't the most important spiritual considerations.

Persistence and joy are.

Note on the Appendices

These appendices explore some principal religious and philosophical ideas about the infinite and eternal. Appendix 1 briefly outlines humanity's fundamental descriptions of the nature of the divine and its relationship to the universe and human beings. It considers defining issues involved in the comparison of any religious systems, with the aim of providing clarity as to the differences and similarities in the beliefs described in the next appendix. Parts 1 through 3 of appendix 2 survey the history of major religious, spiritual, and philosophical conceptions and beliefs regarding the psychospiritual composition of humanity and the totality of the human self, observing historical connections that influenced how these originated and developed. The particular purpose of the appendices is to illuminate the concept of the individual infinite self by noting where it entered into religion, philosophy, or mysticism and looking at the range of perspectives from which spiritual seekers and metaphysicians have experienced and expressed it. Part 4 focuses on a pivotal moment in recent spiritual development, when circumstances and choices increased the dualistic split in the consciousness of the Western mind, leading directly to the crises of our time.

My intent is also to give an overview of how we came to be where we are. This will afford us a better feel for the terrain we stand on and a clearer view of where we're going.

This material is only a sample, meant to give a sense of the range of experiences and conceptions we have record of. It's far from a comprehensive survey.

Examining and comparing the literature on the subject of religious and mystical experience requires the greatest circumspection and humility. Spiritual experience, as distinct from dogma, is difficult at best to put into words; the interior events that occur at the inception of most religions are essentially mystical, and mystical experience by its very nature transcends our means of expression. All writing on this subject is suggestive at best.

When individuals working within a given spiritual tradition compare their experiences, they find that their words mean subtly or even extremely dissimilar things to different people; misunderstanding of meaning compounds when the same words are across diverse traditions. "Soul" is an example (see appendix 1). In classical Hebrew, soul means "the vital force, the life, the person,"[1] while in Christianity it refers to a spiritual element apart from the body, mind, and emotions.

Even a single writer, Plato, uses the Greek term for soul to mean variously "principle of life," "mind," or "self."[2] The problem becomes more complex when translation is involved; the language or religion may be dead, and thousands of years of cultural and psychospiritual change may stand between the writer and the translator. The fact that often both translator and reader haven't had transcendent or mystical experiences and haven't pursued a spiritual discipline that would provide an affinity with these increases the likelihood of confusion and even gross misunderstanding. With a background of such experience or discipline, however, it's possible to glimpse in the words the living experiences forming the basis of the written record and draw some cautious inferences about the original meaning.

Appendix 1. Infinite Possibilities: The Relationship of God, Cosmos, and Humanity

Humanity has created a great diversity of conceptions regarding God's relationship to the natural world. These are important not only for humanity's sense of connection to the divine but, by implication, for finite self's possibility of relationship with infinite self. The following are the major categories.

Monism refers to the idea of the unity of everything, particularly that God and the cosmos are one, experienced mystically as personal union with the divine. **Dualism** stresses the separation of God from the cosmos or of ideal form from matter; it's at the heart of beliefs such as those that sharply differentiate the nature of soul and body. Dualism has *absolute* and *relative* categories. **Pluralism** has its basis in the observation that there is a multitude of things in the world; it sees the universe as lacking an overall unifying factor. Dualism is distinct not only from monism and pluralism but from monotheism and polytheism, although the situation is often ambiguous.

Religious dualism posits two paramount forces, beings, or groups of beings, good and evil, which brought the cosmos into existence. The *absolute* (or *radical*) form of dualism maintains that these two forces or beings are co-eternal, as in Zoroastrianism and Manichaeism. *Relative* (*mitigated*) dualism holds that one being or force is created by or emerges from the other, such as Lucifer, whom Christians see as created by God but later rebelling against him.

Theologians distinguish *eschatological* and *dialectical* dualism. The dialectical form sees a never-ending and often cyclic or historically recurrent opposition of forces or beings. In Western culture, for example in Platonism, this finds expression as an inherent opposition of One and many or of Idea and matter. Eschatological dualism addresses the ultimate fate of man and the cosmos, postulating an end to the current dualistic condition of the universe. History consists of a linear sequence of unique events; at its completion, evil suffers utter defeat. Eschatological dualism occurs in Christianity, Zoroastrianism, and Manichaeism.

God is **immanent** if conceived to be within, pervasive, or at least near at hand but **transcendent** if held to be remote, above, or outside the cosmos. Belief in God's immanence tends to promote a feeling of being able to relate to the divine without any intermediary such as church or priest.

Religions and belief systems vary as regards the reality of the cosmos—whether it is **illusion** or partakes of the **reality** of God. God, in turn, is seen as **absolute**—creator of the cosmos but unaffected by it, eternal, outside of time—or else **relative**, affected by the world and existing in time; God may be a combination of absolute and relative, these conditions pertaining to different dimensions of divinity. In monistic systems, where all is one, God and the world are both absolute; in dualistic systems, God is absolute and the world relative. Almost all religions attribute **eternity** to God, at least in his highest aspects. On the other hand, **time** may be completely an illusion, or it may be a real aspect of the created cosmos only, or else it may be real in the world and as an aspect of God.

The question of human **freedom** in choice and destiny arises if God is all, or at least omniscient. If **determinism** or predestination is the nature of the cosmos, freedom is an illusion.

Finally, if God and the cosmos are one, as in monism, the cosmos is **sacred** in all aspects, but if God and cosmos constitute a duality, then the latter is **secular** or even impure and fallen from grace. In a third option, the most common, only certain places—natural locations or places of worship, for instance—partake of the sacredness of the divine.

Each of these distinctions combines with others to create the principal kinds of religions:

Animism, thought to be the earliest form of religion, holds that the world contains myriad spiritual beings that interact with human beings for good or ill. The "great" religions, which have all developed in historical times, are not animistic but may contain animistic elements. Most tribal religions are animistic, although these may have come to contain polytheistic and monotheistic elements even before the rise of the great religions.

Theism (whether *polytheism*, which posits more than one divinity, or *monotheism*, which asserts there is only one god) involves the belief that the existent cosmos is contingent on something above human understanding that is self-sufficient yet engaged with the world and its affairs. Theism views the divine as ideal, complete, and the source of all creation; the acts of divinity continue to affect creation. God is eternal, omniscient, omnipotent, and has created the world but is unchanged by it. He is detached and apart, yet at the same time concerned, involved, and near at hand, as in the Biblical foundation of Judaism, Christianity, and Islam. This simultaneous engagement and aloofness inevitably raises the question of how people might understand and relate, especially in any personal way, to a distant and enigmatic divinity. Another issue is that in theism, man's freedom is open to question because God is omniscient; theism nevertheless normally affirms it.

Deism credits each individual with innate religious knowledge or the capacity to achieve it through the exercise of reason, because divine creation involves comprehensible rational laws. This is often termed natural religion, in contrast to religious knowledge attained through divine revelation or religious instruction. Deism arose in England early in the seventeenth century; it was prevalent among the American Founding Fathers. The most extreme form of Deism saw God's role as that of original creator only; after creation, God was no longer involved in nature or the course of human development; this contrasts with theism's doctrine of divine immanence and involvement in history.

Pantheism and **panentheism** understand God as encompassing, inclusive, and all embracing, unlike the apartness of divinity that is an aspect of theism. Pantheism and panentheism are nonetheless versions of theism broadly construed, since theism also holds that God is immanent. Pantheism sees God and the world as the same, while panentheism conceives the limited, created cosmos to be within and a part of the divine infinity.

The term pantheism encompasses a variety of specific beliefs: God is identical with the cosmos; the cosmos is within God (e.g., as the body of God) but does not affect the divine; God *is* reality, while the cosmos is an unreal appearance; opposites may be seen to unite in God, which can only be apprehended intuitively, not rationally; or, God, perfect and transcendent, is not the cause of the cosmos, but the cosmos is an emanation of the divine.

Panentheism seeks to resolve certain contradictions and to have the best of both cosmoses by attributing both transcendence and immanence, both the absolute and the relative condition, to God. It views God as omniscient, yet holds the future to be undetermined, so omniscience amounts to awareness of what is possible or probable. The divine is causal but its creation nonetheless affects it. Human beings have freedom of choice and are co-creators with the divine, together engaged in ongoing creation. God is eternal but also temporally engaged.[1]

Soul, Spirit, and Nature

Is the goal of spiritual development a return to God? If we return, are we absorbed into the divine, or do we nonexpressively reside in the eternal presence of God, or else can we look forward to a co-creative relationship with God (or infinite self) involving union but also individual expression? If the spiritual part of humanity is immortal, is it as a limited soul or an infinite self? Is the goal of human spiritual progress directed away from the body and physical world (usually felt to be a temporary and negative place of temptation and struggle), or is the goal an integration of body and spiritual nature? Answers to these fundamental questions about our spiritual destiny vary among religious traditions according to key distinctions regarding the psychospiritual makeup of human beings.

A watershed divides spiritual paradigms that hold human beings to consist of body and soul from those in which our existence comprises at least body, soul, and spirit. Many variations occur within these two basic views, but this distinction has crucial implications.

Depending on the tradition, the word "soul" includes decidedly different aspects of human nature. Traditionally, soul has meant that which continues to exist after death, or the moral aspect of a person, or the essence of something, or the immortal or spiritual element that has no physical existence but governs thinking, willing, and thus behavior. Recently, the tendency has been to apply the word to aspects and functions of the personality (as Thomas Moore employs it in such books as *Soul Mates*) or to "soul music" and other artistic forms created from deep and authentic emotion. Psychologist James Hillman, drawing on Blake and John Keats (1795-1821), speaks of "soul-making" and defines soul as "a perspective rather than a substance, a viewpoint toward things rather than a thing itself."[2] He refers to Georg Wilhelm Friedrich Hegel's (1770-1831) assertion that psychopathology is inherent in the soul.[3] Moore assigns fate a large role in the life of the soul, yet quotes Heraclitus: "The soul is its own source of unfolding," and so with good reason says that the soul is "filled with paradox."[4]

Thus, soul is seen as fated or self-unfolding, an aspect of personality or of spirit, subject to pathology or untainted, and the locus of will, mind, and morals or the source, as Hillman puts it, of "imagination, passion, fantasy, reflection, that is neither physical and material . . . nor spiritual and abstract."[5] In short, it is ascribed a vast and contradictory range of human experience and existence.

Hillman attributes to human beings a tripartite existence of body, soul, and spirit and suggests unfortunate consequences if the latter two are combined. The triune nature he describes is different from what I refer to, however, in a way that usefully illustrates the serious problems arising from the protean meaning of the terms "soul" and "spirit." For him soul, or psyche, is emotional, of the night, feminine, patient, metaphorical, and involved with the myriad phenomena and impressions of everyday living. Spirit is masculine, active, of the light, ascending beyond earth, pure, abstract, intellectual, and, in its own view, superior to soul. He asserts that those disciplines and religions (including most modern ones) emphasizing the spirit try to rise above the problems of the world and that this attempt at transcendence denigrates and represses the "pathologies" of the soul in a way that "is in itself pathological, an exercise in self-deception."[6]

While his critique of spiritual and psychological thought has considerable validity, his descriptions of soul and spirit don't apply to the way the most penetrating and complete psychospiritual descriptions of human beings use the terms. The qualities, strengths, and weaknesses he ascribes to soul and spirit define quite accurately the most rarified aspects of the personality (the knowing, sensing, and emotional faculties) but not the infinite spirit or the higher spiritual aspects of the finite self—or even the soul as traditionally understood. A full account of finite human nature can involve eight or more distinct aspects or dimensions. For our purposes, a tripartite delineation includes: first, body and personality taken together, second, soul and other spiritual aspects of finite self (which are beyond the pathologies and conditioned reflexes of the personality and are unified with and guided by infinite self), and finally, infinite self. (It seems that in some systems the third aspect involves the higher finite spiritual aspect—those attributes that are beyond the soul—alone or in conjunction with infinite self.)

This problem of terminology leads Hillman to criticize a variety of spiritual disciplines based on a misinterpretation. He's correct in saying that what he calls spirit—what I identify as the highest aspect of personality, the closest part to actual soul—does try at times to rise above the pain, puzzlement, and reactivity of what he terms soul. Its attempts to transcend the problems of the lower aspects of personality are rightly suspect, and any discipline that confuses these higher personality characteristics with those of actual soul and spirit merits the criticism he offers. However, the transcendence of true soul and spirit is quite different. Their movement is into the personality and its vicissitudes—more accurately, they are already always interpenetrating, in but not of, and they strive to awaken the person to their presence—so that they can help the individual to acknowledge the cause of a pain or illness or reveal a roadblock to greater expression of actual self. They can then help the personality to choose (which it must do for itself) to release its attachment to the cause of the problem; then they can transmute the cause into something healthier and more actualizing. If we believe them to be aloof, their actual presence may not be registered or their assistance received, so we experience them to be aloof. This leaves body and personality adrift and feeling devalued.

Other significant variations in beliefs about soul and spirit include their time of creation—with the body (or after it), before it but at some point in time, at or before the creation of the cosmos, or after that but before the formation of the earth. If they pre-exist body or cosmos, differences arise as to whether one or both "fell" into earthly existence or chose it, whether soul and/or spirit is always "spiritual" or evolves to that state, and, if evolving, whether one or both exists potently and meaningfully during (or before) life or only comes into its own after death. Beliefs vary as to whether the soul can be lost or damned, whether it is or at least can become close to God, and whether the life of the soul after death is on earth or on a heavenly plane separated from earth or else continuous with it.

Another important watershed in descriptions of human psychospiritual nature involves, on one side, those who believe that the spiritual growth of humanity is movement away from the body and material world and toward the heavenly realms; these usually attribute lesser value to earth and nature than to spirit and may see them as a testing ground or adversary or else simply iniquitous and degrading to inhabit. The other side includes those who see the earth and the cosmic natural order as an expression of the divine or as the body of God. Intermediate is the belief in the resurrection of the body, usually at the end of time and in an altered, purified environment. Those for whom nature and earth are good are further divisible. Some see the spiritual and the natural as two separate realms, the latter being of little importance to us spiritually. Others speak of continuity between them, such that they potentially constitute a whole, the purpose of humanity being to integrate them. In the latter view, our spiritual growth leads to a more caring relationship with body and nature; it asserts that soul or spirit view all creation with the eyes of love and are completely committed to it.

Appendix 2. A History of Religious Beliefs Regarding the Spiritual Nature of Human Beings

Part 1: Prehistory to the Classical World

This survey begins with non-literate cultures and progresses through historical literate cultures to the present. If the experience of an infinite spiritual aspect of human beings occurred in prehistoric times, its transmission in these preliterate cultures would have been oral, leaving no record. Anthropology can give us only the most general sense of early religious belief. In literate societies, the notion of the infinite self arises most frequently when, as now, there is increased intercultural contact, such as when the Roman Empire melded Greek, Middle Eastern, Egyptian, and Latin beliefs, and when ideas from the Islamic world (including Classical texts preserved by Islamic scholars) penetrated Europe due to the Crusades and the reconquest of Spain.

Religions of Non-Literate Cultures

From their earliest development and in their most "primitive" condition, human beings have believed that individual consciousness persists after death; C. E. Vulliamy states that apparently "coeval with humanity itself . . . [is] the belief in the immortality of the soul. . . . In some form or other it is practically universal."[1] Apparently Neanderthals considered themselves immortal, as they buried their dead with attentiveness and goods. Cro-Magnon burials indicate a thoroughly developed, explicit, and certain conviction regarding spiritual existence.[2] We have only physical evidence, however, and cannot infer any specific concepts.

In the last one hundred fifty years, anthropologists recorded that many extant (or then-extant) cultures feel that people possess two or more souls, such as a body-soul and a spirit-soul[3] (cf. Egypt and Taoism below). For example: A New Guinean group holds that there is a "long soul" associated with the shadow and involved in dreams, while a "short soul" leaves the body only after death, passing on to the spirit realm. Solomon Islanders held that a man has one malevolent soul and one that is peaceful and benevolent. A number of West African cultures assert that there is a soul for the body and a soul for the spirit. Groups in Nigeria and Northern Congo believe that there exists a four-fold spiritual nature, these being soul, shadow, life, and double.[4]

Vulliamy maintains that belief in gods may or may not arise entirely from the cult of deceased ancestors but it's certain a belief in gods is contingent on belief in an immortal soul. The very reason for the god is that he or she ensures immortality.[5] (The notion of personal immortality and the idea of an immortal, infinite self are quite different, as will be apparent from examining Taoist beliefs.)

Egypt

Perhaps the infinite self's earliest recorded appearance, albeit partial, occurred in ancient Egypt. For Egyptians, the description of the nonphysical self began with the *ka*, variously described as a man's double or his dual personality,[6] the "spiritual counterpart of the body,"[7] or the "deeper self, residing in the divine world."[8] It was a vital energy focused through the pharaoh, priests, or nobles—in modern terms, the psychic energy of the collective unconscious or a generalized universal life force. However, this *ka* energy, by the time of the Old Kingdom, became individualized for the pharaoh, nobility, and religious hierarchy, and for them, Naydler explains, "the *ka* was more like a protective and inspirational genius or daimon."[9] The *ka* energy absorbed most people at death; the majority of people expected that any individuality would be incorporated into the consciousness of their collective forebears.[10] Only the pharaoh assimilated or integrated the *ka* energy into himself.

The Egyptians had great interest in achieving spiritual transformation, occurring through a properly orchestrated post-death ritual (or, for a select few, through spiritual initiation). In the earliest period, only the loftiest members of society were privy to and could afford this ritual; later it became increasingly widespread among the upper classes.

While the *ka* was, for most, a collective energy that Egyptians related to with detachment or deference, the *ba,* in contrast, was more individual. It was the person in a different configuration than in waking life, operating during sleep, after death, or in the altered consciousness achieved in initiation. Usually translated as the person's "soul," it might be characterized as the individual "in an out-of-body state"; it only functioned in such a condition. By means of the *ba,* a person manifested in spiritual circumstances. Its essential nature was movement directed toward a higher spiritual level. It represented a more unified self-consciousness than was possible, in normal waking life, for Egyptians of that time.[11]

We glimpse the infinite self in the *akh,* "the shining one," the spirit of the pharaoh and of nobles; after the person's death, it lived a godly life of immortality. The ascent of the *ba* was toward the *akh.* If we understand the *ba* to be soul, the *akh* would be spirit, the *ba* made divine. It was, in Vulliamy's words, "immortal, ethereal, and passionless; the ultimately surviving form of the soul."[12] While the *ba's* existence was intermediate between the physical and spiritual realms, the *akh* found its true abode in the heavenly domain. It was in its element in the realm "of spiritual light . . . *akh* conveys notions of light: 'shining,' 'illumination,' 'irradiation'";[13] the elite who became individually immortal did so in the form of stars.[14] A papyrus claims: "A god has been born / now that I have been born."[15]

In his earth life, the pharaoh was both human and an "aspect" of the solar divinity; "the emanation of the divine . . . was present within his temporal, human, dimension."[16] Although the *akh* of the pharaoh could become prominent, even dominant, among the gods, the radiance of the *akh* was derivative, due to becoming united with the sun god Ra, the source of spiritual illumination, or to becoming Ra's son. The *akh* was not pre-existent; it was a condition gained through initiation or after death: its spiritual body, the eternal *sah,* was germinated from the physical body.[17] The *akh* was immortal only as regards future time; it didn't create the body and wasn't present in it, nor did the life of the body seem to interest it. The physical creation's purpose wasn't to manifest the *akh* in life but to be the starting point for the *akh*'s full existence in the spiritual realm.

Mesopotamia

Mesopotamians believed that the gods created humanity to provide them labor and food,[18] keeping eternal life for themselves. Death, however, did not mean cessation of existence, which was no more conceivable to Mesopotamians than to Egyptians. As Cohn notes, the deceased "must, as a disembodied soul, make his or her way down to the lowest level of the world" where there was no light, sound, or motion. These shades could assist the living in return for burial goods and offerings of food; if neglected, they might behave demonically. Mesopotamians had no hope of a happy hereafter or any change.[19] They were much less preoccupied with the afterlife than the Egyptians;[20] the official religion was mostly silent on the subject, although in ancient popular beliefs individuals could achieve the same immortality as the gods.[21]

Despite the prospect of an uninspiring hereafter, Mesopotamians could derive some comfort from the belief that the gods created them from divine material, partaking of divine nature. Humanity was neither radically unlike the gods nor distant from them.

Zoroastrianism

The earliest full appearance of the individual infinite self is the *fravashi* of Zoroastrianism. Zoroaster (Zarathustra) founded this religion in eastern Persia somewhere between the fifteenth and sixth centuries B.C.E. It influenced post-exilic Judaism and thereby Christianity and Islam, and possibly Greek philosophers such as Plato and Pythagoras.

In Zoroaster's vision of our psychospiritual nature, a person is a microcosm, consisting of the body (created after the soul but of "like substance") and spiritual elements that vary in number in different versions. As described by Jacques Duchesne-Guillemin, these include "a vital breath, a faculty of discernment, a conscience, a soul and a Fravashi. When the vital breath leaves the body, discernment and conscience perish; only the soul and the Fravashi have a post-mortem existence."[22] The soul is damnable, its fate dependent on the person's free will choices.

The *fravashi* is a person's fundamental spiritual nature; it shares in the highest divinity's radiant light and goodness. With free will it takes on a body to enter the world to fight for the divine good. It's described by *EB* as a "protective spirit"[23] or "the preexisting external higher soul or essence of a person (according to some sources, also of gods and angels),"[24] and is linked to the highest divinity, Ahura Mazda, from the beginning of creation, partaking of his essence and limitless abundance. *Fravashis,* along with other divinities, support and enhance *asha,* the good or right way for things to happen.

There are three categories of *fravashis*: yet to be born, alive, and deceased. A person's *fravashi* carefully supports her lifelong development of the ability to manifest her spiritual potential. Following death, the redeemed soul and *fravashi* are reunited. Like the *ka* in Egypt,[25] the *fravashi,* according to *EB,* can be seen as a kind of "deity who acts as a protective spirit of each individual and is also an ancestor spirit."[26] The *fravashi* is assigned to a person (and thus apparently doesn't create soul and body), guiding righteous living. Duchesne-Guillemin suggests that *fravashis* are "comparable . . . to Plato's Ideas. . . . Not only has a man's soul a Fravashi, but so has the entire creation, animated or not. The duty of the Fravashi is to see to the prosperity and just growth of the world."[27] Zoroastrians might revere *Fravashis* as deities of clans, families, and fundamental aspects of the natural world but also as souls whose character is benign and noble. Human beings are created to aid in the cosmic battle of good and truth versus evil and falsehood.

Fravashis are the essential confederates of Ahura Mazda in protecting the cosmos and sacred fire against demonic forces; the *fravashi* puts on the body and is in the forefront of the battle to help conquer Ahriman, the evil spirit, who brought death into the world and tries to separate soul and body. *Fravashis* have assurance of ultimate restoration to heavenly existence.

At the body's demise, the soul leaves to receive judgment. The idea of a judgment day is crucial in Zoroastianism. The soul is responsible for how a person lived his life and will be penalized or rewarded accordingly, either descending into the abyss or progressing to a heavenly existence. The abyss is a place of torment and punishment; Zoroaster apparently invented hell,[28] called the "House of Worst Thinking" or "House of Untruth." The worthy soul progresses through several phases, potentially reaching the paradise of infinite lights (the "House of Song"). [29] Between paradise and abyss is a destination for souls whose lives were equally good and evil. Disembodied souls populate heaven; a last judgment and a universal bodily resurrection occur at the end of time, at which point the evil souls will suffer annihilation and the good will live blissfully on earth with their bodies. Zoroastrianism regards people as good by nature and possessed of free will, able to decide their own destinies.

Initially, the idea of the *fravashi* applied only to the upper classes. Later, it included other classes, a progression that occurred in Egypt in the Osiris cult as well as in Greece.

Zoroastrianism's duality between the universal divine forces of good and evil sometimes tended toward radical, or eternal, dualism, though in most periods the dominant belief was that dualistic conflict would definitively conclude with good triumphing at the end of time. This is not a dualism of body and spirit; material creation partakes of the good of Ahura Mazda, who first created the world in spiritual form and then transformed it into materiality. This, remarks Cohn, "was in no sense a fall . . . it was a completion, a fulfillment."[30] The body is an instrument of the soul, created from like substance.

Hinduism

The earliest recorded expressions of Hindu spirituality are the hymns of the Rig Veda, composed mostly around or before 1200 B.C.E. and written down about 600 B.C.E. These hymns indicate early belief that each member of the privileged castes had a spiritual essence—ethereal, breath-like, distinct from the corporeal self—that, at the demise of a devout and virtuous individual, proceeded to heaven to reunite with its body and continue life. Heaven was a "blissful realm . . . full of radiant light, and of harmony and joy. . . . They make love—all the more deliciously because they have been freed from every bodily defect."[31] The bodily life was obviously valued and not divisible from the spiritual; divine and mundane are not separate. The deity Shiva (Siva) expresses the continuity of infinite and finite, being both creator and creation, transcendent and immanent, the all-encompassing at the infinite level of being and creator and destroyer at the finite level.

In later classical Hinduism, *Atman* is the conception most closely approaching the idea of the individual infinite self. In Hindu cosmology, *Brahman* is ultimate reality. Transcending conceptual ability, it is the infinite, fundamental nature or soul of all creation; *Atman* is the term for its presence and expression in the human soul. Sri Aurobindo says that *Atman*, "our true self, is Brahman; it is pure indivisible being, self-luminous. . . . It is timeless, spaceless and free."[32] Swami Nikhilananda (1895-1973) states that *Atman* signifies "the unchanging and transcendental Consciousness in man, present in his every act of cognition, no matter what the level or state of the experience."[33] *Atman* is *Brahman* entering existence as pure consciousness.

Hindu metaphysics thus identifies the true self of a person as cosmic and infinite yet one with *Brahman*, the Supreme Soul. Nikhilananda elucidates: "He who knows the Self is liberated . . . because he has realized himself to be the very Soul (Atman) of the gods. 'He who knows the Supreme Brahman verily becomes Brahman.'" Only *Brahman*, "the one Self or Supreme Soul of the universe," exists, and each soul as well as everything in nature is "non-different from Brahman." An individual soul, called *atman* (lower case) or *jiva*, "is identified with a body, and is the victim of hunger and thirst, pain and pleasure, good and evil. . . . Limited in power and wisdom, it is entangled in the eternal round of *samara* [the impermanence and changeability of the universe] and seeks deliverance from it." It is "insignificant."[34] Aurobindo urges that "we must cease to make . . . this world or even its right, light and beauty our object of pursuit; we must go beyond these to . . . a transcendent Truth, Light and Beauty."[35] The highest aspect of self is nonindividualized *Atman*, while for *atman*, finite self, the emphasis is on overcoming causation and the attachments of body and mind, illusions and desires, not on a growing partnership with infinite self. It too is *Atman*.

While there's little or no suggestion here of a cosmic individuality of identity and purpose, a shift in nuance from emphasis on the oneness of the whole cosmos in *Brahman* to oneness in the sense of *union* in and with the divine opens the way to the potential for individuality in experience and identity. Thus, as Aurobindo stresses, "attainment of the Brahman" enables us to achieve immortality, which isn't overcoming death, "but the finding of our true self of eternal being and bliss. . . . To know and possess [the soul's] true nature, free, absolute, master of itself and its embodiments is the soul's means of transcendence, and to know and possess this is to know and possess the Brahman."[36] The emphasis in this statement is more on the activity and goals of the individual. This statement from Nikhilananda is also suggestive: "While the jiva . . . roams about overcome by the pairs of opposites, 'his immortal Self remains like a drop of water on a lotus leaf.'"[37]

Hinduism doesn't suggest a distinction of soul from immortal self or immortal self from the one divine nature, but neither is it contrary to it. While the idea of the oneness of God or the universal soul would not seem to disallow the possibility of individual infinite selves, there seems to have been no formulation of a notion of the infinite self in Hindu philosophy.

Taoism

For the ancient Chinese, the idea of immortality related strictly to existence in the physical universe. In Taoist philosophy, the spiritual, as distinct from the ethical (Confucian) tradition of China before Buddhism, there was no single, indissoluble soul or spirit. Taoists originally held there to be two souls: one, the *hun*, begins in the upper or celestial realm; the other, the *p'o*, arises from the lower, terrestrial region. These join at birth; life and health depends on maintaining their proper relationship. The dynamic quality of this interaction is *chi*, life-energy or vitality, which keeps the relationship occurring as a unity or person, much as did the Egyptian *ka*.[38]

Immortality concerned the indefinite extension of physical existence by the management of decay and transformation[39] by keeping the *chi* sustained in its proper circulation in the body in order to maintain the dynamic interchange of *hun* and *p'o*. Over time, Taoists further differentiated the two-part soul into a three-part *hun* and seven-part *p'o*, but their essential relationship and the conception of immortality remained the same. In Taoism's earlier phases, immortality had nothing to do with perfecting a transcendental vehicle that leaves the body,[40] as was the Egyptian concern. Joseph Needham explains that unlike the Western conception of an original nothingness from which the world was created, the Chinese posited "an undifferentiated nothing which contained within itself a universal potentiality for the differentiation and appearance of everything"; thus, the demarcation between matter and spirit was quite indistinct. The ancient Chinese conceived of no alternate non-material reality, "no heaven or hell, no creator God, and no expected end of the universe. . . . All was natural, and within Nature."[41] This changed after the introduction of Buddhism; despite the fact that the Buddha disavowed the existence of a soul, the schools of Buddhism that flourished in China included in their teachings the survival of an immortal, non-physical soul surviving in either paradise or hell; Taoism adopted these ideas over time.[42]

Before this development, the continuity of spirit and body within nature led to two Taoist approaches to attaining immortality. The first was through alchemical investigation, possibly as early as the fifth century B.C.E.[43] Needham defines it as a search for "knowledge, drugs or elixirs . . . [to extend life by] rejuvenating the body and its spiritual parts so that the adept . . . can endure through centuries . . . finally attaining the status of eternal life and arising with etherealized body as a true Immortal." The Taoist alchemical adept could hope to enter "the ranks of the invisible bureaucracy of the universe as a Heavenly Immortal . . . or else [become] . . . an Earthly Immortal, purified, ethereal and free, able to spend the rest of eternity wandering as a kind of wraith through mountains and forests, enjoying . . . the cycle of the seasons."[44] Either way, this kind of immortality requires the preservation of the body "in however etherealized or 'lightened' a form." This immortal existence, essentially as a "will o' the wisp" that remains entirely within the confines of physical existence, constitutes one of the great departures in ideas about immortality compared to beliefs in India, Persia, and the West.[45]

In the Chinese conception, immortality occurs on, beneath, or above earth. Regarding the first location, the Taoist notion of the ages-long persistence of the individual in a wraithlike, insubstantial body, in the world but largely avoiding people, has similarities to the beliefs of Native Americans, aboriginal Australians, and others. Underworld beliefs were akin to those of ancient Israel (*She'ol*), Babylonia, and Greece (*Hades*). The Chinese "celestial bureaucracy" in the starry constellations corresponds to an important aspect of Egyptian afterlife.[46]

The second Taoist approach to achieving immortality was more spiritual. The practice of *wu wei*, "not-doing," or more accurately "no action contrary to nature,"[47] aimed to remove the influence of the conceptual mind, which obstructs the complementarity of the *yin* and *yang* principles of natural existence by creating the "ten thousand things," the labyrinth of multiplicity. Spiritual historian Roger Weir elaborates: "yin and yang, without the interference of man . . . become again the *Tao* [the authentic design of existence]; man bridges heaven and earth by taking his interference out of the picture." *Wu wei* enables man to completely and precisely *present* the inner eternal, rather than *represent* cognitively the external. Therefore, human immortality consists of eliminating ideas of immortality and of engendering, through purification, the capacity to experience the eternal—to become a transparent screen for experiences of the inner world. The Taoist then is included in this immortality physically, and his interior world becomes spiritual. Through *wu wei,* heaven and earth occur not in him but *as* him: he *embodies* immortality.[48]

At various times and in different Taoist lineages, immortality was a physical goal, attainable through a chemical and physiological process, or it involved a spiritual existentialism, an embodied experience of the immortality of the cosmic order (and therefore was still a material occurrence). This didn't involve a higher spiritual identity that created, sustained, and guided the individual finite creation—but then there was in ancient China no tradition of a macrocosmic creator identity, either in Taoism or its shamanic roots.

Taoism's this-worldly heavens began to blend with Buddhist otherworldly heavens and hells by the early third century C.E., a transformation that was well advanced by the mid-fourth century; entrance to these depends on how ethically one lives. (Needham observes that Confucians "regarded the whole business [of heaven] as a dangerous diversion from man's earthly duties."[49])

In Chinese folk religion, as per *EB,* following death "the soul becomes either of two spirits: the *shen,* which ascends to the spirit world, or the *kuei,* a dark, passive *yin* spirit, which remains within the grave." The ability of the *shen* to rise hinges on the family performing the proper ceremonies. Lacking these, it becomes frustrated and, as a malicious ghost or *kuei,* it visits its wrath on the living.[50]

Buddhism

Buddhism is the spiritual system that seems most removed from the notion of an individual infinite self. As expressed by Buddhist scholar Edward Conze, it understands occurrences "without any reference to a 'self,' and must explain what actually happens on the assumption that the 'self' is not an active or actual factor." There is knowing but no knower; there are acts but no agent. "The Actual living Buddha is a combination of the impersonal metaphysical principle of Dharma with a 'vile body'. . . . 'Persons' . . . do not exist."[51] Nothing that isn't absolute spirit is real. All things interpenetrate all others, as does the universal principle of existence, in a "'sameness' or identity of everything." Every least thing contains the entirety of the *Dharma*-element, the absolute principle. To comprehend the nature of any one thing is to comprehend each thing and all things.[52] *Dharma* in Buddhism is similar to Hinduism's *Atman* and *Brahman* but is more radical in denying a self—there is no *atman.*

The absolute principle, *Dharma,* manifests in earthly form as a *Tathagata,* a term applied to the Buddha as a type, not an individual. These types manifest in life sequentially at particular times; "each . . . follows the same Path," says Conze. Their variances are insignificant; in their fundamental nature, they are identical. Each entity, organic and otherwise, is a nascent *Tathagata;* the ubiquitous seed of Buddhahood is in all things. "The Absolute in this system is defined as the spotless and translucent Spirit, which is also Suchness . . . the Buddha element." While Nirvana, the goal, is the complete opposite of life as most people know it, a person can achieve Nirvana because it's always within, and she need only definitively remove what has hidden it.[53]

In sum, there is an infinite and eternal principle, *Dharma,* indwelling in all things, but there is no infinite *or* finite self whatsoever, and any experience of either is illusion.

Orphism and the Dionysian Religion

Orphism, a religion centered on the mythologized pre-Homeric poet and musician Orpheus, arose in Thrace, northeast of Greece, apparently in the sixth century B.C.E. Orphism seems to have had a seminal influence on aspects of Western spirituality by way of Pythagoreanism and thereby Plato and others, and so is included here. Orphics believed that the soul is created before the body, is immortal, and partakes of divinity. Some scholars have suggested, controversially, that the Greek idea of the soul's immortality and divinity derived from the ancient Dionysian (Bacchic) mystery religion of Thrace, which thus provided the classical world with its grand conception of human nature and purpose. Thracian tribes were called "those who make themselves immortal." Related to or derived from the Dionysian religion, Orphism believed in the transmigration of souls; they were intensely preoccupied with the afterlife, which, Stoyanov notes, "was to impel some Thracians to weep at the birth of children and to rejoice at the burial of the dead." There was an important Orphic trend in the later Greek mystery religions.[54]

Orphism may have introduced the dualism of body and soul to European religious belief. An Orphic myth relates that the Titans, enemies of Zeus, Dionysus's father, dismembered and ate the baby Dionysus. In vengeance, Zeus destroyed the Titans, and out of their ashes man was created, inheriting both Dionysian and Titanic qualities; human beings are thus of dual nature, the soul partaking of Dionysus's divinity and the body consisting of "evil Titanic material," in Stoyanov's words. Alternately, the Titans were not the source of man's bodily nature; rather, they restricted the soul to their own domain and simply were bad role models. The soul's creation occurs before the body and apart from it; the soul receives punishment in the body until it works off its primeval guilt. This view, in which the body is sepulcher for the immortal soul, has similarities to Gnosticism's emphasis on releasing the "divine spark" from its bodily confinement.[55] The soul, as a divine element, is akin to the gods.

Orphic dualism involved an implicit monism, in that it saw in the profusion of existent things only an illusory annihilation of the divine oneness, from which everything emerges and back to which all is restored.[56] There was no soul or spirit with an eternal distinction from the "One Principle."

Salvation of the soul occurred through self-effort, including ascetic discipline and acquiring esoteric knowledge, rather than by divine aid or grace, as in Christianity, or through ritual magic, as in Egyptian religion. Orphic training involved learning to maintain memory after death, in order to end the transmigration of the soul.

Pythagoras and the Pre-Socratic Greek Philosophers

A seminal Greek mathematician and philosopher, Pythagoras was reputed to have studied for years in Egypt, bringing Egyptian esoteric themes to the Greek world. Pythagoreanism, a more mystical approach to knowledge than Ionian naturalism, had much in common with Orphic thought. It had a marked influence on later Greek philosophers, including Plato, Aristotle, and the Neoplatonics. It began as a religious brotherhood and philosophical school founded by Pythagoras about 525 B.C.E. at Crotona in Southern Italy. Evidence of its beliefs is fragmentary and difficult to understand—members of the cult swore secrecy, and Plato suffered expulsion for breaking this code of silence.

Conceptions of the personhood of human beings developed radically in sixth century Ionia (the western islands and coast of modern Turkey), where Pythagoras spent much of his life. Changes in the laws of the Ionian states promoted a greater sense of individuality and personal responsibility. At the same time, individuals had increasingly direct access to the gods Apollo and Dionysus. The cults of these gods may have helped promote another phenomenon of this period, a new belief regarding the soul's dignity and destiny. Likewise, where previously only a few could expect to receive divine revelation, the *Golden Verses of Pythagoras* (see below) state that Nature will impart revelation to *every* mortal.[57] Previously, Greek culture held the soul to be insignificant and doomed to a shadowy destiny in Hades.[58] Pythagoreans believed the soul to be immortal and able to achieve union with the divine.

To the belief in degrees of divinity and the ability of men to become gods that was current in Greece at this time, Pythagoreanism added that union with the divine was accomplished through philosophical understanding, ethical and virtuous practice, abstinence, the use of ritual and symbols, and the subjective experiences and wisdom received by the initiated. Also important was the understanding that the essential nature of things is form, not substance.

According to commentaries from the early fifth century C.E. regarding the *Golden Verses*, one who has accomplished this spiritual purification can achieve the immortality of a god. (Scholars date the *Golden Verses* anywhere from the fifth century B.C.E., even from Pythagoras himself, to the fourth century C.E.; regardless, they may contain accurate records of original Pythagoreanism.[59]) The exact belief presented in the *Verses* is unclear. Johan C. Thom states: "There is a dynamic tension in the *Golden Verses* between *being* and *becoming* divine"; human beings "have a divine origin."[60] The commentaries refer to the aspirant as being "restored to his primordial state" but also say that his "deification has had a beginning" that is accomplished only gradually; he succeeds when he has been "divested of what is mortal." These enlightened and purified humans, "immortal when they are ascended into Heaven but mortal when they descend upon earth" are a third class of gods, after the immortal gods and angelic beings.[61] They sometimes forget the divine. The predominant theme is immortality achieved. The divine, not an immortal higher self, creates soul and body.

As in Orphism, the author of *The Golden Verses* sees the body as a prison. The soul must be "purified . . . from all the pollutions of matter," If the soul doesn't renounce the desires of the flesh, it's subject to reincarnation as various species, leading to ultimate purification. The *Verses* speak of *Daimons*, souls of humans that the commentaries divide into three categories, according to their truth, virtue, and connection to this world, so-called "because they are full of knowledge and light."[62] Apparently, once having been freed from the wheel of birth, souls can still choose to return to a body.

Philolaus (b. c. 474 B.C.E.), the first Pythagorean from whom there are extant writings and who apparently influenced Plato, thought that everything "is a harmonious compound of Limited and Unlimited elements. . . . All beings are necessarily Limited or Unlimited, or simultaneously Limited and Unlimited."[63] This suggests at least a philosophical sense of the interaction of the infinite and finite within the self.

Contemporaries of Pythagoras in Ionia and Southern Italy also helped lay the foundations for European beliefs regarding humanity's relationship with the divine. While the pre-Socratic philosophers left no statements regarding a concept of the infinite self, they illuminate later views and arguments.

The Ionian philosophers Thales (fl. sixth century B.C.E.) and Anaximander of Miletus (c. 610-546/545 B.C.E.) felt that all things in the universe are living, filled either with gods or with "pneuma," cosmic breath, and thus they made no distinction between the spiritual and material. Heraclitus emphasized a hidden connection between all things, contending that any transformation occurring in the cosmos derives from the dynamic interaction of opposites. Each set of opposites constitutes a unity:[64] hot can't exist without cold or good without evil.

This union of the spiritual and material and of all opposites—and the original unity of what became the separate fields of science, philosophy, and religion—underwent division in the philosophy of Parmenides (b. c. 515 B.C.E.) and the Eleatic school of Southern Italy, which was highly critical of Heraclitus. They posited a divine principle existing beyond humans and gods. This ultimate reality, Eon, transcends description, except for being unlimited, absolute, pure, and unchanging. Eon is unrelated and irrelevant to the constantly varying mundane aspects of life, seen as a lesser order of actuality;[65] the realm of the eternal is separated from the human world. The Eleatic thinkers could not conceive of anything real that was not both accessible to thought and able to be articulated. Research necessitated not only intellectual inquiry but also its verbal formulation.[66] This firm relationship of language to reality set the Eleatic School apart from the Ionians, some of whom were mystically inclined; mystical experience is essentially beyond language. The influence of the Eleaticists led to the ultimate predominance of the rational mode of awareness and investigation in Western experience.

Greek philosophers of the fifth century B.C.E., notably Leucippus (mid-fifth century) and Democritus (c. 460- c. 370) tried to bridge the gap between Ionians and Eleaticists. They maintained, however, the unambiguous distinction between spirit and matter, the latter consisting of elements inherently devoid of life, upon which external spiritual forces, in their essence unlike matter, operated to give rise to physical motion. This led to the Greeks placing inquiry regarding the spiritual world above that regarding matter. For Aristotle, explorations of physical existence were of intrinsically less importance or interest than reflections on the nature of God or the soul. For this reason, Greek science never yielded the kind of technological advances that began in Europe in the seventeenth century. Christianity would make the Eleatic heritage of decisively valuing spirit above matter, as expressed by Aristotle, the foundation of orthodox philosophy until the end of the Middle Ages.

The Greek word for infinity, *apeiron,* meant not only the unbounded but also the infinitely complex, disordered, imperfect, and indefinite—in effect, very messy. The Greeks found it distasteful.

Plato

Plato's description of the spiritual composition of human beings was decisive for the development of subsequent Western portrayals. He viewed the soul as "akin" to the divine, but its sojourn in physical reality is a sort of exile. He refers to an unnamed divinity as the source of the Greek pantheon and the world soul, thus adding to Greek exoteric religion a creator god, a concept new to Greece. He used the old deities in a new cosmic schema, grafting differing religious frameworks.

Plato held that the soul is a composite, having both immortal and mortal parts. The divine creator fashioned the immortal spark in the soul of each living thing. The creator tasked the other gods with creating the remaining two parts of the soul, which are mortal. Plato thus describes the soul as tripart; a person will "learn with one part of [the soul], feel anger with another, and with yet a third desire the pleasures of nutrition and generation" and companionship.[67]

Plato's creator god instructs the other gods, his offspring, about engendering creatures:

> "Unless they are created the world will be imperfect. . . . But if these were created and given life by me, they would be equal to gods. In order therefore that there may be mortal creatures . . . turn your hands . . . to the making of living things, taking as your model my own activity in creating you. And in so far as there ought to be something in them that can be named immortal, something called divine, to guide those of them who are ready to follow you and the right, I will begin by sowing the seed of it and then hand it on to you; it remains for you to weave mortal and immortal together and create living creatures. Bring them to birth . . . and when they perish receive them again."[68]

The creator god mixed the compound from which souls were to be created and "allotted each soul to a star"; the gods "took the immortal principle of the mortal creature, and in imitation of their own maker" combined measures of the four elements.[69]

The immortal soul is immutable and "in the very likeness of the divine." Before incarnating, souls are able to perceive "absolute beauty, and goodness, and an absolute essence of all things."[70] Incarnating, they're subject to the senses; if they govern these, their life will be good, but if governed by them, it will prove evil. The soul does not value the body. It achieves life in the realm of the gods through good practices. If the soul maintains its purity, never while alive choosing attachment to the body, at death it "forever dwells . . . in company with the gods." Souls that "purified themselves with philosophy" are thereafter free of the body.[71]

In changing the Olympic gods to, literally, God children who create microcosms at God's behest in the manner of God's creation of themselves and the macrocosm, Plato produced a scenario similar to the infinite self's creation of and ongoing relationship with the finite self. Also comparable is humanity partaking of both finite and infinite nature. In his description of the creation of the soul, he splits what I call attributes of the infinite self between the higher part of the soul (immortal, having a divine spark) and the lesser gods that create its mortal aspects. However, these God children (referring here to both gods and higher souls) don't predate the physical cosmos, indwell throughout their creations, or love them completely. Worldly sense experience and emotions distract from the joys and beauty of the pure world and are misleading. Plato's message is mixed: mortals are necessary to the world's wholeness, but no self-respecting immortal soul would ever choose to associate with one.

Judaism

In Genesis, God can be present on Earth, "walking in the garden," talking to Abraham, appearing in human form, eating, and having his feet washed as a guest.[72] (In the garden, God is, in fact, hard to avoid; Adam and Eve resort to hiding.) By Exodus, a great distance has arisen between God and man. Moses first encounters God in a burning bush he cannot approach and before which he hides his face in fear. Later, God manifests as a cloudy pillar to speak to Moses. Even though God "used to speak to Moses face to face, as one speaks to a friend," God is still not visible, saying, "you cannot see my face: for no one shall see me and live." Only his back may be viewed.[73] Except in Genesis, the divine largely remains apart and mysterious and is often wrathful; finite humanity could not conceive of washing God's feet or breaking bread with him.

"One of the most remarkable features of Jewish belief in the Hereafter is the absence of any kind of definite information in the Bible," observes theologian Louis Jacobs. This may indicate an attempt by Biblical authors to distinguish Israelite beliefs from surrounding religions that emphasized immortality of the soul as contingent upon identification with their gods after death or upon becoming a god.[74] According to Needham, "the prophets . . . [were] strongly against any emphasis on the life after death. . . . Jahweh . . . was a God of the living and not of the dead."[75] However, Israelite popular beliefs in continuity after death were ancient; they entered "official" religion later. The earliest beliefs held that both the righteous and unrighteous could expect to end up after death in a vague, nebulous region called *She'ol*, "the pit" or "land of oblivion,"[76] receiving neither reward nor punishment. Impurity surrounded death in Biblical times; the divine had no place in *She'ol*.[77]

The incorporation of popular belief in an afterlife into the priestly religion took several centuries, involving, as Needham puts it, "the breakthrough of the soul to God from the realm of death" beginning in the late Biblical period.[78] Job 19:26 (fourth century B.C.E. with older elements) speaks of bodily resurrection. In the words of Ecclesiastes 12:7 (late fourth or early third century B.C.E.): "and the dust returns to the earth as it was, and the breath [alternately, "spirit"] returns to God who gave it." This indicates a change either to a close relationship of the spirit to God or to reabsorption into God. Daniel 12:2-3 (first half of the second century B.C.E.) states: "Many of those who sleep in the dust of the earth shall awake, some to everlasting life, and some to shame and everlasting contempt." Cohn asserts: "This passage . . . marks a decisive break with the traditional Israelite notion of death"; in Daniel, however, as well as in Essene texts, "there is no suggestion . . . the righteous will exist as immaterial souls in an immaterial realm: those crowns of joy and garments of majesty will be bestowed on bodies, which will then become . . . radiant, angel-like."[79] At the end of time, souls and bodies rejoin in an earthly paradise. Greek thought probably strongly influenced the development of the doctrine of the soul's immortality; combined with Persian (Zoroastrian) ideology of resurrection of the dead and with Jewish Messianism, a scenario later developed where the individual soul continues to live in heaven rather than being lost at death.[80]

The Maccabean uprising (168-164 B.C.E.), caused great loss of life among those considered righteous, challenging the traditional view that deeds were rewarded and punished in this life and helping to increase the importance of belief in an afterlife. The *Wisdom of Solomon* (late first century B.C.E., in the Apocrypha) asserted that each human being is immortal and that God "made him to be an image of his own eternity."[81]

Philo of Alexandria, a Jewish philosopher erudite in Greek thought, viewed souls as pre-existing bodily incarnation. With Platonic disdain for the body and its pleasures, he writes that "a heavy dose of sheer ill luck has infected those souls that, nourished in air and the purest ether, migrated to earth, the region of mortality and evil, because they were unable to endure the satiety of divine goods."[82] Matter being, for Philo, irredeemably evil, resurrection of the body was out of the question.[83]

Philo held that "man is located on the frontier between mortal and immortal nature, having a part in each." While the physical nature is mortal, the mind has immortality;[84] the "fully purified" soul is "inextinguishable and immortal."[85] Some souls "have never deigned to associate with any of the parts of the earth. . . . [They serve as] ministers and helpers in [God's] care for mortal man."[86]

Philo describes a two-part soul, one created in God's likeness and the other being earthly. Following the skeptic philosopher Sextus Empiricus (fl. early third century B.C.E.), Philo speaks of the "soul's soul." He refers to the ruling part of the total soul, by which Sextus denoted that which binds and unifies the whole compound.[87] The meaning of the soul's division isn't entirely clear or developed, but it indicates some distinction between soul and spiritual self. Philo placed Forces, similar to Plato's Ideas, in a mediating role between God and material existence. These, infinitely numerous, preexisted the cosmos and act in it as God's creative agency. He considered the Forces to be the equivalent of the *daemons* (*daimons*), a person's soul, higher intellect, or guardian spirit that the Greeks often considered part of the individual.[88]

Philo, holding man to be both mortal and immortal and positing Forces that are both God's agency and higher aspects of human beings, approaches somewhat the idea of the infinite self. He is an example of the highly sophisticated and syncretistic nature of Hellenistic Judaism, which was a major source for Gnosticism and, evidence strongly suggests, was the aspect of Judaism from which Christianity arose.[89] Hellenistic Judaism's development ended late in the first century C.E. with the rise of Rabbinic Judaism following the destruction of the Second Temple. Further changes in Jewish understanding of human psycho-spiritual nature found expression, particularly from the twelfth century on, in the Kabbalah.

Hellenistic and Roman Pagan Beliefs

Plato's notion that each soul is linked to its own star, from which it departs for worldly incarnation and to which it returns after the body's demise, was developed by his follower Heraclides Ponticus (early fourth century B.C.E.) into the idea that the Milky Way is the path souls take on this round trip. This heralded a new view, "celestial immortality," that became widely accepted in the Hellenistic and Roman worlds as the principal conception of the afterlife. This immortality meant that the soul, in David Ulansey's words, "ascends through the heavenly spheres to return to its true home beyond the stars."[90] This seems to have been an important tenet of Mithraism, which originated in Asia Minor in the second or first century B.C.E. and spread throughout the Roman Empire in the first century C.E., becoming Christianity's most important rival to replace the Roman pantheon as the empire's dominant religion.

Plutarch (c. 46 C.E.–d. after 119), a Platonist, viewed the soul as composite and multi-layered.[91] Above this soul, explains historian Peter Brown, "lies a true soul [*daimon*] that is as superior to it as is the soul to the body";[92] therefore, human beings are tripartite: body, soul, and intellect or *daimon.* This vision of multilevel existence prefigures Plotinus. Plutarch, says Ian Kidd, relates "how the soul after death shoots up like a star and becomes a daimon, or deity. . . . In incarnate souls themselves a deity may remain." The *daimon* provides divine guidance. After the body's death, the soul also dies, leaving the *daimon,* untainted, to rise to heaven.[93]

Part 2. From the Beginnings of Christianity to the End of Western Classical Civilization

Early Christianity

Early Christianity is suggestive but unclear regarding an infinite self. Jesus' compelling statement, "You are Gods,"[1] sums up the vision of human nature at the foundation of Christianity. This is amplified by such assertions as "the kingdom of heaven is among [alternately, 'within'] you" and "the one who believes in me will also do the works that I do and, in fact, will do greater works than these"[2] and affirmed in John's letter, "those who abide in love abide in God, and God abides in them."[3] Jesus prefaces "You are Gods" with "Is it not written in your law . . . ?" alluding to Psalm 82:6-7, where the reference is to gods who are called "children of the Most High" and who are being judged by God for lack of justice and who henceforth "shall die like mortals." Jesus has taken a passage understood to be a condemnation of non-Hebrew gods and a demotion of them to mortal status[4] and changed it to a reminder about the potential heights of human nature: "those to whom the word of God came were called 'gods.'"[5]

Paul (10?-67?) wrote in I Thessalonians 5:23: "May the God of peace himself sanctify you entirely; and may your spirit and soul and body be kept sound." Here he envisions that a person's wholeness is tripartite, although even spirit is potentially fallible. The Letter to the Hebrews—almost certainly not by Paul—says that "the word of God is . . . sharper than any two-edged sword, piercing until it divides soul from spirit."[6] The author thus apparently sees soul and spirit as intimately related yet distinguishable and separable from each other, although the context suggests that the distinction requires a level of discernment bordering on the divine.

In Matthew 18:10 Jesus, referring to little children, cautions: "Take care that you do not despise one of these little ones; for, I tell you, in heaven their angels continually see the face of my Father." This is a remarkable statement, first in the assertion that children have their own angels, whose privileged position in heaven rubs off on the children, and second in the singling out of these angels as always beholding the face of God. For angels we might read infinite selves (always unified with God) and remember children are especially open to the infinite.

2 Peter 1:3, 4 avows: "His divine power has given us everything needed for life and godliness. . . . You may . . . become participants of the divine nature." Jesus' sending of the Holy Spirit, which, John declares, will "be with you forever . . . and he will be in you"[7] implies, Jung asserts, "a tremendous change in man's status, for he is now raised to sonship and almost to the position of a man-god." Considering that the Holy Spirit "is the Third Person of the Deity, this is as much as to say that *God will be begotten in creaturely man*. . . . The future indwelling of the Holy Ghost in man amounts to a continuing incarnation of God."[8]

Jesus' willingness to minister to prostitutes, moneychangers, and lepers set the tone for an egalitarianism of the spirit. He declared that all people are spiritually equal with comparable opportunity to achieve heavenly immortality; Christianity's democratic and meritocratic view of the afterlife moved decisively away from the ancient idea that earthly status determined one's spiritual rank in the hereafter, as had the Egyptian, Greek, and Zoroastrian religions previously, to varying degrees. This equality differed from the expectation, common in many other societies, of privileged treatment for kings, priests, and nobles, who were given higher places in the afterlife and even had different kinds of souls than commoners.[9] Christian teaching that the quality of afterlife depends on moral merit enabled people to experience themselves as more spiritually independent of their life circumstances and more an individual spiritual self partaking of divine nature than was possible in most religions of the time. The teaching that the meek would inherit the earth was radical regarding the hereafter as well as earthly society. (The doctrine of predestination would undercut this, especially from Augustine on.)

Apparently, Jesus felt the kingdom of God, which he said was immanent and into which the righteous would enter, would be in this world, but this transformed earth would mirror the condition of heaven: all would be "on earth as it is in heaven." Cohn proposes: "Perhaps, then, heaven and earth will be fused, and all those dwelling in that single realm will be equally glorious? Sometimes Jesus seems to suggest just that . . . men and women will be 'like angels in heaven,' and . . . 'shine like the sun.'" They will belong, "in the very near future, to a community of immortal, transfigured beings."[10] Paul anticipated a kingdom of the spirit in the air inhabited by spiritual bodies of the resurrected. Revelation 21:10-25, in contrast, describes the descent from heaven of the new Jerusalem, which is quite material and even quantifiable, to which the earth's kings shall come but which will be free of worldly defilement.

Several hundred years later Augustine pronounces, "when the judgment is finished . . . this world shall pass away by transmutation, not by absolute destruction. . . . The figure, therefore, passes away, not the nature." Augustine is clear that those who are saved will continue in physical form. "The qualities of the corruptible elements which suited our corruptible bodies shall utterly perish, and our substance shall receive such qualities as shall . . . harmonize with our immortal bodies, so that, as the world itself is renewed to some better thing, it is fitly accommodated to men, themselves renewed in their flesh to some better thing."[11]

The Christian attitude to the body and the earth is mixed: spirit and earth can directly and beautifully relate but not until the world is made new, Paul's view excepted. The righteous must endure the current situation if they are to attain and enjoy a transformed life.

Clement of Alexandria (c. 150-c. 215 C.E.) maintains, "if a man knows himself, he shall know God."[12] He believed, in Chadwick's words, that in "an ascent from faith through knowledge to the beatific vision beyond this life," those who achieve redemption "are one with God" in what he terms a deification.[13] Clement followed Plato in conceiving that human purpose is to achieve "likeness to God so far as possible."[14] He believed that within each human being is an unseen impression of God.[15]

By the second half of the second century, belief in a considerable disparity between God and humanity also appears. The church father Justin Martyr (C. 100-c. 165), upon becoming convinced of a vast difference between the divine and the human mind, gave up Platonic in favor of Christian philosophy. As a Platonist, he saw affinity between humankind and God and believed the soul to be "'divine and immortal, and a part of that very regal mind.'"[16] As a Christian, he came to believe divine revelation is necessary for the mind's illumination, based on the idea that it can't, on its own, realize God within.[17] Irenaeus, Bishop of Lyons, deemed God active and infinite, while humanity is a finite, passive recipient of divine action.[18] His student Tatian (120-173) said that prior to Adam's transgression, human nature included two spirits: the soul and the "image and likeness of God."[19] Historian Roelof van den Broek explains that, according to Tatian, the latter "more powerful spirit" left at the Fall; the human soul "dies with the flesh. Only if the soul obtains knowledge of God is it reunited with the divine spirit, who is called the soul's companion. . . . This spirit-companion of the soul, who helps it to find the way back to God, is identified with the Holy Spirit. . . . [It is] a heavenly counterpart of man, which was considered to be his guardian spirit or angel."[20] The Church condemned Tatian's teachings as heretical.

In summary, Jesus spoke of human beings as "Gods"; some early Christians could articulate the potential of the "godliness" of human beings and their capacity to become "deified" as "immortal, transfigured beings" and to live a heavenly life in the future. However, this was a development of human potential based on actions in this life, not an eternal condition, the soul not existing prior to the body's creation (though Jesus' reference to Psalm 82:6 seems to speak of more). In some views, humans have both soul and spirit. The Christians attitude toward the value of bodily existence varied considerably. We'll return to the significance of the figure of Jesus Christ in relationship to the understanding of the individual infinite self in the last section of this part.

Gnosticism

Gnosticism developed in the first or second century C.E. It's variously considered an independent religious movement, a Christian heresy, or a Jewish heresy or esoteric offshoot. Its diverse sects drew heavily on Judeo-Christian sources; it may have arisen before Christianity, or it may have its basis in proto-Christian sources, developing in parallel with more orthodox Christian sects. It seems to have incorporated elements of Zoroastrianism and Platonism.[21]

Most Gnostic sects believed that the world's formation was a mistake made by emanations, immortal offspring of the Monad, the cosmic creator. Basilides (second century C.E. Alexandria) held that the unbegotten divine creator had hundreds of emanations, varying in degrees of purity or corruptness.[22] Other teachings described numerous levels of creation generated successively by these offspring and their creations before the final making of the world and humankind. The major problem for humanity is to overcome not sin but ignorance, which is the cause of the formation of the world and therefore suffering; this is accomplished through gnosis—knowing or insight, especially self-knowledge—through which one can know God.

Broek describes the Gnostic belief that a person's "soul or mind or divine spark . . . originally belonged to the divine world."[23] Salvation involves the withdrawal of spirit from a person's material nature and even from his soul, through gnosis. Human beings consist of matter, soul, and spirit, but only spirit is of essential value, and many Gnostics regarded the material world as worthless. Like Plato, they believed one should sever attachment to it. Gnostic sects could be ascetic, avoiding worldly temptations, or, having disdain for the world and its conventions, they could be scandalously licentious. They expected that when all created beings had awakened and returned to the pleroma, the material world and its creator (not the Monad) would cease to exist.[24] A Gnostic text instructs that the Gnostic initiates "are supposed to put off their souls, become intellectual spirits, [and] unrestrainably and invisibly enter the fullness [pleroma]."[25] Apparently, not all sects supposed that everyone would return. Thus, from *The Dialogue of the Savior,* a Gnostic gospel: "If one does not understand how [the] body . . . came into existence, he will [perish] with it."[26]

Self-knowledge is equivalent to knowledge of God, given that self and the divine are identical; however, the Gnostic sources seem to disagree whether "identity" meant union with the divine, realizing "the fundamental identity between God and man," being "in God,"[27] or having a divine nature like Christ that makes one a son of God. Those initiated into gnosis experience redemption to the pleroma—the spiritual world or the fullness of the one divine being.

The Gnostic teacher Valentinus (fl. c. 140) contended that fallen angels, or aeons, created humankind. God made known the highest divinity by manifesting as *Anthropos,* seen as humanity's spiritual nature, core, and exemplar. In Valentinus's view, Pagels says, "humanity itself manifests the divine life and divine revelation. . . . [But he] did not use the term in its contemporary sense, to refer to the human race taken collectively. Instead, he and his followers thought of Anthropos (here translated 'humanity') as the underlying nature of that collective entity." Jesus, in calling himself the "Son of Man," thus meant, according to some Gnostics, that he was the Son of *Anthropos.* Christ, considered the purest aeon, taught the secret gnosis by which souls could achieve divinity.[28]

Some groups now labeled as Gnostic sects regarded themselves as true Christians, indeed as *the* true Christian Church, outside of which were those now known as orthodox Catholics. Others were inclusive of Catholics and anyone else who joined them in search of truth. The Catholic Church, however, deemed all Gnostics to be heretics, anathematizing and burning their books. (Some of these texts were hidden in the Egyptian desert at Nag Hammadi and unearthed in 1945). The Gnostics accepted some of these books as gospels containing the "secret" teachings of Jesus that were not recorded in the orthodox texts but given only to the most highly initiated in Jesus' circle and afterward passed on only directly from teacher to disciple. In evaluating these texts, it should be remembered that the accepted Gospels were not written until well after Jesus' death, many non-Gnostic Christian groups had their own gospels, and the orthodox canon took form only in the latter part of the second century and was not formally settled until the fourth. Much of early Church history is a sad chronicle of power politics among competing groups and beliefs; the Church's structure of authority was a significant source of dispute with the Gnostics.[29]

These considerations are important because the Gnostic gospels are the texts most strongly suggesting that some notion of the individual divine self was once part of Christianity. The *Gospel of Thomas* (one of the earliest non-Pauline Christian texts, some of which was perhaps written about 62 C.E. and which in its origins wasn't Gnostic but had Gnostic layers added later[30]) has Jesus teaching: "When you come to know yourselves . . . you will realize that it is you who are the sons of the living Father."[31] Likewise in *Thomas*, "Jesus said, 'He who will drink from my mouth will become like me. I myself shall become he, and the things that are hidden will be revealed to him.'"[32] And "Jesus said . . . 'the . . . elect . . . will find the kingdom. For you are from it, and to it you will return.' . . . 'If they say to you, "Where did you come from?", say to them, "We came from the light, the place where the light came into being . . . and became manifest through their image." If they say to you, "Is it you?" say, "We are its children."'"[33] The Valentinian *Gospel of Truth* conveys that "he [Jesus] discovered them [those to whom he gave knowledge] in himself, and they discovered him in themselves."[34] To Thomas, who has just wisely answered a question put by Jesus to his disciples and addressed Jesus as "Master," Jesus says, "I am not your Master."[35]

Thus, the Gnostic view of human spiritual nature was that a person came from the kingdom and the light and could return. A Gnostic believed he could become one with the Christ nature and its all-knowing mind and thereby himself be a son of the *Anthropos* and thus a God child. Jesus is not Lord, religious historian Elaine Pagels maintains, "unique . . . forever distinct from the rest of humanity," but a "spiritual guide." She adds: "Contrary to orthodox sources, which interpret Christ's death as a sacrifice redeeming humanity from guilt and sin," the crucifixion is "the occasion for discovering the divine self within."[36] Thus, in *Thomas*: "Jesus said, 'That which you have will save you if you bring it forth from yourselves.'"[37]

The *Gospel of Philip* describes the process of self-discovery that brings this about: "You saw the spirit, you became the spirit. You saw Christ, you became Christ. You saw [the father, you] shall become father. So [in this place (the material world)] you see everything and [do] not [see] yourself, but [in that (heavenly) place] you do see yourself—and what you see you shall [become]."[38] To see divinity is to become it; the trick is to know where to look.

These passages imply a penetrating vision of the fullness of human spiritual stature. Gnostics did not accord this stature to all created things; they didn't match the Buddha's revelation that all beings are Buddhas. Humans are, in part, divine children of God, but only humans—and of those, only initiates—could claim this status. As Pagels puts it: "Humanity itself, in its primordial being, was disclosed to be the 'God over all'. . . . Plotinus, who agreed with . . . Plato. . . . that nonhuman intelligences, including the stars, share in immortal soul, castigated the gnostics for 'thinking very well of themselves, and very ill of the universe.'"[39]

In contrast to the vision of human existence suggested in this book, that is, to the idea of the goodness of all aspects of human existence and of a purposeful partnership between finite and infinite aspects of self, for Gnostics the purpose of self-realization was to remove self from material nature and even from the soul. They understood self-realization or gnosis as progress through time toward an eschatological vision, the end of the material universe. Many Gnostics believed in achieving a higher spiritual status or returning to it, rather than it being an estate that some aspect of self continuously enjoys during the life of finite self as well as before and after. Instead of self-realization leading to a mutual relationship of finite and infinite selves serving to bring heaven into earth in an eternal here-now, the Gnostics, simply put, wanted out.

Plotinus and Neoplatonism

The third century C.E. Neoplatonic philosopher Plotinus synthesized Platonic, Stoic, and Aristotelian thought in an intellectually rigorous but mystically based description of human psychospiritual nature. Though not Christian, his system significantly influenced Christian and Islamic mystics and thinkers. Born in Egypt, he studied in Alexandria; his work is preserved in transcriptions of lectures given in Rome. These are difficult to understand in the original and quite challenging to translate, in part because they're founded in personal mystical experiences of union with the divine.

Plotinus taught that human existence reaches from the divine to the material worlds without diminishing its divinity. He argues that there are archetypes of each individual rooted in an aspect of the divine; all attributes of this divine aspect exist in the individual soul. To return in awareness to the divine does not mean absorption in it. Living as one's highest self means to exist as divinity.

He proposed a trinitarian godhead, consisting of three hypostases. The first of these is the One, absolutely unknowable and indescribable, transcending all possible qualities including even that of being. Strictly speaking, it can't be described as the cause of all else; as translator MacKenna explains, while the way that we think and speak necessitate conceiving of it as cause, this is valid only insofar as "its Perfection implies . . . a 'generation' of something other than It self."[40]

The second hypostasis, thus generated or emanated, is the divine mind or cosmic Intellectual-Principle, the loftiest aspect of divinity we can reach with our understanding. It can also be thought of as "Spirit" and includes—in fact, is—the cosmos we can know: the Intelligible Universe. It corresponds to the Platonic Ideas; it could also be termed the realm of archetypes. The Intelligible Universe includes, or is, all specific minds or intelligences, which are representations of divine mind. The essence of all creation exists eternally here. In Plotinus's words, the "Intellectual-Principle . . . is all. . . . It has all by other means than having, for what It possesses is still Itself, nor does any particular of all within It stand apart; for every such particular is the whole and in all respects all, while . . . still distinct. . . . The Good [the first Hypostasis] remains stationary within itself, but the Intellectual-Principle acts in relation to It and, as it were, lives about It."[41]

Translator A. H. Armstrong describes the lively interaction within the second hypostasis:

> Intellect is for Plotinus . . . the Platonic World of Forms, the totality of real beings. . . . [It] is an organic living community of interpenetrating beings which are at once Forms and intelligences, all "awake and alive," in which every part thinks and therefore in a real sense is the whole; so that the relationship of whole and part in this spiritual world is quite different from that in the material world, and involves no sort of separation or exclusion. This unity-in-diversity is the most perfect possible image of the absolute unity of the One. . . . Intellect is itself infinite in power and immeasurable . . . composed of . . . definite, limited realities.[42]

Physical things cannot occupy the same space, but "unbodied" entities lack this constraint, as Plotinus puts it: "their separation is solely that of otherness, of differentiation; in the absence of otherness, it is similars mutually present."[43] This is akin to the relationships of infinite selves with the divine as well as with one another in union.

Paul Henry says Intellect is infinite in a different way than is the One, the first hypostasis, because the former's nature is infinitely divided; each aspect is "identical with Intellect as a whole," but these aspects can stay "severally distinct."[44] (Cf. the description of transfinite numbers in chapter 7.)

The third hypostasis is the All-Soul, the emanation of the second. This generates the lower universe of matter, based on the example of divine mind. "The Soul, outside [the Intellectual-Principle], circles around the Intellectual-Principle, and by gazing upon it, seeing into the depths of It, through It sees God," in Plotinus's words.[45] He often speaks of the All-Soul as if divided into a Celestial Soul (Intellective-Soul) contemplating the Intellectual-Principle, and a Generative Soul or Logos that creates material existence.

Each level of existence, except the first, contemplates and seeks to return to the level that generated it. Each generates the level below it in a dynamic relationship where all in a sense partakes of the nature of all. At the same time, they are a unity, one divine nature; while the Intellectual-Principle is the unity's divine mind and envisioning capacity, the All-Soul is its dynamic, expressive quality. The cosmic Intellectual-Principle and All-Soul together correspond to the level of existence of infinite selves.

The individual soul has three divisions. The highest, the Intellective-Soul, is almost completely uninvolved with matter or the body, in which it differs from the Reasoning-Soul and the Unreasoning-Soul. Its function can be understood as "intellection, or intuition, or True-Knowing of Real Existences," as described by MacKenna. It forever reflects on the divine, but a person is unaware of its contemplation. He can awaken only through the practice of "philosophical morality," enabling the person to wholly identify with his most spiritual nature. "To live by the First-Soul, the Intellectual-Principle [the human Intellectual-Principle is identical with the Intellective-Soul] is to live as a God."[46]

The Godhead is present in human nature; we extend through all levels of existence with our full divinity. Plotinus states: "For the Soul is many things, and all things, both the things above and the things below down to the limits of all life, and we are each one of us an intelligible universe, making contact with this lower world by the powers of Soul below, but with the intelligible world [second hypostasis] by its powers above . . . and we remain with all the rest of our intelligible part above, but by its ultimate fringe we are tied to the world below, giving a kind of outflow from it to what is below, or rather an activity, by which that intelligible part is not itself lessened."[47] Each person has a Form or archetype whose "origin and principle" is in the All-Soul. This hypostasis encompasses all souls, but they maintain individual existence within it. Whatever is true of the All-Soul is true for the individual soul.[48]

The Intellectual-Principle of each individual, originating in the higher division of the All-Soul, is eternally existent and unified with God (like the All-Soul, in contemplation of the divine) regardless of the awareness or actions of the person. A person's growth requires becoming aware of this already-existing aspect of self, so that he can actualize his always-present divine potential. A person's purpose (and most profound motivation) is to strive to identify with this highest self. It is thereby possible to achieve, in MacKenna's words, "the 'possession' of the God-head in an ineffable act of identification, becoming . . . one with God, actually God, and foretasting the blessedness of the final Return after which he is for all the space of eternity to be with the God-head, to be Divine, or to be God."[49]

Plotinus proposes that every person has the divine Intellectual-Principle, or second hypostasis, in its completeness in his highest soul.[50] Each soul contains many levels of reality, experience, and action, down to the level of matter, on any one of which a person may elect to live,[51] although ultimately only the highest will prove fulfilling. We can be active at every level of existence. The individual soul in its various levels corresponds to the finite self.

In portraying the continuity of the levels of cosmos and soul, Plotinus demonstrates how the person can rise, if she chooses, by gradually refining, cleansing, and simplifying, finally achieving union with God. As Armstrong summarizes: "There are two movements in Plotinus's universe, one of outgoing from unity to an ever-increasing multiplicity, and the other of return to unity."[52] The highest gathers the lower existences to it; they simultaneously seek to rise to it,[53] so that cosmic evolution involves a mutual relationship of creator and creation reaching toward each other.

Our existence reaches the realm of All-Soul, and by way of it the Intellectual-Principle, in exact semblance of the latter. Armstrong explains that in the world of the second hypostasis, "where the laws of space and time do not apply and the part is the whole, we are Being and the All." Becoming or being Intellect does not mean that the lower self ceases to exist; rather, it involves the lower self's "return to its perfect archetypal reality, distinguished in unity from all other archetypal realities, individual and universal," retaining its identity.[54]

The core of our being even extends to the One. Return to unity involves movement in consciousness. As Plotinus taught: "Thus the Supreme as containing no otherness is ever present with us; we with it when we put otherness away. . . . We reach towards the Supreme; it is we that become present. We are always before it: but we do not always look."[55] We must redirect our energy from the world around us toward what is within, focusing energy rather than scattering it. We return to our actuality through great discipline of mind and morality, making ourselves ready and remaining so until the Supreme responds within us.[56] In proposing that our own action helps return us to God, not Divine Grace exclusively, Plotinus is at variance with later Augustinian Christian orthodoxy. He claims that the soul's authentic movement is to rotate around its own originating center or source, "for to be a god is to be integral with the Supreme; what stands away is man still multiple, or beast. Is then this 'centre' of our souls the Principle for which we are seeking? We must look yet further: we must admit a Principle in which all these centres coincide. . . . [The soul's] primal nature (wholeness) is within it and about it. . . . We . . . hold through our own centre to the centre of all the centres."[57]

Plotinus, depending on the direction from which he approaches the issue, puts forth differing views as to the goodness or evil of the material world, but either way, he sees matter as necessary to the whole and therefore positive. The soul (but not its highest part) "falls" into materiality to seek self-identity. To return to our divine nature we have to disengage from matter, for it is unproductive and fails to return to the levels above it. At times Plotinus approaches dualism, but preponderantly he suggests existence has unity and continuity in which humankind participates at every level. While at times he holds matter to be the location of evil and almost completely lacking in any real existence, he allows even it is capable of being given shape and thus moving in the direction of true existence—Soul and Intellect; it even has some remote connection with the first hypostasis. For Plotinus, human evil is less an issue of disobeying or resisting the higher levels of existence than of fatigue and confusion. A person achieves salvation when she brings into awareness an experience of who she most deeply is, so that "Intellect which is beyond the virtues identifies itself with true being," as Henry explains.[58]

Often Plotinus seems to be self-contradictory or trying to have it both (or three) ways because he's trying to speak with intellectual clarity about that which is inherently paradoxical; to attempt to speak of such with completeness is to have to say it both ways, as we must describe light as both wave and particle. These different descriptions point to another, higher or more fundamental, order of existence than either conveys, one that contains both.

Plotinus's dying words were, "Strive to bring back the god in yourselves to the Divine in the universe."[59] This "bringing back" differs from the Gnostics' return journey to the kingdom or pleroma. For Plotinus, that journey is a movement of focused awareness through aspects of self that already manifest at every level of existence.

Plotinus's description of the human spiritual dimension, based especially on his four mystical experiences of union with the divine, provides an extremely clear expression of the essentials of infinite selves: divine beings (eternal Forms at the cosmic Intellectual-Principle and All-Soul levels), generated by the highest divine, unifying with other similar beings, themselves generating further levels of existence that are in their image and likeness—the levels of individual soul that mirror cosmic existence. While the condition of the Forms and their eternal union with the divine don't depend on what the personal self does, Plotinus considers that the possibility of experiencing union and living fully remains only a potential until a person has withdrawn himself from his material existence. This is distinct from the idea of living as an infinite self that is able to and desirous of manifesting purposefully in the physical world by way of the finite self, and from the idea that our potential is the full interaction of infinite self and all aspects of finite self.

Plotinus's vision of the richness, range, and possibilities of human existence is grand in scope and empowering in its implications. It yields a view of humankind at once material and spiritual, finite and infinite, mundane and divine, and able to choose and help bring about its destiny.

Origen and the Eastern Christian Mystical Tradition

Origen, a third-century Alexandrian Christian theologian who studied under the same teacher as Plotinus, carried on Clement's line of thought. His teachings were seminal for the Christian mystical tradition in the Eastern Church and, by way of the monastic movement, for Western Christianity.

Trained in Neoplatonism, he accepted the Platonic idea of the soul being akin to God. He held that before creating the cosmos, as historian Henry Chadwick describes it, God brought into being "a realm of spiritual beings endowed with reason and free will"[60] yet dependent on God, a domain, in Origen's words, of "rational beings . . . living a bodiless life in a blessed state."[61] The entirety of human nature engages in a long process of falling away from God and at last finding redemption,[62] achieving a mystical marriage with the Logos (Plotinus's second hypostasis, embodied as Christ). Origen's entire theology hinges on God's goodness and the free will of his creatures; he held that God creates beings that may share in His goodness through realization of His nature. The rational beings are peers existing outside of time, being eternal. They have kinship with the World Soul and so have the capacity to partake of higher wisdom; although they are creations, they're completely involved in God via the Word (Logos).

Following Philo's idea, Origen taught that the rational beings grew "sated" with their bliss; by degrees their love of the divine "cooled." They fell away from God through forgetfulness, tedium, and disregard of the divine in favor of lesser things. Origen compares their fall to a physician who, not keeping up with his discipline, loses his ability. In cooling, the rational natures became souls.[63] Souls exist before the body.

Due to the souls' fall, God created the world for humankind as a place of beginning education and preparation. It's not designed as a place of comfort, though God's goodness suffuses it in the form of organization and beauty; its difficulties serve to gradually and constantly reform and redeem the person to redirect him toward the creator. This allows the person to exercise his free will, particularly considering God does not coerce; creation entailed, for God, some self-restriction. The physical cosmos is conditional; the soul's sojourn in it is merely a part of its far greater life prior to and after inhabiting the body. Following this life, it continues to learn and grow, to atone and purify. All souls have the capacity for perfection and restoring their godly identity. We as souls may know God; we exist in his image, will be united with him in love, and, explains translator Rowan A. Greer, will "see Him face to face. . . . The goal of the Christian life is to be made divine." Greer notes: "The real difficulty with Origen's view is that it tends to obscure the distinction between God and the rational natures."[64]

Origen believed that evil powers fell for the same reasons as well as from pride, which inhibited their repenting forthwith. Nonetheless, they still have free will and the ability to reason; Origin believed, therefore, that even Satan has some capacity to acknowledge the truth and so could repent at any time, up to the end of the world. This would bring about the annihilation of his rebellious and evil aspects and the lifting up and restoration of his divine nature to God. Completion of the divine plan occurs only when all are resurrected so that, as put by Chadwick, "God is all in all." This does not seem to be inevitable, however, considering that the gift of free will is incontrovertible. Thus, Origen has to admit to the possibility that even those who've reunited with God may again diminish in their love of God and so fall again, and again achieve redemption, endlessly. Origen "cannot know, because he cannot believe either that freedom is lost or that love can fail."[65] Greer provides another interpretation of Origen's belief: due to their learning and perfecting, the redeemed rational beings are at a higher level from which they can't fall again. Recurrent falling is also prevented because, after evil's final defeat and the restoration and atonement, souls will have new corporeal bodies ("resurrection bodies"); the physical form has no resurrection. In any case, because of what they've gone through on their journeys, they can "ply the Word with endless questions and . . . maintain their interest in His teaching" and thus not cool again in their adoration.[66] Souls, originally peers, now have rank, perhaps based on their experiences.

After his death, Origen's teachings became suspect as heretical and were condemned in 553. The doctrines most in question were of the preexistence of souls, their return to the condition of pure spirits, the flesh being the spirit's prison, the spiritual nature of the resurrected body, and the possibility of world cycles rather than a definitive end to world history with a final triumph of Good over Evil.

Origen differs from Plotinus and this book's premise in his belief that only God's prompting and support moves us to begin our spiritual return to our actual nature. Despite the fact that we have free will and despite the fact that our success hinges on our soul's own valor and fortitude, only God can give us the power to transcend ourselves. For Plotinus and in the view presented in this book, it is a partnership; for Origen it is also mutual effort but with the deciding factor being God's grace.

Origen, like Plotinus and all those influenced by Plato, felt it vital to segregate the soul from the worldly and material. The body isn't necessary to understanding what it is to be human; Origen believed what's essentially human is mind or soul, in contrast to this book's contention that the body is the locus and means for the indwelling infinite self to manifest its goodness, beauty, and truth in the world. Unlike Plotinus, Origen does not posit a spirit distinct from the soul; for him, the rational mind/soul's entry into the body is a fall of the whole self, so there is no higher aspect that remains unified with God. The whole self is involved in a historical process that doesn't seem to allow either for the instant awakening envisioned by the Buddha or the simultaneous experience of separation and union inherent in Plotinus's system and the one presented here. Nevertheless, Origen, with his "rational spiritual beings" that participate in God, anchors in Christian thought a view of human nature as God-like, eternal, free, and able to know divine truth.

Origen profoundly influenced the Christian East. Around 200, Eastern Christian mysticism began to articulate its experiences in forms dependent on Platonic philosophy. Plato's idea of deification seemed to match Christian beliefs about becoming sons of God and to be consistent with the promise of "becom[ing] participants of the divine nature."[67] Eastern Christianity could then import the Neoplatonist concept of union, expressed as union with God. Origen's theology, infused with Neoplatonism, was instrumental in giving form to the earliest important movement in Christian mysticism, which is still dominant in the East and was the foremost influence on all Western Christian mysticism until around 1200.

Eastern Christian mysticism makes a distinction between God's nature and his divine qualities (or attributes), the latter seen as energies permeating cosmic existence. As with Plotinus, the universe exists through a progressive emanation, in which God is conveyed out of himself to inhabit the center of all creation. The fourth-century theologian and mystic Gregory of Nyassa (c. 335-c. 394) averred that God created people as "the living image of the universal King."[68] He shared Origen's expectations of universal salvation.

Another mystic extremely influential for both Eastern and Western Churches was Pseudo-Dionysius the Areopagite (the pseudonymous writer was probably a fifth or sixth century Syrian monk, using the name of Paul's Athenian convert). His objective was to join Christian mysticism and theology more fully with Neoplatonism. He described the potential of human beings to slowly rise through a hierarchical universe, lifted by divine love; the material world and its creations are stripped away and left behind through a process of unknowing, that is, of surcease of the reasoning mind's function in favor of the actuality of spirit. They can go beyond hierarchy and knowledge to enter, as the darkness of unknowing, mystical union with God; there they encounter light from God's completely indefinable and inexpressible nature, the "Divine Dark." The soul achieves divinization through contemplative prayer, culminating in the ecstasy of experiencing the divine light. Any description of the highest divine is inadequate and misleading.

The divine darkness beyond cognition resembles Plotinus's first hypostasis, which is beyond all attribute or description. This negative approach involves dismissing anything material or conceptual that one might identify as the ultimate because the divine transcends all finite identification or characterization. God is nothing, no-thing; God is anything *and* its opposite. Pseudo-Dionysius's approach is entirely paradoxical.

In Pseudo-Dionysius's words, "it is the very nature of that God Which is the Supreme Cause of all to call all things to Participation in Itself in proportion to the capacity and nature of each."[69] He saw God as the soul's foundation of existence; an inner path is available to all via a person's own experience, allowing the soul to know its purpose and completely achieve its "Divine Likeness." The soul can attain the status of coworker with the celestial hierarchies. Pseudo-Dionysius affirms that humans can have celestial knowledge, unite with God, and achieve sonship of and friendship with the divine.[70] Even members of the celestial hierarchies, however, only reflect God, having a divine likeness rather than an inherent divine aspect. Angels get divine illumination directly and pass it on to rational human beings, who get it partially.[71] In this, Pseudo-Dionysius differs from Plotinus, for whom humans exist at all levels and can attune to the Intellect within them. He differs also in that he puts decisive weight on God assisting human beings in their rise toward divinity; for Plotinus, a person rises by way of a mutual reaching out, requiring much discipline and effort on the part of the individual. Pseudo-Dionysius describes God as desirous of and drawn toward the created universe while also remaining self-contained, unlike the totally aloof Greek cosmic divinity.

The emphasis in Eastern Christian mysticism on the divinization of humanity provides continuity in Christianity of the sense of human divine potential. However, rather than recognition of *being* infinite and eternally unified with God, this involves *becoming* divine through a spiritual life.

Manichaeism

Mani was born in Babylon in 216 C.E.; his family adhered to a Judeo-Christian sect. His "Religion of Light" syncretized Zoroastrian, Christian, Buddhist, Egyptian, and Jewish traditions in a formulation that had millions of followers and spread across Central Asia to China, where it continued into the seventeenth century. It also had a strong influence on Christian heresies during the middle ages, most notably the Bogomils and Cathars.

Manichaeism in the Western Roman Empire involved a dualism in which a war of light and dark substances occasioned the creation of the world; the conflict included a battle for the human soul, seen as a fragment of light caught up in darkness. Mani's followers considered themselves the true Christians. For them, Christ served to redeem particles of light trapped in matter, enabling them to return to where they belong. The "elect," the most dedicated Manichaeans, were celibate and ascetic, believing that return to the divine required freedom from body and materiality.

In Mani's dualism there are two primal, utterly opposed principles of good and evil. At the beginning of the Present Time, the principle of evil invaded the Realm of Light. To counter this demonic assault, the Father of Greatness caused the evocation of Primal Man and dispatched him to oppose the Prince of Darkness, bearing as weapons the five elements of the Light Sphere. In the ensuing battle, the forces of darkness prevailed, and while the Primal Man swooned in the bondage of Darkness, these forces devoured some of the luminous elements. Through this cosmic ingestion, the Father of Greatness ultimately trapped the forces of Darkness, who became, in Stoyanov's words, "poisoned but addicted to the Light elements they had swallowed." Then another cohort of divine beings was brought forth in the Realm of Light, including the Living Spirit, who freed the Primal Man by taking him by his right hand to lift him from his captivity (thereby establishing our familiar handshake greeting). The Living Spirit commenced the process of redeeming the Light elements: the "'Living Soul' imprisoned in . . . matter." The creation of the world was a way to redeem the Light elements from mixture with darkness. Humanity is the principal battleground between the forces of Light and Dark.[72]

In this cosmology, the soul is a fragment of the highest realm, not an image of it; the soul, a Light element, remains light and ultimately returns to the divine through the aspirant's efforts. It does not, however, seem to be a spiritual self with identity or creativity; it's simply an element of the Good needing the aspirant's help to go back to its source, although there's an implication of something more defined and individual, at least as regards Mani. One Manichaen codex speaks of a divine messenger to the youthful Mani; this turned out to be his guardian angel or Twin, and Manichaen teaching represents this, in Johannnes van Oort's words, as "an emanation of the Jesus of Light (who is in turn an emanation of the Nous or Divine Intellect)."[73] As in Gnostic systems, Manichaeism involves a complete negation of the material world's value, evil forces having created humanity as a physical race.

Augustine and Western Christianity

Augustine of Hippo provided the synthesis of Platonic philosophy and New Testament theology that dominated Western Christian thought for a thousand years. A youthful adherent of Manichaean dualism, profoundly influenced by Neoplatonism and especially Plotinus, and a student of Paul's writings in his mature life as a bishop, he helped give Christian thought an emphasis on humanity's propensity to sin, its fallen, subordinate, and dependent position relative to God, and its need for divine grace.

His view of humanity was Platonic, seeing the soul as superior to the body and independent of it. He taught that to return to God, a person must escape from the body. He couldn't ignore, however, the differences between Neoplatonic philosophy and the Christianity of Paul. Although the Bible agrees with Plotinus that one can find God within oneself, the Christian understanding is that this presence takes the form of a changeable image of the divine upon the soul, while for Neoplatonists the soul is itself a lesser form of the divine. Thus, Augustine could find God within, but not as an aspect of humanity's own nature. A further difference was his belief was that there are no beings free of potential sin save the Trinity.

Augustine proposes that knowledge is impossible without God's illumination of the human mind. He largely agrees with Plotinus that the soul receives illumination from the higher hypostases, the One and the Intellect, and this enables human beings to know the divine and eternal. Augustine differs in drawing a more severe distinction between God the creator and his creations. While he can allow that humans participate in the divine and there is a likeness and correspondence to the divine in the self-governing actions of the soul, he claims religious thought can only occur because of divine presence. While humanity can participate in divine love, even human love is directly dependent on God. Human nature is analogous to, or a reflection of, the divine, as for Pseudo-Dionysius.

Augustine strongly opposed Pelagius (c. 354-d. after 418), who rejected the doctrine of original sin. Pelagius emphasized the actuality of human freedom, despite human weakness, and the responsibility this entails. He argued that, absent such true freedom to choose the good, God's meting out of justice, as either retribution or recompense, would be unwarranted. Pelagius, like Plotinus, thought that a person's return to union with the divine requires the individual's effort and abilities. Augustine countered that God gives all good, and this does not allow raising oneself to righteousness through one's own struggle. For Augustine, while original sin stemmed from humanity's rejection of its allotted position in creation—the rebellion of the flesh against spirit—and while we have fallen by our own will, we aren't able to reverse this by a similar act of will. Only the grace of God's love can accomplish this. Augustine grants that a person's love for God has to be a free will choice, but he follows Paul in saying that the love of God arises as a gift of the Holy Spirit. Augustine had increasing difficulty in maintaining a place for a free will response to the gift of love in his doctrine of grace, holding that only God causes a person to open to good, and divinity is not intrinsic to our nature. Although God is the font of all human goodness, understanding, and strength, it was Augustine's belief that humanity doesn't retain or embody these qualities and so couldn't express them on its own, depending instead on God as their constant source. The Church ultimately condemned Pelagius's teachings as heretical and embraced Augustine's positions.

For Augustine, ever since the rebellious angels were ejected from heaven, two forces, faith and non-belief, have competed for the loyalty of God's creatures. These forces manifest as self-love with contempt for God and love of God involving disdain for self. For Augustine, these loves are mutually exclusive—despite the fact that God creates self, and in Augustine's view all creation is good.

Augustine's brilliance assured that his philosophy would provide a foundation for centuries of Christian thought. While largely affirming the goodness of God's physical creation and humanity, he was subject to dark extravagance in his depiction of human beings as completely dependent on the divine and pre-ordained for damnation or redemption, beyond any effect of free will action by the individual. Augustine didn't invent the doctrine of predestination but gave it great impetus. This immediately translated into dependence of the person on the Church and its dogma, as compared, for instance, to the Christian Gnostics' emphasis on continued revelation and a less hierarchical church. The stature which Plotinus and, to a lesser degree, Origen accorded the human spirit was gravely diminished by Augustine. This lost ground wouldn't be recovered in the West for hundreds of years, beginning when Peter Abelard gave renewed dignity to the rational mind and mystics such as Hadewijch and Meister Eckhart again soared to heights of vision, insight, and love.

The Christ Archetype in Late Antiquity

No existing religion is as crucially centered on its founder's identity, life, manner of death, and what happened to him after death as Christianity. Judaism is more concerned with the events Moses facilitated in the history of his people and his interactions with God than with his identity or the particulars and meaning of his existence. While the history of Muhammad's (c. 570-632) life is very important to Muslims, Islam's foundation is the Qur'an, which provides little coherent biography.

Yet, while Christianity rests as much on occurrences in the life of a man as on his teachings, the Biblical stories of Jesus have little historical corroboration. He left no writings, and scholars using textual analysis place the composition of the Gospels decades after his death, in the late first century, so that whether eyewitnesses wrote them comes sharply into question. Such textual analysis indicates that the earliest material in the Gospels is from the 50s—sections called the "Book of Q," for *quelle,* German for "source"—and these formed the core of Matthew and Luke. The non-canonical *Gospel of Thomas,* probably from the early 60s, shares some of the Q material.[74]

These first texts consist largely of Jesus' sayings; they give little of his life story, their earliest layer providing virtually none at all. Some scholars interpret them to indicate that Jesus was a teacher in the manner of the Hellenistic Cynic philosophers. These were not cynics in the modern sense; they were in the vein of Zen or Sufi teachers, often outrageous and provocative in behavior and words and given to using paradoxical questions or stories to challenge the conventional mindset and status quo.[75] Other scholars see Jesus as a radical social and economic reformer following the tenets of Judaic belief in a just and righteous God, responding to the effects on the peasants of Galilee of the Roman Empire's economic "globalization" and urbanization.[76] These early sayings don't depict the people of Galilee who recorded them as thinking of Jesus as Christ; neither do they speak of a resurrection. Jesus comes across as a sage using aphorisms to show people how to live morally and ethically together[77] and to survive as a community while beset by forces of change. The Pauline groups of northern Syria and Asia Minor developed the doctrine of the Christ.[78]

Whatever Jesus' teachings were and however his original followers viewed him, the obvious lack of consistency among the Gospels and their extended, late period of composition highlight the fact that Jesus' story and the doctrine of the Christ were developed and fleshed out by many people. As with almost all religions, Christianity's formation was decidedly a group undertaking, involving a wealth of differing interpretations over time that led eventually to the difficulties between Gnostic and orthodox sects and still later had to be sorted out in church councils from the fourth century on. Thus, however it's considered theologically, the figure of Christ is also a true archetype in the Jungian sense, complex and rich, satisfying the new eon's developing psychospiritual needs.

By the time the early Church councils had established the dogmas of the nature of Christ and the Trinity, and by the time Augustine had helped define Western orthodoxy and Origen had been excommunicated, the figure of Jesus Christ not only embodied all aspects of the infinite self but also had become, for orthodox Christians, their only receptacle. For those who prevailed in the council debates (and for most modern Christians), Jesus was seen as the Son of God from eternity, eternally unified with God, a divine being in human form, pre-existing that form and continuing after it as more than a soul, inheriting all the attributes of God and able to manifest these in physical form as the teacher, messenger, and embodiment of God's love—a description that almost completely matches that of the infinite self. (Of course, Trinitarian doctrine declared Jesus to be more than this: the same as God, of one substance with the Father).

The complex origins of the Christ figure and its nature as an archetype (from a psychological perspective) mean that it transcends rational comprehension and expression. In the early centuries of Christianity, this produced endless disputes about the relationship of Christ to God, whether Jesus was a man only, divine only, or both, and whether Christ was actually crucified. Christianity's establishment as the Roman state religion in the fourth century required greater unity and less contentiousness. A series of councils tried to definitively codify Christian belief; Christ's nature was established by compromise and vote; the bishops decreed dissenting groups such as the Arians and Nestorians to be heretical. Even within the newly established orthodoxy, however, the settlements were never to everyone's satisfaction; reinterpretations created new controversies and ultimately the Eastern and Western Churches divided on the issue rather than allowing room for a living, intuitive sense of Christ as a mystery beyond fathoming by the finite mind.

In the first decades and centuries after his death, some Christians felt Jesus intended his teachings to enable them to experience and manifest their own truth and actual selves. Elaine Pagels states that Gnostic

Christians believed a "disciple who comes to know himself can discover, then, what even Jesus cannot teach."[79] A Gnostic text proposes that each Gnostic is to be a "disciple of his [own] mind" which "is the father of the truth."[80] Another text has Jesus instruct, "Have a great number of friends, but not counselors. . . . Entrust yourself to God alone as father and as friend"; it has Jesus refer to "the divine and the teaching which are within you."[81] In other Gnostic tracts, Jesus is depicted as a teacher turning aside queries to aim his questioners toward pursuing their own realizations: Jesus says "I set forth the action for you. Indeed the understanding dwells in you";[82] Jesus' disciples ask him, "What is the place to which we are going?" Sounding more like a teacher than a savior, he answers, "Stand in the place you can reach!"[83]

The doctrine that became orthodox, however, had Jesus pointing to himself alone as the way to God and salvation. Thus, in John 14:6 Jesus proclaims, "I am the way, and the truth, and the life. No one comes to the Father except through me." Psychologically, this meant the projection of the believer's own infinite self onto Jesus Christ, diminishing the nature of the individual. Thenceforward, it would be difficult for a Christian to accept experiences of her own infinite self as such. The actual nature of the individual infinite self received elucidation as never before but could be expressed only in the figure of Jesus Christ. It effectively was held in trust and could be reclaimed only partially, or heretically, or in periods when orthodoxy's sway diminished for some parts of the population, particularly around the twelfth and in the twentieth centuries.

While the pagan initiatory mysteries, such as the Eleusinian, were for the few, pagans felt the relationship with the spiritual and supernatural realm involved everyone, just as, in the early Church, it could involve any Christian. The gods would appear to all alike, in visions or dreams, regardless of distinctions such as class; an oracle or prophet was simply a useful medium for communicating the divine message.[84] A particular individual, such as an oracle, might have a closer relationship, but this was not consistent; rather, it involved, in Brown's words, "the discontinuous plucking of the fingers of God on his soul."[85] Everyone could relate to the divine directly (in a routine, non-initiatory way), though the divine was seen as external. Similarly, in early Christianity, any individual could engage with the divine; itinerant charismatics and prophets presented themselves as moved by the Holy Spirit, and the community accepted them on their merits. "The primitive Christians perpetually trod on mystic ground," as historian Edward Gibbon remarks.[86] People of the Mediterranean two millennia ago inhabited a world that included powerful spirits with whom they must interact, in the same way they had to get on with their more tangible human associates. The spiritual world was mundane, real, and present; it could be taken for granted exactly as could the material world—it was no more stressful to deal with a divinity than with the person next door. Interactions were casual.[87] "Divine and human, eternal and temporal, heaven, earth, and Hades were marvelously porous and open to one another," according to historian John Dominic Crossan, and it wasn't considered unseemly for gods to beget offspring with humans.[88]

The problem for pagans and Christians alike was that this equal-opportunity relationship with the divine meant there was no differentiation between an average man, a holy man, or a nefarious sorcerer, and competition for spiritual status was constant and indecisive, creating social instability.[89] Determining whether charismatics and prophets were genuine produced considerable stress for Christians trying to decide whether to follow them; it also created tension within communities.[90] In response, between 200 and 400 C.E. more and more inhabitants of the Mediterranean region, both Christian and pagan, began to fervently believe that divine forces and faculties were not only available to traditional religious entities (oracles, etc.) and to the common person but also to a few remarkable people who had been given the ability to manifest divine power within their groups, due to their enduring and steady connection with the divine, a connection readily apparent to their coreligionists. Such an exceptional individual was called a *hyperanthröpos*, a "superman" or "divine man," the image of which took definite shape in the circles of pagan philosophers such as Plotinus.[91]

Thus, by later Antiquity God was believed to have conveyed permanent, consistent powers to certain personages due to their spiritual development and holy lifestyle. These "specialists," according to Optatus of Milevis (fourth century), "brought down the binding force of Heaven from the sky."[92] Christians were well ahead of pagans in this attitudinal shift, and it helped them to gain the upper hand in the Roman world.[93] Their edge may have stemmed from Christianity's Jewish roots, specifically the tradition of the Hasidim, men of God, considered to have begun with Abraham and Moses, continuing through Elijah and Elisha, and still very alive in the centuries around Jesus' life. Their devotion and unworldliness gave them a special connection to God, empowering them to work miracles.[94]

There were both losses and gains in this arrangement. While the *hyperanthröpos* embodied what was formerly in the sphere of the divine, the rest of society, which had been able to approach the divine directly in shrines, dreams, and visions, increasingly had to go through these elite "specialists"; most people were themselves more removed from the divine. For the group around the specialist, however, this degradation of position was mitigated by their being, in their own eyes, distinguished from and placed above non-believers, now seen by the group as having no connection to the divine whatsoever. Having a secure and lasting proximity to the specialist and thus the divine, his associates basked in the heavenly radiance he grounded and dispersed, muted, to the group.[95]

Many pagans found this development abhorrent because in their tradition divinity was openly and continually available to all and they had long held that the divine and material worlds co-existed and interacted comfortably and peacefully. The authority of the pagan mysteries was founded on an intricate pattern of correlations and interconnections with the structure of the cosmos; Christianity shredded this pattern and sense of connectedness that was crucial to pagan faith.[96]

This new situation was quite paradoxical. Brown argues that while only the "divine men," such as the Egyptian Christian ascetics of the fourth century, were deemed, based on their extreme lifestyle or the institutions they founded, to continuously and demonstrably wield heavenly power on earth, this power wasn't to be used to apprehend the divine. While the *hyperanthröpos* joined heaven and earth within himself, not only was his divine power not available to everyone, he created an upper limit to the ability to interact with the divine.[97] He separated himself from "the shimmering, tantalizing presences of the other world"[98] by creating a "wall of darkness" based on his perception of himself as by nature sinful.[99] But while his power was never to be used or, at most, employed only to help others become aware of their own hearts and sins, he "gained more power through rejecting it." Increasingly, the *hyperanthröpos* employed divine power in the world only to wield authority over others, as in founding monasteries. "The Christians looked to the earth alone. They claimed power from heaven; but they had made that heaven remote and they kept its power to themselves, to build up new separate institutions among upstart heroes on earth."[100]

A profound and permanent alteration had occurred for Christians, individually and collectively, in their beliefs regarding human potential vis-à-vis the divine, disconnecting them from their early traditions and the pagan present and sanctioning their recently elevated status as the Church of the Roman world. The select few, those in authority and those seen as filled with spirit, were now positioned between the celestial realm and a world from which divine presence was freshly removed.[101] This was in part accomplished by sharpening the split of self and body begun in classical Greek philosophy. Christian ascetics, who proved their proximity to "heavenly" energy through harsh and pitiless overcoming of their "earthly" nature, increased this split. Pagans, in contrast, mostly maintained a sense that human flesh was open to and pervaded by the divine.[102]

In the third and fourth centuries, the Christian charismatics, prophets, and others who had been sources of social stress and spiritual uncertainty were brought within Church structure, forced into a sort of exile in isolated monastic communities, or else anathematized. This limited the number and kind of individuals who could embody aspects of the divine. (Crossan suggests this institutionalization began in rural Syria as early as the second half of the first century. This is where the Pauline emphasis on Jesus as Christ, not sage or teacher, began.) Thus, Jesus fully integrated divine and human (infinite self and finite self) in himself and taught that his followers could also attain this; it became widely recognized as a human potential (though not accepted in theory, the spirit aspect of self—as distinct from soul— remaining theologically controversial). However, in practice this potential's fulfillment was limited to the few who lived non-normal lives and imposed on themselves and their followers a restricted relationship with the divine and separation from the carnal world. Jesus would remain the only example of complete and unlimited access to and embodiment of the divine allowed in Christendom. Ironically, from its origins within the context of the pagan situation of an initiate few and the divinely-visited many, Christianity had evolved through a time of highly democratic spirituality to a period in which it instituted another group of divinely powerful men. At the end of this process, the masses were further removed from the divine than before, and heaven had become more inaccessible and distant.

It's not clear whether this restriction was inevitable. An alternative was available, less limiting than the *hyperanthröpos.* This was the multilayered, composite soul that Plutarch and other pagans spoke of, especially the superior "true soul" above each soul. Brown reports this true soul was seen in Late Antiquity as "an invisible and intimate protector, the personal *daimon*, the *genius*, the guardian angel . . . conceived of, very largely, as an upward extension of that individual."[103] Jerome (347-419/20) saw the guardian angel as the principle of a person's identity.[104] A superior man had a more powerful *daimon* and had a higher degree of mergence with its identity. This invisible companion or celestial twin was one of the most emotion-laden, highly developed, and refined aspects of religion in Late Antiquity, a "private line" to the divine apart from the temple or oracle and consistently within the person.[105] The relationship with the *daimon* kept open the boundaries between the human and divine worlds. We may see in the *daimon* either the highest aspect of the finite self, an intuition of the infinite self, or an undifferentiated conflation of the two.

The *daimon* was part of Christian thought throughout its early centuries; Origen brought it to prominence. He felt it and other angelic presences protected him from the demonic, guiding his spiritual growth. For Origen, as expressed by Brown, "upward ceilings of earlier thought have been removed. . . . Men and women might yet live . . . according to a higher identity that merged with angelic beings." With Origen we find in Christianity an optimistic view of the "angelic life" on earth in which the spiritual aspects of the identity gradually emerge. Origen was however, driven from Egypt; his enemies, who would define the ascetic movement, overcame his followers. The potential integration fragmented; heaven and earth were divided and layperson and "divine man" made distinct and separate. From Origen's "loving invisible presences,"[106] the focus shifted to the temptations and torments of a *hyperanthröpos* such as Anthony (251-356) in the Egyptian desert, beset by the demons of his unintegrated shadow self.[107] The more democratic relationship with the divine that the *daimon* facilitated and the larger vision of human spiritual nature it expressed went by the wayside.

Did this have to occur? I've drawn on Brown extensively because he offers a rare, detailed window on a culture's response to a major development in psychospiritual evolution that included a new understanding of human potential. He suggests that Mediterranean society could not handle the stresses of a freewheeling and open spirituality and the consequent social instability, uncertainty, and competition or the kind of individual that developed in response to those stresses, such as early Christian charismatics. This inability had its roots in the rampant individual ambition already undermining the Roman social structure.[108] Roman society couldn't assimilate this new, spiritually powerful man ("new women" in Christianity were beyond consideration after the early decades) without making him an institution—*hyperanthröpos*—and thereby limiting his impact and scope for expressing individual truth.

This suggests that it's difficult for a society to integrate the kind of quantum leap in the conception of human nature and potential that occurred in Classical times and more difficult still to make that potential realizable for everyone, even given a few centuries. Perhaps it takes a millennium or two. (Jung and others have suggested that the human psyche develops in cycles that seem to last two thousand-plus years.) In the meantime, those in power may feel compelled to try to contain and constrain, often harshly, those embodying the new potential. Modern civilization has begun to face aspects of this situation, which will unfold over the next few centuries. Hopefully, we can avoid repeating how Late Antiquity handled it, despite the fact that societal stresses are remarkably similar: globalization, heads of multinational corporations acting as did ambitious members of the Roman upper classes, concentration of power, disparity of economic circumstances, charismatics, and mesmerizing, authoritarian spiritual leaders. By examining historical parallels in social circumstance and spiritual change, we may be able to mitigate the effects of these stressors and integrate the new spiritual potentials and those individuals who will embody them, this time choosing less severe and limiting alternatives for the many "new men and women" and not idealizing and making institutions of the few (such as televangelists and gurus). The essential first step is to identify and understand these challenges and potentials and recognize they've begun to play out.

Part 3.
The Medieval and Renaissance Eras

Zen Buddhism

Zen Buddhism developed in the sixth century C.E. from Buddhism's encounter with Taoism in China; it entered Japan in the twelfth century. Zen's disposition toward spiritual psychology is summed up by D. T. Suzuki (1870-1966), the preeminent interpreter of Zen to the West, regarding the question of the soul's relationship to the body: "The best way to come to a real understanding of the matter is 'not to ask the question.'" This approach applies to spiritual identity, if treated as the identity of something with something: this "presupposes [an] original opposition of two terms"; therefore Zen's goal is "to restore the experience of original inseparability . . . to the original state of purity and transparency"[1] that existed before consciousness divided and gave rise to such a question. Along these lines a Zen master said, "The soul is the body and the body is the soul, and as they are identical there is no destruction of either." However, Zen has plenty of room for vigorous disagreement: another master contended, "the soul distinguishable from the body disappears with the disappearance of the latter."[2]

Zen speaks of "the invisible spirit keeping the mind, body and limbs in full activity . . . like the spirit or energy (*ki, ch'i*) of heaven and earth," in Suzuki's words. Spirit, while transcending material existence, is the operative factor in our lives.[3]

True Self is both Buddha and Mind. Zen Master Shin'ichi Hisamatsu (1889-1980), in conversation with Jung, distinguished the nature of *Atman*, which has substance, from True Self or Original Self, which is without form or substance. "Ultimately, to become 'The Formless Self' . . . is the essence of Zen."[4] Hisamatsu, in a commentary on this conversation, noted that Self is "perfect liberation" and "unbounded self-awakening."[5]

Zen holds that everything is perfect in itself, manifesting the One. Suzuki remarks that the prime Zen experience of Reality is expressed as "All in One and One in All"; "One" is the realm of the Absolute, *sunyata* ("emptiness"), and "All" is "the world of particulars," *tathata* ("suchness").[6] Yet, in Zen it's not that simple, since there's no One in Zen, in the sense of being distinct from All. Thus, "All is the One and One is the All"—"Not Two!" but also "Not One either!"[7]

This gives the flavor of Zen's approach, which seeks to eliminate dualistic thinking so the practitioner experiences the nondistinction of subject and object. Because it emphasizes direct intuitive and sensory experience unmediated by cognition, assisted by thinking the unthinkable, it would seem to allow for awareness of and interaction with one's infinite self but would not distinguish it from finite self, or from God, or from anything in any way. There's no sense of a mutual relationship between infinite self and finite self, for this would introduce a distinction foreign to Buddhism. Undefined, infinite self's presence would enter experience; that's enough. The most advanced Zen practitioner, however, has shifted orientation from finite self's viewpoint to having awareness focused firmly in infinite or True Self, or, more accurately, to having experience *as* the infinite or True Self, inclusive of all aspects of self. While one may understand Nothingness as Mind, this does not mean something exterior to oneself or different from other aspects of self; rather, Richard DeMartino observes, "Mind is Myself and . . . I am that Mind. This Mind is not the Mind which is seen, but is, on the contrary, the Mind which sees."[8] Masao Abe, in comparing Western psychology to Zen, notes: "Zen does not discuss the unconscious or so-called 'No Mind' from the side of consciousness [as does the Western approach]. . . . It is the way of Zen to go deep into the unconscious and break through its bottom through *zazen*, seated meditation and struggling with *koan*. . . . True Self in Zen . . . is none other than the self-awakening which is realized through such breaking-through of the framework of self."[9]

True Mind doesn't enter into normal consciousness. Hitoshi Kataoka declares: "It thinks, but does not become the object of thought. . . . [One grasps True Self] by becoming one with the undifferentiated whole of the phenomena and the act of consciousness." Oriental Nothingness, or "No Mind," involves awareness that's completely present and of supreme clarity.[10]

Zen Buddhism has a here-now focus that differs from the Buddhist goal of extricating oneself from this world of forms, *Maya*. This difference holds even for Mahayana Buddhism, in which the Bodhisattva vows to postpone entry into Nirvana until all other sentient beings, which he serves, have preceded him: the goal is still to leave this world. Master Seigen Ishin's (seventh or eighth century) famous statement sums up Zen's essence: "When I had not yet practiced Zen, to me a mountain was a mountain, and water was water; after I got an insight into the truth of Zen through the instruction of a good master, I thought a mountain was not a mountain and water was not water; but now that I have really attained to the abode of rest, as before a mountain is just a mountain, and water is just water."[11]

The Zen practitioner aims to overcome the sense of a personal self or any sort of identity; the experience sought is the Formless Self or Mind present in the world, unencumbered by a feeling of, or investment in, a personal destiny or purpose. It emphasizes awareness of existence without differentiating its aspects; thus, their interrelationships aren't consciously addressed or developed.

Islam and Sufism

Orthodox Islam's attitude to any idea of an eternal self is easy to describe. Sufism's is much more difficult to discern.

The orthodox view is summarized in the statement, "There is no God but God." Titus Burckhardt suggests that the correct translation of Islam's most basic tenet should be, "there is no divinity if it be not The Divinity." Islamic theology rejects any differentiation within the nature of God, as well as any other divine entities. Divine Names and Divine Attributes are merely "extrinsic" characteristics of God.[12] The Qur'an states,

> Say: He, Allah, is One.
> Allah is He on Whom all depend.
> He begets not, nor is He begotten.
> And none is like Him.[13]

Muhammad serves as the exemplar of human development, but Islam does not consider him an incarnation of God in the manner orthodox Christianity views Jesus Christ; he is purely and simply God's Prophet. Islam denies completely any movement of God down into man. Muhammad is "the perfect man . . . the prototype of creation." He is the paragon of humanity's potential spiritual attainment. This amounts to a reflection or symbol of the divine. The Prophet, understood esoterically as the Universal Man, is the whole of the cosmos and, in Burckhardt's words, "the synthesis of the divine radiance" within it, completely passive in his relationship with the divine. Muhammad, as well as humankind esoterically understood, is "in essence the Spirit . . . [that] emanates directly from God . . . [God's] unique and universal 'beloved.'"[14]

For Muslims, then, Muhammad signifies the perfectibility of human beings in their relationship to God; for Christians, Christ is God born as man, although for some esoteric Christians, Christ represents the divine aspect of humanity. While Divine Sonship has no place in Islam because Islam holds the divine to be without internal differentiation, the idea of humanity esoterically understood as Spirit that "emanates directly from God" is not essentially different from the idea of God children, considering that these are creations of the divine, not divisions within it as Christ is seen by Islam to be a belief in God divided. Islam holds a firm line on divine unity, but in its more mystical expressions it approaches the paradoxical understanding of creator and creation as being both distinct and continuous. Islam is theistic, with a personal deity—adamantly held to be transcendent—as its core belief, and it repudiates as blasphemy any doctrine of incarnation; yet, paradoxically, in maintaining that God is all, Islam, particularly Sufic mysticism, can present the entirety of human activity as the function of God acting within him, which comes close to equating man with God.

Most scholars concur that Sufism arose as an ascetic response to the worldliness that developed early in Islam. It promoted self-development and spiritual awakening, maturing gradually as it incorporated aspects of Gnosticism, Neoplatonism, Hellenistic culture and other Middle Eastern spiritual influences, and perhaps Zoroastrianism and Egyptian Hermeticism. Speculation pushes its origins earlier. "Though commonly mistaken for a Moslem sect," Robert Graves asserts, "the Sufis are at home in all religions. . . . They even dislike being given any inclusive name which might force them into doctrinal conformity. . . . The characteristic Sufic signature is found in widely dispersed literature from at least the second millennium B.C."[15]

Idries Shah, a Sufi, advises that anything written about Sufic teaching is incomplete. "Sufism is known by means of itself"; a student can only deeply understand the discipline by learning directly from an instructor.[16] It is a methodology for human evolution and ascertaining truth, not a body of doctrine; whatever ideas regarding man's psychospiritual makeup it may embrace are reserved for those advanced in the training and only hinted about to others. We'll examine a few hints.

Within Islam, Sufism progressed through several stages, the last a theosophical pantheism tending to equate God and creation. In the pantheistic period, the union of soul with the divine was portrayed as a single drop of water released into the sea. The mystery of divine oneness and multiplicity was represented as mirrors reflecting the various attributes of God or as clear light given hue by prisms. According to a *hadith qudsi* ("holy tradition," a non-Qur'anic Divine Word revealed through Muhammad), God, finding himself alone—"'I was a hidden treasure and wanted to be known'"—desired, as described by *EB*, "manifestation" and so brought forth the universe "by effusing being upon the heavenly archetypes" to create an earthly materialization of the divine.[17] Another *hadith qudsi* affirms: "When I [Allah] love him [Allah's servant] I become the hearing with which he hears and the eye with which he sees and the hand with which he grasps." The philosopher and mystic Muhyiddin Ibn 'Arabi (1165-1240) declares, "all things are the faces of God."[18]

'Arabi was the prime exponent of the theory of "Unity of Being," in which all life and the cosmos are one, an expression of the divinity that is their foundation, but his teaching emphasized a clear difference between the divine One and his self-manifestation.[19] For 'Arabi, the essence of self-understanding is "*Thou art He.*" Anything else would be polytheism. He writes: "Thou art non-existent now as thou wast non-existent before the Creation. . . . God . . . can have no partner nor like nor equal." The fact that Thou art He, however, means that "it is permitted to him who is united to Reality to say, 'I am the Truth,' and to say, 'Praise be to Me.' But none attains to union except he see his own attributes to be the attributes of God."[20] 'Arabi expresses this in a hymn, while also emphasizing the unalterable distinction between creator and creation:

> My essence is His essence in truth, without defect or flaw.
> There is no becoming between these two, and my soul it is which manifests that secret.
> . . . .
> I did not lose to Him my soul.[21]

There is an apparent tension between 'Arabi's pantheism and this distinction, a tension that perhaps resolves only by understanding our paradoxical nature.

Shah contends, "Every Sufi experience is an experience . . . in qualitative infinity," and we are infinitely perfectible. He specifies four human conditions; the last is "Absorption . . . referring to the condition of 'divinity' in another sphere," and speaks of the "Sacred Heart," the aspect of a person that "partakes of the essence of divinity."[22] Sufis understand angels as "representations of man's higher faculties." We have only "quasi divinity" and are different from the *houris,* the *"creatures of light"* of paradise.

The soul pre-exists the body and continues after; an unidentified Sufi states: "Before garden, vine or grape was in the world . . . our soul was drunken with immortal wine."[23] 'Abdul-Karim Jili (1365-1408) talks about a tripartite nature of man as body, soul, and spirit and of "the Realm where you were before your physical existence, in the form of an atom among a crowd of spirits. And you knew what God wished of you in this Realm . . . He had designated your singularity. . . . Then when you descended . . . to the depths of the world of bodies, you forgot that Realm and what happened to you in it."[24] Making this descent, 'Arabi attests,

> I bore witness to you as King before our existence
> . . . .
> At the time of testimony there was no deception,
> The road I took was plainly and joyfully taken.
> I was not a prisoner in the grip of confinement.[25]

In a passage suggestive of the cosmic learning game, 'Arabi writes: "It is as if the experience of the one who is aware enters his heart through

He whose being is infinite, imposing a finiteness upon him for the sake of the manifestation thus made possible in him." Jili adds: "His attributes are not completed except in us. So we give Him the attributes, and He gives us being."[26] Although 'Arabi's and Jili's statements are about Allah, they parallel the relationship between an infinite self and its creation and the purpose for that creation. Jili likewise evokes the relationship and differences we have posited between God and God children and between God children and the finite world, recounting, "God sends to the people of the Garden a message. . . : 'A letter from the Life Everlasting to the Life Everlasting. I say to a thing "Be," and it is, and I have made you to say to a thing "Be," and it is,'—and they do not say to a thing 'Be' except that it is. This is the essence of the manifestation of vice-regency, and the world is not suitable for that. For this world is the house of work and responsibility."[27] But while Sufi metaphysics distinguishes Being from "principial possibilities" ('Arabi's term), Burkhardt notes that this differentiation is, quoting 'Arabi, "'non-existent as such, though permanent'" and "does not at all envisage distinct cosmic entities. . . . This distinction of Being from the principial possibilities or immutable essences—a distinction which is at the very limit of what is conceivable and is resolved in the Divine Infinity" lets the divine reaffirm itself "as one in each manifested possibility and as alone in all, whereas the possibilities as such establish diversity without ever being essentially detached from the One."[28]

Sufis do not separate spirit from the physical, considering them connected, according to Shah, in "a continuum of refinement of matter . . . until it becomes what has been generally considered to be separate—spirit." He says that the material and spiritual aspects of self can join when total balance between them has been attained.[29] Unwilling to separate humankind or cosmos from God, the Sufis envision a lofty attainment for human beings as partaking of the infinite and divine; they value materiality positively as a manifestation of God. Within the Islam's orthodox framework, however, they don't establish an eternal and unique individual human creative spiritual identity. Though spirit precedes the existence of the body (and, as indicated by Jili's suggestive statement, partakes of God's creative capabilities) and continues after it, only God is eternal.

Medieval Christianity

Many ideas about the makeup and destiny of spiritual aspects of humanity were condemned following orthodoxy's codification by the early church councils, and books containing these beliefs, such as the Nag Hammadi texts, were burned or buried. During the Middle Ages, esoteric groups including Gnostic and Manichaean sects maintained the continuity of these ideas.[30] Arabic texts, for example the *Ghayat al-hakim* ("The Aim of the Wise," circa twelfth century, Latin *Picatrix*), confirm the continuance during this period of themes from Neoplatonism, hermeticism, and late classical religions. These include, in Gershom Scholem's words, the personal "spiritual being," that is, "man's 'perfected nature,'" a version of the Greek notion of the personal *daimon.*[31] These themes reemerged in the West in Kabbalah and in alchemical and hermetic studies, beginning in the twelfth and thirteenth centuries with figures such as Robert Grosseteste (1168-1253) and his student Roger Bacon (1220-1292). Grosseteste, like Bacon a founder of empirical science, spoke of "the infinite generation of light."[32] He was referring not to the light we see but to something almost spiritual that provides for continuity in the natural world and unifies body and soul.[33] Bacon's studies earned him an accusation of witchcraft; he had to show that he had a formula for an explosive—black powder, invented in China and just then reaching the West—to demonstrate the propriety of his endeavors.

These esoteric ideas and studies flourished when the *Corpus Hermeticum* and other esoteric texts became available in the West after Constantinople's fall to the Turks in 1453. They made significant contributions to Renaissance humanism.

John Scotus Erigena (810-c. 877), an Irishman at the court of Charlemagne's successor, Charles the Bald, and among the most audacious and innovative thinkers of medieval Europe, introduced to Western Europe the tradition of Christian Greek Platonism as developed by Pseudo-Dionysius and others, translating their works into Latin. He systematized Western Christian belief and philosophy, using Neoplatonism as a basis. He drew upon early Celtic Christianity's positive and life-loving attitudes, in which, summarizes Thomas Cahill, "God's pleasure and man's are reunited," the entire world is holy and filled with divine messages, and this holiness extends to the entire body.[34] The divine enters creation and thereby becomes known; God is the source of all creatures and in the last days will reabsorb them. For Erigena, "there is no useful distinction between natural and supernatural. . . . Reality is a continuum, and all God's creatures are theophanies of God himself, for God speaks in them and through them." He is pantheistic, and, like Origen, proposes that all will achieve salvation, even devils.[35] Erigena believed in the divinity of humanity (and all creation) and its divine destiny, though not the idea of eternal existence as distinct spiritual creators of finite creations. The Roman Church condemned his opinions as heretical in 1210; the pope ordered the burning of his book *De Divisione Naturae,* though his ideas, and through him those of Pseudo-Dionysius, influenced Western mysticism.

The West's understanding of the divine aspect of human beings was further crippled, and remained so until the Renaissance, by the Eighth Ecumenical Council (or Fourth Council of Constantinople), concluded in 870. The council anathematized all who ascribed to the "dogma that a human being has two souls," which had been "growing like some loathsome form of weed."[36] Given the vigor with which weeds grow and spread, the condemned doctrine would seem to have been both popular and threatening to the Church. This decree removed an important remnant of Plotinus's vision of human spiritual existence from Catholic dogma: the multifaceted spiritual nature that is a microcosm of the divine. It closed the door to entertaining the idea or experience of a tripart psychospirituality of body, soul, and spirit; it degraded the possibility of an individual spirit, leaving only a reference to an intellectual aspect of the soul. Walter Stein contends: "At this Council the Trinity within the human being was extinguished."[37] Strong antecedents to this decree appear in Augustine and the reactions to Origen and the Gnostics; it is apparent from this action centuries later that belief in or experience of an aspect of human nature higher than the soul had proved enduring and hard to suppress.

Left with only body and soul, Christians saw themselves, accordingly, as fundamentally non-creative, spiritually passive, and fully damnable, while for Plotinus and those in alignment with his legacy, the individual spirit is always unified with God and God's will and thus could never suffer eternal loss of soul or damnation. The tendency of Christian dogma to disempower believers affected even the forms of worship at mass. The congregants' role in the sacraments decreased in significance relative to the priest's function in the mystery; the latter became increasingly distant. This occurred particularly after the fourth century when the Eastern part of the Church, not yet divided from Rome, began veiling the altar so that the congregation couldn't see it. By no later than the 700s, it became customary for the priest to speak the canon of the Latin mass too softly for the congregants to hear.[38] The concealed altar and subaudible mass made tangible the changing status of the worshipers, increasingly separated from divinity by church teaching and practice.

Catharism

Bogomilism, a Balkan dualistic heresy similar to Manichaeism, arose in the tenth century, based in part on hidden apocryphal manuscripts, passed on via eastern Christendom, that survived from the first centuries C.E.[39] Bogomil doctrines, in turn, influenced the medieval European Cathar heresy and its precursors. These often claimed to convey Jesus' true teachings. Most of what we know of their beliefs come to us through their inquisitors, clearly a biased source, so their exact sense of human spiritual nature is uncertain.

Around 1025 in northwest Italy, a heretical group apparently believed in a Trinity involving God the Father, the Son (Jesus Christ, who, in the words of medieval sources, they believed to be "the soul of man beloved of God"), and the Holy Ghost.[40]

Something close to the idea of the divine self appears in the beliefs of Catharism, which included dualistic heretical Christian groups in France, Italy, and Germany in the early centuries of the last millennium. Italian Cathars held human beings to have five distinct aspects. As described by Stoyanov, "the God of Light . . . created his heavenly people, comprising the [spiritual] body, soul and spirit, the spirit being outside the body and serving as the custodian of the soul." These were in the heavenly realm, apart from the earth, the creation of the God of Darkness. Satan led astray some of these souls and entrapped them "in the prison of the [second, earthly] body."[41] According to Broek, such a soul retains its original "divine nature." That soul, however, is distinct from "our present soul, which is identical with our blood and will perish together with our body." Earthly man consists of this lower soul plus the physical body and a lower spirit that "is identical with the soul of his heavenly counterpart." Salvation occurs when the lower spirit separates from the lower soul and physical body and reunites with the higher aspects, restoring the heavenly person.[42] The spirit must free itself from material existence.

The human heavenly spirit is essentially the same as the Holy Spirit; in the Cathar belief, God had created numerous Holy Spirits, so that "the Third Person of the Trinity is at the same time the collective of all heavenly spirits and the individual divine spirit." This spirit-custodian is free of sin.[43] The *consolamentum*, the Cathars' sacrament, was the only way the incarcerated soul could regain its heavenly custodian spirit. At the end of time, all souls that had atoned would return to their dwelling places in heaven and recover their spiritual bodies.[44]

Catharism was radically dualistic, as regards not only good and evil but also spirit and matter. Cathars believed spirit would abandon the world; the body would not undergo resurrection. Stoyanov recounts: "In some Cathar accounts the God of Darkness was regarded as the Lord of Genesis, the Creator of . . . the visible heaven . . . and everything on earth. . . . The God of Light was the Creator of everlasting, eternal things" who also fashioned his own new universe.[45]

These beliefs involved a lofty human spiritual heritage and destiny and a tripartite vision of human nature. While the Cathars devalued physical existence, they elevated the status of the human spirit and asserted its divinity, but its individuality is ambiguous.

The Albigensian Crusade (early thirteenth century) exterminated the Cathars of France, the largest group; the Inquisition eliminated those in Italy and Germany.

Medieval Christian Mystics

Bernard of Clairvaux (1090-1153) drew upon Origen in declaring, "being united in a holy kiss [with Christ], we are by his condescension made to be one Spirit in him."[46] Bernard became an early defender of the mystical, intuitive faculty against the methods of the rational, skeptical mind when the latter, as espoused by Peter Abelard, first began its long rise to eventual dominance of the Western mind. Bernard attacked Abelard's dialectical Scholasticism as holding itself beyond what it supposed to be faith's restrictions even though, according to Bernard, Abelard's was but one among many methods of investigation and debased the mysteries of the divine. He said: "We search in a worthier manner, we discover with greater facility through prayer than through disputation." He held love to be the prime necessity to understand God.[47]

Hadewijch was an early thirteenth century Flemish Beguine. (Beguines were the women's movement of the time, devoted to spiritual lives without taking vows as nuns.[48]) Lost until the nineteenth century, her poems and visions establish her as "the most important exponent of love mysticism and one of the loftiest figures in the Western mystical tradition," asserts Paul Mommaers.[49]

In one vision an angel says to her, "you have conquered the powerful and strong God, from the origin of his Being, which was without beginning; and with him you shall wield power over eternity in eternity!" Her divine Beloved, Jesus, reveals, "you are standing in me, from all eternity, entirely free and without fall."[50] In another, the Holy Spirit calls her "ancient one" and tells her, "you shall not live less than what I, Love, am . . . until the death that will make you alive. . . . Go forth, and live what I am; and return bringing me full divinity."[51] In her vision of her mystical marriage with her divine Beloved, she learns that she possesses "true life" and discovers "the eternity of . . . [her] domain." Jesus informs her: "You shall suffer everything to the end with what I am, and we shall remain one."[52]

In a letter she says those "ready to content Love are . . . eternal and unfathomable. For their *conversation is in heaven*." In another, she attests to the soul being "a bottomless abyss in which God suffices to himself; and his own self-sufficiency ever finds fruition to the full in this soul, as the soul, for its part, ever does in him. Soul is a way for the passage of God from his depths into his liberty; and God is a way for the passage of the soul into its liberty, that is, into his inmost depths."[53]

In these passages, if we read the individual infinite self in place of the Beloved or God, they give precise expression to the relationship of finite and infinite selves. In the language of love, Hadewijch articulates a union of soul and divinity where the soul is not absorbed or made insignificant but rather enters a mutually fulfilling relationship in which each is realized through the other. A human being is capable of love through which she can "live what I am" and can "bring me full divinity." The human spiritual essence is co-eternal with God; although it is capable of sin, evil is alien to its nature, and it falls beneath it as beneath a burden. However, divinity is not pre-existent but achieved through a life lived in love of the divine. Hadewijch does not distinguish soul and spirit, but, given the constraints of orthodoxy, her vision is remarkable in elevating the human spiritual essence in relationship to divinity.

Hadewijch influenced Jan van Ruysbroeck (Flemish, 1293-1381), who wrote, "What we are, that we behold; and what we behold, that we are; for in this pure vision we are one life and one spirit with God."[54] For him, union with Christ meant the soul melts, as Brian Riggs puts it, "into the Unity; and . . . into the life of God."[55] Ruysbroeck, along with Bernard, views human beings as by their nature capable of union with the divine. The predominant feeling given by these two is that by union the divine absorbs the human soul, or the two become non-distinct; human effort and volition seem little involved. Ruysbroeck's German contemporary, the mystic Henry Suso (1295?-1366), imparts a different sense of human beings involving separation between God and man: "There is an *image* of God in the soul which can rise to the Divine Essence, or Source, and which, unhindered by the clouds and veils of created things, may *contemplate*, in silent darkness . . . the marvels of Divinity."[56]

Meister Eckhart (German, 1260-c. 1328) put forward the radical vision of the "God-man." Influenced by Augustine and Pseudo-Dionysius, he advocated a highly innovative pantheistic theology; his most contentious idea was that each person has a divine essence in the soul, allowing him to enter union with and have an intimate understanding of God.

He took Jesus' reference to "my Father" seriously and rather literally, in effect as a blood relationship: "We are not God, yet God's blood flows in our veins," in translator Raymond B. Blakney's words. His great theme is that God and humanity have an "essential unity" that is so close there's "no room for a priest in between." While emphasizing the fundamental difference between God and man, he saw them as at least "of the same genus." He felt that people have a spark of divinity that God "concealed within the shell of selfhood"; our spark transcends our earthly lives as much "as heaven is high above earth." It "is the germ of eternal life and the seed of God."[57] As Eckhart himself put it, his conviction was that God does not "beget differently in me than in eternity."[58] Likewise, he writes: "There is something uncreated, something divine in the soul," so that the necessary focus for any study of the divine is the ancient Greek charge to "know thyself." Eckhart maintains: "God never tied man's salvation to any pattern of life. . . . So one must be permeated with the divine Presence . . . so that he may radiate that Presence without working at it." Eckhart was determined to confirm the generative, foundational wellspring of existence in the sole location where a person can apprehend it directly, in the human spiritual core.[59]

The reformation arguably had its religious and intellectual roots in Eckhart. His fervent and uncompromising expression of his doctrine of the God-man, the divine and eternal human essence, threatened the church establishment; Eckhart ultimately was brought before the Inquisition and posthumously condemned.

Kabbalah

New sources of knowledge, both exoteric and esoteric, entered the medieval West, due partly to the access to the eastern Mediterranean established by the Crusades and to Islamic learning available in Spain as Christians reconquered it. During this period, Sufi and Christian mysticism blended with and impacted Jewish spiritual inquiry.[60] The beginning of the Jewish Kabbalah tradition is marked by the publication of *Sefir Bahir* ("Book of Brilliance") in 1175 in Provence, when the Cathars also flourished there. Kabbalah is considered to contain esoteric wisdom of the unwritten Torah, God's revelation to Moses and Adam. While adherence to the written Law is fundamental to the Jewish faith, Kabbalah allows for a more immediate experience of God. The influential text *Sefer ha-zohar* ("Book of Splendour"), composed in Spain late in the thirteenth century by Moses de Leon (1250-1305), describes a human being, in Scholem's words, "as the most perfect shape—'the form that contains all forms' . . . through which alone all things exist. . . . The lower, earthly human being and the upper, mystical human being, in which the Godhead is manifested as shape, belong together and are unthinkable without one another in a well-ordered world." An individual's purpose is to cultivate his interior image of God. In the *Sefir Bahir,* the Sefiroth, holy forms important for the formation and maintenance of the cosmos, "appear in the form of Primal Man . . . which corresponds to that of earthly man."[61]

Another thirteenth-century development within Kabbalah borrowed from the Platonic psychology of the tripartite soul and related this to biblical concepts, identifying the Platonic "vegetative soul" with the biblical *nefesh* (life soul), the "vital" or "animal" soul with the *ruah* (spirit), and the "speaking" or "rational" soul with the *neshamah,* the highest, which leads and uplifts. The lowest form of soul, *nefesh,* contains the other two as "potentialities," and, as Scholem explains, "whether or not . . . [everyone] will succeed in bringing down his own *ruah* and *neshamah* from the treasure-house of souls, or some other heavenly source where these higher forms of his own soul abide, depends upon his own choice and spiritual development." Mystics accomplish this through extensive spiritual preparation and reflection on the Torah's esoteric aspects. The Zohar describes the highest aspect of soul as fundamentally beyond sin and probably free from transmigration. Later Kabbalistic thought posited five souls (adding two higher souls) and five worlds each inhabited by one of these.[62]

Thus, in Kabbalah we find the idea of a higher self expressing God in finite form and existing in a mutually necessary relationship with the earthly man. Kabbalah also contains and develops the tradition of multiple aspects of the psychospiritual self, the highest of which is purely spiritual and perhaps unaffected by past error. Human effort is fundamental to spiritual integration.

Celtic Paganism

The Catholic Church never completely suppressed traditional religions, despite its best efforts to incorporate some of their elements and its persecution of what resisted assimilation or didn't fit. These religions were necessarily secretive and often transmitted orally. Our knowledge of the nuances of their metaphysics and psychospiritual systems is limited and mostly of recent collection; although some acolytes assert an unbroken tradition of ancient origin, the lineages of present-day witchcraft, paganism, Wicca, Faery lore, etc., are much in question. The source material we have is interesting and suggestive, but some studies are the product of looking at these religions through a modern filter. In addition, we have no way of knowing what syncretism occurred during the religions' long and unhappy coexistence with Christianity; neither do we know their interactions with Judaism and Kabbalah, Christian heretical movements, or Islam. (Modern paganism regards its teachings as the essential core of all human religion, so for its adherents such syncretism would be only of historical interest and not a dilution or alteration of its nature.) Although the origins of at least some of the extant pagan traditions predate Christianity, the earliest existing written records are from the mid to late Middle Ages, so this section is presented at this point in our survey.

Folklorist Lewis Spence states that British Celts did not believe that people have numerous nonphysical bodies; in this system, there is no spiritual aspect that is already divine. The soul progresses rather mechanically and inevitably through many incarnations to gain understanding of all aspects of life and, in Spence's words, "of every operation and power and condition of evil and good," not so much by moral effort as by accumulation of experience.[63] By means of transmigration, the soul progresses through three planes of existence: "*Annwn*, the plane of germinal existence, *Abred*, the earth-plane, and *Gwynvyd*, the plane of justified spirits." The divine plane, *Ceugent*, was the inaccessible abode of God.[64] Although early Celts believed only heroes and other exceptional individuals reincarnate as "divine beings reborn on the human plane of life,"[65] this evolved to include all living things. All make it to *Gwynvyd* in the end, permanently, although there can be backsliding along the way from plane to plane, including angels who fall from *Gwynvyd* to *Abred* because they attempted to reach *Ceugent*.[66] The Celtic view of immortality, according to Spence, was largely a perpetuity achieved by way of ongoing transmigration, viewed as a positive process rather than as punishment or reparation such as obtained in Pythagorean and Hindu doctrine.[67] It should be remarked that scholarly historians deem Spence a "tremendous romantic," albeit a "good folklorist,"[68] and he uses as sources eighteenth-century writers of considerable imagination.

Starhawk writes that in the beliefs of Celtic Faery tradition (particularly in Wales, Cornwall, Ireland, and Scotland), "the Deep Self or God Self . . . is the Divine within, the ultimate and original essence, the spirit that exists beyond time, space, and matter. It is our deepest level of wisdom and compassion" which is held to consist of the union of the consciousness of male and female. She compares this Deep Self to the Kabbalistic *neshamah*.[69] As we've just seen, Scholem says this is incapable of sin and free from rebirth.

If these two traditions derive from the same source, there would seem to be a part of self that through many reincarnations ultimately achieves divinity or angelic existence, as well as a higher, already-divine, infinite, and eternal part that doesn't fall or incarnate.

Cahill, drawing on pre-Christian Irish epics committed to writing in the medieval period, observes that shamanic aspects of the religion of that time, such as shape-shifting, suggest that individuals experienced "no fixed identity but . . . [were], like the rest of reality, essentially fluid—essentially inessential. Of course, the Irish had no way of expressing such ideas directly. One needs a sense of identity before one can complain of its absence."[70]

This small sampling indicates considerable divergence either within

Celtic beliefs or among writers' and scholars' interpretations of the available material.

Renaissance Humanism

In fifteenth century Europe, newly available Greek and Roman manuscripts and translations, social and economic changes that produced affluent, autonomous urban centers where thought could develop relatively freely, and wealthy patrons who supported such inquiry yielded a period lasting a century and a half that envisioned humanity as having glorious earthly and spiritual potentials. Part of the modern fascination with the Renaissance mind arises from its reintegration of earth and heaven, with humanity assuming a central role in this physical-spiritual cosmos. The period is paradoxical in that, even though its philosophers looked consistently backward to the golden age of Greece, Rome, and Egypt, it laid the foundation for the modern era. It transformed how people viewed scientific efforts and technological development, turning the practical application of science into a worthy and acceptable pursuit—an acceptance that, ironically, it didn't receive in the Classical world revered by these humanists.[71] The Renaissance synthesis of interests in religion, science, philosophy, technology, magic, art, and indeed the whole of human endeavor would not survive the first half of the seventeenth century; these remain painfully sundered. Only in the past century have we begun to explore and embrace human nature as fully as did the humanists; perhaps we are ready to transcend their vision.

Marsilio Ficino (1433-1499), who headed the Florentine Platonic Academy established by Cosimo de Medici, produced complete translations of Plato and Plotinus. Ficino gave his era a Plato colored by his own medieval and Neoplatonic studies, involving, as he puts it, "a hierarchy of substances that descends from God to matter." In this, the human soul holds an essential position, such that "the soul through its universal, infinite aspirations and thoughts links the highest with the lowest beings and acts as a bond and knot of the universe."[72] Ficino saw in every human being the representation of God, reckoning both man and cosmos would become divine. For Ficino, Platonic theology affirmed that everything consists of finite and infinite compounded. Immaterial forms, including the rational soul, are immortal.[73] In Ficino's words, "it was for the limitless alone that He [God] created men, who are the only beings on earth to have rediscovered their infinite nature." Man's soul is divine.[74]

Ficino sought to prove this immortality and godliness. He found ample reason for declaring human divinity in humanity's independence of the physical world, in its domination and development of it, and in the likeness of this to God's dominion.[75] A soul that is able to return to itself comes to know its divine nature.[76] As Ardis Collins puts it, Ficino, like Thomas Aquinas (1224/5-1274), thinks of the destiny of humankind as a complete union with the divine, where God lifts the soul "beyond its limitations revealing himself not through an image or representation, but through direct presence."[77]

Ficino, however, follows Christian doctrine in viewing the soul as entire, unlike Plotinus's upper soul, which is an element of a greater whole.[78] Contrary to Plato, he felt that the soul's creation does not precede the body's, but vice versa. God gives infinite life, although Ficino questions whether this occurs from one eon to another or from a given point to the conclusion of time. In Ficino's view, the soul is midway between the eternal and temporal.[79] He finds nothing in human psycho-spiritual existence beyond the soul, nothing truly eternal that is outside time and that pre-exists bodily life.

Ficino also translated the *Corpus Hermeticum,* supposedly written by Hermes Trismegistus, a legendary Egyptian sage thought by some to predate and be seminal for all religions, though the *Corpus* subsequently proved to be written much too late for that. It exerted an important influence on Renaissance science, medicine, and humanism, encouraging emphasis on individualism and the dignity of humanity. It proposed that human beings are the microcosmic image of the macrocosm. The following are some of the tenets of the *Corpus*: "Unless you make yourself equal to God, you cannot understand God: for the like is not intelligible save to the like. Make yourself grow to a greatness beyond measure, by a bound free yourself from the body; raise yourself above all time, become Eternity. . . . Believe that nothing is impossible for you, think yourself immortal and capable of understanding all."[80] Confidence in this capacity for understanding, as well as the notion that individuals have the qualities of mind necessary for self-refection and critical analysis of their world, led to the conviction, prevalent in the Renaissance, that human beings could take their fate into their own hands and perfect themselves.

Giordano Bruno (1548-1600), an Italian mathematician, astronomer, and philosopher with strong interests in the occult, combined Copernican astronomy with Neoplatonism to create theories prefiguring modern science. Transcending Copernicus's belief in a finite universe, he proposed an infinite cosmos wherein the soul could achieve union with the infinite divine; his theorized that opposites come together in infinity. Expressing the Renaissance ethos, he urged attaining truth and virtue and asserted, "in every man . . . there is a world, a universe."[81]

Ficino, a century earlier, still distinguished humanity from nature and placed it in the superior position, identifying human nature as consisting of the rational soul differentiated from the body.[82] Bruno, however, joining form and matter, articulated scientifically the unity of all and the continuity or non-separation of divinity and the physical. Humankind can attain divinity, as in Ficino's vision, but for Bruno the person as a whole, not only his soul, can unify with God.

Renaissance hermeticism and alchemy were marriages of proto-science, metaphysics, and philosophy, which together enabled practitioners to work on themselves in ways that married spiritual discipline and empirical investigation. Bruno's theory uniting form and matter was the culmination of this. For a brief time, the humanists transformed the largely negative regard for physical existence that characterized the Orphics, Pythagoras, Plato, the Neoplatonists, the Gnostics, and medieval Christianity into an affirming embrace of life; Ficino and others declared humanity's incomparable position and potential on this earth. (This occurred, however, for only a few people; the uneducated and a good portion of the educated classes could not or would not enter into this new world. They still believed physical life to be different from and less than the life of the soul and far inferior to the divine, and they continued to hold that the soul's perfection involves leaving the body behind.)

Renaissance humanism didn't posit an infinite, pre-existing aspect of self that is in eternal union with the divine, eternally partakes of divine attributes, and expresses these throughout its finite creation. Humanism's breakthrough was to conceive the movement of the soul as opposite to the Christian and even the Neoplatonic conceptions. Instead of trying to go beyond earthly life to seek union with God, in humanism's pantheistic view the soul expresses itself fully in life and thereby achieves its divinity and its union with God within earthly existence.

Part 4.
Modern Dualism: The Seventeenth-Century Split between Scientific Materialism and Religion, and Its Aftermath

The Inquisition burned Bruno in 1600, a marker for the declining primacy of the Renaissance ideal and the initiation of a profound change in how Western Europeans viewed themselves and their relationship to God and physical existence. The scientific endeavors of the humanists had aimed to understand the natural order and achieve the wisdom to live with it harmoniously. The 1600s saw this turned on its head, so that beginning with Francis Bacon (1561-1626), the aim of science was more narrowly to discover how to govern nature and exploit it for humanity's ends.[1]

The seventeenth century was pivotal for the development of the modern world. It began with an expanding vision of the potential for the physical manifestation of human existence's full finite and infinite spectrum. This would come about through a marriage of science and religion, or more accurately, through science in the service of a religious ideal of a millennial period on earth. While we don't encounter any clear notion of the infinite self or the paradoxical nature of human existence, a number of people in the early seventeenth century envisioned the possibility of humankind creating a divine order on earth expressing humanity's unbounded possibilities. This would occur by means of spiritual study and education in science and art. The humanists saw science and religion (or spiritual advancement) as partners mutually supporting and illuminating each other or simply as one endeavor. (This attitude resembles sixth-century B.C.E. Greece before the philosophies of Pythagoras and Parmenides split spirit and matter.) Psychospiritually this meant, in effect, that the infinite self exists entirely within the physical cosmos, recognizable strictly as an infinite capacity within human beings to improve their circumstances and the world in the image and service of the divine.

The Renaissance's faith in humanity's destiny and capacity for progress took root in profound confidence about what science could accomplish in service of spiritual aims. During the early seventeenth century, a principal motivation for scientific endeavor was a perceived need for a renewal of spiritual life. According to historian Frances Yates, this holistic approach to man, the world, and divinity envisioned "a new general reformation" of the world, based on Christian brotherly love, Hermeticism and Kabbalah, and "turning towards the works of God in nature in a scientific spirit of exploration." A deeply religious purpose pervaded the study of the natural order. "God has imprinted his signs and characters in the Book of Nature. In contemplating that Book we contemplate God Himself."[2]

The relationship between science and religion changed drastically during the first decades of the seventeenth century. The development of science was abruptly removed from its spiritual context and its original significance, boundaries, and guidance. Thus orphaned, it could find meaning only in unlimited scientific advancement and technological achievement, rather than in supporting the expression of the divine nature of humankind.

Continuously from the classical period through the Middle Ages, religion and philosophy held spiritual reality to be primary, and conjectures about the nature of the physical world had to conform with accepted spiritual beliefs. This began to change when the monk Roger Bacon, an early exponent of experimental science, proposed that valid data could be obtained not only through divine inspiration and mystical experience but by way of the senses, adding objective perceptions to spiritual insight and reasoning as legitimate means of acquiring knowledge. Later scientists reciprocated by retaining divine illumination and mystical insight as sources of scientific understanding. Religion and science were in the same camp—until the seventeenth century. Then the converse of the situation before Bacon became standard belief: the means and methods by which science could prove something lay exclusively in the physical realm.

Magic, which the medieval Church entirely proscribed and which nearly everyone during the Middle Ages regarded negatively, achieved a new respectability in the Renaissance when it bifurcated into two distinct endeavors: black magic, which humanists disavowed, and natural magic, the study of divine forces in nature. Natural magic became a wholly acceptable pursuit for many Renaissance philosophers, and this permitted increased scientific interest in the natural world. Its practitioners began to see in mathematics a potential for effective operations, that is, for the application of philosophical and theological speculation to transforming the physical world through technology. Greek philosophers having placed questions about the spiritual world above those regarding matter, Greek science, despite many discoveries in mechanics, never produced much in the way of technological applications. In the Middle Ages, the desire to operate raised suspicions of satanic motivation.[3] Renaissance Europeans such as Pico della Mirandola (1463-1494), however, believed that celestial forces, in the words of science historian Charles Webster, "might be brought to bear on the terrestrial world in order to perform natural works rather than to seek miracles";[4] they moved from philosophy and theology to applied science and operations. As Yates puts it, "Man" was no more merely "the pious spectator of God's wonders"; now he sought "to draw power from the divine and natural order." That humanity should exercise all its capacities became "dignified and important," and humanists considered this to be in alignment with divinity's intent. "Magic as an aid to gnosis . . . [began] to turn the will in the new direction. . . . The will to operate, stimulated by Renaissance magic, could pass into, and stimulate, the will to operate in genuine applied science."[5] Yates notes the great irony that "the growth of mechanical science, through which arose the idea of mechanism as a possible philosophy of nature, was itself an outcome of the Renaissance magical tradition."[6] Inspired by the Kabbalah and by the *Corpus Hermeticum* and its supposed authority as the seminal religious document, the Renaissance hermetic magus was the locus of the transformation that developed the will and desire to operate. This magus appears in Shakespeare, for instance in *The Tempest*; his plays mark the pinnacle of European civilization's synthesis of art, spirit, inquisitiveness, and the excitement of new possibilities revealed by Renaissance science. Shakespeare died the year before the beginning of the events that would undo this synthesis.

Science served and was holistically wedded to concerns that transcended it. Accurate medical comprehension, for instance, required focusing on, Webster observes, "all the workings of heaven—to be a theologian, philosopher and physician"; to separate one aspect from another would affront God.[7] This holistic approach, Yates relates, required renovation of society as well as religious reformation because philosophers perceived that their nascent scientific approach had its perils and "its diabolical as well as its angelical possibilities."[8] Parliamentarian England most clearly discerned this risk and the need for reform; Webster recounts concerns there regarding Cartesian and other mechanistic philosophies, including "the materialistic dangers of science" and "the divorce between God and His universe."[9] However, political upheaval precluded taking action, and following the Restoration, as Yates says, "science was allowed to develop in isolation from . . . the idea of a reformed society, educated to receive it. The comparative disregard . . . was surely unfortunate for the future."[10] The costs of failing to include the renovation of society can be seen, for instance, in the medical consequences of a wide gap in wealth among its members. Statistical studies show that the most important factor contributing to the health of its citizens is not the wealth of a nation or the amount spent on health care; it's the degree of income disparity.

The Movement Destroyed

Several events combined to undermine the impetus for a moral, spiritual, and aesthetic science embedded in a progressive, reformed society and to create a split in the Western psyche that only now may be starting to heal. In 1614 the composition of the *Corpus* was shown to have occurred no earlier than the second century C.E. and therefore could not have been a source for Pythagoras, Plato, Christianity, and other religions; it lost the authority of its alleged antiquity. Given that "progress" in the Renaissance meant eliminating medieval superstition and drawing on the earliest and purest sources, its late date called into question the validity of its hermetic tenets, such as that man the microcosm reflects the macrocosm as part of a system of universal harmonies and that the inner world of man is connected with the outer world of nature. Belief in these was vital to the union of science and religion and to the movement for individual and societal development based on it. Dating the *Corpus*, Yates concludes, was "a watershed separating the Renaissance world from the modern world."[11]

Another pivotal event was the horrific Thirty Years War (1618-1648). Around 1620, forces of the Counter-Reformation devastated and depopulated areas of Bohemia and Germany that were a center for the promulgation of humanism's marriage of science and spirit and for the flowering of a religiously tolerant and open-minded utopian movement.

The third event was an intensified persecution of witches, whose targets included those committed to this utopian integration of religion and science as well as others accused of practicing the diabolical magic that was confused with the natural magic forming the nourishing medium for the development of science.[12] This forced those involved in scientific investigation to go to great lengths to separate their studies of the physical world from any activity that even appeared unacceptable in this less tolerant religious environment. The horrors of war, disillusionment following the discrediting of the *Corpus*, and fear of persecution produced an unnecessary and unnatural segregation of science and technology from their prior inclusive, spiritual, and humane context, divorcing in the European mind the material and divine worlds and dividing the scientific intellect from the intuitive, moral, and spiritual matrix it had been born in. Bruno's union of form and matter and all opposites in the infinity of Beingness would henceforth apply only to the physical universe.

The effects of these events unfolded over the following decades. In his youth, mathematician and philosopher Rene Descartes (1596-1650) found himself accused of involvement in the utopian movement of the early 1600s. The charge could have brought him to the stake; he denied it, though it was possibly true.[13] He proceeded to declare science and religion completely separate areas of study. He was seminal in the development of the mechanistic view of the physical universe, helping to produce the modern radical separation of human consciousness from the external world. Fear also influenced the monk Marin Mersenne (1588-1648), Descartes's friend and a prominent supporter of mechanical philosophy. Mersenne "had to protect his own interest in mathematics and mechanics from any taint of conjuring. This gave an asperity to his anti-Renaissance movement which, in less excited times, might have been conducted more gently and with less loss of the more valuable aspects of the Renaissance," says Yates. [14]

Despite these events, the relationship between scientific investigation and spiritual beliefs died slowly. Just as earlier groundbreaking scientists like Johannes Kepler (1571-1630) had, according to Webster, "animistic conceptions of the earth, moon, planets and stars," so Newton, until the end of his life in 1727, pursued scriptural prophecy and alchemical studies, considering these essential elements of his scientific pursuits. Webster remarks: "The idea of harmony in nature, parallelism between the macrocosm and microcosm, the pervasiveness of forces akin to sympathy and antipathy . . . and . . . emanations and hierarchies that bridged the gulf between the material and non-material world remained viable explanatory options . . . [for] forward-looking thinkers throughout the seventeenth century,"[15] such as the pioneering chemist Robert Boyle (1627-1691). The founders of modern science were extremely dedicated to their alchemy and astrology.

Nevertheless, the events of the seventeenth century produced a separation that persists to this day in mainstream Western thought. This has left spiritual inquiry to rely on what has become perforce a blinded faith, bereft, in the eyes of scientists, of any legitimacy in its application to empirical inquiry while holding itself above scientific examination. (This has contributed to the remarkable disconnect between many Christians' literal reading of the Bible and the historical understanding of scripture gained from one hundred fifty years of textual analysis, archaeology, and the discovery of new sources.) The primacy granted the "rational" soul of Plato and of Platonizing Christianity now resides in the rational function of the physical mind, and many scholars and scientists regard religion as essentially irrational. The scholastic, alchemical, and hermetic manifestations of the rational self in the service of spiritual humanity that occurred before this split appear, on the basis of our modern materialistic and scientific biases, to be bizarre and laughable. We may consider the combining of astronomy and astrology to be silly and misguided, and in terms of our modern scientific and technological goals, it clearly is. The intent of Renaissance science and technology was different, more holistic, more cautious about what humankind ought to do with science and more concerned about what might happen if intellect were severed from spiritual guidance and context. With good reason: in the absence of such guidance, science has created the means to place humanity's existence and the viability of the biosphere in jeopardy. This split allowed science and technology to develop at full speed, out of phase with and unfettered by the spiritual development necessary to structure them morally and envision them as part of the entirety of human and planetary life.

The split receives rigorous enforcement. Biologist Jacques Monod (1910-1976) laments, "any mingling of knowledge with values is unlawful, forbidden." In sociologist Max Weber's (1864-1920) words: "Whoever lacks the capacity to put on blinders, so to speak . . . may as well stay away from science." Regarding the nineteenth century, science historian Steve J. Heims states, "any consideration of social responsibility in connection with scientific research became a direct violation of the standards and values of the profession."[16] We invent things because we can; the advancement of science and technology has become its own moral imperative.

This critique does not imply regret about science's development. I would rather live in the early twenty-first century than in the sixteenth, but I suspect there is good reason to prefer living now to living fifty or one hundred years on, when the social and environmental debts incurred by technology's amoral application seem likely to come due. The relocating of man's infinity to his mental and technological capacities has produced the belief that we can always keep ahead of science's negative effects by developing technological fixes *ad infinitum.* Science's claim to be the pinnacle of rationality is ironic, considering that many scientists have what amounts to a blind faith that whatever problems science and technology create they can solve by such patches; this faith lacks justification, given the historically brief period in which we've (perhaps) managed to stay ahead of those problems. It seems more likely that healing the harmful consequences of science and technology will require re-integrating spirit and science and necessitate understanding what our paradoxical, infinite nature and potential is and is for. I don't think our highest estate is to be consumers of endlessly multiplied goods and services.

The dis-integration of the European psyche in the seventeenth century and its divorce of science and religion further distanced the mainstream of Western humanity from the possibility of experiencing, much less understanding, the full human psychospiritual nature including the infinite self, already difficult throughout the Middle Ages and Renaissance although the divine realms had still been close and real. This situation persisted until the nineteenth-century introduction of Eastern religious ideas, which led to popular interest in comparative religion and, in recent decades, helped to produce the array of pursuits collectively called New Age. This forum of world religious and spiritual views and experiences has fostered, as it did in the then-unprecedented cultural cross-fertilization during the Hellenistic and Roman period and almost did in the Renaissance, a new ability to conceptualize and experience humanity's full dimension.

The European psyche had been freed in some ways by the Renaissance and aspects of the Reformation and remained poised to embrace the inspired sense of human potential that fifteenth-century through early seventeenth-century spirituality had been leading toward. Many deeply spiritual and mystical statements from the late seventeenth and eighteenth centuries offer evidence of this.

The Pietist Gottfried Arnold (1666-1714) provides an example. "Know and believe that this noble Sophia is not distant from you, but . . . wishes to be much closer to you than you are to yourself, if you do not drive her off. . . . Every spirit created according to God's image may find the divine virgin in himself . . . This virgin was in the first man . . . as a seed of his spiritual birth . . . and awakened in him all imaginable joy and desire. Adam should have been satisfied with this and willing to live with this pure bride in paradise." He continues, "The full marriage day. . . she keeps until man's full perfection."[17] (Sophia is the feminine personification of divine Wisdom, associated with Mary in Catholic doctrine.) This aspect of divinity is within each person, closer than he is to himself from the beginning in his living spirit but separated from him by his dissatisfactions. This has resonances with the idea of the divine self within, which seeks, above all, the union with finite self that is the goal of finite self's evolution ("perfection"). The major differences are that the "pure bride" is not explicitly an individual divine entity within each person, and instead of an individual simply losing the capacity to be aware of her, Sophia can be driven off (although she remains close by); the infinite self never departs.

The American Vision

America's foundation rests on a compelling image of human possibilities, which from the beginning emphasized the freedom of the individual to combine religious experience and rational and scientific understanding in his own way. A person's infinity lay in unlimited possibilities for self-advancement in a land of endless new horizons and resources. Instead of the interaction of finite and infinite selves determining what manifests, in America it has been the relationship of the individual to the unbounded frontier.

The transcendentalist philosopher Ralph Waldo Emerson (1803-1882) articulates an essential American sensibility: "If a man is at heart just, then in so far is he God; the . . . immortality of God, the majesty of God, do enter into that man with justice."[18] Emerson described his view of the relationship of the finite to the infinite in the following way: "We live in succession, in division, in parts, in particles. Meantime within man is the soul of the whole . . . to which every part and particle is equally related; the eternal ONE." "There [is] no bar or wall in the soul, where man, the effect, ceases, and God, the cause, begins."[19] We partake of divinity if we live properly, but it is God's divinity. Emerson's idea of a person's spiritual existence includes only a soul; this can have a one-to-one relationship to the divine, which embraces it and is the "common heart" of all existence; the soul evolves in this relationship. Questions regarding the soul's immortality are themselves sinful; the soul properly finds it in the infinity of the moment.[20]

In Mormon doctrine, promulgated by Joseph Smith (1805-1844) beginning in the 1830s, human beings are literally children of God, begotten in spirit form by God and a heavenly Mother. God was originally as humans are now but evolved to divine stature. Human beings come into existence as spirits and then are born into bodies. After death, they continue as spirits together with the spirits of their earthly families; all have the capacity and opportunity to progress in power and knowledge, potentially toward divine status. Although spirit is pre-existent to the body, this doctrine does not posit a higher self that is always divine and united with God; it is a belief in becoming divine.

In the last two centuries, material from the East and from archaeological discoveries has exposed us to the tremendous breadth of human spiritual understanding and how that developed. For the first time in history, the more esoteric descriptions of the nature and dimensions of human existence are available to a large number of people in forms that are relatively intelligible. We are in a period of digesting this; as in previous melds of diverse societies and their ideas and religious beliefs, this is yielding new religions and some rather far-out metaphysical notions. Our spiritual smorgasbord resembles the one that flourished for centuries until a new state religion in Rome codified orthodoxy.

Prior to the sixteenth century, books were expensive and rare, esoteric teachings concealed and their adherents often persecuted, unorthodox texts destroyed or hidden, and orthodox scripture and doctrine purged of any substantial references to humankind's full spiritual stature. Hermetic and alchemical writings, from Antiquity through the eighteenth century, were highly symbolic and allegorical, and understanding them usually required direct training from an initiate; without this instruction they were impenetrable and seemed weird and fantastical. This was by design, in part for protection from persecution; it served, at least some of the time, to bring mere ridicule or disregard to the teachings, so that their students might have safety and relative peace. The increase in freedom of thought in many parts of the world during the last two centuries, the growing awareness of other religions and spiritual traditions, and the discovery of material such as the Nag Hammadi and Dead Sea texts have made accessible and understandable much that previously was lost or suffered suppression or lack of attention. Writers such as Madame Blavatsky (1831-1891), Alice A. Bailey (1880-1949), Rudolf Steiner (1861-1925), and C. G. Jung have imported, explained, and synthesized a multitude sources and contributed to an unprecedented efflorescence of readily available critiques and interpretations producing an understandable modern exposition of what until recently was a highly arcane understanding of man's spiritual dimensions.

Currently, Western students of the human spirit have little concern about religious repression, although fundamentalism increasingly raises concerns. A clear understanding of the human paradox and the infinite self is more at risk from this very profusion of ideas. A common thread in New Age thought is an idea of a higher self, in too many manifestations to survey here. Arising intuitively in these disparate beliefs, this frequently envisions the higher self helping to direct life, connecting people at a higher level, and providing healing ability, creative insight, and inspiration,[21] but the idea lacks explicit delineation. That it frequently fails to receive rigorous exposition is unsurprising in a movement that is often at odds with the products and processes of the analytic mind. Disinclination to critical thinking and the desire primarily to promote a positive attitude and a loving and accepting nature mark many sincere New Age pursuits. Though seekers take in much information, they sometimes poorly digest it. In this context, the idea of a higher self does not necessarily engage a strong sense of the responsibility for the hard choices that need to flow from it, including moving beyond dualistic thinking, employing to one's best ability the power of the infinite self to help create new conditions, respecting other views but also critiquing them, rigorously examining and challenging one's mental habits and beliefs and working with one's shadow side, and acknowledging and integrating all aspects of self.

As we've seen, the divine responds to our need for renewed balance, for a synthesis of all we've learned and our new potentials, by creating new symbols. These transcend verbal capacity to convey meaning, allowing us to understand who we are and what we're becoming. The notion of the individual infinite self (in whatever form this idea finds expression) is one such symbol. The spiritual realization expressed by this symbol is not new, but how we conceive it, sense it, and feel about it are novel and timely.

In this appendix, we have caught elusive glimpses of the individual divine self in several religions, spiritual traditions, and philosophies, plus a few clearer sightings, as in Zoroastrianism, Plotinus's philosophy, and esoteric Christianity. We've noted how religious politics and orthodoxy have constrained or shut off development of this insight, and we've found many instances where there was only the barest suggestion or a complete absence of it. This overview, in itself, does not provide a compelling reason to think that the description is a necessary one. All that's definite is that humanity consistently considers itself to be more than the physical body and is convinced that this supraphysical existence can impact the physical world and those in it and, usually, that a person's actions can likewise affect the supraphysical self, how it relates to the finite world, and its destiny. Nonetheless, we can state that there's a hint of the individual infinite self in religions, mystical experiences, and philosophies from many periods, a thread that can be traced from ancient Persia and Egypt, through Antiquity in the Near East and Mediterranean, to the modern West, never completely lost and increasingly a part of current non-orthodox thought. How it and other insights and symbols evolve will have a great influence not only on spiritual development but also on all aspects of our future. We are all involved in how this spiritual evolution plays out; the more conscious we are of all our developing symbols, the more positive an effect we can have.

Notes

Citations from *The Nag Hammadi Library* use the abbreviation *NHL*; bibliographic information for this source is listed under James M. Robinson. Citations from the *Encyclopædia Britannica* (*Britannica CD 97*) use the abbreviation *EB*. All Bible quotations are from the New Revised Standard Version (NRSV) unless otherwise noted. When a reprint edition is cited, page citations are to that edition.

Preface

1. Johan Huizinga, *Homo Ludens: A Study in the Play-Element in Culture* (1950; reprint, Boston: The Beacon Press, 1955), page unnumbered.

2. Plotinus, *The Enneads*, abr. ed., trans. Stephen MacKenna, abr. John Dillon (London: Penguin Books, 1991), 402, V.5.11.

3. Rudy Rucker, *Infinity and the Mind: The Science and Philosophy of the Infinite* (1982; reprint, New York: Bantam Books, 1983), 46.

4. David Bohm, *Wholeness and the Implicate Order* (1980; reprint, London: Routledge, 1995), 172.

Chapter One

1. "Ode. Intimations of Immortality from Recollections of Early Childhood," I.1-4, 9; V.59-63, 65-69.

2. Physicist David Bohm suggests that the Western way of encountering the world has its basis in a mental-perceptual illusion that conditions us to view things as separate and so to fragment what is by nature indivisible. He argues that quantum and relativity theories, in contrast, imply that we must see the cosmos in terms of "an *undivided whole*, in which all parts of the universe, including the observer and his instruments, merge ... in one totality" (Bohm, *Wholeness and the Implicate Order*, 1-8, 11.) Bohm proposes the concept of undivided wholeness in a flowing movement that preexists the objects of our world that take shape and disperse in the flow, where "mind and matter are not separate substances." Consciousness and body are projections of a higher dimension, a more fundamental reality (*ibid.*, 209); this precisely matches how the infinite and finite selves relate.

In both Buddhism and Hinduism, the highest metaphysical realities, *Dharmakaya* and *Brahman* respectively, suffuse material existence, mirrored in the finite minds of human beings as enlightened wisdom, or *bodhi*. They are therefore simultaneously both gross and spiritual; the most sublime reality is indivisible from the forms in which it enters existence. Lao Tzu referred to the Tao, ultimate existence, as beyond description but everywhere. One can't be outside it or get perspective on it; one can experience it but can't know it, can practice it but not understand it.

3. A. Schmölders, *Essai sur les ecoles philosophiques chez les Arabes*, abr. (Paris, 1842), 210, qtd. in William James, *The Varieties of Religious Experience* (1902; reprint, New York: Penguin Books, New American Library, Mentor Books, 1958), 322.

Chapter Two

1. C. G. Jung, *Memories, Dreams, Reflections,* rev. ed., ed. Aniela Jaffe, trans. Richard and Clara Winston (1961; reprint, New York: Random House, Vintage Books, 1965), 256-57.

Chapter Three

1. Bohm, *Wholeness and the Implicate Order,* 177.
2. Ibid., 149.
3. Qtd. in P. A. Schilpp, ed., *Albert Einstein, Philosopher-Scientist* (Evanston, Ill.: The Library of Living Philosophers, 1949), 114, qtd. in Fritjof Capra, *The Tao of Physics,* 3rd ed., expanded (Boston: Shambhala, 1991), 185.
4. Capra, *The Tao of Physics,* 292.
5. Plotinus, *Plotinus,* vol. 1, *Porphyry on the Life of Plotinus and the Order of His Books, Enneads I. 1-9,* trans. A. H. Armstrong (Cambridge, Mass.: Loeb Classical Library, 1966), xxiii.

Chapter Four

1. Jn. 14:12.
2. H. W. Brands, *The First American: The Life and Times of Benjamin Franklin* (2000; reprint, New York: Random House, Anchor Books, 2002), 665.
3. Lk. 22:22.
4. Rucker, *Infinity and the Mind,* 231.
5. Bohm, *Wholeness and the Implicate Order,* 25.

Chapter Five

1. Marion Woodman, *The Crown of Age: The Rewards of Conscious Aging* (Boulder, Colo.: Sounds True no. W528D, 2002), CD.
2. Robert Johnson, *We: Understanding the Psychology of Romantic Love* (San Francisco: HarperCollins, HarperSanFrancisco, 1983), 157-160.
3. Ibid., 160.
4. Ibid., 162.
5. Ibid., xi-xii.
6. Ibid., xiii.
7. Ibid., 44-45.
8. Ibid., 51.
9. Ibid., 53-54.
10. Gottfried von Strassburg, *Tristan: With the Surviving Fragments of the Tristan of Thomas,* trans. A. T. Hatto (1960; reprint with revisions, London: Penguin Books, 1967), 192, 194-95.
11. Johnson, *We,* 150.
12. Ibid., 142-43.
13. Qtd. in Rebecca Armstrong, "The Metaphysical Function of Mythology; Man and Woman: The Odyssey," in Joseph Campbell Foundation Website Archive, *Myth Letter* (February 2003), available from www.jcf.org/myth_letter.

14. Johnson, *We,* 183.

15. Wolfram von Eschenbach, *Parzifal,* trans. Helen M. Mustard and Charles E. Passage (New York: Random House, Vintage Books, 1961), 415.

16. "The Ballad of Reading Gaol," VI.649.

17. Susan Pierce provided this parallel.

Chapter Six

1. Mt. 6:14.

2. Mt. 7:7.

3. Rom. 12:19.

Chapter Seven

1. Rucker, *Infinity and the Mind,* 102.

2. C. G. Jung, *Aion,* 2nd ed., trans. R. F. C. Hull, Bollingen Series XX (Princeton, N.J.: Princeton University Press, 1968), 267.

3. Heinrich Zimmer, *The King and the Corpse,* Bollingen Series XI (1948; reprint, Princeton, N.J.: Princeton University Press, 1971), 212.

4. Friedrich Nietzsche, *The Portable Nietzsche,* trans. Walter Kaufmann (New York: The Viking Press, 1954), 435, *Thus Spoke Zarathustra.*

5. Zimmer, *The King and the Corpse,* 34-35.

6. Jung, *Memories, Dreams, Reflections,* 36-40.

7. Caitlin Matthews, *Sophia: Goddess of Wisdom, Bride of God* (1991; reprint, Wheaton, Ill.: Theosophical Publishing House, Quest Books, 2001), 276.

8. Norman Cohn, *Cosmos, Chaos and the World to Come: The Ancient roots of Apocalyptic Faith* (New Haven, Conn.: Yale University Press, 1993), 68.

9. Jean Piaget, *The Origins of Intelligence in Children,* trans. Margaret Cook (1952; reprint, N.Y.: W. W. Norton, The Norton Library, 1963), 39.

10. Zimmer, *The King and the Corpse,* 87-88.

11. Lao Tzu, *Tao Te Ching,* trans. D. C. Lau (Middlesex, England: Penguin Books, 1963), 85, XXVIII.

12. Susan Pierce, unpublished notes.

13. The effects of the growing feminine influence are welcomed as beneficial by some but reviled by others. We have only fragmentary evidence of living conditions during a supposed previous eon of feminine ascendancy, lasting until perhaps four thousand years ago (see Eisler, Stone); some ascribe it an Eden-like quality, while others describe unmitigated squalor and struggle. Recent findings, such as the Neolithic man frozen for forty-four hundred years in a glacier in the Alps, suggest that people were technologically sophisticated and worked merely two hours a day to make their living. For that period, at least, the evidence doesn't support the case for a life of extreme difficulty.

In the second millennium B.C.E., patriarchal Indo-European peoples from Central Asia, worshipers of bellicose thunder deities, conquered societies believed to have been more peaceful and matrilineal or at least less masculine-dominant. The history of Indo-Aryan tribes that subjugated parts of north India in the second half of that millennium is recorded in mythic form in the Rig Veda. In these myths, benevolent superhuman beings called *Adityas* battled equally powerful magical demons. The *Adityas* were the offspring of a goddess whose name probably meant "freedom"; these divinities represented, Cohn writes, "wide-open nature, free from all restriction and obstruction," qualities the masculine values; the demons, in contrast, were "restraining, binding, obstructing" (Cohn, *Cosmos, Chaos and the World to Come,* 62), qualities that the masculine typically resents and fears in the feminine. Likewise, Mesopotamian mythology portrays the goddess Tiamat as a monster inimical to life, inducing sterility and inertia; she is killed (by a male deity) so a new order can be established. (Yet, she was mother of the gods and originally their defender, which may indicate that the conquerors of the people for whom she was a benevolent deity altered her to elevate their own deities) (*ibid.*, 65.)

Tiamat and the demons may have been deities of matrilineal or feminine-oriented societies, and the conquering peoples may have found this kind of social order to be constraining and hostile to movement, uninhibited action, and free growth (at least the conquerors' movement and freedom). In the Rig Veda, we may find preserved a glimpse of the process of change from the age of feminine ascendancy to that of masculine dominance that is suggested for that time. The feeling of constraint and need to overcome it did not necessarily have anything to do with actual characteristics or flaws in the older societies. The sense of constraint may have had more to do with a felt need to express a new archetypal pattern of consciousness and psychological energy becoming predominant in the deep psyche of all peoples at that time, a pattern that the war-like Indo-Europeans seem to have been on the cutting edge of. Those moved by the new energy wanted freedom from the old order; their myths and conquests suggest that they were intoxicated with it, producing urgency to act without restraint and to expand without restriction. The negative traits attributed to Tiamat and the demons may have been projections of the conquerors' social or psychological conflicts. The way the new archetype was expressed, through violent subjugation of older societies, can't have been the only way this change from feminine to masculine polarity could have occurred; it was probably influenced by particular historical circumstances. Similarly, at our point in psychospiritual history, the way the archetypal feminine comes into expression will be determined by current circumstances.

We may well suspect that there were imperfections, limitations, and imbalances in the prior matrilineal order that needed change, and that humanity was ready to grow in new directions. It seems reasonable to expect that toward the end of an eon, that period's archetypal pattern of consciousness and the old order's dominant characteristics deteriorate into depleted, negative, or corrupt expression. (Some see this occurring now at the end of a masculine, patriarchal era felt to be increasingly destructive and obsolete.) If the feminine archetype was deteriorating, the perceived constraints and limitations that the masculine often dislikes in its relations with the feminine (for example, the requirements of fidelity, commitment, and foregoing the freedom to roam) may have been particularly prominent then, as the myths suggest. (Feminine energy manifests especially in form and structure, which are often viewed, inaccurately, to be more limited and limiting than masculine, dynamic energy.)

As human consciousness evolved, there arose from the deep psyche a move toward the other polarity, opening new possibilities for psychosocial development. However, the degree of male ascendance and privilege, aggression and dominance, that was established and has held sway until the present would seem to have been a terribly extreme cure for any faults of the previous order.

14. Stephen Hawking, *A Brief History of Time: From the Big Bang to Black Holes* (Toronto: Bantam Books, 1988), 46.

15. For examples of continuities, see physicist Fritjof Capra's *The Tao of Physics* for parallels between Eastern philosophy and mysticism and physics, such as the concept that "all things are seen as interdependent, inseparable, and as transient patterns of the same ultimate reality" (329). See Bohm's *Wholeness and the Implicate Order* concerning comprehending the universe and consciousness together "as a single unbroken totality of movement" (172), for the idea of the infinite multidimensionality of existence (186-87) and for the concept of the plenum, a multidimensional sea of infinite energy, perceived as void but from which all matter arises (189-92). Perhaps spiritual reality occurs at the highest end of the frequency spectrum of radiant energy, beyond visible light and cosmic radiation and beyond our current capacity to measure but still on the continuity of that spectrum.

16. Capra, *The Tao of Physics,* 310-11.

17. Ibid., 320.

18. Ibid., 68.

19. Ibid., 290.

20. Stephen Hawking, *The Universe in a Nutshell* (New York: Bantam Books, 2001), 78.

21. Hawking, *A Brief History of Time,* 129.

22. Qtd. in ibid.

23. Bohm, *Wholeness and the Implicate Order,* 69.

24. The horizon of the infinite coming into finite form can perhaps be specified. The Planck length (10 to the minus 35 meters,) is theorized to be the shortest possible, "the smallest distance to which we can probe without creating a black hole" (Hawking, *The Universe in a Nutshell,* 199). Beyond this boundary, random quantum foam is so violent as to make nonsense of time or space measurement.

25. Rucker, *Infinity and the Mind,* 173.

26. Ibid., 8.

27. Ibid., 10.

28. Georg Cantor, *Gesammelte Abhandlungen,* ed. Abraham Fraenkel and

Ernst Zermelo (Berlin: Springer Verlag, 1932), 378, qtd. in Rucker, *Infinity and the Mind*, 10.

29. Rucker, *Infinity and the Mind*, 54.

30. Ibid., 53.

31. Ibid., 87.

32. Ibid., 54.

33. Cantor, *Gesammelte Abhandlungen*, 374, italics added, qtd. in Rucker, *Infinity and the Mind*, 46.

Chapter Eight

1. This is expressed in the codes of Lipit-Ishtar in Sumer and Akkad and of Hammurabi in Babylon (early nineteenth and early eighteenth centuries B.C.E.)

2. Mt. 7:12.

3. The Analects.

4. Udana-Varga 5,1.

5. Mahabharata, bk. 5, ch. 49, v. 57.

6. *Tobit* 4:14-15.

7. Babylonian Talmud, Shabbat 31a.

8. Bohm, *Wholeness and the Implicate Order*, 177.

Chapter Nine

1. Plotinus, *The Enneads*, c.

Chapter Ten

1. Thich Nhat Hanh, *Cultivating the Mind of Love: The Practice of Looking Deeply in the Mahayana Buddhist Tradition* (Berkeley, Ca.: Parallax Press, 1996), 80-81, 83.

2. Qtd. in James, *The Varieties of Religious Experience*, 296.

3. Jung, *Memories, Dreams, Reflections*, 338.

4. Capra, *The Tao of Physics*, 190.

5. Bohm, *Wholeness and the Implicate Order*, 143.

6. William Blake, *The Complete Poems*, ed. Alicia Ostriker (London: Penguin Books, 1977), 181.

7. Fynn, *Mister God, This Is Anna* (New York: Holt, Rinehart and Winston, 1975), 42-43.

Chapter Eleven

1. Dudley Young, *Origins of the Sacred: The Ecstasies of Love and War* (1991; reprint, New York: HarperCollins, HarperPerennial, 1992), 409-13.

2. Bohm, *Wholeness and the Implicate Order*, 210, 52, 190-92.

Chapter Thirteen

1. Huizinga, *Homo Ludens,* 7-10.
2. Ibid., 5.
3. Ibid., 152, 156.
4. Ibid., 10, 11.
5. Ibid., 17.
6. Plato, *The Collected Dialogues of Plato: Including the Letters,* ed. Edith Hamilton and Huntington Cairns, Bollingen Series LXXI (1961; reprint with corrections, Princeton, N.J.: Princeton University Press, 1963), 1375, *Laws* VII:803.
7. Huizinga, *Homo Ludens,* 14.
8. Ibid., 10.
9. James Hillman, *Re-Visioning Psychology* (1975; reprint, New York: Harper and Row, Harper Colophon Books, 1977), 12.
10. Huizinga, *Homo Ludens,* 6.

Chapter Fourteen

1. Cohn, *Cosmos, Chaos and the World to Come,* 3, 57.
2. Ibid., 107.
3. Ibid., 26.
4. Jeremy Naydler, *Temple of the Cosmos: The Ancient Egyptian Experience of the Sacred* (Rochester, Vt.: Inner Traditions, 1996) 62.
5. Cohn, *Cosmos, Chaos and the World to Come,* 77.
6. Ibid., 82-84, 96-99.
7. Ibid., 146-47.
8. Ibid., 180, 145.
9. John Dominic Crossan, *The Birth of Christianity: Discovering What Happened in the Years Immediately after the Execution of Jesus* (New York: HarperCollins, HarperSanFrancisco, 1998, 461-62.
10. Cohn, *Cosmos, Chaos and the World to Come,* 178, 189.
11. Richard Laurence, trans., *The Book of Enoch the Prophet,* Secret Doctrine Reference Series (1883; reprint with index, San Diego, Ca.: Wizard's Bookshelf, 1983), 25, *1 Enoch* XVIII:15-16.
12. Rev. 2:26, 3:10.
13. Plotinus, *The Enneads,* xcvii.
14. Joseph Needham, with the collaboration of Lu Gwei-Djen, *Science and Civilization in China, Vol. 5: Chemistry and Chemical Technology, Part II: Spagyrical Discovery and Invention: Magisteries of Gold and Immortality* (Cambridge: Cambridge University Press, 1974), xxvii.
15. Hawking, *A Brief History of Time,* 143-44.
16. Rucker, *Infinity and the Mind,* 11.
17. Lama Anagarika Govinda, *Foundations of Tibetan Mysticism* (New York: Samuel Weiser, 1974), 116, qtd. in Capra, *The Tao of Physics,* 185-86.
18. Henry David Thoreau, *Walden and Other Writings,* ed. Brooks Atkinson (New York: Random House, Modern Library, 1937), 15, *Walden.*

19. Qtd. in James, *The Varieties of Religious Experience,* 317.

20. Jung, *Memories, Dreams, Reflections,* 295-96.

21. Karl Rahner, "The life of the dead," chapter 14 in *Theological Investigations,* Vol. 4 (London: Baltimore, 1966), 347-54, qtd. in Louis Jacobs, *A Jewish Theology* (West Orange, N.J.: Berman House, 1973), 89.

22. Naydler, *Temple of the Cosmos,* 62.

23. Thoreau, *Walden and Other Writings,* 7, *Walden.*

24. William Butler Yeats (1865-1939) lays out a fascinating view of this relationship in his book *A Vision,* describing a historical periodicity containing twenty-eight phases that occur over one-thousand-year spans. He describes each phase in terms of the kind of art created and the psychological type prominent in each. Published in 1937, the book has accurately predicted dominant currents in art. Jung, discussing the archetypes of the collective unconsciousness, tells how the Anthropos, or archetype of the self, timeless yet evolving, takes a new form in each eon. See *Memories, Dreams, Reflections,* 220-221, and his *Aion.*

25. Nietzsche, *The Portable Nietzsche,* 330, *Thus Spoke Zarathustra.*

Chapter Fifteen

1. Young, *Origins of the Sacred,* 50-51, 67.

2. Ibid., 70-71.

3. Ibid., 76, 119.

4. Neanderthals buried their dead at least eighty thousand years ago.

5. Sharon Begley, Science Journal, "Scans of Monks' Brains Show Meditation Alters Structure, Functioning" (*Wall Street Journal,* November 5, 2004).

Chapter Sixteen

1. Young, *Origins of the Sacred,* 301.

2. Martin Buber, *Good and Evil: Two Interpretations,* 2nd ed., (New York: Charles Scribner's Sons, 1953), 138.

3. Ibid., 111.

4. Cohn, *Cosmos, Chaos and the World to Come,* 182.

5. Ibid., 161.

6. Ibid., 181-82.

7. Henry Chadwick, *The Early Church,* The Pelican History of the Church, vol. 1 (Harmondsworth, Middlesex, England: Penguin Books, 1967), 104.

8. This discussion draws on Woodruff, Paul, and Wilmer, Harry A., *Facing Evil: Confronting the Dreadful Power behind Genocide, Terrorism and Cruelty* (Chicago: Open Court, 1988).

9. Martin Buber, *The Knowledge of Man* (New York: Harper, 1966), 181.

10. Friedrich Nietzsche, *Beyond Good and Evil,* trans. Marianne Cowan (Chicago: Henry Regnery, Gateway, 1955), 2-3.

11. Milton C. Nahm, *Selections from Early Greek Philosophy,* 4th ed. (New York: Meredith Publishing, Appleton-Century-Crofts, 1964), 71.

12. Jung, *Memories, Dreams, Reflections,* 329.

13. C. G. Jung, *The Undiscovered Self,* trans. R. F. C. Hull (1958; reprint, New York: Mentor, 1959), 113.

14. Mt. 6:22-23 speaks of the dire effect of splitting polarities: "If . . . thine eye be single, thy whole body shall be full of light. But if thine eye be evil, thy whole body shall be full of darkness" (King James Version; NRSV has "healthy" for "single" and "unhealthy" for "evil.") The eye, the capacity to perceive existence, must be "single" or it will be Evil.

15. C. G. Jung, *Answer to Job,* trans. R. F. C. Hull (1954; reprint, Cleveland: World Publishing, Meridian Books, 1960), 87, 28.

16. Ibid., 110-11.

17. Ibid., 206 n. 8.

18. Ibid., 110.

19. Job 2:10.

20. Jung, *Answer to Job,* 111.

21. Ibid., 98-99.

22. In the Hebrew *1 Enoch,* written as early as the second century B.C.E., a section (possibly composed by a Christian writer and interpolated in the second century C.E.) has an angel expelling "the Satans" from the presence of God, prohibiting them from making accusations against human beings, the job apparently having been eliminated (Laurence, *The Book of Enoch the Prophet,* 45, XL:7.

23. Jung, *Answer to Job,* 99.

24. Buber, *Good and Evil,* 74-78.

25. Ibid., 91-92.

26. Ibid., 125-26.

27. Ibid., 79-80.

28. Ibid., 94-95, 97.

29. Ibid., 121, 128.

30. Ibid., 39-40.

31. Ibid., 57, 34.

32. Young, *Origins of the Sacred,* 75.

33. Webster's New Universal Unabridged Dictionary, deluxe 2nd ed.

34. Gen. 1:26.

35. Edgar Allan Poe, *Complete Tales and Poems of Edgar Allan Poe* (New York: Modern Library, 1938), 225.

36. Young, *Origins of the Sacred,* 285, 308.

37. Eric A. Havelock, *The Muse Learns to Write: Reflections on Orality and Literacy from Antiquity to the Present* (New Haven, Conn.: Yale University Press, 1986), 96.

38. Homer, *The Odyssey,* trans. Robert Fitzgerald (1961; reprint, Garden City, N.Y.: Doubleday and Company, Anchor Books, 1963), 239-40.

39. Ibid., 91.

40. Ibid., 240.

41. Plotinus, *The Enneads,* c.

42. Nietzsche, *Beyond Good and Evil,* 138.

43. See Rowan A. Greer, *Introduction to Origen: An Exhortation to Martyrdom, Prayer, First Principles, Book IV, Prologue to the Commentary to the Song of Songs, Homily XXVII on Numbers,* The Classics of Western Spirituality (New York: Paulist Press, 1979), 16.

44. Job 1:11, 2:5.

45. Karl E. Weick, "Small Sins and Large Evils," in Woodruff and Wilmer, *Facing Evil,* 88.

46. Raul Hilberg, "The Holocaust," in Woodruff and Wilmer, *Facing Evil,* 99-117.

47. Qtd. in Zimmer, *The King and the Corpse,* 230.

48. Nietzsche, *Beyond Good and Evil,* 86.

49. Young, *Origins of the Sacred,* 292-96.

50. Ibid., 323.

Chapter Seventeen

1. Naomi H. Rosenblatt and Joshua Horwitz, *Wrestling with Angels: What the First Family of Genesis Teaches Us about Our Spiritual Identity, Sexuality, and Personal Relationships* (New York: Delacorte, 1995), 45.

2. Gen. 3:6.

3. Ibid., 2:16-17.

4. Ibid., 3:22.

5. Ibid., 1:26.

6. Ibid., 3:10.

7. Heb. 11:3.

8. Ibid., 11:1.

9. Mt. 7:16.

Chapter Eighteen

1. Piaget, *The Origins of Intelligence in Children,* 33, 35-37.

2. Ibid., 35-37.

3. Erik H. Erikson, *Childhood and Society,* 2nd ed., rev. and enl. (New York: W. W. Norton, 1963), 250.

4. Ibid., 85.

5. Ibid., 252-53.

6. Ibid., 253.

7. Ibid., 254.

Chapter Nineteen

1. Akkadian Councils of Wisdom.

Introduction to Appendices

1. Jacobs, *A Jewish Theology,* 305.

2. G. S. Kirk, J. E. Raven, and M. Schofield, *The Presocratic Philosophers: A Critical History with a Selection of Texts,* 2nd ed. (Cambridge: Cambridge University Press, 1983), 220.

Appendix One

1. The main source for this section is *EB*, s.v. "Systems of Religious and Spiritual Belief."

2. Hillman, *Re-Visioning Psychology*, ix-x.

3. Ibid., 70.

4. Thomas Moore, *Soul Mates* (New York: HarperCollins, 1994), xiii, xvi.

5. Hillman, *Re-Visioning Psychology*, 68.

6. Ibid., 68-70.

Appendix Two, Part One

1. C. E. Vulliamy, *Immortality: Funerary Rites and Customs* (1926; reprint [orig. pub. as *Immortal Man*], London: Random House UK, Senate, 1997), 1.

2. Ibid., 79, 84.

3. Ibid., 205, 35.

4. Ibid., 5-6.

5. Ibid., 67.

6. E. A. Wallis Budge, *From Fetish to God in Ancient Egypt* (1934; reprint, New York: Dover Publications, 1988), 328-29.

7. Vulliamy, *Immortality*, 144.

8. Naydler, *Temple of the Cosmos*, 199.

9. Ibid., 198-99.

10. Ibid., 196.

11. Ibid., 200-03.

12. Vulliamy, *Immortality*, 145.

13. Naydler, *Temple of the Cosmos*, 207.

14. Budge, *From Fetish to God in Ancient Egypt*, 326.

15. E. A. Wallis Budge, *The Egyptian Book of the Dead (The Papyrus of Ani): Egyptian text, Transliteration and Translation* (1898; reprint, New York: Dover, 1967), 174, qtd. in Naydler, *Temple of the Cosmos*, 208.

16. John Ray, *Reflection of Osiris: Lives from Ancient Egypt* (Oxford: Oxford University Press, 2002), 9.

17. Naydler, *Temple of the Cosmos*, 209.

18. Cohn, *Cosmos, Chaos and the World to Come*, 36.

19. Ibid., 55, 56.

20. G. F. Moore, *History of Religions*, vol. I (Edinburgh, 1950), 228-29, qtd. in Jacobs, *A Jewish Theology*, 302-03.

21. Jacobs, *A Jewish Theology*, 301.

22. Jacques Duchesne-Guillemin, *Symbols and Values in Zoroastrianism: Their Survival and Renewal*, Religious Perspectives, vol. XV (1966; reprint, New York: Harper and Row, Harper Torchbooks, 1970), 4.

23. *EB*, s.v. "Religious Doctrines and Dogmas—Zoroastrianism and Parsiism"; "Ancient Middle Eastern Religions."

24. Ibid., s.v. "Fravashi."

25. Naydler, *Temple of the Cosmos*, 193, 196-97.

26. *EB*, s.v. "Ancient Middle Eastern Religions"; "Religious Doctrines and Dogmas—Zoroastrianism and Parsiism."

27. Duchesne-Guillemin, *Symbols and Values in Zoroastrianism*, 4.

28. Cohn, *Cosmos, Chaos and the World to Come*, 96.

29. Yuri Stoyanov, *The Hidden Tradition in Europe* (London: Penguin Books, Arkana, 1994), 11.

30. Cohn, *Cosmos, Chaos and the World to Come*, 85.

31. Ibid., 59, 75-76.

32. Sri Aurobindo, *Wisdom of the Upanishads* (Wilmont, WI.: Lotus Light Publications, 1988), 12, 18.

33. Swami Nikhilananda, *The Upanishads*, abridged ed. (1963; reprint, New York: Harper and Row, Harper Torchbooks, Cloister Library, 1964), 31.

34. Ibid., 63, 384, 54-55.

35. Aurobindo, 22.

36. Ibid., 21.

37. Nikhilananda, *The Upanishads*, 55, quoting from the Svetasvatara Upanishad.

38. Needham and Lu, *Science and Civilization in China, Vol. 5*, 85, 82; Roger Weir, *Taoism—Part 3*, Lecture July 15 (Los Angeles: privately published, 1986), Audiocassette.

39. Needham and Lu, *Science and Civilization in China, Vol. 5*, xxvii.

40. Holmes Welch, *Taoism: The Parting of the Way*, rev. ed. (1957; reprint, Boston: Beacon Press, 1966), 112.

41. Needham and Lu, *Science and Civilization in China, Vol. 5*, 92-93, 98 footnote c.

42. Welch, *Taoism*, 112.

43. Needham and Lu, *Science and Civilization in China, Vol. 5*, 8-9.

44. Ibid., 11-12.

45. Ibid., 82, 96 footnote b, 71.

46. Ibid., 77-80.

47. Ibid., 83.

48. Weir, *Taoism*.

49. Needham and Lu, *Science and Civilization in China, Vol. 5*, 111.

50. *EB*, s.v. "Shen."

51. Edward Conze, *Buddhist Thought in India: Three Phases of Buddhist Philosophy* (1962; reprint, Ann Arbor: University of Michigan Press, Ann Arbor Paperbacks, 1967), 103, 104, 171.

52. Ibid., 242, 228-29.

53. Ibid., 172, 229-30.

54. Stoyanov, *The Hidden Tradition in Europe*, 13.

55. Ibid., 15-16, 3.

56. *EB*, s.v. "Systems of Religious and Spiritual Belief."

57. Johan C. Thom, *The Pythagorean Golden Verses: With Introduction and Commentary*, Religions in the Graeco-Roman World, vol. 123 (Leiden: E. J. Brill, 1995), 204-07.

58. J. A. Philip, *Pythagoras and Early Pythagoreanism,* Phoenix, Journal of the Classical Association of Canada, suppl. vol. 7 (Toronto: University of Toronto Press, 1966), 175-77.

59. Thom, *The Pythagorean Golden Verses,* 4-11.

60. Ibid., 209, 207.

61. Pythagoras, *The Golden Verses of Pythagoras, with the Commentary of Hierocles,* adapted from trans. of N. Rowe (Santa Barbara, Ca.: Concord Grove Press, 1983), 88-89.

62. Ibid., 86, 32-33.

63. Kenneth Sylvan Guthrie, trans., and David Fideler, ed., *The Pythagorean Sourcebook and Library: An Anthology of Ancient Writings Which Relate to Pythagoras and Pythagorean Philosophy* (Grand Rapids, Mich.: Phanes Press, 1988), 167; Philolaus qtd. in, 168.

64. Capra, *The Tao of Physics,* 20.

65. *EB,* s.v. "Western Philosophical Schools and Doctrines."

66. Ibid.

67. Plato, *The Collected Dialogues,* 678, IV.436a.

68. Plato, *Timaeus and Critias,* trans. Desmond Lee (Harmondsworth, Middlesex, England: Penguin Books, 1971), 56-57, *Timaeus* 41.

69. Ibid., 58-59, *Timaeus* 42.

70. Plato, *Five Great Dialogues,* trans. B. Jowett, ed. Louise Ropes Loomis (New York: Walter J. Black, 1942), 114-15, *Phaedo.*

71. Ibid., 149, 110.

72. Gen. 3:8, 17:1-22, 18:1-8.

73. Ex. 3:4-6, 33:9, 33:11, 33:20, 23.

74. Jacobs, *A Jewish Theology,* 301-03.

75. Needham and Lu, *Science and Civilization in China, Vol. 5,* 78-79 footnote b.

76. Cohn, *Cosmos, Chaos and the World to Come,* 174.

77. Jacobs, *A Jewish Theology,* 303.

78. Needham and Lu, *Science and Civilization in China, Vol. 5,* 78-79 footnote b.

79. Cohn, *Cosmos, Chaos and the World to Come,* 174, 193.

80. Jacobs, *A Jewish Theology,* 306-07.

81. *The Apocrypha according to The Authorised Version* (Oxford: Oxford University Press, n.d.), 109, 2:23.

82. Philo of Alexandria, *Philo of Alexandria: The Contemplative Life, The Giants, and Selections,* trans. David Winston, The Classics of Western Spirituality (New York: Paulist Press, 1981), 118-19, *Quis Rerum Divinarum Heres Sit* 240.

83. Jacobs, *A Jewish Theology,* 308.

84. Philo, *Philo of Alexandria,* 103, 135, *De Opificio Mundi.*

85. Ibid., 122, *Quis Rerum Divinarum Heres Sit.*

86. Ibid., 63, *The Giants* II.12-13.

87. Ibid., 120-21, *Quis Rerum Divinarum Heres Sit* 55-57; 346 n.65.

88. Theodore Vrettos, *Alexandria* (New York: The Free Press, 2001), 167-68.
89. Burton L. Mack, *The Lost Gospel: The Book of Q and Christian Origins* (1993; reprint, New York: HarperCollins, HarperSanFrancisco, 1994), 57-58.
90. David Ulansey, *The Origins of the Mithraic Mysteries: Cosmology and Salvation in the Ancient World* (1989; reprint, New York: Oxford University Press, 1991), 86.
91. Plutarch, *Essays,* trans. Robin Waterfield, intro. and anno. Ian Kidd (London: Penguin Books, 1992), 343-44, "On Socrates's Personal Deity" 591d-e.
92. Peter Brown, *The Making of Late Antiquity* (1978; reprint, New York: Barnes and Noble Books, 1998), 68.
93. Plutarch, *Essays,* 301, 306.

Appendix Two, Part Two

1. Jn. 10:34.
2. Lk. 17:21, Jn. 14:12.
3. 1 Jn. 4:16.
4. Crossan, *The Birth of Christianity,* 207-08.
5. Jn. 10:35.
6. He. 4:12.
7. Jn. 14:16-17.
8. Jung, *Answer to Job,* 136.
9. Vulliamy, *Immortality,* 179, 5.
10. Cohn, *Cosmos, Chaos and the World to Come,* 199 qtg. Mark 12:25 and Matt. 13:43, 209.
11. St. Augustine, *The City of God,* trans. Marcus Dods (New York: Random House, Modern Library, 1950), 732, Bk. XX Ch. 14; 734, Ch. 16.
12. Paed. iii. 1, qtd. in Plotinus, *The Enneads,* lxxvii.
13. Chadwick, *The Early Church,* 97.
14. Qtd. in Greer, *Introduction to Origen,* 25.
15. Elaine Pagels, *Adam, Eve, and the Serpent* (New York: Random House, 1988), 51.
16. Elaine Pagels. *The Gnostic Gospels* (1979; reprint, New York: Random House, Vintage Books, 1989), 122.
17. Pagels, *Adam, Eve, and the Serpent,* 37.
18. Pagels, *The Gnostic Gospels,* 121-22.
19. *Oratio ad Graecos,* qtd. in Roelof van den Broek, "The Cathars: Medieval Gnostics?" in *Gnosis and Hermeticism from Antiquity to Modern Times,* ed. Roelof van den Broek and Wouter J. Hanegraaff (Albany, N.Y.: State University of New York Press, 1998), 101.
20. Broek, "The Cathars: Medieval Gnostics?"
21. Pagels, *The Gnostic Gospels,* xxx, xxxii.
22. Brian Riggs, "The Storm in Alexandria," in *Gnosis* 45 (fall 1997), 24.
23. Broek, "Gnosticism and Hermeticism in Antiquity: Two Roads to Salvation," in Broek and Hanegraaff, *Gnosis and Hermeticism,* 11.
24. Matthews, *Sophia,* 151.

25. Ibid., 152, quoting an unidentified text.
26. NHL, 250, 134.11-14, first brackets added.
27. Broek, "Gnosticism and Hermeticism in Antiquity," 1.
28. Pagels, *The Gnostic Gospels,* 122-23.
29. See Ibid., 102-118.
30. Crossan, *The Birth of Christianity,* 252-53.
31. NHL, 126, 32.26-33.2.
32. Ibid., 137, 50.28-30.
33. Ibid., 132, 41.27-42.3.
34. Pagels, *The Gnostic Gospels,* 144.
35. NHL, 127, 35.5.
36. Pagels, *The Gnostic Gospels,* xx-xxi, 95.
37. NHL, 134, 45.30-31.
38. Ibid., 147, 61.29-35, brackets are in qtd. material; words in parentheses added.
39. Pagels, *The Gnostic Gospels,* 144-45.
40. Plotinus, *The Enneads,* xxxii.
41. Ibid., xxxiii; 57, Ennead I.8.2.
42. Plotinus, *Plotinus,* vol. 1, xx-xxi.
43. Plotinus, *The Enneads,* 544-45, Ennead VI.9.8.
44. Ibid., liv.
45. Ibid., xxxiii; 57, Ennead I.8.2.
46. Ibid., xxxvi.
47. Plotinus, *Plotinus,* vol. 3, *Enneads III. 1-9,* trans. A. H. Armstrong (Cambridge, Mass.: Loeb Classical Library, 1967), 149-50, Ennead III.4.3. The translator notes (150-51n) that, while Plotinus here is at pains to indicate the continuity of our divine nature through all dimensions, later Neoplatonists, such as Proclus (c. 410-485), separated the levels so that man is in his one proper place, as these saw it: low in the cosmic hierarchy.
48. Plotinus, *The Enneads,* 406, Ennead V.7.1.
49. Ibid., xxxix.
50. Ibid., 9, Ennead I.1.8.
51. Plotinus, *Plotinus,* vol. 3, 140.
52. Plotinus, *Plotinus,* vol. 1, xi-xii.
53. Lloyd P. Gerson, ed., *The Cambridge Companion to Plotinus* (Cambridge Companion Series (Cambridge: Cambridge University Press, 1996), 55-56.
54. Plotinus, *Plotinus,* vol. 1, xxi-xxiii.
55. Plotinus, *The Enneads,* 544-45, Ennead VI.9.8.
56. Plotinus, *Plotinus,* vol. 1, xxvi.
57. Plotinus, *The Enneads,* 544-45, Ennead VI.9.8.
58. Ibid., xcvii, xxxv, xlvi-xlvii.
59. Ibid., lii.
60. Chadwick, *The Early Church,* 104.
61. *Commentary on John* 1.17, qtd. in Riggs, "The Storm in Alexandria," 23.
62. Chadwick, *The Early Church,* 105.

63. Ibid., 104.
64. Greer, *Introduction to Origen,* 24-25, 10-11.
65. Chadwick, 107.
66. Greer, *Introduction to Origen,* 16.
67. 2 Pet. 1:4.
68. Pagels, *Adam, Eve, and the Serpent,* 98.
69. Dionysius the Areopagite, *The Mystical Theology and The Celestial Hierarchies of Dionysius the Areopagite: With Commentaries by the Editors of The Shrine of Wisdom and Poem by St. John of the Cross,* trans. The Editors of the Shrine of Wisdom (Fintry, Brook, nr. Godalming, Surrey, Great Britain: The Shrine of Wisdom, 1949), 40.
70. Ibid., 8, 25-27.
71. Ibid., 37, 40-41.
72. Stoyanov, *The Hidden Tradition in Europe,* 93-95.
73. Johannes van Oort, "Manichaeism," in Broek and Hanegraaff, *Gnosis and Hermeticism,* 41.
74. Crossan, *The Birth of Christianity,* 239, 248.
75. Mack, *The Lost Gospel,* 114-21; Idries Shah, *The Sufis* (1964; reprint, New York: Doubleday, Anchor Books, 1971), xxi, 443.
76. See Crossan, *The Birth of Christianity,* esp. Part V.
77. Mack, *The Lost Gospel,* 4-5.
78. Ibid., 215-16.
79. Pagels, *The Gnostic Gospels,* 131.
80. NHL, 453, *The Testimony of Truth* 44.2, 43.26.
81. Ibid., 386, *The Teachings of Sylvanus* 97.18-19, 98.8-10; 382, 87.22-24.
82. Ibid., 322, *The Discourse on the Eighth and the Ninth* 52.15-16.
83. Ibid., 253, *The Dialogue of the Savior* 142.16-19.
84. Brown, *The Making of Late Antiquity,* 36, 24.
85. Ibid., 13.
86. Edward Gibbon, *The History of the Decline and Fall of the Roman Empire,* new ed. with index, vol. 1 (Philadelphia: Henry T. Coates, 1845), 542.
87. Brown, *The Making of Late Antiquity,* 9-10, 65.
88. Crossan, *The Birth of Christianity,* 29.
89. Brown, *The Making of Late Antiquity,* 65-66.
90. Crossan, *The Birth of Christianity,* 373-82.
91. Brown, *The Making of Late Antiquity,* 12, 25, 59.
92. Qtd in ibid., 17.
93. Ibid., 62.
94. For a description of these Jewish men of God, see Geza Vermes, *The Changing Faces of Jesus* (2000; reprint, New York: Penguin Compass, 2002), 252-263.
95. Brown, *The Making of Late Antiquity,* 14.
96. Ibid., 99-100.
97. Ibid., 92-94, 96-98.
98. Ibid., 92.

99. Ibid., quoting *Apophthegmata Patrum,* Ammoe 4, 128A.
100. Ibid., 92-93, 100.
101. Ibid., 97-98, 101.
102. Ibid., 68, 86, 91.
103. Ibid., 68-69.
104. Ibid., 121 note 68.
105. Ibid., 69.
106. Ibid., 70-71.
107. Late Roman culture focused on the demonic, due not to viewing demons as hostile but to their indefinite and uncertain standing. For Plutarch, says Brown, this presented "a benign ambiguity: the demons were an 'elegant solution' for the incongruities that arose from the joining of heaven and earth." By the end of Antiquity, however, they represented a font of delusion (ibid., 20). For Christians, they were not only hostile *to* man but "summed up all that was anomalous and incomplete *in* man. Demons, incomplete creatures, sought completion through human complicity" (ibid., 90).
108. Ibid., chapter 2.

Appendix Two, Part Three

1. Suzuki, *Zen and Japanese Culture,* Bollingen Series LXIV (1959; reprint, Princeton, N.J.: Princeton University Press, 1970), 407, 359.
2. Ibid., 407.
3. Ibid., 159.
4. Jung and Shin'ichi Hisamatsu, "Self and Liberation: A Dialogue Between Carl G. Jung and Shin'ichi Hisamatsu," in *Self and Liberation: The Jung-Buddhism Dialogue,* ed. Daniel J. Meckel and Robert L. Moore (New York: Paulist Press, 1992), 112, 113.
5. Shin'ichi Hisamatsu, "Hisamatsu's Commentary on the Conversation," in Meckel and Moore, *Self and Liberation,* 117.
6. Suzuki, *Zen and Japanese Culture,* 27, 35-36.
7. Ibid., 32.
8. Koji Sato, Hitoshi Kataoka, Richard DeMartino, Masao Abe, and Hayao Kawai, "What is the True Self? A Discussion," in Meckel and Moore, *Self and Liberation,* 120.
9. Ibid., 121-22.
10. Ibid., 122, 123.
11. Ibid., 125.
12. Titus Burckhardt, *An Introduction to Sufism,* trans. D. M. Matheson (1976; reprint [orig. pub. as *An Introduction in Sufi Doctrine*], London: HarperCollins, Thorsons, 1995), 53, 78.
13. Qur'an, Surah CXII, The Unity.
14. Burckhardt, *An Introduction to Sufism,* 77-78.
15. Shah, *The Sufis,* vii-viii.
16. Ibid., xxvi, xxiii.

17. *EB*, s.v. "Muhammad and the Religion of Islam."

18. Muhyiddin Ibn 'Arabi, *Journey to the Lord of Power: A Sufi Manual on Retreat, with Notes from a Commentary by 'Abdul-Karim Jili,* trans. Rabia Terri Harris (Rochester, Vt.: Inner Traditions International, 1989), 5, 102.

19. *EB*, s.v. "Muhammad and the Religion of Islam: The teachings of Ibn al-'Arabi."

20. 'Arabi, *"Whoso knoweth himself ...": from the treatise on Being,* trans. T. H. Weir (1976; reprint, Abingdon, Oxon: Beshara Publications, 1988), 5,6, 9-10.

21. Ibid., 25.

22. Shah, *The Sufis,* 158, 416-17, 439.

23. Ibid., viii, xvi-xvii, 30.

24. 'Arabi, *Journey to the Lord of Power,* 86, 72-73.

25. Ibid., 73.

26. Ibid., 103.

27. Ibid., 80.

28. Burkhardt, *An Introduction to Sufism,* 60-61.

29. Shah, *The Sufis,* 181, 27.

30. Gershom Scholem, *On the Mystical Shape of the Godhead: Basic Concepts in the Kabbalah,* trans. Joachim Neugroschel, ed. Jonathan Chipman (New York: Schocken Books, 1991), 198.

31. Ibid., 255.

32. Robert Grosseteste, *On Light (De Luce),* trans. Clare C. Riedl, Mediaeval Philosophical Texts in Translation, no. 1 (Milwaukee, WI.: Marquette University Press, 1942), 13-14.

33. Ibid., 5, 6, 8.

34. Thomas Cahill, *How the Irish Saved Civilization* (1995; reprint, New York: Doubleday, Anchor Books, 1995), 144, 133, 135.

35. Ibid., 209-10.

36. Norman P. Tanner, ed., *Decrees of the Ecumenical Councils,* vol. 1, *Nicea I to Lateran V* (Washington, D. C.: Georgetown University Press, 1990), 175, eleventh decree.

37. Walter Johannes Stein, *The Ninth Century: World History in the Light of the Holy Grail,* updated and rev. ed. with index, trans. Irene Groves (London: Temple Lodge Press, 1991), 203.

38. Chadwick, *The Early Church,* 286.

39. Stoyanov, *The Hidden Tradition in Europe,* 126.

40. Ibid., 153.

41. Ibid., 220.

42. Broek, "The Cathars: Medieval Gnostics?" 96.

43. Ibid., 97-98.

44. Stoyanov, *The Hidden Tradition in Europe,* 220.

45. Ibid.

46. Bernard of Clairvaux, *The Song of Songs* (London: Huddle and Stroughton, 1990), 38, qtd. in Riggs, "The Storm in Alexandria," 26.

47. Qtd. in *EB,* s.v. "Bernard de Clairvaux, Saint."

48. Hadewijch, *Hadewijch, The Complete Works,* trans. Mother Columba Hart, The Classics of Western Spirituality (New York: Paulist Press, 1980), 3.
49. Ibid., xiii.
50. Ibid., 264, 268, "The Garden of Perfect Virtues."
51. Ibid., 272, "What and Who is Love."
52. Ibid., 287-88, "The Bride in the City."
53. Ibid., 70, 86.
54. Qtd. in Dionysius the Areopagite, *The Mystical Theology,* 22.
55. Riggs, "The Storm in Alexandria," 26.
56. Qtd. in *ibid.,* 22, italics added.
57. Johannes Eckhart, Meister, *Meister Eckhart: A Modern Translation,* trans. Raymond B. Blakney (New York: Harper and Row, Harper Torchbooks, 1941), xx-xxiii.
58. Ibid., 296, *The Defense.*
59. Ibid., xxvii, xvii, xxi.
60. Edward Hoffman, *The Way of Splendor: Jewish Mysticism and Modern Psychology* (Boulder, Colo.: Shambhala Publications, 1981), 11.
61. Scholem, *On the Mystical Shape of the Godhead,* 45, 220, 43.
62. Ibid., 218, 219, 230.
63. Lewis Spence, *The Mysteries of Britain: Or the Secret Rites and Traditions of Ancient Britain,* 3rd ed. (London: Rider, n.d.), 183, 101.
64. Ibid., 179.
65. Lewis Spence, *The History and Origins of Druidism* (New York: Barnes and Noble, 1949), 93-94.
66. Spence, *The Mysteries of Britain,* 101, 182-83, 102.
67. Spence, *The History and Origins of Druidism,* 98.
68. Ronald Hutton, *The Pagan Religions of the Ancient British Isles: their Nature and Legacy* (Oxford: Blackwell Publishers, 1991), 141.
69. Starhawk, *The Spiral Dance: A Rebirth of the Ancient Religion of the Great Goddess,* 10th anniv. ed. with a new introduction and chapter by chapter commentary (New York: HarperCollins, HarperSanFrancisco, 1989), 35-36. In the 1979 1st ed. of *The Spiral Dance,* the author uses "High Self" instead of "Deep Self."
70. Cahill, *How the Irish Saved Civilization,* 129.
71. Frances A. Yates, *Giordano Bruno and the Hermetic Tradition* (1964; reprint, Chicago: University of Chicago Press, 1991), 155-56.
72. *EB,* s.v. "Ficino, Marsilio."
73. Ardis B. Collins, *The Secular is Sacred: Platonism and Thomism in Marsilio Ficino's Platonic Theology,* International Archives of the History of Ideas, vol. 69 (The Hague: Martinus Nijhoff, 1974), 46-48.
74. Marsilio Ficino, *Meditations on the Soul: Selected Letters of Marsilio Ficino,* trans. members of the Language Department of the School of Economic Science, London (1996; reprint, Rochester, Vt.: Inner Traditions International, 1997), 25, 46.
75. Charles Trinkaus, "Marsilio Ficino and the Ideal of Human

Autonomy," in *Ficino and Renaissance Neoplatonism*, ed. Konrad Eisenbichler and Olga Zorzi Pugliese, University of Toronto Italian Studies 1 (Ottowa: Dovehouse Editions Canada, 1986), 142, 148.

76. Ficino, *Meditations on the Soul*, 43.

77. Collins, *The Secular is Sacred*, 96.

78. Laura Westra, "Love and Beauty in Ficino and Plotinus," in Eisenbichler and Pugliese, *Ficino and Renaissance Neoplatonism*, 177.

79. Ficino, *Meditations on the Soul*, 40, 52, 41.

80. *Corpus Hermeticum* XI, qtd. in Yates, *Giordano Bruno and the Hermetic Tradition*, 198.

81. Qtd. in Yates, *Giordano Bruno and the Hermetic Tradition*, 220.

82. Trinkaus, "Marsilio Ficino and the Ideal of Human Autonomy," 143.

Appendix Two, Part Four

1. Capra, *The Tao of Physics*, 334-35.

2. Frances A. Yates, *The Rosicrucian Enlightenment*, (1972; reprint, New York: Barnes and Noble Books, 1996), 139, 97.

3. Yates, *Giordano Bruno and the Hermetic Tradition*, 155-56.

4. Charles Webster, *From Paracelsus to Newton: Magic and the Making of Modern Science* (1982; reprint, New York: Barnes and Noble Books, 1996), 58-59.

5. Yates, *Giordano Bruno and the Hermetic Tradition*, 144, 150.

6. Ibid., 113.

7. Webster, *From Paracelsus to Newton*, 42, 21.

8. Yates, *The Rosicrucian Enlightenment*, 233.

9. Webster, *From Paracelsus to Newton*, 65.

10. Yates, *The Rosicrucian Enlightenment*, 233.

11. Yates, *Giordano Bruno and the Hermetic Tradition*, 398.

12. Webster, *From Paracelsus to Newton*, 75-103.

13. Yates, *The Rosicrucian Enlightenment*, 114-16.

14. Ibid., 113.

15. Webster, *From Paracelsus to Newton*, 89-92, 10, 68-69.

16. Monod, Weber, and Heims qtd. in John T. Nichols, "What Is a Naturalist, Anyway?" in *Natural History* (November 1992), 10.

17. Gottfried Arnold, "The Mystery of the Divine Sophia: On the Arrival and First Voice of Sophia in Man," in *Pietists: Selected Writings*, ed. Peter C. Erb, The Classics of Western Spirituality (New York: Paulist Press, 1983), 219, 226.

18. Ralph Waldo Emerson, *The Portable Emerson*, ed. Carl Bode in collaboration with Malcolm Cowley (1946; reprint, New York: Penguin Books, 1981), 74, "Divinity School Address."

19. Ibid., 210-11, 212, "The Over-Soul".

20. Ibid., 219.

21. Ted Peters, Viewpoint, "Seeing No Evil: A Lutheran Minister Critiques the New Age," *Common Boundary* (November/December, 1991), 29.

Bibliography

Page references in the text refer to reprint editions, when listed.

The Apocrypha according to The Authorised Version. Oxford: Oxford University Press, n.d.

'Arabi, Muhyiddin Ibn. *"Whoso knoweth himself . . .": from the treatise on Being.* Trans. T. H. Weir. 1976. Reprint, Abingdon, Oxon: Beshara Publications, 1988.

———. *Journey to the Lord of Power: A Sufi Manual on Retreat, with Notes from a Commentary by 'Abdul-Karim Jili.* Trans. Rabia Terri Harris. Rochester, Vt.: Inner Traditions International, 1989.

Armstrong, Karen. *A History of God.* 1993. Reprint, New York: Random House, Gramercy Books, 2004.

Armstrong, Rebecca. "The Metaphysical Function of Mythology; Man and Woman: The Odyssey." In Joseph Campbell Foundation Website Archive. *Myth Letter,* February 2003. Available from www.jcf.org/myth_letter

Arnold, Gottfried. "The Mystery of the Divine Sophia: On the Arrival and First Voice of Sophia in Man." In *Pietists: Selected Writings,* ed. Peter C. Erb. The Classics of Western Spirituality. New York: Paulist Press, 1983.

Augustine, St. *The City of God.* Trans. Marcus Dods. New York: Random House, Modern Library, 1950.

———. *Confessions.* Trans. E. B. Pusey. New York: Barnes and Noble Books, 1999.

Aurobindo, Sri. *Wisdom of the Upanishads.* Wilmont, Wis.: Lotus Light Publications, 1988.

Barks, Coleman. *Rumi: Voice of Longing.* Boulder, Colo.: Sounds True no. W240, 1994. Audiocassette.

Begley, Sharon. Science Journal, "Scans of Monks' Brains Show Meditation Alters Structure, Functioning." *Wall Street Journal,* November 5, 2004.

Bernard of Clairvaux. *The Song of Songs.* London: Huddle and Stroughton, 1990. Quoted in Brian Riggs, "The Storm in Alexandria," *Gnosis* 45 (fall 1997): 26.

Blake, William. *The Complete Poems.* Ed. Alicia Ostriker. London: Penguin Books, 1977.

Blumenthal, H. J. *Plotinus' Psychology: His Doctrines of the Embodied Soul.* The Hague: Martinus Nijhoff, 1971.

Bly, Robert, Hillman, James, Meade, Michael, eds. *The Rag and Bone Shop of the Heart: Poems for Men.* 1992. Reprint, New York: Harper Collins, HarperPerennial, 1993.

Bohm, David. *Wholeness and the Implicate Order.* 1980. Reprint, London: Routledge, 1995.

Boyle, Robert. "Of the high veneration man's intellect owes to God." In *Works.* Vol. 5, 1685. Quoted in Charles Webster, *From Paracelsus to Newton: Magic and the Making of Modern Science* (Reprint of 1982, New York: Barnes and Noble Books, 1996), 93.

Brands, H. W. *The First American: The Life and Times of Benjamin Franklin.* 2000. Reprint, New York: Random House, Anchor Books, 2002.

Broek, Roelof van den. "Gnosticism and Hermeticism in Antiquity: Two Roads to Salvation." In *Gnosis and Hermeticism from Antiquity to Modern Times,* ed. Roelof van den Broek and Wouter J. Hanegraaff. Albany, N.Y.: State University of New York Press, 1998a.

———. "The Cathars: Medieval Gnostics?" In *Gnosis and Hermeticism from Antiquity to Modern Times,* ed. Roelof van den Broek and Wouter J. Hanegraaff. Albany, N.Y.: State University of New York Press, 1998b.

Brown, Peter. *The Making of Late Antiquity.* 1978. Reprint, New York: Barnes and Noble Books, 1998.

Buber, Martin. *Good and Evil: Two Interpretations,* 2nd ed. New York: Charles Scribner's Sons, 1953.

———. *The Knowledge of Man.* New York: Harper, 1966.

Budge, E. A. Wallis. *The Egyptian Book of the Dead (The Papyrus of Ani): Egyptian text, Transliteration and Translation.* 1898. Reprint, New York: Dover, 1967. Quoted in Jeremy Naydler, *Temple of the Cosmos: The Ancient Egyptian Experience of the Sacred* (Rochester, Vt.: Inner Traditions, 1996), 208.

———. *From Fetish to God in Ancient Egypt.* 1934. Reprint, New York: Dover Publications, 1988.

Bulfinch, Thomas. *Bulfinch's Mythology,* illus. ed. New York: Avenal Books, 1978.

Burckhardt, Titus. *An Introduction to Sufism.* Trans. D. M. Matheson. 1976. Reprint (orig. pub. as *An Introduction in Sufi Doctrine*), London: HarperCollins, Thorsons, 1995.

Cahill, Thomas. *How the Irish Saved Civilization.* 1995. Reprint, New York: Doubleday, Anchor Books, 1995.

Cantor, Georg. *Gesammelte Abhandlungen.* Ed. Abraham Fraenkel and Ernst Zermelo. Berlin: Springer Verlag, 1932. Quoted in Rudy Rucker, *Infinity and the Mind: The Science and Philosophy of the Infinite* (Reprint of 1982, New York: Bantam Books, 1983), 46, 10.

Capra, Fritjof. *The Tao of Physics,* 3rd ed., expanded. Boston: Shambhala, 1991.

Chadwick, Henry. *The Early Church.* The Pelican History of the Church. Vol. 1. Harmondsworth, Middlesex, England: Penguin Books, 1967.

Chopra, Deepak. *The Higher Self,* abr. ed. New York: Simon and Schuster Audio Division, Sound Ideas no. 87028-9, 1989. Audiocassette.

Cohn, Norman. *Cosmos, Chaos and the World to Come: The Ancient roots of Apocalyptic Faith.* New Haven, Conn.: Yale University Press, 1993.

Collins, Ardis B. *The Secular is Sacred: Platonism and Thomism in Marsilio Ficino's Platonic Theology.* International Archives of the History of Ideas. Vol. 69. The Hague: Martinus Nijhoff, 1974.

Conze, Edward. *Buddhist Thought in India: Three Phases of Buddhist Philosophy.* 1962. Reprint, Ann Arbor: University of Michigan Press, Ann Arbor Paperbacks, 1967.

Crossan, John Dominic. *The Birth of Christianity: Discovering What Happened in the Years Immediately after the Execution of Jesus.* New York: HarperCollins, HarperSanFrancisco, 1998.

(Dionysius the Areopagite: see also Pseudo-Dionysius)

Dionysius the Areopagite. *The Mystical Theology and The Celestial Hierarchies of Dionysius the Areopagite: With Commentaries by the Editors of The Shrine of Wisdom and Poem by St. John of the Cross.* Trans. The Editors of the Shrine of Wisdom. Fintry, Brook, nr. Godalming, Surrey, Great Britain: The Shrine of Wisdom, 1949.

———. *The Works of Dionysius the Areopagite: Part 1. Divine Names, Mystical Theology, Letters, &c.* Trans. John Parker. 1897-99. Reprint, Merrick, N.Y.: Richwood Publishing, 1976.

Duchesne-Guillemin, Jacques. *Symbols and Values in Zoroastrianism: Their Survival and Renewal.* Religious Perspectives. Vol. XV. 1966. Reprint, New York: Harper and Row, Harper Torchbooks, 1970.

Eckhart, Johannes, Meister. *Meister Eckhart: A Modern Translation.* Trans. Raymond B. Blakney. New York: Harper and Row, Harper Torchbooks, 1941.

The Economist. "Survey: Manufacturing Technology: The Multiplication of Labor," 5 March 1994, 18.

Eisler, Riane. *The Chalice and the Blade: Our History, Our Future.* 1987. Reprint, with new epilogue, San Francisco: HarperCollins, HarperSanFrancisco, 1995.

Emerson, Ralph Waldo. *The Portable Emerson.* Ed. Carl Bode in collaboration with Malcolm Cowley. 1946. Reprint, New York: Penguin Books, 1981.

Erikson, Erik H. *Childhood and Society,* 2nd ed., rev. and enl. New York: W. W. Norton, 1963.

Eschenbach, Wolfram von. *Parzifal.* Trans. Helen M. Mustard and Charles E. Passage. New York: Random House, Vintage Books, 1961.

Ficino, Marsilio. *Meditations on the Soul: Selected Letters of Marsilio Ficino.* Trans. members of the Language Department of the School of Economic Science, London. 1996. Reprint, Rochester, Vt.: Inner Traditions International, 1997.

Fynn. *Mister God, This Is Anna.* New York: Holt, Rinehart and Winston, 1975.

Galilei, Galileo. *Dialogues Concerning Two New Sciences.* Trans. Henry Crew and Alphonso De Salvio. 1914. Reprint, New York: Dover Publications, 1954.

Gerson, Lloyd P., ed. *The Cambridge Companion to Plotinus.* Cambridge Companion Series. Cambridge: Cambridge University Press, 1996.

Gibbon, Edward. *The History of the Decline and Fall of the Roman Empire,* new ed. with index. Vol. 1. Philadelphia: Henry T. Coates, 1845.

Govinda, Lama Anagarika. *Foundations of Tibetan Mysticism.* New York: Samuel Weiser, 1974. Quoted in Fritjof Capra, *The Tao of Physics,* 3rd ed., expanded (Boston: Shambhala, 1991), 185-86.

Greer, Rowan A. *Introduction to Origen: An Exhortation to Martyrdom, Prayer, First Principles, Book IV, Prologue to the Commentary to the Song of Songs, Homily XXVII on Numbers.* The Classics of Western Spirituality. New York: Paulist Press, 1979.

Grimal, Nicolas. *A History of Ancient Egypt.* 1992. Reprint, New York: Barnes and Noble Books, 1997.

Grosseteste, Robert. *On Light (De Luce).* Trans. Clare C. Riedl. Mediaeval Philosophical Texts in Translation, no. 1. Milwaukee, Wis.: Marquette University Press, 1942.

Guthrie, Kenneth Sylvan, trans., and Fideler, David, ed. *The Pythagorean Sourcebook and Library: An Anthology of Ancient Writings Which Relate to Pythagoras and Pythagorean Philosophy.* Grand Rapids, Mich.: Phanes Press, 1988.

Guthrie, W. K. C. *A History of Greek Philosophy.* Vol. 1, *The Earlier Presocratics and the Pythagoreans.* Cambridge: Cambridge University Press, 1962.

Hadewijch. *Hadewijch, The Complete Works.* Trans. Mother Columba Hart. The Classics of Western Spirituality. New York: Paulist Press, 1980.

Hafiz. *The Gift: Poems by Hafiz The Great Sufi Master.* Trans. Daniel Ladinsky. New York: Penguin/Arkana, 1999.

Havelock, Eric A. *The Muse Learns to Write: Reflections on Orality and Literacy from Antiquity to the Present.* New Haven, Conn.: Yale University Press, 1986.

Hawking, Stephen. *A Brief History of Time: From the Big Bang to Black Holes.* Toronto: Bantam Books, 1988.

———. *The Universe in a Nutshell.* New York: Bantam Books, 2001.

Hesse, Hermann. *Magister Ludi: (The Glass Bead Game).* Trans. Richard and Clara Winston. 1969. Reprint, New York: Bantam Books, 1970.

Hilberg, Raul. "The Holocaust." In *Facing Evil: Confronting the Dreadful Power behind Genocide, Terrorism and Cruelty,* ed. Paul Woodruff and Harry A. Wilmer. Chicago: Open Court, 1988.

Hillman, James. *Re-Visioning Psychology.* 1975. Reprint, New York: Harper and Row, Harper Colophon Books, 1977.

Hisamatsu, Shin'ichi. "Hisamatsu's Commentary on the Conversation." In *Self and Liberation: The Jung-Buddhism Dialogue,* ed. Daniel J. Meckel and Robert L. Moore. New York: Paulist Press, 1992.

Hoffman, Edward. *The Way of Splendor: Jewish Mysticism and Modern Psychology.* Boulder, Colo.: Shambhala Publications, 1981.

Homer. *The Odyssey.* Trans. Robert Fitzgerald. 1961. Reprint, Garden City, N.Y.: Doubleday and Company, Anchor Books, 1963.

Huizinga, Johan. *Homo Ludens: A Study in the Play-Element in Culture.* 1950. Reprint, Boston: The Beacon Press, 1955.

Hutton, Ronald. *The Pagan Religions of the Ancient British Isles: their Nature and Legacy.* Oxford: Blackwell Publishers, 1991.

Jacobs, Louis. *A Jewish Theology.* West Orange, N.J.: Berman House, 1973.

James, William. *The Varieties of Religious Experience.* 1902. Reprint, New York: Penguin Books, New American Library, Mentor Books, 1958.

Jedin, Hubert. *Ecumenical Councils of the Catholic Church: An Historical Outline.* Trans. Ernest Graf. New York: Herder and Herder, 1960.

Johnson, Robert. *We: Understanding the Psychology of Romantic Love.* San Francisco: HarperCollins, HarperSanFrancisco, 1983.

Jung, C. G. *Answer to Job.* Trans. R. F. C. Hull. 1954. Reprint, Cleveland: World Publishing, Meridian Books, 1960.

———. *The Undiscovered Self.* Trans. R. F. C. Hull. 1958. Reprint, New York: Mentor, 1959.
———. *Memories, Dreams, Reflections,* rev. ed. Ed. Aniela Jaffe, trans. Richard and Clara Winston. 1961. Reprint, New York: Random House, Vintage Books, 1965.
———. *Symbols of Transformation: An Analysis of the Prelude to a Case of Schizophrenia,* 2nd ed. with corrections. Trans. R. F. C. Hull. Bollingen Series XX. 1967. Reprint, Princeton, N.J.: Princeton University Press, 1976.
———. *Aion,* 2nd ed. Trans. R. F. C. Hull. Bollingen Series XX. Princeton, N.J.: Princeton University Press, 1968.
———. *The Portable Jung.* Ed. Joseph Campbell, trans. R. F. C. Hull. 1971. Reprint, New York: Penguin Books, 1976.
——— and Hisamatsu, Shin'ichi. "Self and Liberation: A Dialogue Between Carl G. Jung and Shin'ichi Hisamatsu." In *Self and Liberation: The Jung-Buddhism Dialogue,* ed. Daniel J. Meckel and Robert L. Moore. New York: Paulist Press, 1992.
Kirk, G. S., Raven, J. E., and Schofield, M. *The Presocratic Philosophers: A Critical History with a Selection of Texts,* 2nd ed. Cambridge: Cambridge University Press, 1983.
Kübler-Ross, Elisabeth. *On Death and Dying.* 1969. Reprint, New York: Macmillan Publishing, Collier Books, 1970.
Kyber, Manfred. *The Three Candles of Little Veronica: The Story of a Child's Soul in this World and the Other, new ed.* Trans. Rosamond Reinhardt. Garden City, N.Y.: Waldorff Press, 1975.
Lao Tzu. *Tao Te Ching.* Trans. D. C. Lau. Middlesex, England: Penguin Books, 1963.
Laurence, Richard, trans. *The Book of Enoch the Prophet.* Secret Doctrine Reference Series. 1883. Reprint with index, San Diego, Ca.: Wizard's Bookshelf, 1983.
Los Angeles Times, 24 December 1996.
Lucretius. *On the Nature of the Universe.* Trans. W. Hannaford Brown. New Brunswick, N.J.: Rutgers University Press, 1950a.
———. *On the Nature of Things.* Trans. Ronald E. Latham. Harmondsworth, England: Penguin Books, 1950b. Quoted in Rudy Rucker, *Infinity and the Mind: The Science and Philosophy of the Infinite* (Reprint of 1982, New York: Bantam Books, 1983), 16.
Mack, Burton L. *The Lost Gospel: The Book of Q and Christian Origins.* 1993. Reprint, New York: HarperCollins, HarperSanFrancisco, 1994.
Margull, Hans Jochen, ed. *The Councils of the Church: History and Analysis.* Trans. Walter F. Bense. Philadelphia: Fortress Press, 1966.
Matthews, Caitlin. *Sophia: Goddess of Wisdom, Bride of God.* 1991. Reprint, Wheaton, Ill.: Theosophical Publishing House, Quest Books, 2001.
Meckel, Daniel J., and Moore, Robert L., eds. *Self and Liberation: The Jung-Buddhism Dialogue.* New York: Paulist Press, 1992.

Moore, G. F. *History of Religions.* Vol. I. Edinburgh, 1950. Quoted in Louis Jacobs, *A Jewish Theology* (West Orange, N.J.: Berman House, 1973), 302-03.
Moore, Thomas. *Soul Mates.* New York: HarperCollins, 1994.
More, Henry. *A Collection of Several Philosophical Writings of Henry More,* 2nd ed. London, 1662. Quoted in Frances A. Yates, *Giordano Bruno and the Hermetic Tradition* (Reprint of 1964, Chicago: University of Chicago Press, 1991), 423.
Morrison, Philip. Book Reviews. "Three Dimensional Words." *Scientific American,* November, 1992, 132-34.
Nahm, Milton C. *Selections from Early Greek Philosophy,* 4th ed. New York: Meredith Publishing, Appleton-Century-Crofts, 1964.
Nhat Hanh, Thich. *Cultivating the Mind of Love: The Practice of Looking Deeply in the Mahayana Buddhist Tradition.* Berkeley, Ca.: Parallax Press, 1996.
Naydler, Jeremy. *Temple of the Cosmos: The Ancient Egyptian Experience of the Sacred.* Rochester, Vt.: Inner Traditions, 1996.
Needham, Joseph, with the collaboration of Lu Gwei-Djen. *Science and Civilization in China, Vol. 5: Chemistry and Chemical Technology, Part II: Spagyrical Discovery and Invention: Magisteries of Gold and Immortality.* Cambridge: Cambridge University Press, 1974.
Ni, Hua-Ching. *The Taoist Inner View of the Universe and the Immortal Realm.* Malibu, Ca.: The Shrine of the Eternal Breath of Tao; Santa Monica, Ca.: College of Tao and Traditional Chinese Healing, 1979.
Nichols, John T. "What Is a Naturalist, Anyway?" *Natural History,* November, 1992, 6-12.
Nietzsche, Friedrich. *The Portable Nietzsche.* Trans. Walter Kaufmann. New York: The Viking Press, 1954.
———. *Beyond Good and Evil.* Trans. Marianne Cowan. Chicago: Henry Regnery, Gateway, 1955.
Nikhilananda, Swami. *The Upanishads,* abridged ed. 1963. Reprint, New York: Harper and Row, Harper Torchbooks, Cloister Library, 1964.
O'Donohue, John. *Anam Cara.* Boulder, Colo.: Sounds True no. AF00039, 1996. Audiocassette.
Oort, Johannes van. "Manichaeism." In *Gnosis and Hermeticism from Antiquity to Modern Times,* ed. Roelof van den Broek and Wouter J. Hanegraaff. Albany, N.Y.: State University of New York Press, 1998.
Pagels, Elaine. *The Gnostic Gospels.* 1979. Reprint, New York: Random House, Vintage Books, 1989.
———. *Adam, Eve, and the Serpent.* New York: Random House, 1988.
Peters, Ted. Viewpoint. "Seeing No Evil: A Lutheran Minister Critiques the New Age." *Common Boundary,* November/December, 1991, 26-30.
Philip, J. A. *Pythagoras and Early Pythagoreanism.* Phoenix. Journal of the Classical Association of Canada. Suppl. Vol. 7. Toronto: University of Toronto Press, 1966.
Philo of Alexandria. *Philo of Alexandria: The Contemplative Life, The Giants, and Selections.* Trans. David Winston. The Classics of Western Spirituality. New York: Paulist Press, 1981.

Piaget, Jean. *The Origins of Intelligence in Children.* Trans. Margaret Cook. 1952. Reprint, N.Y.: W. W. Norton, The Norton Library, 1963.

Plato. *Five Great Dialogues.* Trans. B. Jowett, ed. Louise Ropes Loomis. New York: Walter J. Black, 1942.

———. *The Collected Dialogues of Plato: Including the Letters.* Ed. Edith Hamilton and Huntington Cairns. Bollingen Series LXXI. 1961. Reprint with corrections, Princeton, N.J.: Princeton University Press, 1963.

———. *Timaeus and Critias.* Trans. Desmond Lee. Harmondsworth, Middlesex, England: Penguin Books, 1971.

Platt, Rutherford H. Jr., ed., and J. Alden Brett, asst. ed. *The Forgotten Books of Eden.* 1927. Reprint, New York: Bell Publishing, 1980.

Plotinus. *Plotinus.* Vol. 1, *Porphyry on the Life of Plotinus and the Order of His Books, Enneads I. 1-9.* Trans. A. H. Armstrong. Cambridge, Mass.: Loeb Classical Library, 1966.

———. *Plotinus.* Vol. 3, *Enneads III. 1-9.* Trans. A. H. Armstrong. Cambridge, Mass.: Loeb Classical Library, 1967a.

———. *Plotinus.* Vol. 4, *Enneads IV. 1-9.* Trans. A. H. Armstrong. Cambridge, Mass.: Loeb Classical Library, 1967b.

———. *The Enneads,* abr. ed. Trans. Stephen MacKenna, abr. John Dillon. London: Penguin Books, 1991.

Plutarch. *Essays.* Trans. Robin Waterfield, intro. and anno. Ian Kidd. London: Penguin Books, 1992.

Poe, Edgar Allan. *Complete Tales and Poems of Edgar Allan Poe.* New York: Modern Library, 1938.

(Pseudo-Dionysius: see also Dionysius the Areopagite)

Pseudo-Dionysius. *Pseudo-Dionysius; the Complete Works.* Trans. Colm Luibheid with collaboration by Paul Rorem. The Classics of Western Spirituality. New York: Paulist Press, 1987.

Pythagoras. *The Golden Verses of Pythagoras, with the Commentary of Hierocles.* Adapted from trans. of N. Rowe. Santa Barbara, Ca.: Concord Grove Press, 1983.

Radhakrishnan, S. *Indian Philosophy.* New York: Macmillan, 1958. Quoted in Fritjof Capra, *The Tao of Physics,* 3rd ed., expanded (Boston: Shambhala, 1991), 190.

Rahner, Karl. "The life of the dead." Chapter 14 in *Theological Investigations.* Vol. 4. London: Baltimore, 1966. Quoted in Louis Jacobs, *A Jewish Theology* (West Orange, N.J.: Berman House, 1973), 89.

Ray, John. *Reflection of Osiris: Lives from Ancient Egypt.* Oxford: Oxford University Press, 2002.

Riggs, Brian. "The Storm in Alexandria." *Gnosis* 45 (fall 1997): 22-26.

Rilke, Rainer Maria. *The Notebooks of Malte Laurids Brigge.* Trans. M. D. Herter Norton. 1949. Reprint, New York: Capricorn Books, 1958.

Rist, J. M. *Plotinus: The Road to Reality.* Cambridge: Cambridge University Press, 1967.

Robinson, James M., gen. ed. *The Nag Hammadi Library in English,* 3rd, compl. rev. ed. 1978. Reprint, New York: HarperCollins, HarperSanFrancisco, 1990.

Rosenblatt, Naomi H., and Horwitz, Joshua. *Wrestling with Angels: What the First Family of Genesis Teaches Us about Our Spiritual Identity, Sexuality, and Personal Relationships.* New York: Delacorte, 1995.

Rucker, Rudy. *Infinity and the Mind: The Science and Philosophy of the Infinite.* 1982. Reprint, New York: Bantam Books, 1983.

Sagan, Carl. *The Dragons of Eden.* 1977. Reprint, New York: Ballantine Books, 1978.

Sato, Koji, Kataoka, Hitoshi, DeMartino, Richard, Abe, Masao, and Kawai, Hayao. "What is the True Self? A Discussion." In *Self and Liberation: The Jung-Buddhism Dialogue,* ed. Daniel J. Meckel and Robert L. Moore. New York: Paulist Press, 1992.

Schilpp, P. A., ed. *Albert Einstein, Philosopher-Scientist.* Evanston, Ill.: The Library of Living Philosophers, 1949. Quoted in Fritjof Capra, *The Tao of Physics,* 3rd ed., expanded (Boston: Shambhala, 1991), 185.

Schmölders, A. *Essai sur les ecoles philosophiques chez les Arabes,* abr. Paris, 1842. Quoted in William James, *The Varieties of Religious Experience* (Reprint of 1902, New York: Penguin Books, New American Library, Mentor Books, 1958), 322.

Schofield, Russell Paul. *Imprint Unmistakable.* Los Angeles: privately published, 1970.

Schofield, Russell Paul, and Schofield, Carol Ann. *Basic Principles of Actualism,* rev. ed. Solana Beach, Ca.: Actualism, 1993.

Scholem, Gershom. *On the Mystical Shape of the Godhead: Basic Concepts in the Kabbalah.* Trans. Joachim Neugroschel, ed. Jonathan Chipman. New York: Schocken Books, 1991.

Seife, Charles. *Zero: The Biography of a Dangerous Idea.* 2000. Reprint, New York: Penguin Books, 2000.

Seneca. *Moral Essays.* Vol. II. Trans. John W. Basore. Cambridge: Harvard University Press, 1965.

Shah, Idries. *The Sufis.* 1964. Reprint, New York: Doubleday, Anchor Books, 1971.

Sonsino, Rifat, and Syme, Daniel B. *What Happens After I Die?: Jewish Views of Life After Death.* New York: UAHC Press, 1990.

Spangler, David. *The Laws of Manifestation.* Findhorn, Moray, Scotland: Findhorn Publications.

Spence, Lewis. *The Mysteries of Britain: Or the Secret Rites and Traditions of Ancient Britain,* 3rd ed. London: Rider, n.d.

———. *The History and Origins of Druidism.* New York: Barnes and Noble, 1949.

Starhawk. *The Spiral Dance: A Rebirth of the Ancient Religion of the Great Goddess,* 10th anniv. ed. with a new introduction and chapter by chapter commentary. New York: HarperCollins, HarperSanFrancisco, 1989.

Stein, Walter Johannes. *The Ninth Century: World History in the Light of the Holy Grail,* updated and rev. ed. with index. Trans. Irene Groves. London: Temple Lodge Press, 1991.

Steiner, Rudolf. *Christianity as Mystical Fact.* Trans. Andrew Welburn. Hudson, N.Y.: Anthropsophic Press, 1997.

Stone, Merlin. *When God Was a Woman.* 1976. Reprint, San Diego: Harcourt Brace Jovanovich, 1993.
Stoyanov, Yuri. *The Hidden Tradition in Europe.* London: Penguin Books, Arkana, 1994.
Strassburg, Gottfried von. *Tristan: With the Surviving Fragments of the Tristan of Thomas.* Trans. A. T. Hatto. 1960. Reprint with revisions, London: Penguin Books, 1967.
Suzuki, Daisetz T. *Zen and Japanese Culture.* Bollingen Series LXIV. 1959. Reprint, Princeton, N.J.: Princeton University Press, 1970.
Tanner, Norman P., ed. *Decrees of the Ecumenical Councils.* Vol. 1, *Nicea I to Lateran V.* Washington, D. C.: Georgetown University Press, 1990.
Thom, Johan C. *The Pythagorean Golden Verses: With Introduction and Commentary.* Religions in the Graeco-Roman World. Vol. 123. Leiden: E. J. Brill, 1995.
Thoreau, Henry David. *Walden and Other Writings.* Ed. Brooks Atkinson. New York: Random House, Modern Library, 1937.
Tolstoy, Leo. *War and Peace.* Trans. Ann Dunnigan. New York: Penguin Books, Signet Classic, 1968.
Trinkaus, Charles. "Marsilio Ficino and the Ideal of Human Autonomy." In *Ficino and Renaissance Neoplatonism,* ed. Konrad Eisenbichler and Olga Zorzi Pugliese. University of Toronto Italian Studies 1. Ottowa: Dovehouse Editions Canada, 1986.
Ulansey, David. *The Origins of the Mithraic Mysteries: Cosmology and Salvation in the Ancient World.* 1989. Reprint, New York: Oxford University Press, 1991.
Vermes, Geza. *The Changing Faces of Jesus.* 2000. Reprint, New York: Penguin Compass, 2002.
Vrettos, Theodore. *Alexandria.* New York: The Free Press, 2001.
Vulliamy, C. E. *Immortality: Funerary Rites and Customs.* 1926. Reprint (orig. pub. as *Immortal Man*), London: Random House UK, Senate, 1997.
Waters, Chris, Jones, Bucky, and Shapiro, Tom. "Come Back (When You Can Stay Forever)." Nashville, Tenn.: Sony/ATV Cross Keys Publishing/ASCAP, 1983.
Watkin, E. I. *The Church in Council.* London: Darton, Longman and Todd, 1960.
Watts, A. W. The Way of Zen. New York: Pantheon Books, 1957.
Webster, Charles. *From Paracelsus to Newton: Magic and the Making of Modern Science.* 1982. Reprint, New York: Barnes and Noble Books, 1996.
Weick, Karl E. "Small Sins and Large Evils." In *Facing Evil: Confronting the Dreadful Power behind Genocide, Terrorism and Cruelty,* ed. Paul Woodruff and Harry A Wilmer. Chicago: Open Court, 1988.
Weir, Roger. *Taoism—Part 3.* Lecture July 15. Los Angeles: privately published, 1986b. Audiocassette.
———. *Jesus in Alexandria.* Series of 39 lectures. Los Angeles: privately published, 1987. Audiocassettes.
———. *Rise of the Mysterious Person Archetype.* Series of 26 lectures. Los Angeles: privately published, 1987-88. Audiocassettes.

———. *Mysterious Person: New Age Spiral.* Lecture Nov. 22. Los Angeles: privately published, 1988. Audiocassette.

———. *Roots of Hermetic America.* Lecture no. 2, *Trithemius,* May 11; no. 7, *John Dee,* May 16; no. 11, *Comenius,* June 13. Los Angeles: privately published, 1991. Audiocassettes.

Welch, Holmes. *Taoism: The Parting of the Way,* rev. ed. 1957. Reprint, Boston: Beacon Press, 1966.

Westra, Laura. "Love and Beauty in Ficino and Plotinus." In *Ficino and Renaissance Neoplatonism,* ed. Konrad Eisenbichler and Olga Zorzi Pugliese. University of Toronto Italian Studies 1. Ottowa: Dovehouse Editions Canada, 1986.

Woodman, Marion. *Dreams: The Language of the Soul.* Boulder, Colo.: Sounds True no. AW00131, 1991. Audiocassette.

———. *The Crown of Age: The Rewards of Conscious Aging.* Boulder, Colo.: Sounds True no. W528D, 2002. CD.

Woodruff, Paul, and Wilmer, Harry A. *Facing Evil: Confronting the Dreadful Power behind Genocide, Terrorism and Cruelty.* Chicago: Open Court, 1988.

Yates, Frances A. *Giordano Bruno and the Hermetic Tradition.* 1964. Reprint, Chicago: University of Chicago Press, 1991.

———. *The Rosicrucian Enlightenment.* 1972. Reprint, New York: Barnes and Noble Books, 1996.

Yeats, William Butler. *A Vision.* A reissue with the author's final revisions. 1956. Reprint, New York: Macmillan Publishing, Collier Books, 1966.

Young, Dudley. *Origins of the Sacred: The Ecstasies of Love and War.* 1991. Reprint, New York: HarperCollins, HarperPerennial, 1992.

Zimmer, Heinrich. *The King and the Corpse.* Bollingen Series XI. 1948. Reprint, Princeton, N.J.: Princeton University Press, 1971.

INDEX

ORDER FORM

Please send ______ copies of *Living in the Infinite*
@ $17.00 US (25.00 CAN) = $__________

Add 7.25% sales tax ($1.23 US, $1.81 CAN per copy) __________

Shipping: within US, first copy @ $3.50 = __________

each additional copy @ $1.75 = __________

Total: = $ __________

Please include your check or money order in US dollars payable to Lucia Press. Please allow two to four weeks for delivery.

Address you would like your order sent to:

____
NAME

____
ADDRESS

____
CITY STATE/PROVINCE ZIP

____
PHONE

____
E-MAIL

Mail your order to: Lucia Press
77 Spruce Way
Carmel, CA 93923-9609

Questions, please email: stan smith1@sbcglobal.net
or call: (510) 482-6454

Thank you for your order.

Printed in the United States
87284LV00004B/343-423/A